TRANSLATING
CHINESE LITERATURE

TRANSLATING CHINESE LITERATURE

Edited by

Eugene Eoyang and Lin Yao-fu

INDIANA UNIVERSITY PRESS

Bloomington and Indianapolis

The paper used in this publication meets the minimum requirements of
American National Standard for Information Sciences—Permanence of
Paper for Printed Library Materials, ANSI Z39.48-1984.

Manufactured in the United States of America

Library of Congress Cataloging-in-Publication Data

Translating Chinese literature / edited by Eugene Eoyang and Lin
Yao-fu.
        p.   cm.
    Includes papers presented at the first International Conference on
the Translation of Chinese Literature held in Taipei, Nov. 19–21,
1990.
    Includes index.
    ISBN 0-253-31958-7
    1. Chinese literature—Translations into English—History and
criticism—Congresses.   I. Eoyang, Eugene Chen.   II. Lin, Yao-fu,
date   III. International Conference on the Translation of Chinese
Literature (1st : 1990 : Taipei, China)
PL2658.E1T73   1995
428′.02951—dc20   94-18309

        1   2   3   4   5   00   99   98   97   96   95

CONTENTS

PREFACE

In November 1990 the Council for Cultural Development and Planning, the Chiang Ching-kuo Foundation, and National Taiwan University joined together to convene the first International Conference on the Translation of Chinese Literature. More than forty scholars from abroad were invited to Taipei to interact with their counterparts and colleagues from Taiwan, Hong Kong, and Southeast Asia. More than one hundred papers were presented over a three-day period, November 19–21, 1990. This volume presents a selection of the papers. Unfortunately, it wasn't possible to publish every paper presented: such a volume would have exceeded three thousand pages. Many worthy contributions had to be omitted, not to mention many worthy contributors. We explored different criteria for selection. Our publisher not unexpectedly selected papers that concentrated on the translation of Chinese literature into English. This linguistic chauvinism can be easily criticized, except that it does reflect the greater preponderance of expertise at the conference, and is very likely to reach the greatest audience of readers.

The translation of Chinese literature has, in a generation, progressed to such a stage that we no longer have only a handful of variously gifted practitioners ranging throughout the historical corpus. Now we have specialists translating the *Shih chi*, the *Wen hsüan*, the *Shih-shuo hsin-yü*, the *San-kuo chih*, the *Yüan ch'ü*, the *Shih-tou chi* (Hung-lou meng), even the *Lumudan*. Such a gathering of practitioners provided an excellent chance to share workshop notes. Many of the participants took advantage of this opportunity of sharing their frustrations and their all too infrequent triumphs, to the edification of all. Whatever differences emerged in the conference, those attending were unanimous about the fragility of the translator's art, and the precarious position of the translator. Still, there was a special sense of encouragement for each translator-participant to confer and to commiserate with fellow agonizers over the arduously bilingual art known as translation.

In a sense, the conference marked the maturation of translation from the Chinese. In the past, the purveyors of Chinese literature in Western languages were isolated in their solitary studies or in libraries, ensconced in their bookish endeavors: there would scarcely have been enough critical mass to convene anything so grandiose as an international conference. (Indeed, some would have been too shy to attend such a public event.) Each translator had an Olympian air about him, and was usually surrounded by admirers who did not know Chinese at all, and who were ignored by those who were familiar with the original, the Chinese, either for reasons of tact, perhaps tinged with cultural superiority, or because they were unsure of their command of English. In this past generation, a cadre (if one may be allowed to "recuperate" that overpoliticized word) of translators has emerged with greater command of the "other" language, whether of Chinese by Westerners or of Western languages by Chinese. This has permitted a dialogue, a discourse, on the problems of translation that would hardly have been possible half a century ago. In the case of Chinese literature, it almost appeared as if those who translated it had no interest in the present-day Chinese (Waley, notoriously, refused to visit contemporary China, though he would have been delighted to visit—by some form of time machine—earlier periods). And the contemporary heirs of Chinese literature seemed indifferent to how it was being presented to outsiders.

All this has changed, and the intense interest in present-day China, either in the Republic of China or the People's Republic of China, includes even those more enamored of traditional than of modern Chinese culture. And the Chinese are intensely concerned with how they are being presented in other languages. The Foreign Languages Press in Beijing is producing translations of Chinese literature, contemporary and modern, at a voluminous rate. Conferences on translation and on comparative literature now normally attract Chinese scholars whose primary field of expertise is in Chinese literature from both the Republic of China and the People's Republic of China.

This collection has been divided into three sections: working notes, anthologizing, and critical surveys. The first section includes essays on specific encounters with particular texts; the second addresses the shape of the material as presented by certain definitive collections; and the third assesses, either theoretically or pragmatically, the state of the art of translation.

We are indebted to the Council for Cultural Development and Planning, not only for its support of this 1990 conference and a second conference held in December 1992 but also for its generous help with the publication of this volume. In due course, a second volume, consisting of the papers presented at the 1992 conference, will also appear. Professor Lin would also like to thank the Professor Lilian Chao Cultural and Educational Foundation for its support of the 1990 conference.

Eugene Eoyang
Lin Yao-fu

Working Notes

Reflections of a Working Translator

CYRIL BIRCH

I am deeply grateful for the honor of this invitation to address the conference today, but what really excites me is that an event such as this conference can occur at all. I believe it is a genuine milestone in a progress to which many of us here have dedicated our working lives, the bringing of the great gift of Chinese literature within the reach of those peoples of the world who do not have the good fortune of knowing the Chinese language. At this opening stage of our proceedings I would like, on behalf of all here, to congratulate and thank the initiators and organizers of the conference and to express our appreciation for the very generous support of the Council for Cultural Planning and Development, the Chiang Ching-kuo Foundation, and the National Taiwan University.

Upon reaching a milestone, it is natural to look back at the way one has come. So I would ask you to indulge me if I take you back for a moment to my own situation as a recent graduate in Chinese studies, London circa 1950, the midpoint of this bustling century. No doubt it was a very salutary experience for me to be able to find so little satisfaction from the English translations of Chinese literature in existence—let alone in print—at that date. I am not suggesting that I read at that time every English translation that had ever been made; but a reader with enough *Sitzfleisch*, a sufficiently well-padded seat, probably could have done so and still have obtained only the sketchiest idea of the breadth and sweep of Chinese literature. Yes, in

This essay was delivered as the keynote address at the International Conference on Translation of Chinese Literature, Taipei, November 1990.

retrospect I suppose it was good for my soul to be forced to actually read things in the original because the translations either didn't exist or were basically unreadable. The case was surely the same or worse with other languages of Europe—with practically every language, in fact, except for the special case of Japanese.

Of course there were delights among the translations that had been made. I wish it were possible for me here to pay tribute to the many worthy pioneers—to Julien for French, Bernhard Karlgren for Swedish, Jaroslav Prusek for Czech—but let me limit myself to the English translators. Of them, from the great James Legge on down, I shall make brief mention only of Giles and Waley. Herbert Giles, a Cambridge professor at the turn of the century, wrote what I imagine must have been the first history of Chinese literature in any language (including Chinese), produced handsome Edwardian verses from Tang and other originals, and rendered Chinese prose in an English style that carried one along in a sort of airy canter. He also had a rather idiosyncratic way with a footnote. I remember laughing out loud in the hush of a college library when I was looking through some translations from old tales—I think it was probably Giles's *Strange Stories from a Chinese Studio*, his Liaozhai selections. The charms of a fair maiden were being catalogued in conventional fashion, and when the text arrived at the slenderness of her tapering fingers, the usual "onion-shoot" simile was used. At this point the translator—as I say, I think it must have been Giles—supplied a footnote. I don't have the book at hand, but approximately it read: "Onion-shoots: when sauteed lightly with a little ginger, these are esteemed a particular delicacy by the Chinese." Now, I'm all for adding local color. One great virtue of footnotes is that they can help bring to the outsider some of the cultural advantages enjoyed by the native reader. But Giles is far from the only translator who has included wildly incongruous or irrelevant material in footnotes.

One way, incidentally, to keep footnotes to a minimum and thereby reduce the irritation they inevitably cause is to incorporate explanatory information in the text itself. Let me give a simple instance. When Du Liniang, in scene 3 of *Mudanting*, first greets her parents, she has the following lines, among others, in her aria:

> Zhu xuanhua chunshu
> Suize shi zi sheng chimu
> shoudejian zhe pantao shu.

> 祝萱花椿樹
> 雖則是子生遲暮
> 守得見這蟠桃熟

We might translate these lines more or less word for word:

> Wish that lily and cedar
> Though child born late in evening
> May see me raised to ripen as fairy peach.

I suppose this is understandable as it is, but footnotes would make it a little less cryptic. I chose instead to build the minimum information required into my English text, as follows:

> O mother gentle as lily,
> father as cedar strong,
> though the faery peach comes only
> after thirty centuries to fruit
> and even so I your child
> was born of your evening years
> yet with careful guarding
> may you see me brought to ripeness.

I have made eight lines here out of three, and perhaps this is unforgivable, especially with a text as long as *Mudanting* is to begin with; but I wanted a version of Liniang's lines that would retain the arboreal imagery and still be intelligible, without distracting the reader into sifting through yet another mass of little numbers at the bottom of the page.

But to return to Herbert Giles. People, it appeared, certainly read him for pleasure, because it was with Giles that my own model and mentor, Arthur Waley, had to compete when he first began to publish. The duel between the two of them over the question of rhymed iambics versus free verse and sprung rhythms in English versions of Chinese poems caught the interest of literary circles of the twenties and did more than anything else to put Chinese poetry on the English literary map.

Should we use rhyme when we translate? Always? Sometimes? Never? To pick away for a minute at this knot I would like to revert again to my usual practice as a teacher of literature and use a specific example. My intention is to illustrate two convictions of mine that conflict with each other: first, that Chinese poems that rhyme should be translated into English verse that rhymes, whenever this is possible; and second, that Arthur Waley was a giant figure in our past even though he set his face against the use of rhyme in translation and sternly criticized the kind of thing Giles had been producing. Waley, after all, came along at a time when most young poets were experimenting with rhymeless verse after Whitman, sprung rhythms after Gerard Manley Hopkins, and so on, and so it is hardly surprising that he developed his particular kind of line, which has had such a universal impact on the practice of subsequent translators into English. And yet if a translator is working from a rhymed original in French, German, or most other languages, it is most unlikely that the resulting English version will not be rhymed.

The example that shows both that Chinese verse can be translated into rhyming English with superb success and that, paradoxically, Waley could do this himself if he wanted to, is his version of the famous "Wang Jiang-nan" *ci* by Li Houzhu:

> Duoshao hen.
> Zuoye menghun zhong
> Hai si jiushi you Shangyuan:
> Che ru liushui ma ru long,
> Hua yue zheng chunfeng.

> 多少恨
> 昨夜夢魂中
> 還似舊時遊上苑
> 車如流水馬如龍
> 花月正春風

Waley's version:

> Immeasurable pain!
> My dreaming soul last night was king again.
> As in past days
> I wandered through the Palace of Delight,
> And in my dream
> Down grassy garden ways
> Glided my chariot, smoother than a summer stream;
> There was moonlight,
> The trees were blossoming,
> And a faint wind softened the air of night,
> For it was spring.

I have seldom read an English translation of a Chinese poem that had this kind of verbal magic about it. Unfortunately the translation is obviously far from perfect; indeed, some of Waley's decisions here seem headed for disaster. Why no dragons? The dragons are absolutely central both to the royal persona and to the dreamlike setting of the original. And where do the grassy garden ways come from? Kensington Palace, surely, rather than any Chinese royal park. In fact, it is tempting to speculate that the word *grassy* is in the poem because the graph *yuan* in *Shangyuan*, Li Yu's third line, is topped with a grass radical, *caozitou*— perhaps even Waley was not quite immune from the visual semantics bug that Fenollosa brought in to bite Pound, Florence Ayscough, and others. But looking at how the pluses of Waley's translation outweigh the minuses, how grateful we should be that the atmosphere of Li Yu's last line is so perfectly captured in the English, even though it took daring as well as great skill to expand five syllables into four whole lines of English, lines whose uneven length recalls the metrical pattern of the original but only in a generic, not a precise, sense. It goes without saying that a quatrain, *jueju*, or an eight-line *lushi* would be destroyed if one played around with the number of lines like this. It would be like translating a sonnet by Michelangelo into seventeen or twenty-three English lines—no one would think of doing such a thing. But when translators have to tackle a lengthy and semantically packed line of a *ci*, or worse still a *qu*, they will almost certainly have to consider departing from the attempt to represent the metrical form of the original quite so slavishly.

In the end it is a different magic from Li Yu's that one derives from Waley's poem, and perhaps from the difficulty of the decisions Waley had to make here one can see how he developed his distrust of rhyme. I have belabored this one lyric long enough—but it seems to me to be only through intensive consideration of this kind of text that one can think through some of the problems involved in the audacious, presumptuous, and ultimately humbling business of translating from Chinese into English.

As I have been suggesting, way back in 1950 we could afford to quibble at this kind of length about the intricacies of translation simply because we had so few models before us. Forty years later we have, praise be, a very different situation. One can teach a college-level literature-in-translation course nowadays with a fairly respectable reading list. Anthologies of poetry no longer come in slim volumes with wide margins and a terminal point somewhere in the Tang dynasty. It is possible for the reader of English to gain familiarity with a fair sampling of the oeuvre of a number of individual poets, especially of the Tang and Song dynasties. The level of readability is often high and the quality and quantity of annotation impressive; translators no longer confine themselves to the more colloquial lyrics, free from allusions and self-explanatory in English.

In the area of fiction, every one of the six great classical novels, the *Sida qishu* plus *Hongloumeng* and *Rulin waishi*, is now or soon will be accessible in a respectable—sometimes a brilliant—translation, and of course the number of traditional novels well worth reading and available in English versions is by no means limited to six. There are readable translations of plays of various generic types. *Yuan zaju* have received the most attention, as is only proper when we reflect that it is now two and a half centuries since William Hatchett published *The Chinese Orphan: a Historical Tragedy...*, *Interspers'd with Songs, after the Chinese Manner*, his version of *Zhaoshi guer* retranslated from the French of Father Prémare. By this time we have English versions of perhaps some thirty *zaju* altogether, though the quality of translation varies rather violently. This again is understandable, since Chinese dramatic forms are hospitable to the widest imaginable range of language levels, from classical-style lyric through parallel prose down to dialect slang and gutter invective. Perhaps this might explain why after all this time there is still no single volume on the market of representative *zaju* plays, translated in full into idiomatic English.

I shall have a little more to say later about the long Ming *chuanqi* plays, but in surveying what has been done already we may note that several of the best-known plays are now available in English. The only other dramatic genre that·has been translated in more than specimen form is Peking opera, and here again we have available a handful of the minority of these plays that are in fact readable as literary and not just as theatrical pieces.

You will have noticed, I'm sure, that I am using a highly Westernized definition of what sort of writing counts as literature. It would take me too far afield to argue the case here for historical, philosophical, or other texts, but let me simply comment that, again, a fair sampling is possible in English of the more "literary" of such works, the *Shiji*, the Mencius, and so on, and I suppose the number of English-language versions of the *Laozi* must have passed two hundred long ago.

A really startling boom has been under way for some time now in the area of contemporary writing. Two obvious reasons for this are the rise in quality of the writing itself, in Taiwan since the sixties and on the mainland in the post-Mao years, and the exponential growth in the number of British and American students of modern Chinese. A considerable pool of qualified language experts is now a reality, with the result that the sorts of works that used to be translated by travelers and journalists are now being tackled by well-trained professional scholars. Surely the younger Chinese writers of today, whether publishing in Taiwan or on the mainland, are accessible to the Anglophone reader to a degree undreamed of by any preceding generation. Without question, fiction writers have fared better than poets or dramatists in this regard and important and exciting pieces in all genres wait still to be discovered, but it is truly heartening to see Chinese writers on the way to crashing the language barrier and taking their place on the world literary scene as Japanese and Latin American writers did in the sixties.

The speed and breadth of this expansion of the field of translation, welcome as it is, naturally give rise to concern about a corresponding improvement in quality. For if there is one fundamental truism about the translation of literary works, it is that a bad translation is much worse than no translation at all. I'm sure many here have known the frustration of having a non-Chinese-reading friend comment in lukewarm fashion on a favorite piece that the friend has read in a flat, wooden English version. One wants to cry: "But if only you could read the original! This really isn't what Chinese poetry is like!"

In this regard I should like to use this platform, which really is what Teddy Roosevelt would have called a bully pulpit, to put forward a plea and a prayer. The plea is for help in the elucidation of literary texts from scholars across the entire field of humanistic studies, and the prayer is that future translators from Chinese will be blessed not just with linguistic skill but with a passion for literature.

First, the plea for help. The most immediate form of assistance that I have in mind is a very obvious one, the reprinting of reliable texts and the provision of copious annotation. And here I can speak with true feeling, because I have been the beneficiary of aid of this kind. I launched out on a complete translation of *Mudanting* (The Peony Pavilion) realizing that I was probably doing a very foolhardy thing, and in the face of certain passages I suppose I came close to despairing of ever finishing the task. But I could never have begun if it had not been for the appearance in the late fifties of a generously annotated edition of a reliably complete text of the play.

Over and above the immediate help of annotated cribs, translators depend on scholarship from many sides. First-rate critics help them select their material, historians of literature help them place it in perspective. Comparatists who make analogy studies between totally unrelated literary traditions make possible a stronger sense of genre, and if translators have these studies, then the required tone will come much more naturally to them, whether it be the distinctive tone of satire, polemic, lyrical reminiscence, comic romance or heroic tragedy, naturalist fiction, or fairytale.

From other fields of scholarship, the work of historians in general helps translators develop the necessary depth of understanding of the cultural context, the work of linguists can refine their appreciation of the kind of choices of diction that were available to the original author—style, in any language, being a matter of choices made between alternative intelligibilities. Reference aids of all kinds are indispensable—the *Zhongwen da cidian* alone has made possible a quantum leap in our ability to cope with obscurities. And yet no form of aid is more absolutely precious to us than the work of annotation, by means of which the innocent outsider can avoid the nightmarish traps of ignoring allusions, translating proper names, and all the other horrors that bring cold panic to the translator's sweating brow.

So much for the plea; now for the prayer. It is that translation be undertaken by men and women with a genuine passion for literature, people who read texts for fun and not just because they get paid to teach them. I don't want to sound cynical, but I suspect all of us have come across colleagues as well as students who set up as translators but whose true interests may be historical, linguistic, in fact anything but literary, who in fact would find it hard to recall the last work of imaginative literature they actually read for pleasure. And I'm not speaking just of Chinese literature. A good translator should be able to command a considerable range of English styles, chatty, stately, vulgar, pompous, nervous, virile, lyrical, ascetic, sentimental, whatever. And the only way I can think of to develop this kind of range is to read, as a matter of love and habit, both the classics of the past and the inventors of the new English styles of today.

Above all, an obvious prerequisite of good translation is to be in love with the text one is translating. That is why I have always deeply appreciated the freedom of choice that is accorded a Free World academic. If I were translating for a government bureau, or for money to pay the rent, or as part of some kind of master plan devised by someone else, I don't believe I could infuse into my work the sense of relish for the original that I hope it at least sometimes conveys. For this reason, the old expression "a little of what you fancy does you good" aptly describes my first principle of translation. What I mean by this is that if I try to translate only things that hold a special attraction for me, then the chances are that my translations will repay to other readers some of the debt of pleasure I've owed to the original creators. Also, because the saying calls for only a little of what you fancy, I have tried to make it a rule not to go on working at the actual putting into English (though I might continue some of the donkey work of dictionary thumping and allusion chasing) after I've begun to feel tired or bored.

Compiling an anthology of translations from Chinese literature was for me an unalloyed delight, since I could choose all the juicy texts to translate myself and use the work of other translators to represent pieces which I thought should be in a representative anthology but which didn't excite my own particular tastes—things like prose essays of a philosophical bent, for example. And when I speak of "unalloyed delight," I am thinking also of the fact that I could do things like take from a particular poet those pieces that I thought I understood and ignore others, however worthy, that would need interpretation by an expert more erudite than myself.

And now, although in these rambling remarks I have been discussing literature in general, I should like to spend the rest of my time considering a specific question, the question of abridgment or partial translation of a text, and to discuss this question in relation to one type of text in particular, the Ming *chuanqi* play.

Somehow I have never felt happy about abridgments—I remember the feeling I had of being cheated when as a schoolboy I read *The Brothers Karamazov*, by discovering only after I had finished the book that it was an abridged English version of Dostoyevsky's work, edited by Somerset Maugham, and not the complete text. And until the wonderful Hawkes-Minford *Story of the Stone* came out it was always with apologetic discomfort that one urged one of the various abridgments of *Dream of the Red Chamber* on eager undergraduates.

And yet, when it comes to the late-Ming playwrights I have to think of a remark made by an English critic about some of those endless verse tragedies written by Romantic poets and rapidly consigned to well-deserved oblivion: "They had the right to take their time," said our critic; "the question is, do they have the right to take mine?" That sounds like a very arrogant remark, but after all life is short and art is long, and those unemployed or underemployed mandarins of seventeenth-century China were writing, often enough in the tranquil comfort of their garden studios, for a public that had a lot more time for reading and far fewer masterpieces available to them than most of us have. In the history of world drama, the plays which failed and today are lost or simply unread must outnumber the hits by some astronomical ratio. The French Revolution, for example, was swiftly followed by an extraordinarily prolific period of writing for the stage; but which of these predecessors of the great Victor Hugo is performed, read, or recalled at all now by any but historians of literature?

So why bother with late Ming effusions? Because, obviously, they contain passages and sometimes whole scenes that are still alive with wit, lyrical beauty, stirring sentiments, and insights into the human condition. But oh, the length and oh, the uneven quality of the writing! Even *The Peony Pavilion*, for which I have almost unqualified admiration, has its longueurs, its scenes that just about any intelligent director would abridge or delete, its passages that the translator, having committed to doing the whole thing, will delay facing up to until some morning when he or she is feeling unusually daring or desperate.

Discriminating Western readers surely are entitled to have placed in their hands a complete version of a play like *The Peony Pavilion* so that they may gauge for themselves the wit or dullness of the often pedantic examination humor, the nobility or sheer vainglory of the martial interludes, even the moving tenderness or the cloying sentimentality of the domestic scenes. We now have reasonably representative English renderings of a handful of *chuanqi* plays, and beyond argument we need complete translations of more.

But however it may go against the grain to contemplate abridgment or the mining of a long text for its precious gems, I believe there is a case also for the translation of selected scenes from certain plays, to do in fact for English translation what Chinese managers have done for centuries in stage performance by isolating single scenes which then became known as *zhezi-xi*. This might indeed be the best possible strategy for laying Ming *chuanqi* plays in translated form before the English-reading public, to present a sampling of selected scenes, with the kind of introductory material which would appropriately locate each scene within its dramatic context, before challenging the reader with the thirty-odd or forty-odd scenes of a complete individual work. The hope would be, obviously, that the reader of the selection, hooked and clamoring for more, would go on to read complete plays and eventually, in some future decade we can only dream of now, to the complete oeuvre of a Tang Xianzu or a Li Yu.

It would try your patience too far if at this point I were to launch into a full-scale discussion of which kind of play deserves full translation and which might well be abridged. For the present I will argue the case by considering two plays by Wu Bing: *Xiyuanji*, and *Lumudan*. Though both are comedies and very obviously the work of one man, they seem to me to call for very different treatments if they are to be presented to the English-reading public, which so far as I know can have no notion of their existence beyond the listing by Josephine Huang Hung in her *Ming Drama*. I shall plead for complete translation of Wu Bing's *Xiyuanji* but then try to suggest how *Lumudan* might be introduced to the English-reading public, and shown to contain much wit, sharp satire, and some very effective stagecraft, without necessarily confronting this public with a full-length translation, which might indeed, to someone without a considerable background in traditional Chinese life and letters, prove virtually unreadable.

If it is fair to characterize many late Ming *chuanqi* plays as interminable and uneven, these terms certainly cannot be applied to *Xiyuanji*. Not one of the thirty-three scenes of this play deserves to be cut. The opening scene (following the brief prologue) presents the *sheng* hero, as is obligatory, but immediately involves him in action and gives scope for a mime spectacle by having his pleasure boat rammed by that of the *jing* villain. Scene 3, again in obligatory fashion, brings on the *dan* heroine in a mood of boudoir lassitude that delicately recalls Du Liniang. Very soon comes scene 6, bringing the hero's misidentification of the heroine, which is the springboard of the action of the entire play. A succession of scenes from 9 onward poignantly contrast moods of gaiety and pathos: love idylls, the teasing of the hero by his friends, and the lamentations of the dying *xiaodan*. Highlights of later scenes include the complex feelings, on both sides, that accompany the act of adopting an orphan girl in the attempt to compensate for the premature death of one's own daughter (scene 18); coarse slapstick (immediately following, and again used for contrast of mood) as the villain prepares for examination and reminds us of the kind of abuses satirized at greater length in *Lumudan*; the superb lyrical evocation of ghostly wooing, hardly inferior to the *Mudanting* scenes on which these scenes, 23 and 26 especially, are patterned; and a scene of high comedy, 29, in which just about everyone assumes everyone else is a ghost and reacts in terror—a scene for which the only parallel that comes to mind is from the modern Western stage, in Noel Coward's *Blithe Spirit*. Scenes 31 and 32 economically clear up the multiple misunderstandings of Zhang's relationship with *dan* and *xiaodan*, and the grand finale of scene 33 strikes the absolutely appropriate note as the *xiaodan*, in ghostly form, attends the Buddhist mass for her salvation and communicates her thanks to each of the other principals through their common dream.

I am still in the process of reading Wu Bing's five plays, and not all critics consider this one his masterpiece, but I am convinced it would richly repay complete translation. Wu Bing in this play stays refreshingly clear of many of those irritating late Ming conventions of obligatory martial scenes, parting scenes, examination scenes, and so on; he gets on with his not-too-far-fetched plotting in a direct and economical manner, and his plot itself has witty twists that seem almost to prefigure the entertainments of Li Yu.

I am much less sure about *Lumudan*. This is again a stylish romantic comedy, but with an edge of satire in place of the pathos of the young *xiaodan*'s death that makes *Xiyuanji* that much the more absorbing as a work of drama.

In *Lumudan*, the prime criterion for the pairing of lovers is wit. In this regard the work resembles *Much Ado About Nothing* probably more than any other English play. But what makes it unique and quintessentially Chinese is its preoccupation with the traditional system of examinations for the bureaucracy, to the extent that we must redefine wit in this connection as the potential for examination prowess. The lover here enters the lists for his fair lady not by wielding his sword on the battlefield but by plying his brush in supervised literary composition.

And from this very preoccupation with the satirically presented catalogue of examination abuses stems the problem with the play for a modern English reader, the problem of the monotonous reiteration of a whole series of examination scenes. For the present purpose I will limit my comments on the play to a brief mention of three scenes, strategically placed through the action, which are basic to the characterization of the clownish pseudoscholars, *jing* and *chou*, and in this way central to Wu Bing's satiric purpose. All are examination scenes. Ostensibly they depict friendly literary contests held under club rules in a domestic setting; in fact the audience is perfectly aware of the parallel with the official halls of examination, in the provincial or national capital, where the prize will be not the hand of a local beauty as in Wu Bing's comedy but entrance into the imperial bureaucracy with its open avenues to wealth and fame.

Scene 5, "Club Meeting," sets the pattern for the chicanery of the two clowns, as their servants smuggle into the examination room the poems their surrogates have composed for them. The meat of this scene is the set of rules enunciated by the hero, rules outlawing various forms of cheating that were evidently a major source of concern to honest scholars of late-Ming times. Scene 25, "Examination by the Rules," is essentially a repeat performance of this scene, with the difference that on this occasion the rules against leaving the room or communicating with outsiders are strictly enforced. Scene 18, "Alcove Quiz," is the central major comic scene in which the essential stupidity of the two clowns is exposed, and this is the single scene I would choose to present in translation to the English reader as a fitting representation of the entire play.

"Alcove Quiz" turns the poor *jing* Liu Wuliu inside out. He is onstage throughout, most of the time seated at his examination desk, where he shows every sign of embarrassment and discomfort. He is a rich idler, overfed and overdressed, ill fitted to the confines of the scholar's desk. Being totally incapable of literary composition, he can only stretch and yawn, drum his fingers, and pretend to be humming his lines over; in fact he is dividing his time between waiting for his crony to bring him the answer his tutor (the hero of the play) has promised to ghostwrite for him and trying to crane his neck round the curtain to catch a glimpse of the delectable Che Jingfang, his examiner, his intended bride, and the *dan* character of the play. Behind the curtain, Miss Che is accompanied by her old nurse. Miss

Che, as is only proper, never leaves the privacy of her alcove, but the nurse emerges from time to time to bully poor Liu, especially at the point where he is strutting and mincing round his half of the stage in the absurd attempt to impress the young lady with his elephantine "elegance." The comings and goings from the alcove to the "examination hall" proper are complicated also by Miss Che's brother, the *chou* clown who is Liu's crony. He serves as a sort of go-between in this scene, smuggling in the crib to the hapless examinee, skulking onstage and off in an attempt to avoid detection, and finally entering the alcove to plead, in vain, the virtues of Liu's ghosted poem before his sister. By the end of the scene, even the *chou* has given up on Liu, who is left alone on stage completely discomfited. All in all, the construction of the "alcove" scene is a fine example of Chinese dramaturgy, wherein the absence of sets and scenery of any kind beyond a couple of poles supporting a simple curtain and the groupings and movements on stage are skillfully orchestrated for maximum comic effect. In the climactic concluding lines of the scene, the heroine Che Jingfang finally condescends to read out loud the "poem," actually an absurd piece of doggerel which the hero has conned the hapless villain into submitting as his own work and in which poor Liu Wuliu unwittingly ridicules himself as a turtle, i.e., a cuckold.

At least in the case of this one play, then, I would consider partial translation far more likely to win friends among the English-reading public than a complete translation, which would risk seeming oppressively pedantic, repetitious, and boring. My own recommendation would be for complete translation of the scene I have just described, "Alcove Quiz," introduced by a reasonably lengthy explanation of what has been going on earlier in the play, a brief biographical sketch of Wu Bing, some comments on the examination system itself and its late Ming abuses, and whatever other background information one might consider helpful. Add to this a suggestive description of the parallels in the use of comic devices between *Lumudan* and *Much Ado About Nothing*, and the Anglophone reader might perhaps begin to feel sufficiently at home really to relish the flavor of this priceless piece of Chinese dramatic satire.

In these scattered remarks I have restricted myself to my personal prejudices, my likes and dislikes. I hope I have not opened the floodgates to young translators itching to use rhyme but ready to sacrifice rhythm, accuracy, and naturalness in the process. I hope people will not stop making complete translations as a result of my support of partial ones. I hope my rapid survey of the scope of the translations already made from Chinese literature will not give the impression of complacency—in a certain sense, almost everything still waits to be done. But above all I hope I have provided some contentious observations that will help stimulate discussion.

The Implied Reader and Translation

The *Shih chi* as Example

WILLIAM H. NIENHAUSER, JR.

Despite the title, this essay is not really of a theoretical nature. It is primarily a status report on the progress of a project in which I am involved to translate a portion of the *Shih chi* 史記 (Records of the Grand Historian). Besides myself, four other scholars are participating in the work: Chan Chiu-Ming 陳照明, Cheng Tsai-Fa 鄭再發, Lu Zongli 呂宗力, and Robert Reynolds (all of the University of Wisconsin). The theoretical portion of this essay consists mainly of my reflections on the work at this point in time.

Our project is one of six recent large-scale efforts—five ongoing—to render China's best-known early narrative, Ssu-ma Ch'ien's 司馬遷 (145–ca. 85 B.C.) *Shih chi*, into a modern tongue. The *Shih chi* is a fascinating work which attracted admirers almost from the time of its completion (ca. 90 B.C.). In modern times, a number of translators have shared this fascination. Yet of those who have turned their attention to this massive collection of materials—more than half a million words in the original—not a single one has produced a completely successful translation. In fact, to date no complete Western-language translation exists. Before turning to the question of "the implied reader," therefore, let me briefly address these translation texts—past and present—and their methods.[1] Out of convention I will present them in chronological order.

Previous Translations

In the mid–nineteenth century the Austrian sinologist August Pfizmaier
(1808–1887) rendered twenty-four chapters of the *Shih-chi* into German.
Pfizmaier published his work in a number of separate issues of the *Sitzungs-
berichte der Wiener Akademie der Wissenschaften* and seems never to have had a
grand plan to translate the complete *Shih-chi*. Another attempt at the end of
the century, by Léon de Rosny and H. J. Allen,[2] was even less successful.

It took the indefatigable Edouard Chavannes (1865–1918) to begin what
could be called the first project to translate the *Shih-chi* in its entirety. From
1895 to 1905 his carefully annotated translation of the first forty-seven
chapters appeared.[3] As numerous reviews of the time attest, Chavannes's
scholarship exemplifies the best in the French tradition of sinology. Nevertheless, his undertaking remained unfinished.

During the 1930s there were several desultory attempts to pick up where
Chavannes left off: Derk Bodde translated some chapters relating to the
Ch'in period,[4] while two German scholars rendered a number of other
chapters (mostly unpublished).[5] The 1950s also witnessed two smaller-scale
Shih chi translation projects, by the Russian scholar V. Panasjuk[6] and the
American Frank A. Kierman.[7]

The second major attempt to render the *Shih-chi* into a Western language,
undertaken by the American Burton Watson, also began during the 1950s.
Watson translated sixty-six chapters (fifty-seven in full and nine in part),
selecting that portion of the work which he felt demonstrated its excellence
as narrative literature, for his massive *Records of the Grand Historian* (2 vols.,
New York, 1961). Watson's versions are intended for the general reader and
have little annotation.

Thus, despite the work of over a dozen Western translators, there remain
thirty chapters with no adequate translation into any Western language.[8]

Current Projects

As mentioned, there are six recent projects to translate the *Shih chi*. Two of
these undertakings began in the 1970s. Although I cannot be certain which
came first, I will begin with Rudolf Vsevolodovich Viatkin's Russian translation, *Syma Tsyan, Istoricheskie zapiski (Shi Tsi)* (Ssu-ma Ch'ien, Historical
Records [Shih Chi]). The specifics of this work are known to me only with
the help of a colleague at the University of Wisconsin who reads Russian.
Viatkin's efforts began nearly twenty years ago. Although he collaborated
with an expert on the Hsiung-nu, V. S. Taskin, on the first two volumes, he
has carried out most of the work alone.[9] This project, which has been called
"the largest ongoing translation today from Chinese literature into a Western language,"[10] has resulted in annotated, scholarly renditions of the basic

annals, tables, treatises, and hereditary houses. Still to be translated are the seventy "biographies." Yet already Viatkin has done more of the text (about 64 percent) than his most prolific Western predecessors, Chavannes (who did about 57 percent) and Watson (36 percent).[11]

A second large translation project was also begun in the early 1970s by a team of scholars in Peking. Although the work—to be titled *Shih chi i-chu* 史記譯註 —is still unpublished, I have been in contact with one of the team's leaders, Wu Shu-p'ing 吳樹平 of the Academy of Social Sciences, and he has kindly provided me with a few pages of galley proofs of the team's *chüan* 6, the "Basic Annals of the First Emperor of Ch'in." From these few pages the general approach can be surmised. Following the main text (which, I was told, has been collated with important modern editions in a manner in which the 1959 Chung-hua *Shih chi* text was not)[12] are a number of extensive notes, primarily on proper nouns found in the text (names, place names, etc.). Then a modern Chinese translation is appended.[13] The style of the modern Chinese is rather literate, as the following example may illustrate:

Original: 莊襄王爲秦質子趙, 見呂不韋姬, 悅而取之, 生始皇.

Translation: 莊襄王在趙國作爲秦國人質時, 看見呂不韋的姬妾, 很喜觀, 就把她要了過來, 生子始皇

Projecting a total from the size of the small section provided me (in comparison with the number of pages used for the same text in the Chung-hua edition of the *Shih chi*), this new translation is likely to total more than 10,000 pages. No publication date has been set, but the entire project is now in press.

Although Wang Li-ch'i's 王利器 name graces the title page of the *Shih chi chu-i*, Wang himself had nothing to do with the work. He explained to me in summer 1990 that the work was the fruit of three or four years' labor by former students of his and their students, now mostly located in Hunan. Indeed, the front and back matter of the book reveals that many of the forty-five translators were teaching in high schools in Hunan. The key figure in the organization of the project seems to have been one of the three assistant editors, Chang Lieh 張烈, born in 1932 in I-yang 益陽 County in Hunan and a 1964 graduate of the History Department at Peking University who works for Chung-hua Book Company in Peking. His background ties him to the other Pei-ta History Department graduates in the project (Ch'en Ping-ts'ai 陳秉才, also an assistant editor of the *Shih chi chu-i* and a fellow 1964 graduate; Ch'i Nien-tseng 祁念曾, a 1968 graduate and a member of the eight-person editorial board; and Ch'i Ch'ing-ch'ang 齊慶昌, another 1964 graduate) and the Hunan participants. Ts'ao Hsiang-ch'eng 曹相成, a seventy-year-old retired high school teacher and the third of the assistant editors of the volumes, is representative of this latter group.

The preface, from Ts'ao's hand, reveals that the intent of the work is to make the *Shih chi* and the long period of history ·it records available to Chinese youth. Although the preface is not a scholarly document, two other studies in the front matter, by Wang Li-ch'i and I Meng-ch'un 易孟醇 (an editor of Hunan Jen-min ch'u-pan-she), on the text and editions of the *Shih chi* respectively, are important studies. But the scholarship reflected therein has not always been incorporated into this translation.

The *T'i-li* 體例 (Stylesheet) explains that the Chung-hua 1959 edition of the *Shih chi* was used as the base text but that the punctuation was emended in a number of places. It does not deal with questions of authenticity, interpolations, etc. The notes are intended as explanatory. The text uses short-form Chinese characters, but names, titles, and other items likely to be confused are given in normal characters.

Although the translations are more carefully done than previous *pai-hua* renditions, the varied ages of the translators (the oldest was seventy when the work appeared, most were in their fifties, and two only in their twenties) has produced a variety of styles. Still, when we compare the rendition of the passage from the forthcoming *Shih chi i-chu* by Wu Shu-p'ing et al., this version (by Hsia Po-yen 夏伯炎, a retired lecturer from Hunan who was born in 1926, and Ku Ch'ien-fan 谷千帆, a lecturer born in 1940 who is now at a small school in I-yang, Hunan) seems more colloquial, defying Wu's claims to the contrary: 莊襄王作爲秦國的質子到趙國, 看見了呂不韋的 一個小妻, 因爲喜愛就娶了她, 生下始皇.

Yet another ongoing translation which began in the 1970s was conceived by Yoshida Kenkō 吉田賢抗. The work was based on Takigawa Kametarō's 漳川龜太郎 (1881–1945) *Shiki kaichū kōshō* 史記會註考證 and Tanaka Tokujitta's 田中篤實他 *Sōtei Shiki hyorin* 增訂史記評林 (published by Gyokuzan Do 玉山堂 in 1869), but a number of other editions were also consulted. The first volume appeared in 1973. Since that time volumes 2 (*pen-chi* 本紀), 5–7 (all *shih-chia* 世家), and 8 (*lieh-chuan* 列傳) have been published. The latter was translated by Takigawa's protégé, Mizusawa Toshitada 水沢利忠. These volumes are extremely thorough. Following a brief general introduction to each chapter, the original *Shih chi* text is presented at the top of each page over a *furigana* Kambun reading of it. A general translation follows, to which are attached notes explicating names, concepts, places, and, in some cases, linguistic aspects of the original. At the end of each chapter is a long comment by the translator.

The fifth project is ongoing, but my information is entirely secondhand. A colleague has told me that Burton Watson is rendering the biographies of men of the Ch'in era under a grant from the Centre for Translation of the Chinese University at Hong Kong.

Finally, there is our undertaking to render into English the thirty chapters that have no satisfactory Western-language translation. These chapters are all "biographies" (列傳), primarily from the Spring and Autumn and Warring States eras. To date we have draft translations of nine chapters.

Ssu-ma Ch'ien's Implied Reader

Watson's recent project provides an apt transition to the major focus of this study: the implied reader of a translation.[14] Watson, of course, is a master translator, the most prolific and successful at making Chinese literature and history available to the English-speaking audience since Arthur Waley. Scholars as well as general readers have read his work with pleasure and profit. Yet, as Pokora observes concerning his *Shih chi* translation, Watson chose "to write for the general public and to venture a more or less free translation not addressed to the specialist." In the same passage Pokora calls for a "complete scholarly translation."[15] Here I'd like to focus on the word *complete* and its significance for the reader our project has in mind: a student of ancient China from a Western background. At the same time I would like to point out that Ssu-ma Ch'ien also had his reader firmly in mind when he wrote. In his comments to the biography of Kuan Chung and Yen Ying 管晏列傳 (ch. 62), Ssu-ma Ch'ien observes:

> I have read Mr. Kuan's "Shepherding the People," "The Mountains are High,"[16] "Chariots and Horses,"[17] "Light and Heavy,"[18] and "Nine Bureaus"[19] and the *Spring and Autumn of Master Yen.*[20] With such detail have they spoken of things.[21] Since I have seen their writings, I wanted to observe the way they put things into practice[22] and have for this reason composed[23] historical accounts of them.[24] *As for their writings, many people today have copies, and because of this I will not discuss them, but rather comment on those extraneous stories.*[25]

The italicized sentence is meant to emphasize what I see as one of Ssu-ma Ch'ien's historical principles in the *Shih chi*: to avoid repeating texts or information from texts that are widely known to his reader.[26]

In the realm of translation, however, this principle implies that the translator of the *Shih chi* should follow a course directly opposite to that of Ssu-ma Ch'ien. Rather than omitting material we know our reader to possess (as Ssu-ma Ch'ien did), we modern translators of the *Shih chi* must provide our readers with all the material we know they *should* possess to reach an equal footing with the reader Ssu-ma Ch'ien had in mind.

In our work to date we have become convinced that only through a thoroughly annotated text (and thus one addressing concerns slightly different from those of a modern Chinese translation aimed at a Chinese audience) can the *Shih chi* be properly and "completely" translated (complete in the sense of also preparing our reader in the fashion Ssu-ma Ch'ien intended)[27] for the scholarly audience. As Ssu-ma Ch'ien was concerned with what his readers were *familiar* with, we must not ignore what our readers will be *unfamiliar* with. It is this concern that has led us to reject some initial reactions to our early translation work by scholars who called for a simplification of our scholarly apparatus, an apparatus that is somewhat cumbersome.

An Example of a *Shih chi* Translation for
Ssu-ma Ch'ien's Implied Reader

I close on a practical note with a sample chapter of our work—the biography of Kuan Chung from the "Kuan [Chung] Yen [Ying] lieh-chuan" 管晏列傳 (ch. 62). This draft was completed by Chan Chiu-Ming, Cheng Tsai-Fa, and myself. It is interspersed (see the sections set in smaller type) with additional personal comments and queries that were directed at colleagues attending the conference on translation, with the expectation that they would participate in the presentation by offering comments, corrections, and suggestions. The original text (Chung-hua edition) appears at the end of this chapter as appendix 2. Numbers in brackets refer to the corresponding page numbers of the Chung-hua edition.

Kuan [Chung] and Yen [Ying] [28]

[2131]

Kuan [agnomen] Chung [ca. 720–645 B.C.] [praenomen] I-wu[29] was a native of the Ying River region.[30] When he was young, he associated with[31] Pao Shu-ya,[32] so that Pao Shu[-ya] knew that he was worthy. Though Kuan Chung was impoverished and often took advantage of Pao Shu[-ya], Pao Shu[-ya] always treated him well, never deigning to mention any of this.[33]

> Here it seems from Ssu-ma Ch'ien's offhand reference to Kuan Chung's taking advantage of Pao Shu-ya, a situation of great consequence to his overall theme of friendship in this chapter, that he assumed his reader was familiar with the details we provide in note 31.

Shortly thereafter, Pao Shu[-ya] served the Noble Scion[34] Hsiao-po, while Kuan Chung served the Noble Scion,[35] Chiu.[36]

> Here, although we have supplied supplemental materials on these events in notes 34 and following, Ssu-ma Ch'ien has provided a broad outline which seems to indicate he did *not* expect his reader to be completely familiar with the story.

When Hsiao-po was established as Duke Huan [r. 685–643 B.C.], Noble Scion Chiu died[37] and Kuan Chung was imprisoned.[38] Thereupon, Pao Shu recommended Kuan Chung [to the Duke].[39] Once employed, Kuan Chung was entrusted with the administration of Ch'i and Duke Huan thereby became Grand Duke,[40] assembling the feudal lords together[41] and completely rectifying the world.[42] These things all resulted from the counsel of Kuan Chung.

Kuan Chung once remarked, "Earlier when I was in adversity, I engaged in trade with Pao Shu[-ya], and in dividing the profits, I gave myself

more, but Pao Shu never considered me greedy, because
[2132]
he knew I was impoverished.[43]

Whether the reader of the *Shih chi* would react as Hsiang Tsung-lu does to this passage (see note 41) is debatable. Ssu-ma Ch'ien's readers were expected to be able to bring a thorough background in related texts to the *Shih chi*, but at the same time not expected to be too ready to reject the underlying historical validity of a text such as this.

I counseled Pao Shu on affairs and they became worse, but knowing that for all affairs there are opportune and inopportune times, Pao Shu never considered me ignorant. Thrice[44] I gained office and thrice was dismissed by my lords, [but] Pao Shu did not consider me unacceptable, because he knew that my time had not come. I was thrice in battle and thrice I ran,[45] but Pao Shu did not consider me cowardly, because he knew that I had an aged mother.[46] When the Noble Scion Chiu was defeated, Shao Hu died for him while I suffered the humiliation of being imprisoned,[47] but Pao Shu did not consider me shameless, because he knew that I would not be embarrassed by these trivial observances [of social codes], but would consider it shameful if my accomplishments and fame were not made known to the entire world.[48] It was my parents who gave birth to me, but it is Master Pao who appreciates me."[49]

Here (note 46) we find another example of the expectations Ssu-ma Ch'ien has of his reader. Although we have used Lu Chung-lien's letter to augment our annotation, the reader of the *Shih chi* would need to recall the entire story even to understand the allusion in the letter.

After he had recommended Kuan Chung, Pao Shu himself worked under Kuan. His descendants for generations received official emoluments in Ch'i, those who were given fiefs held them for more than ten generations,[50] and often they became famous high officials. Throughout the world people did not praise Kuan Chung's worthiness, but Pao Shu's being able to appreciate men.[51]

Once Kuan Chung was put in charge of the administration and became prime minister[52] of Ch'i, with the tiny territory of Ch'i on the seacoast[53] he exchanged commodities so as to accumulate wealth, enriching the country and strengthening its armies, sharing with the common people their likes and dislikes. Therefore he proclaimed:[54] "When the granaries are full, the people will understand [the value of] social codes and moderation. When their food and clothing are adequate, they will understand [the distinction between] honor and disgrace.[55] If the sovereign practices the restrictions [set by the social codes],[56] the six relationships will be secure.[57] If the four ties are not extended, the nation will perish.[58] The orders handed down are like the source of a river [which follows a natural course] so that they will be in accord with the hearts of the people."[59] For this reason, what he advocated was modest and easy to put into effect.[60] Whatever the masses desired, he would accordingly give them. Whatever they rejected, he would accordingly abolish.

> Here there is ample opportunity to provide examples of Kuan Chung's actions. But, presumably because they are detailed in the *Kuan-tzu*, Ssu-ma Ch'ien chose not to do so.

[2133]

As for his political strategies, he excelled in creating blessings from disasters and in turning failure into success.[61] He gave great importance to the weight [of coins] and was careful about the standards of scales.[62] When Duke Huan was truly angry with Shao-chi and raided south into Ts'ai,[63] Kuan-chung took advantage of the situation to launch a punitive expedition against Ch'u, which he accused of failing to present "bound reeds" as tribute to the Chou House.[64]

> This is a more salient example of the necessity for a detailed annotation. Ssu-ma Ch'ien expected his reader to know the fascinating anecdote of the young girl frightening her liege by rocking his boat!

When Duke Huan was in fact leading a campaign north against the Jung [tribe] of the Mountains,[65] Kuan Chung took advantage of the situation to order the lord of Yen to cultivate the [model] government of Duke Shao.[66]

> Once again Ssu-ma Ch'ien demands that his reader be familiar with the interesting story of Duke Huan's fastidious adherence to the social codes of the time—a tale which he himself tells elsewhere in the *Shih chi* (see note 66)!

At the convention of K'o, Duke Huan intended to break his agreement with Ts'ao Mo [after the convention of K'o], Kuan Chung took advantage of the situation and made him [appear] faithful to his word,[67] and through this the feudal lords all submitted to Ch'i.[68]

> This passage is intriguing. Were Ssu-ma Ch'ien not expecting his reader to be able to provide the key to his cryptic comments here, we could almost see him using the conventions of the Chinese novelist centuries later telling his readers to turn to the next chapter if they wanted to know what happened next.

Therefore, it is said that "Knowing that 'to give is to receive' is the most precious thing in governing."[69]

[2134]

Kuan Chung's wealth was comparable to that of a ducal house. He held [the privilege of] the "three returns"[70] and that of using the cup-stand,[71] but the people of Ch'i did not consider him extravagant. After Kuan Chung died, the country of Ch'i followed his policies and Ch'i was often stronger than the other feudal states. Over a hundred years later, there was Master Yen.[72]

[Here the biography of Yen Ying is omitted.]

Kuan Chung was what the world refers to as a worthy official, but Confucius belittled him.[73] Could it be because he considered that the Way of the Chou House was in decline and Duke Huan was worthy, yet Kuan Chung did not exhort him to become king, but rather to proclaim himself Grand Duke? The saying goes: "[A gentleman] guides [his ruler] in accordance with [his ruler's] merits and rectifies [him] in order to redeem him from his excesses.[74] For this reason the one above and the one below are able to develop a close relationship."[75] Doesn't this refer to Kuan Chung?

[Historian's comment on Yen Ying is also omitted.]

Conclusion

There may have been many things which struck the reader about this translation (neologisms such as "Grand Duke" and "Noble Scion," for example). However, I hope that it has become clear through the sample translation that the *Shih chi* is not only an integrated work in the sense that the various sections—annals, tables, treatises, hereditary houses, and biographies—are meant to be read and cross-referenced, but that Ssu-ma Ch'ien also considered it an integral part of the other source materials then available on his subject. It may not be true that every Han reader could fall back on knowledge of every event or narrative when Ssu-ma Ch'ien demanded, but it is apparent that Ssu-ma Ch'ien expected his ideal reader to be able to do so. For this reason, it is vital to provide an annotative context for all translations intended for the modern scholarly reader. Our modern reader has, of course, the option of referring to or neglecting the relevant context given in our apparatus. While we recognize the tremendous loss in style and flavor the *Shih chi* suffers in any translation, we hope in this way at least to retain some of the spirit of Ssu-ma Ch'ien's historiography in our rendition.

APPENDIX 1

A Sample of the Kind of Note Appended to Each Chapter of Our Translation

Translator's Note

Though Ssu-ma Ch'ien presents only several incidents with which to depict Kuan Chung and Yen Ying, he has thereby revealed some striking parallels between the two men. Both were, of course, ministers to the dukes of Ch'i who brought their lords and their nation glory. In this respect, Kuan's achievements exceeded Yen's. Yet Ssu-ma Ch'ien, in speculating about Confucius's motive in belittling Kuan, observes that Duke Huan was a worthy man whom Kuan Chung could have helped to rise even higher than he did.

Another point which calls for comparison is the relationship between the two protagonists and their colleagues. Kuan Chung's career comes as a result of Pao Shu-ya's appreciation of his talents—after he had been bound and imprisoned. Kuan Chung himself is not shown to be able to appreciate others and his lack of judgment in this respect is perhaps suggested by his underevaluation of Duke Huan. Yen Ying, on the other hand, was able to appreciate both the Elder Yüeh Shih, who was also bound and imprisoned, and his driver.

The reader is also referred to David Johnson's "Epic and Early China: The Matter of Wu Tzu-hsü" (*Journal of Asian Studies* 40, no. 2 [February 1981], 255–271) which posits a theory concerning the formation of a "matter" (*matière,* or "collection of incidents and characters associated with someone") concerning Wu Tzu-hsü during the pre-Ch'in and early imperial eras which could also be applied to Kuan Chung, Yen Ying, and other pre-Ch'in figures; to Sydney Rosen's Ph.D. dissertation, "In Search of the Historical Kuan Chung" (University of Chicago, 1973), and to her article with the identical title (*Journal of Asian Studies* 25 [1976], 431–440), which attempt to identify a tradition early in the process of creating a *matière* for Kuan Chung by restricting her research to the *Tso-chuan* and *Kuo-yü* traditions; to Allyn Rickett's introduction to his *Guanzi,* in which the rich summary of the development of Kuan-tzu the man and the work suggests a number of possibilities for applying an approach such as Johnson's to Kuan Chung; to Alfred Forke's "Yen Ying, Staatsmann und Philosoph, und das Yen-tse Tsch'un-tch'iu" (*Asia Major,* Hirth Anniversary Volume (London: Probsthain, 1924), 101– 144); to R. L. Walker's "Some Notes on the *Yen-tzu Ch'un-ch'iu*" (*Journal of the American Oriental Society* 73 [1953]: 156–163); and to the front matter of Rainer Holzer's *Yen-tzu und das Yen-tzu ch'un-ch'iu* (Frankfurt: Lang, 1983; "Yen-tzus Biographie," 2–7, in which Holzer translates the opening paragraphs of the *Shih chi* biography as well as the remarks of the Grand Historian, and "Untersuchungen zur Textgeschichte," 8–16).

Fuller versions of these lives, also instructive concerning Ssu-ma Ch'ien's motives, are Liang Ch'i-ch'ao's 梁啓超 *Kuan-tzu chuan* 管子傳 (Biography of Kuan-tzu [rpt. Taipei: Chung-hua, 1963]) and the extensive biographies of both men in the *T'ung-chih* 通志. Translations include Georges Margouliès, "Biographies de Kouan [Tchong] et de Yen [Ying]," *Le Kou-wen chinois* (Paris: Geuthner, 1926), 77–83; V. A. Panasjuk, *Syma Czjan', Izbrannoe* (Moscow, 1956), 51–55; and Evan Morgan, "The Lives of Kuan Chung and Yen Tzu," in *A Guide to Wenli Styles and Chinese Ideals* (London: Probsthain, 1931), 117–127.

APPENDIX 2

Original Text from the Chung-hua 1959 Shih chi

史記卷六十二

管晏列傳第二

管仲夷吾者，潁上人也。〔二〕少時常與鮑叔牙游，鮑叔知其賢。管仲貧困，常欺鮑叔，〔三〕鮑叔終遇之，不以為言。已而鮑叔事齊公子小白，管仲事公子糾。及小白立，為桓公，公子糾死，管仲囚焉。鮑叔遂進管仲。〔三〕管仲既用，任政於齊，〔四〕齊桓公以霸，九合諸侯，一匡天下，管仲之謀也。

〔一〕索隱 潁，水名。

〔二〕索隱 地理志潁水出陽城。漢有潁陽、臨潁二縣。今亦有潁上縣。 正義 韋昭云：「夷吾，姬姓之後，管嚴之子敬仲也。」

〔三〕呂氏春秋：「管仲與鮑叔同賈南陽，及分財利，而管仲嘗欺鮑叔，多自取。鮑叔知其有母而貧，不以為貪也。」

〔三〕齊世家云：「鮑叔牙曰：『君將治齊，則高傒與叔牙足矣。君且欲霸王，非管夷吾不可。夷吾所居國國重，不可失也。』於是桓公從之。」韋昭云：「鮑叔，齊大夫，娰姓之後，鮑叔之子叔牙也。」

〔四〕 正義 管子云：「相齊以九惠之教，一曰老，二曰慈，三曰孤，四曰疾，五曰獨，六曰病，七曰通，八曰賑，九曰絕也。」

管仲曰：「吾始困時，嘗與鮑叔賈，〔二〕分財利多自與，鮑叔不以我為貪，知我貧也。吾嘗為鮑叔謀事而更窮困，鮑叔不以我為愚，知時有利不利也。吾嘗三仕三見逐於君，鮑叔不以我為不肖，知我不遭時也。吾嘗三戰三走，鮑叔不以我為怯，知我有老母也。公子糾敗，召忽死之，吾幽囚受辱，鮑叔不以我為無恥，知我不羞小節而恥功名不顯於天下也。生我者父母，知我者鮑叔也。」

〔一〕 正義 音古。

鮑叔既進管仲，以身下之。子孫世祿於齊，有封邑者十餘世，〔一〕常為名大夫。天下不多管仲之賢而多鮑叔能知人也。

〔一〕索隱　按：系本云「莊仲山產敬仲夷吾，夷吾產武子鳴，鳴產桓子啟方，啟方產成子孺，孺產莊子盧，盧產悼子其夷，其夷產襄子武，武產景子耐涉，耐涉產微，凡十代」。系譜同。

管仲既任政相齊，〔二〕以區區之齊在海濱，〔三〕通貨積財，富國彊兵，與俗同好惡。故其稱曰：〔三〕「倉廩實而知禮節，衣食足而知榮辱，上服度則六親固。〔四〕四維不張，國乃滅亡。〔五〕下令如流水之原，令順民心。」故論卑而易行。〔六〕俗之所欲，因而予之；俗之所否，因而去之。

〔二〕正義　國語云：「齊桓公使鮑叔為相，辭曰：『臣之不若夷吾者五：寬和惠民，不若也；治國家不失其柄，不若也；忠惠可結於百姓，不若也；制禮義可法於四方，不若也；執枹鼓立於軍門，使百姓皆加勇，不若也。』」

〔三〕正義　齊國東濱海也。

〔三〕索隱　是夷吾著書所稱管子者，其書有此言，故略舉其要。

〔四〕正義　上之服御物有制度，則六親堅固也。六親謂外祖父母一，父母二，姊妹三，妻兄弟之子四，從母之子五，女之子六也。王弼云「父、母、兄、弟、妻、子也」。

〔五〕集解　管子曰：「四維，一曰禮，二曰義，三曰廉，四曰恥。」

〔六〕正義　官為政令卑下鮮少，而百姓易作行也。

其為政也，善因禍而為福，轉敗而為功。貴輕重，〔一〕慎權衡。〔二〕桓公實怒少姬，〔三〕南襲蔡，管仲因而伐楚，〔四〕責包茅不入貢於周室。桓公實北征山戎，而管仲因而令燕修召公之政。於柯之會，〔五〕桓公欲背曹沫之約，〔五〕管仲因而信之，〔六〕諸侯由是歸齊。故曰：「知與之為取，政之寶也。」〔七〕

〔一〕索隱　輕重謂錢也。今管子有輕重篇。

〔二〕正義　輕重謂恥辱也。權衡謂得失也。

〔三〕索隱　按：謂怒蕩舟之姬，歸而未絕，蔡人嫁之。

〔三〕正義　有恥辱甚貴重之，有得失甚戒慎之。

〔四〕正義　今齊州東阿也。

〔五〕索隱　沫音昧，亦音末。左傳作「曹劌」。正義　沫，莫葛反。

〔六〕正義　以劫許之，歸魯侵地。

〔七〕索隱　老子曰「將欲取之，必固與之」，是知此為政之所寶也。

管仲富擬於公室，有三歸、反坫，〔二〕齊人不以為侈。管仲卒，〔三〕齊國遵其政，常彊於諸侯。後百餘年而有晏子焉。

〔一〕正義　三歸，三姓女也。婦人謂嫁曰歸。

〔二〕正義　括地志云：「管仲冢在青州臨淄縣南二十一里牛山之河。」說苑云『齊桓公使管仲治國，管仲對曰：「賤不能臨貴。」桓公以為上卿，而國不治。曰：「何故？」管仲對曰：「貧不能使富。」桓公賜之齊市租，而國不治。桓公曰：「何故？」對曰：「疏不能制近。」桓公立以為仲父，齊國大安，而遂霸天下。』孔子曰：『管仲之賢而不得此三權者，亦不能使其君南而而稱伯。』

晏平仲嬰者，萊之夷維人也。〔一〕事齊靈公、莊公、景公，〔二〕以節儉力行重於齊。既相齊，食不重肉，妾不衣帛。其在朝，君語及之，即危言；〔三〕語不及之，即危行。〔四〕國有道，即順命；無道，即衡命。〔五〕以此三世顯名於諸侯。

〔一〕集解　劉向別錄曰：「萊者，今東萊地也。」索隱　名嬰，平謚，仲字。父桓子名弱也。正義　晏氏齊記云齊城三百里有夷安，即晏平仲之邑。漢為夷安縣，屬高密國。應劭云故萊夷維邑。

〔二〕索隱　按：系家及系本靈公名環，莊公名光，景公名杵曰也。

〔三〕正義　謂已謙讓，非云功能。

〔四〕正義　行，下孟反。謂君不知己，增脩業行，畏責及也。

〔五〕正義　衡，秤也。謂國無道則制秤量之，可行即行。

越石父賢，在縲絏中。〔二〕晏子出，遭之塗，解左驂贖之，載歸。弗謝，入閨。久之，越石父請絕。晏子懼然，〔二〕攝衣冠謝曰：「嬰雖不仁，免子於戹，何子求絕之速也？」石父曰：「不然。吾聞君子詘於不知己而信於知己者。〔三〕方吾在縲絏中，彼不知我也。夫子既已感寤而贖我，是知己；知己而無禮，固不如在縲絏之中。」晏子於是延入為上客。

〔一〕【正義】縲音力追反。縲，黑索也。絏，繫也。晏子春秋云：「晏子之晉，至中牟，覩美冠反裘負薪，息於途側，晏子問曰：『何者？』對曰：『我石父也。苟免飢凍，為人臣僕。』晏子解左驂贖之，載與俱歸。」按：與此文小異也。

〔二〕【正義】懼，林縛反。

〔三〕【索隱】信讀曰申，古周禮皆然也。申於知己謂以彼知我而我志獲申。

晏子為齊相，出，其御之妻從門閒而闚其夫。其夫為相御，擁大蓋，策駟馬，意氣揚揚，甚自得也。既而歸，其妻請去。夫問其故。妻曰：「晏子長不滿六尺，身相齊國，名顯諸侯。今者妾觀其出，志念深矣，常有以自下者。今子長八尺，乃為人僕御，然子之意自以為足，妾是以求去也。」其後夫自抑損。晏子怪而問之，御以實對。晏子薦以為大夫。〔一〕

〔一〕【集解】皇覽曰：「晏子家在臨菑城南菑水南桓公冢西北。」

【正義】注皇覽云：「齊桓公墓在青州臨淄縣東南二十三里鼎足上。」又云：「齊晏嬰冢在齊子城北門外。」晏子云『吾生近市，死豈易吾志』。乃葬故宅後，人名曰清節里。」按：恐皇覽誤，乃管冢也。

太史公曰：吾讀管氏牧民、山高、乘馬、輕重、九府，〔二〕及晏子春秋，〔三〕詳哉其言之也。既見其著書，欲觀其行事，故次其傳。至其書，世多有之，是以不論，論其軼事。〔三〕

〔一〕【集解】劉向別錄曰：「九府書民閒無有。」【正義】〔山高一名形勢。〕

〔二〕【索隱】皆管氏所著書篇名也。按：九府，蓋錢之府藏，其論鑄錢之輕重，故云輕重九府。餘如別錄之說。七略云管子十八篇，在法家。

〔二〕〔索隱〕按：嬰所著書名晏子春秋。今其書有七篇，故下云「其書世多有」也。〔正義〕七略云晏子春秋七篇，在儒家。

〔三〕〔正義〕軼音逸。

管仲，世所謂賢臣，然孔子小之。豈以爲周道衰微，桓公既賢，而不勉之至王，乃稱霸哉？〔一〕語曰「將順其美，匡救其惡，故上下能相親也」。〔二〕豈管仲之謂乎？

〔一〕〔正義〕言管仲世所謂賢臣：孔子所以小之者，蓋以爲周道衰，桓公賢主，管仲何不勸勉輔弼至於帝王，乃自稱霸主哉，故孔子小之云。

〔二〕〔正義〕言管仲相齊，順百姓之美，匡救國家之惡，令君臣百姓相親者，是管之能也。蓋爲前疑夫子小管仲爲此。

方晏子伏莊公尸哭之，成禮然後去，〔一〕豈所謂「見義不爲無勇」者邪？至其諫說，犯君之顏，此所謂「進思盡忠，退思補過」者哉！假令晏子而在，余雖爲之執鞭，所忻慕焉。〔二〕

〔一〕〔索隱〕按：左傳崔杼弒莊公，晏嬰入，枕莊公尸股而哭之，成禮而出，崔杼欲殺之是也。

〔二〕〔索隱〕太史公之羨慕仰企平仲之行，假令晏生在世，已雖與之爲僕隸，爲之執鞭，亦所忻慕。其好賢樂善如此。賢哉良史，可以示人臣之炯戒也。

【索隱述贊】夷吾成霸，平仲稱賢。粟乃實廩，豆不掩肩。轉禍爲福，危言獲全。孔賴左衽，史忻執鞭。成禮而去，人望存焉。

NOTES

1. The treatment here is selective. Only translations into major Western languages, modern Chinese, and Japanese are considered. Similarly, each of these projects must have been related to an attempt to render the entire text or a strongly representative portion thereof. Several important Japanese translations (including those mentioned in Timoteus Pokora, "Bibliographies des traductions du *Che ki*," in *Les Mémoires historiques de Se-ma Ts'ien*, by Edouard Chavannes [Paris: Adrien Maisonneuve, 1969], v. 6, 113, n. 1) are not discussed herein, primarily because the current project by Yoshida Kenko and Mizusawa Toshitada transcends all previous efforts. This survey owes an additional debt to Pokora for the comments in his review of Burton Watson's *Ssu-ma Ch'ien, Grand Historian of China* and Watson's *Records of the Grand Historian of China* which appeared in *T'oung pao* 50 (1963), 294–323.

2. Their translation of the first two chapters of the *Shih-chi* was published in the *Journal of the Royal Asiatic Society* (1894): 278–295 and 93–110.

3. The five volumes were published as *Les Mémoires historiques de Se-ma Ts'ien, traduits et annotés* (Paris). In 1969 three more chapters (48–50) appeared posthumously, along with two rendered by Max Kaltenmark (51–52) in a sixth volume (see n. 2). Chavannes completed a draft translation of the entire *Shih chi* during his early years in China, but his interest in Buddhism led him away from the work of revision (see Pokora, "Bibliographies des traductions du *Che ki*," 115–116); the remaining drafts are rumored to be in the Musée Guimet.

4. Derk Bodde, *Statesman, Patriot, and General in Ancient China* (New Haven, 1940).

5. I refer to Erich Haenisch (1884–1975) and Fritz Jäger (1866–1957)—see Pokora, "Bibliographie des traductions du *Che ki*," 114. Two publications by Haenisch include *some* of his renderings: "Gestalten aus der Zeit der chinesischen Hegemoniekämpfe, Übersetzungen aus Sze-ma Ts'ien's Historischen Denkwürdigkeiten," in *Abhandlungen für die Kunde der Morgenlandes* 34, no. 2 (1962), and "Der Aufstand von Ch'en She im Jahre 209 v. Chr.," Asia Major, N.S. 2 (1951): 72–84.

6. Panasjuk's translations of seventeen chapters—intended for the general reader —were published in his *Syma Czjan', Izbrannoe* (Moscow, 1956).

7. Kierman published renditions of four chapters in his *Ssu-ma Ch'ien's Historiographical Attitude as Reflected in Four Late Warring States Biographies* (Wiesbaden, 1962).

8. I.e., chapters 62–80, 83, 85–88, 105–106, 110, 126, and 128–129. For a list of translations of the *Shih-chi* through the late 1960s, see Pokora, "Bibliographie des traductions du *Che ki*." Since the 1960s only a handful of careful translations have been completed, including two exemplary works, Chauncey S. Goodrich's "Ssu-ma Ch'ien's Biography of Wu Ch'i," *Monumenta Serica* 35 (1981–1983), and Timoteus Pokora's "Shih chi 127, the Symbiosis of Two Historians," in *Chinese Ideas about Nature and Society: Studies in Honour of Derk Bodde*, ed. Charles Le Blanc and Susan Blader (Hong Kong: Hong Kong University Press, 1987), 215–234.

9. To date, five volumes have appeared; see reviews by Timoteus Pokora in *Orientalistische Literaturzeitung* 82, no. 3 (May–June 1987): 229–239, and Derk Bodde, *Journal of the American Oriental Society* 110, no. 1 (January–March 1990): 183.

10. Derk Bodde made the claim in his brief review of volumes 4 and 5 (see n. 9).

11. See Bodde's review.

12. The Chung-hua text was ostensibly edited by Ku Chieh-kang 顧頡剛 (1893–1980). Yet Wu Shu-p'ing, formerly an editor at Chung-hua, tells me it is common knowledge that the work was done by Sung Yün-pin 宋雲彬, a scholar who had been purged following the Hundred Flowers Movement of the late 1950s, and then picked up by Chung-hua. Sung used only the Chin-ling shu-chü 金陵書局 edition in his work. Ku Chieh-kang may have reviewed Sung's efforts, but Wu Shu-p'ing doubts that he could have read over the entire text. Although the *Shih chi i-chu* editors are consulting several other editions, the sample text I have been given is identical with that of the Chung-hua 1959 edition.

13. This translation was done by Wu Shu-p'ing and Lu Zongli.

14. Here I am going to disregard existing scholarship on the implied reader. The definition of this term is that which can be determined from Ssu-ma Ch'ien's comments. I remain less concerned with this concept in theory than with its practical application in our project.

15. Pokora, review of Watson in *T'oung pao* 50 (1963): 321.

16. *Shan-kao* 山高 are the first words in the second chapter of the present *Kuan-tzu* text, known today as "Hsing-shih" 形勢 (On Conditions and Circumstances; cf. W. Allyn Rickett, trans., *Guanzi* [Princeton: Princeton University Press, 1985], 6, n. 13).

17. As Rickett (*Guanzi*, 114) points out, the term *ch'eng ma* 乘馬 appears in the titles of chapters I.5, XXI.68, 69, and 70 (the last mentioned is no longer extant). A widely accepted reading understands *ch'eng* and *ma* as accounting terms and the chapter title as "on government finances." Rickett proposes to read 乘 as *sheng* and believes the term refers to an early system of military taxes (*sheng-ma chih fa* 乘馬之法).

18. Rickett (*Guanzi*, 6, n. 15) observes that some scholars feel the "Ch'ing chung" 輕重 section (which contains the last nineteen chapters of the present text) was written during the Han dynasty and that Ssu-ma Ch'ien may be referring to other chapters here. Yet it is also possible that Ssu-ma Ch'ien's statement here lends support to scholars such as Hsü Ch'ing-yü 徐慶譽 who believe the "Ch'ing chung" predates *Han Fei tzu*.

19. This chapter has been lost. The *Cheng-i* 正義 (*Shih chi* (Peking: Chung-hua, 1959), 7:62:2136) cites Liu Hsiang's 劉向 (ca. 79–ca. 6 B.C.) *Pieh-lu* 別錄: "The text [entitled] 'Chiu-fu' does not exist among the people." 九府書，民間無有. The *So-yin* 索隱 (ibid.) argues that the "Chiu-fu" were treasuries. In the "Huo-chih liehchuan" 貨殖列傳 (*Shih chi*, 10:129:3255) Kuan Chung is said to have "set up the [system of] light and heavy and the nine bureaus" 設輕重九府. The *Cheng-i* argues that "light and heavy" here refers to money and that the bureaus were financial agencies (cf. also Rickett, *Guanzi*, p. 6, n. 16). On the general textual history of the *Kuan-tzu*, see Rickett, *Guanzi*, 3–25.

20. Wu Tse-yü 吳則虞 (*Yen-tzu ch'un-ch'iu chi-shih* 晏子春秋集 [Peking: Chunghua, 1982], vol. 1, 18–21) believes the text was compiled in the mid–third century B.C. by a scholar from Ch'i, possibly Ch'un-yü Yüeh 淳于越.

21. Here the *chih* 之, literally "those things," presumably refers to the subjects discussed in the *Kuan-tzu* and *Yen-tzu ch'un-ch'iu* which both Ssu-ma Ch'ien and his readers know so well they need not be mentioned.

22. Possibly paraphrasing Confucius's comments on assessing men (Yang Po-

chün 楊伯俊, *Lun-yü i-chu* 論語譯註 [hereafter *Lun-yü*; Peking: Chung-hua, 1988], 5.10, 45–46):

> Tsai Yü was taking a nap. The Master said, "Rotten wood cannot be carved, a wall of dung-filled earth cannot be troweled. As for Yü, what use is there to reprimand him?"
>
> [Another time] the Master said, "At first [my attitude] towards people was to listen to their words and then trust them to put them into action. Now [my attitude] towards people is to listen to their words and then observe their actions. On Tsai's account I have changed this."
>
> 宰子晝寢. 子曰：朽木不可雕也，糞土之牆不可杇也；於予與，何誅.
>
> 子曰：始吾於人也，聽其言而信其行；今吾於人也，聽其言而觀其行. 於予與，改是.

23. *Tz'u* 次 here should not be read "to arrange" as some scholars have argued (Wang Li-ch'i, *Shih chi chu-i*, p. 1613, for example). It means, as do other related terms such as *hsü* 序 or *lun* 論, "to put words into order," i.e., "to compose," as in the translation by Chang Ta-k'o 張大可 (*Shih chi lun-tsan chi-shih* 史記論贊集釋 [Sian: Shan-hsi jen-min, 1986], 251: *pien-hsieh* 編寫).

24. *Chuan* 傳 is read here similar to its use in the title *Tso chuan*. Ssu-ma Ch'ien seems to suggest that his *chuan* will focus on the actions of Kuan Chung and Yen Ying, thereby complementing their words as recorded in the *Kuan-tzu* and *Yen-tzu ch'un-ch'iu*.

25. *I* 軼 is literally "scattered" or "lost" *shih* 事 "stories." *I* refers to texts which were not included in standard texts, as in the following passage from the "Po I lieh-chuan" 伯夷列傳 (*Shih chi*, 6:61:2122): "I am sorrowed by Po I's meaning, when I read this 'extraneous' poem I find I can marvel in it." 余悲伯夷之意，睹軼詩，可異焉. The *So-yin* (6:61:2123) comments here: "[*I*] means the texts of poems which have been lost ... [this poem] was not included in the three hundred pieces [*Shih ching*], and for this reason it is called an 'extraneous poem.'" 謂見逸之詩，…不編入三百篇.

26. Whether this is a consistent principle of Ssu-ma Ch'ien throughout the *Shih chi* I am not prepared to argue at this time, but it is clearly so in the present context.

27. The question of author's intent is a thorny one in Western criticism. Yet determining author's intention has been—and remains for me at least—one of the more successful methods employed by native and Western sinologists on the Chinese corpus.

28. We should like to thank Professors C. S. Goodrich, Hsu Cho-yun, W. Allyn Rickett, and C. K. Wang for their comments and suggestions. All errors remain the responsibility of the translators.

29. Kuan 管 was the surname; the Kuans had the royal cognomen Chi 姬. I-wu 夷吾 was the praenomen. Chung 仲 was Kuan's nomen. Ching 敬 was his posthumous name. Although throughout history generally known as Kuan Chung (cf. Takigawa Kametarō, *Shiki kaichū kōshō* 史記會註考證 [Rpt. Taipei, 1980], p. 850C), he is referred to with his full name here. See also Wang Shu-min 王叔岷, *Shih chi chiao-cheng* 史記斠證 [hereafter, Wang Shu-min; Taipei, 1982], 7:62:2013, and Fang Hsüan-chen 方炫琛, "*Tso-chuan* jen-wu ming-hao yen-chiu" 左傳人物名號研究, Ph.D. dissertation, Cheng-chih University [Taiwan], 1983, entry 1920, 557–558.

30. Here we follow Wang Li-ch'i (1611) in reading *Ying* 穎 as the name of the river and *shang* indicating "along" or "on the shores of." Although the Chung-hua

Shih chi editors, Wang Shu-min (2013), and other modern scholars treat Ying-shang as a place name (perhaps misreading the *So-yin* [2131], which says Kuan was born near what was in T'ang times [and today is] Ying-shang County 潁上縣, located near the confluence of the Ying and the Huai 淮 rivers in the western part of modern Anhwei), in the late eighth century B.C. when Kuan Chung was born, there was no place named Ying-shang (cf. Ch'ien Mu 錢穆, *Shih chi ti-ming k'ao* 史記地名考 (Rpt. Taipei: San-min, 1984), 439, and T'an Ch'i-hsiang 譚其驤, ed., *Chung-kuo li-shih ti-t'u* 中國歷史地圖 (hereafter Li-shih ti-t'u; Shanghai: Ti-t'u ch'u-pan-she, 1982), vol. 1, 29–30). In the seventh century B.C. this region was occupied by several small states, but the Ying generally divided Sung 宋 from Ch'u 楚 (cf. *Li-shih ti-t'u*, vol. 1, 21, 29–30). Kuo Sung-t'ao 郭嵩燾 (1818–1891) claims this was the territory of the state of Cheng 鄭, but he doubts that Kuan Chung's lineage can really be traced to Ying-shang (cf. his *Shih chi cha-chi* 史記札記 [Taipei: Shih-chieh, 1963], 5:234–235).

31. Here we read 常 as a phonetic loan for 嘗; indeed, the *Momijiyama* 楓山 and *Sanjō* 三條 editions have 嘗. Pao Shu-ya and Kuan Chung were involved in trade in Nan-yang 南陽 (see also n. 41), a statelet just north of the Eastern Chou capital (in modern northern Honan).

32. In this text and elsewhere Pao is often referred to as Pao Shu 鮑叔, although Shu-ya 叔牙 is apparently his praenomen, since in the "Ch'i T'ai-kung shih-chia" 齊太公世家 (Hereditary House of Ch'i T'ai-kung [Wang], hereafter "House of Ch'i") of the *Shih-chi* (5:32:1486) Pao referred to himself as Shu-ya. The *Cheng-yin* (*Shih chi*, 7:62:2131) cites a commentary from Wei Chao 韋昭 (208–273) which supports this reading. Fang Hsüan-chen, entry 2214, 626–627, believes that Shu designates his generational rank ("third brother") and Ya was the praenomen.

33. The *So-yin* (5:62:2131) cites a passage from the *Lü-shih ch'un-ch'iu*: "Kuan Chung and Pao Shu engaged in trade together at Nan-yang. When they divided the profits, Kuan Chung often took advantage of Pao Shu and got a bigger share. Pao Shu, knowing that he had a mother [to support] and that he was poor, did not consider him greedy." However, this passage cannot be found in modern editions of the *Lü-shih ch'un-ch'iu*; cf. Chiang Wei-ch'iao 蔣維喬 et al., *Lü-shih ch'un-ch'iu hui-chiao* 呂氏春秋彙校 (Shanghai: Chung-hua, 1937), 664.

34. Noble Scion (*Kung-tzu* 公子) is a formal title given to all legitimate male offspring of any feudal lord except the designated successor, who was called Greatest Scion (*T'ai-tzu* 太子), (Yang Po-chün, *Ch'un-ch'iu Tso-chuan tz'u-tien* 春秋左傳詞典 [hereafter *Tz'u-tien*; Peking: Chung-hua, 1985], 99). Both Hsiao-po and Chiu were sons of Duke [Hsi] of Ch'i [r. 730–698 B.C.] by a concubine.

35. Chiu 糾 was older than Hsiao-po 小白 (cf. Yang Po-chün, *Ch'un-ch'iu Tso-chuan hui-chu* 春秋左傳會註 [hereafter—*Tso-chuan*; Peking: Chung-hua, 1981], vol. 1, 176, commentary). It is generally accepted that they were brothers, but in *Kuan-tzu* 管子 ("Ta-k'uang" 大匡, *SPPY*, 7:1b) Kuan Chung said: "The people of this country detest Jiu's [Chiu's] mother and extend this [detestation] to Jiu himself, whereas they pity Xiaopo [Hsiao-po] for being motherless" 管仲曰：國人憎惡糾之母以及糾之身，而憐小白之無母也, [trans. by Rickett, *Guanzi*, 1985, 285]. Their half-brother, Chu-erh 諸兒, was probably older (cf. the order in which the brothers are listed in the "Ta K'uang" chapter of *Kuan-tzu* [7:1a]). He was the son of the Duke's legiti-mate wife, succeeded his father, Duke Hsi, in 698 B.C. and ruled as Duke Hsiang until he was murdered in 686 B.C. His murderer, a cousin of the brothers named

Wu-chih 無知, usurped power in Ch'i until he too was killed by the people of Ch'i in the spring of 685 B.C. (*Tso-chuan*, 177). Wu-chih's death precipitated the struggle between Chiu and Hsiao-po.

36. There are several passages which describe these events in more detail. The *Tso-chuan* (176) notes that when Duke Hsiang 襄公 first took office he was "without constancy" (*wu ch'ang* 無常). This has been interpreted as referring either to his administration (Tu Yü 杜預) or to his personal morals (as in Ssu-ma Ch'ien's account of how he murdered Duke Huan of Lu among others and slept with Huan's wife and a number of other women in the "House of Ch'i" (*Shih chi*, 5:32:1485). Indeed, his entire reign was constant only in the improprieties and illegalities he perpetrated. The *Tso-chuan* proceeds to tell that Pao Shu-ya foresaw a rebellion and fled to the tiny principality of Chü (near modern Chü County in southeastern Shantung) with Hsiao-po, while Kuan Chung fled with Chiu to Lu 魯. Their destinations proved of consequence. Hsiao-po was nearer to the Ch'i capital in Chü and subsequently the first to reach Lin-tzu 臨淄 after Wu-chih's death. His brother Chiu sought the support of the larger state of Lu and was able to lead their troops against Hsiao-po. Yet the decision to flee to Lu was perhaps a poor one, since under Duke Hsiang relations between Lu and Ch'i were very bad and the people of Ch'i were certain to reject anyone attempting to gain power supported by Lu.

37. After Duke Huan soundly defeated the army of Lu, which was supporting Chiu, he forced them to put Chiu to death.

38. According to the *Tso-chuan* (180), Pao Shu-ya led the Ch'i army into Lu and asked the Duke of Lu to execute Chiu and to turn over Kuan Chung to Pao Shu-ya. The Duke agreed and Kuan Chung was held as a prisoner until Pao Shu-ya had returned to T'ang-fu 常阜, on the Ch'i-Lu border, where he was released.

39. The *Cheng-i* cites the "House of Ch'i" (*Shih chi*, 5:32:1486): Pao Shu-ya said [to Duke Huan]: "If milord wishes to rule Ch'i, Kao Hsi [a fellow official] and I will be sufficient. But if you would serve as Grand Duke to the king, you must have Kuan I-wu. In whatever country Kuan I-wu resides, that country will be weighty, so we should not lose him. At this Duke Huan went along with him." 鮑叔牙曰：君將治齊, 則高傒與叔牙足矣. 君且欲霸王, 非管仲不可. 夷吾所居國, 國重, 不可失也. 於是桓公從之.

40. See Glossary.

41. Reading *chiu* 糾 (**kjəgw*) "assembled" for *chiu* 九 (**kjəgw*), as in the *Pei-t'ang shu-ch'ao* 北堂書鈔 citation of the passage (cf. Wang Shu-min, 2014). As Takigawa notes (850D), the phrase *chiu-ho chu-hou* 九合諸侯 can be found in the *Lun-yü* (*Lun-yü*, 14:16, p. 151): "The Master said: 'Duke Huan assembled the feudal lords together not through his weapons and chariots, but the strength of Kuan Chung.'" 子曰：桓公九合諸侯, 不以兵車, 管仲之力也.

42. *I-k'uang t'ien-hsia* 一匡天下 can also be found in the *Lun-yü* (Yang, *Lun-yü*, 14:17, 151) in a well-known passage: "The Master said, 'When Kuan Chung served as chief minister to Duke Huan, [the latter] became Grand Duke over the feudal lords and completely rectified the world. Down to the present day people have received benefits from him. If there had been no Kuan Chung, we might be wearing our hair unbound and buttoning our coats from the left [both as the barbarians do].'" 子曰：管仲相桓公, 霸諸候, 一匡天下. 民到于今受其賜. 微管仲, 吾其被髮左衽矣. Although there is a parallelism between *chiu* 九, literally "nine," and *i* 一, literally "one," which Wang Shu-min (2014) observes is not uncommon in early texts, this parallelism operates here only at the surface level.

43. The *Momijiyama* and *Sanjō* editions read, "I engaged in trade with Pao Shu[-ya] at Nan-yang." The *So-yin* (appended to the preceding paragraph, 6:62:2131) cites a parallel passage from the *Lü-shih ch'un-ch'iu*: "Kuan Chung and Pao Shu engaged in trade together at Nan-yang. When they divided the profits, Kuan Chung often took advantage of Pao Shu and got a bigger share. Pao Shu, knowing that he had a mother [to support] and that he was poor, did not consider him greedy" (see also n. 29). In the comment on yet another similar passage in the *Shuo-yüan* ("Fu-en p'ien" 復恩編, *Shuo-yüan chiao-cheng* 說苑校證 [Peking: Chung-hua, 1987], 6:132), the modern scholar Hsiang Tsung-lu 向宗魯 notes several other parallel versions for this entire speech in various pre-Ch'in works and concludes that this narrative is allegorical.

44. As in some early English narratives, "thrice" is conventional for a number of times.

45. For *tsou* 走 "ran" the *T'ai-p'ing yü-lan* 太平御覽 (409:1b:2016) and several other sources have *pei* 北 "was put to rout" (Wang Shu-min, 2015).

46. In Hsü Kan's 徐幹 (170–217) *Chung-lun* 中論 (*SPPY*, B:29b) we are told that "In ancient times Kuan I-wu fought three battles and every time was put to rout, so that the people all said he was without courage" 昔管夷吾嘗三戰而皆北, 人皆謂之無勇. Wang Shu-min wryly observes that perhaps Pao Shu-ya was the only person who did not consider Kuan Chung cowardly (2015).

47. Shao Hu 召忽 was a friend of Kuan Chung and Pao Shu-ya. He had gone with Kuan Chung to Lu in support of Noble Scion Chiu. His own decision to die is described in *Kuan-tzu* ("Ta-k'uang," 7:5a–b). There he provides in essence one of the pretexts which have been used to explain Kuan Chung's unconventional acceptance of a position under the lord who defeated his own liege:

> I have not died because I have been waiting for the situation to be settled. Now that it has been settled, [the new duke] will make you chief minister of the left in Ch'i. He would certainly make me chief minister of the right, but for him to employ me after killing my prince would be a double shame for me. You become a live minister, but I shall be a dead one. I shall die knowing that I might have had [charge of] the government of a 10,000-chariot [kingdom]; in this way, Noble Scion Chiu may be said to have had a minister who died for him. But you will live [to raise to power] a Grand Duke; in this way, Noble Scion Chiu may be said to have had a minister who lived for him....
> And so as they were crossing the border into Ch'i, he cut his own throat and died.... (Trans. revised slightly from Rickett, *Guanzi*, 291–292].
> 吾不蚤死, 將胥有所定也. 今既定矣, 令子相齊之左, 必將令忽相齊之右. 雖然, 殺君而用吾身, 是再辱我也. 子爲生臣, 忽爲死也. 忽也知得萬乘之政而死; 公子糾可謂有死臣矣. 子生而霸諸候, 公子糾可謂有生臣矣. 死者成行, 生者成名. 名不兩立, 行不虛至. 子其勉之. 死生有分矣.
> 乃行, 入齊境, 自刎而死⋯

48. In "Ta-k'uang" chapter of *Kuan-tzu* (7:4a) this is explained more explicitly in the words of Pao Shu, "That I-wu [Kuan Chung] did not die for Noble Scion Chiu was because he wanted to make Ch'i's altars of Land and Grain [i.e., the state] secure." 夷吾之不死糾也, 爲欲定齊國之社稷也. (Slightly revised from Rickett, *Guanzi*, 290.) Ssu-ma Ch'ien also records Lu Chung-lien's 魯仲連 sympathetic attitude toward Kuan in a letter Lu wrote to a general of Yen: "Kuan-tzu did not take it as shameful to be tied up in prison; he was only ashamed that the empire was not in order. He did not consider not dying for Noble Scion Chiu as shameful; he

was only ashamed that his prestige had not spread among the feudal lords." 管子不恥身在縲絏之中而恥天下之不治， 不恥不死公子糾而恥威之不信於諸侯. (*Shih chi*, 8: 83:2467–2468.) Takigawa (850D) is of the opinion that Ssu-ma Ch'ien, who also chose to live under what some considered ignoble circumstances, is "speaking of himself" here.

49. Only this paragraph has been translated by Alfred Forke, *Geschichte der alten chinesischen Philosophie* (Hamburg: Friederichsen, 1927), 67–68; there is no translation of the complete text or of the epilogue as Timoteus Pokora ("Traductions," 129) suggests.

50. Takigawa (p. 851A), following Hung Liang-chi 洪亮吉 (1746–1809), notes that the *So-yin* erroneously lists ten generations of the Kuans here, when actually the text suggests that Pao Shu's descendants are meant. Takigawa identifies two of these descendants, Pao Mu 牧 and Pao Yen 晏, both officials of Ch'i.

51. Duke Huan himself was grateful to Pao Shu for his recommendation of Kuan Chung. Every time Kuan Chung completed some great achievement, the Duke would reward Pao Shu first (see "Tsan-neng" 贊能 in *Lü-shih ch'un-ch'iu* [*SPPY* 24:3b]).

52. Sydney Rosen has shown that in the *Tso chuan*, the earliest depiction of Kuan Chung's career, *hsiang* 相 likely meant only "to hold office as a general advisor, with perhaps special advisory functions in the field of interstate relations" (see her "Historical Kuan Chung," *Journal of Asian Studies* 35, no. 3 [May 1976]: 431).

53. This language echoes that in the "Ch'in Shih-huang pen-chi" 秦始皇本紀 (*Shih chi*, 1:6:282): "Yet Ch'in with the tiny piece of land [that it originally held] and with the power of [only] one thousand chariots, summoned the eight territories [to itself] and caused those which were of the same rank to come to pay it homage for over one hundred years." 然秦以區區之地, 千乘之權, 招八州而朝同列, 百有餘年矣 (Cf. the translation by Chavannes, 2:6:231). Chavannes also notes the similarity of the language here to that of Chia I's 賈誼 (200–168 B.C.) "Kuo Ch'in lun" 過秦論, cf. *Wen-hsüan* 文選 (*SPPY*), 51:5a. In ancient times China was divided into nine *chou* 州 or "territories": Yung 雍 (Ch'in territory), Chi 冀, Yen 兗, Ch'ing 青, Hsü 徐, Yang 揚, Ching 荊, Yü 預, and Liang 梁 (cf. Wang Li-ch'i, 1:6:142).

54. The *So-yin* comments here: "This is that which I-wu had written into a book which is called *Kuan-tzu*. As his book contains these words, [Ssu-ma Ch'ien] briefly cites their essential points" 是夷吾著書所稱管子, 其書有此言, 故略舉其要 (*Shih chi*, 7:62:2133). Rickett (*Guanzi*, "The Origin of the Present Text," 14–24) has carefully outlined the development of the current text of the *Kuan-tzu*. This first chapter Rickett believes to be "certainly one of the earlier chapters" (51), and dates it "from the early or middle part of the fourth century B.C." (52).

55. Rickett (*Guanzi*, 52, n. 2) observes that "Jung ju" 榮辱 (Honor and Disgrace) is the title of chapter II, 4 of the *Hsün-tzu* and discusses comments by Hsün-tzu and Meng-tzu on "honor and shame."

56. This passage also occurs at the onset of the first section ("Mu-min" 牧民 [Shepherding the People]) of the *Kuan-tzu* (*SPPY*, 1:1a). Fang Hsüan-ling's 房玄齡 (578–648) commentary glosses *fu* 服 as *hsing* 行, "to carry out, to practice," and *tu* 度 as *li-tu* 禮度, "restrictions of the social norms." Although there are a number of explications of this passage in the various *Shih chi* commentaries, our translation follows Fang's reading, which addresses the text in its fuller context. The translation is revised accordingly from Rickett, *Guanzi*, 52.

57. We follow Wang Pi's 王弼 (226–249) opinion quoted in the *Cheng-i* (*Shih chi*, 7:62:2133): "[The six relationships are those with] father, mother, elder brother, young brother, wife, and children." 父, 母, 兄, 弟, 妻, 子也. Cf. Rickett, *Guanzi*, 52, n. 3.

58. This is a quotation from the first chapter of the *Kuan-tzu*, "Mu-min" (trans. modified slightly from Rickett, *Guanzi*, 52–53). The *ssu-wei* 四維 or "four ties," refers "to the four guy lines or ropes used to support a target or lines attached to the four corners of a fish net to pull it in" (Rickett, 52, n. 4). They are subsequently explained in "Mu-min" as *li* 禮 (social codes), *i* 義 (righteousness), *lien* 廉 (honesty) and *ch'ih* 恥 (sense of shame). Rickett thus renders the term "the four cardinal virtues."

59. This last section is slightly revised from *Kuan-tzu*, 1:2b and is again rendered in a version based on Rickett, *Guanzi*, 55.

60. The *Cheng-i* (*Shih chi*, 7:62:2133) presents another reading: "Which is to say 'His administrative orders were humble and few, and the common people were easily able to put them into effect.'" 言爲政令卑下鮮少, 而百姓易作行也.

61. Similar language is found in the "Yen-ts'e" 燕策 of the *Chan-kuo ts'e* (9.3b): "A sage in regulating events would turn calamity into a blessing and take advantage of failure to make it into success. This is how Duke Huan could turn his back on the woman sent to be his wife yet make this the means of gaining more honor" 聖人之制事也, 轉禍而爲福, 因敗而爲攻, 故桓公負婦而名益尊. (cf. James I. Crump, trans., *Chan-kuo Ts'e* (2d ed. rev., San Francisco: Chinese Materials Center, 1979), 508; cf. also the "Su Ch'in lieh-chuan" 蘇秦列傳 (*Shih chi*, 7:69:2270).

62. The *So-yin* (*Shih chi*, 7:62:2133) comments: "'Light and heavy' refers to coins. In the present *Kuan-tzu* there is a 'Light and Heavy Section,'" 輕重謂錢也, 管子有 輕重編. The *Cheng-i* (ibid.), however, reads this passage metaphorically: "Light and heavy refer to shame and dishonor; the weight and beam [of the scale] refers to gains and losses. When there were [matters involving] shame and dishonor, he took them as very important; when there were [matters involving] gains and losses, he was very cautious [in dealing with] them." 輕重謂恥辱也, 權衡謂得失也, 有恥辱甚 貴重之, 有得失甚戒愼之. This section is one of eight into which an unknown person (possibly Liu Hsiang) divided the *Kuan-tzu*; "Light and Heavy" makes up the final sections of the work (*SPPY*, ch. 24) and is concerned mainly with economics (cf. Rickett, *Guanzi*, 5). It appears "to be quite late" and is "often associated with the scholars representing the tradition of the famous Salt and Iron debates in 81 B.C." (Rickett, "*Kuan-tzu* and the Newly Discovered Texts on Bamboo and Silk," in *Chinese Ideas about Nature and Society*, ed. Charles LeBlanc and Susan Blader (Hong Kong: Hong Kong University Press, 1987, 243, n. 18). In personal correspondence Rickett concurs that our reading for *ch'ing-chung* might be correct here, but cautions that "in the *Guanzi* [the term] is much more complex. There it refers to the manipulation of goods to control prices and production. It also appears to involve a rudimentary quantitative theory of money."

63. Shao-chi 少姬, literally the "minor" or "younger consort," is referred to elsewhere as Ts'ai-chi 蔡姬, "the consort from Ts'ai." The *So-yin* (7:62:2133) comments: "It is our opinion that this refers to his being angry with the 'rocking-boat consort,' who when she was sent back [to Ts'ai] was not divorced. The people of Ts'ai had her remarried." 按：謂怒蕩舟之姬, 歸而未絕, 蔡人嫁之. The basic story is told in the *Tso-chuan* (656 B.C.; Yang, *Tso-chuan*, 286): "The Marquis of Ch'i [Duke Huan]

was boating with the Ts'ai Consort in [his] park when she rocked the duke. The duke was frightened, changed color, and forbade her [from this], but she wouldn't stop. The duke became angry and sent her back [to Ts'ai] without divorcing her. The people of Ts'ai remarried her." 齊侯與蔡姬乘舟于囿, 蕩公. 公懼變色, 禁之. 不可. 公怒, 歸之, 未之絕. 蔡人嫁之. Ts'ai is located near modern Hsin Ts'ai 新蔡 on the Ju River 汝水 in today's southeastern Honan about 360 miles southwest of the Ch'i capital at Lin-tzu 臨淄 on the northeastern border of Ch'u (cf. *Li-shih ti-t'u*, 1:20–21 and 29–30). Therefore, to attack Ch'u the allies would have to pass through (or very near to) Ts'ai. In several later accounts, including those in the "House of Ch'i" and the "Kuan, Ts'ai shih-chia" 管蔡世家 (Hereditary Houses of Kuan and Ts'ai) in the *Shih chi* (32:1489 and 35:1566, respectively), this event is amplified and related to the concerted attack on Ts'ai by the feudal lords reported in the account of the following year (656 B.C.) in the *Tso-chuan*. Yang Po-chün (*Tso-chuan*, 289) recounts several versions of this story in his notes, including that which says Duke Huan summoned the feudal lords on the pretense of wanting to punish Ch'u, but then swung his armies about and attacked Ts'ai. But he concludes that these are merely accounts by later "persuaders" (*shuo-k'e* 說客) and that the *Tso-chuan*, which does not link the two incidents, should be considered the most reliable account.

64. *Fa* 伐, "to launch a punitive expedition against" (see Glossary under "campaign"), were undertaken on behalf of the Chou king. The reason given here is that Ch'u had stopped submitting *pao-mao* 包茅 or 苞茅 (the *Momijiyama* and *Sanjo* editions both read *ching-mao* 菁茅 here; see Wang Shu-min, 2017), reeds which were bound to filter wine for sacrifice.

65. The Shan-Jung 山戎 or Mountain Jung (a northern non-Chinese tribe), also known as the Pei-Jung 北戎, lived along the lower reaches of the Luan River 灤河 in what is today eastern Hopeh (30–40 miles east of T'ang-shan 唐山).

66. According to the "House of Ch'i" in the *Shih chi* (5:32:1488), "In the twenty-third year [of Duke Huan, i.e., 663 B.C.] the Jung [tribe] of the Mountains made a punitive expedition against Yen, and Yen reported the danger to Ch'i. Duke Huan of Ch'i went to Yen's rescue, leading a punitive expedition against the Jung of the Mountains and reaching Ku-chu 孤竹 [near the modern city of Lu-lung 盧龍 on the Luan River in extreme eastern Hopeh; *Li-shih ti-t'u*, 1:28] before returning. Duke Chuang of Yen then saw off Duke Huan until they entered the Ch'i border. Duke Huan said, 'Unless it is the Heavenly Son [see Glossary], the feudal lords in seeing one another off do not leave their borders. I cannot act outside the social code towards Yen.' Thereupon, he demarcated the land the lord of Yen had reached with a ditch and gave it to Yen, ordering the lord of Yen to reinstate the government of Duke Shao and to pay tribute to Chou as in the days of [kings] Ch'eng [ca. 1040–ca. 1005 B.C.] and K'ang [ca. 1005–ca. 977 B.C.]. When the feudal lords heard of this, they all followed Ch'i." 二十三年, 山戎伐燕, 燕告急於齊. 齊桓公救燕, 遂伐山戎, 至於孤竹而還. 燕莊公遂送桓公入齊境. 桓公曰: 非天子, 諸侯相送不出境, 吾不可以無禮於燕. 於是分溝割燕公所至與燕. 命燕公復召公之政, 納貢於周, 如成康之時.

67. These events took place in the fifth year of Duke Huan's rule (681 B.C.). None of the sources, which provide two basically different accounts, is without errors of some sort (cf. *Tso-chuan*, 193–194, esp. the commentary on 194). Nevertheless, the accounts agree that Duke Chuang of Lu 魯莊公 (r. 693–662 B.C.) met with

Duke Huan at K'o 柯 (southwest of Tung-K'o hsien 東柯縣 in present-day north-western Shantung, Wang Li-ch'i, 1080) "to swear a covenant" (see Glossary) as a means to settle hostilities between Lu and Ch'i. Lu presented Ch'i with the city of Sui 遂 (twenty miles southeast of T'ai-an 泰安 at the foot of Mount T'ai, ten miles north of the Wen River 汶河 and some forty miles north of Ch'ü-fu 曲阜, the Lu capital [ibid.]). Some texts (including the "House of Ch'i," *Shih chi*, 5:32:1487) then describe how Ts'ao Mo 曹沫 (also known as Ts'ao Kuei 劌) leapt onto the earthen altar (see Glossary) and held a dagger to Duke Huan to compel him to return the city to Lu. After the duke had consented and Ts'ao Mo had released him, he wanted to renege on his agreement and kill Ts'ao Mo. Kuan Chung, however, pointed out the larger gain of support from the feudal lords which could be had by the duke's keeping his word. Liang Yü-sheng (*Chih-i*, ch. 27, 1184–1185) points out that all three of these events (i.e., the raid on Ts'ai, the campaign against the Mountain Jung, and the incident with Ts'ao Mo) are not verifiable.

68. The seventh year of Duke Huan's reign (679 B.C.) is generally accepted as the year he became Grand Duke (cf. "House of Ch'i," *Shih chi*, 5:32:1487). Sydney Rosen ("Changing Conceptions of the Hegemon in Pre-Ch'in China," in *Ancient China: Studies in Early Civilization*, ed. David T. Roy and Tsuen-hsuin Tsien [Hong Kong: Chinese University Press, 1978], 99–114) has summarized the final steps in Ch'i's ascendancy as follows: "In 684 Duke Huan extinguished the small state of T'an, the ruler of which had offended him. In 683 he married a Chou princess. In 681 there was a meeting of the states to consider disorder in Sung. Commentators assert that it was called by Ch'i, although that is not clear in the text of the *Tso-chuan*. The little state of Sui did not send a representative and that summer Ch'i extinguished Sui. In the winter of the same year Lu concluded a peace pact with Ch'i. The Ch'i ruler requested troops from the king and thus, with royal armies, led the feudal lords under the king's banner, in a disciplinary action, against Sung. The state of Sung submitted. And in 679, at a meeting of the feudal lords, Ch'i 'for the first time was *pa*' [citing the "House of Ch'i" here]."

69. This saying is also found in the "Mu-min" chapter of *Kuan-tzu* (*SPPY*, 1:2b; trans. by Rickett, *Guanzi*, p. 54). A similar saying is also found in *Lao-tzu* (36: 143–4): "If you wish to snatch something from it [the Way], you must certainly give something to it" 將欲奪之, 必固與之 (trans. Robert G. Henricks, 88). The current text of the *Lao-tzu* reads *to* 奪 "to snatch" for *ch'ü* 取 "to take." Chu Ch'ien-chih (*Lao-tzu*, 144) reviews the various arguments and texts concerning these variant readings and settles on *to* 奪. Here *ch'ü* may be used because of the rhyme with *yü* 與 "to give." Regardless of the exact wording, our text refers to Kuan Chung's strategy of giving back to Lu what it wanted so as to gain for Ch'i the confidence of other feudal states, including eventually Lu itself.

70. *San-kuei* 三歸 "three returns" has been variously interpreted. The *Cheng-i* (7: 62:2134) says: "The 'three returns' are women of three cognomens. A woman refers to getting married as a 'return' [to her home]." 三歸, 三姓女也. 婦人謂嫁曰歸. V. A. Panasjuk (*Syma Czjan', Izbrannoe* [Moscow, 1956], 55) follows this reading. But Kuo Sung-t'ao refutes the *Cheng-i* (in his *Shih chi cha-chi*, 5A: 235–6) claim, pointing out that this explanation is based on a commentary (by Ho Yen 何晏 [d. 249]) to the *Lun-yü* (3:22). Kuo goes on: "According to the social code, when the feudal lords first took a wife, a country of the same cognomen used her nieces as servants [for the bride]. [But] in one marriage [to take] wives of three surnames, was unheard of

according to the social code...." 禮, 諸侯始娶, 同姓之國以姪娣媵；一娶三姓女, 於禮 未聞. Kuo's conclusion is that *san-kuei* referred to a *return* of *three* parts of ten from profits in the marketplace and he cites passages from the "Ch'ing-chung" section of the *Kuan-tzu* (*SPPY*, 24:2b) and several other supporting texts. Wang Li-ch'i (1612) assembles most of the other theories concerning "three returns," which include (1) the name of a tower, (2) the name of a city, and (3) three homes (to return to). Wang Li-ch'i prefers the "three homes." Wang Shu-min (2018), however, endorses Kuo Sung-t'ao's conclusions, as do we.

71. Takigawa (p. 851C) observes that *fan-tien* 反坫 were "cup-stands" placed between two pillars where the lords placed empty cups after drinking to seal a pledge or vow. Cheng Hsüan 鄭玄 (127–200) argues in his commentary to the *Li chi* (*SPPY*, 8:3a) that the stands were used after a toast to a visiting lord. This *Li chi* passage is in the context of various privileges which had been usurped from the king by the feudal lords. Perhaps in response to this, Confucius criticized Kuan Chung for having both a cup-stand and the three returns (cf. *Lun-yü*, 3:22).

72. As Wang Li-ch'i (1612) observes, Kuan Chung died in 645 B.C., while Yen Ying was first appointed to a position in Duke Ling's court in 556 B.C., only eighty-nine years after Kuan's death. However, since Yen-tzu served in the Ch'i court for a long period (he died in 500 B.C.—*Shih chi*, 5:32:1505), Ssu-ma Ch'ien might have intended here that "over one hundred years later Yen-tzu was there [in charge of the Ch'i government]."

73. As Takigawa (852C) observes, this probably refers to Confucius's comment, "Small indeed was Kuan Chung's capacity!" 管仲之器小哉 (*Lun-yü*, 3.22, 31). Margouliès (82, n. 33) believes that Confucius may have been jealous of the grandeur that Kuan Chung gave to Ch'i, a rival of Confucius's home state of Lu.

74. The *Cheng-i* commentary understands *ch'i* 其 as referring to the people and the state (*Shih chi*, 6:62:2136), thus "[A gentleman] guides [his ruler] in accordance with the merits of the people [or "the state"] and rectifies [him] in order to redeem their excesses...." Panasjuk (55) follows this interpretation in his rendition.

75. This is from the *Hsiao ching* (*SPPY*, 8:2a–b). The entire passage reads: "The Master said, "'A gentleman in serving his ruler, exhausts his every thought in how to be loyal as he comes to court, and in how to remedy his [ruler's] faults as he withdraws. [He] guides [his ruler] in accordance with [his ruler's] merits,...'" 君子 之事上也, 進思盡忠, 退思補過. 將順其美, 匡救其惡.

Problems of Translation

The *Wen hsüan* in English

DAVID R. KNECHTGES

In 1981 I referred to my effort to translate the *Wen hsüan* as "a bold, perhaps even foolhardy undertaking."[1] If I were to recast this statement today, I would remove the word *perhaps*, for I am now even more daunted by the task of attempting a complete annotated translation of this difficult and massive work. So far I have managed to publish only two of the projected eight volumes. Volume 3, which includes the rest of the *fu* section, is nearly finished. I also have finished draft translations of approximately half of the remaining portion. However, my pace continues to be excruciatingly slow, and I would well deserve the title of the world's slowest translator.

The causes of my lentitude are two: the nature of the *Wen hsüan* itself, and my own approach to translation. The *Wen hsüan* (Selections of Refined Literature) is not only a huge corpus; it is a work of considerable variety of genres, styles, authors, and content. It thus presents numerous problems to anyone who attempts to translate the entire work. In this essay I discuss some of the problems and the solutions I have devised to deal with them.

The size of the *Wen hsüan*, which was compiled circa 530, is daunting indeed. In its present form it consists of 761 pieces in sixty *chüan*. The length of these pieces ranges from short poems of no more than ten lines to long *fu* and prose essays extending to over a thousand lines. In addition, the compilers of the *Wen hsüan* intended it to be an anthology representative of the major works of literature, which they collected into thirty-seven genres. Anyone who would translate the entire collection must master all of these genres, which include such poetic forms as *fu* 賦 (rhapsody), *shih* 詩 (lyric poetry), *sao* 騷 (selections from the *Ch'u tz'u*), and various prose types such as memorials (*piao* 表), letters (*shu* 書), proclamations (*hsi* 檄), prefaces to the classics ·and literary collections (*hsü* 序), praise poems (*sung* 頌), imperial edicts (*chao* 詔), encomia for famous men (*tsan* 贊), historical, philosophical and political disquisitions (*lun* 論 and *shih lun* 史論), threnodies and laments for the dead (*lei* 誄, *pei* 碑, *ai* 哀), even examination essays (*ts'e-wen* 策問). Thus I have spent considerable time studying the histories of these forms of literature to understand their conventions and become familiar with the special type of language that pertains to each genre. For example, the memorials and court documents use various formulae and bureaucratic terms that were de rigueur in state writings. There are plenty of passages like this excerpt from the opening lines of the "Memorial Urging the Succession" by the Chin dynasty writer Liu K'un 劉琨 (271–318):

> In the fifth year of Chien-hsing, in the third month with a *kuei-wei* day as the first day, on *hsin-ch'ou*, the eighteenth day, the Commissioner Bearing Credentials, the Cavalier Attendant In-Ordinary, the Inspector of Military Affairs of the three provinces north of the Yellow River, Ping, Chi, and Yu, the General Directing and Protecting the Army, Commander of Gentleman of the Hsiung-nu, Minister of Works, Inspector of Ping-chou, Marquis of Kuang-wu, your servant K'un; the Commissioner Bearing Credentials, Palace Attendant, Inspector General of Military Affairs for Chi-chou, the General Controlling the Army, Inspector of Chi-chou, Worthy King of the Left, Duke of Po-hai, your servant P'i-ti, knocking our heads on the ground and at risk of death, submit the following memorial.[2]

> 建興五年,三月癸未朔十八日辛丑,使持節散騎常侍都督河北并冀幽三州諸軍事,領護軍匈奴中郎將,司空,并州刺史,廣武侯臣琨,使持節侍中都督冀州諸君事,撫軍大將軍,冀州刺史左賢王,渤海公臣磾,頓首死罪,上書。

Although it is a tedious chore, one must devise translations for all of the official titles enumerated in such passages, which are more common than one would like. Compounding the problem is that not all of them can be found in the Western language studies of bureaucratic terms. The bureaucratic terms for the Six Dynasties period are poorly studied in Western sinology, and except for those terms discussed by Michael Rogers in his translation of chapter 114 of the *Chin shu* and Richard Mather's glossary appended to his translation of the *Shih-shuo hsin-yü*, there is no handy source of ready-made renderings of official titles for this period.[3] One is then left to his own devices to research the title himself and devise an appropriate English equivalent.

One genre that contains special bureaucratic terminology is the "Memorial of Impeachment" (*t'an shih* 彈事), which uses numerous legal terms. The "Tsou t'an Liu Cheng" 奏彈劉整 ("Impeachment of Liu Cheng") by

Jen Fang 任昉 (460–508) is filled with such expressions, to which several scholars have devoted special studies.[4] The same piece also is interesting for the verbatim citation of affidavits, which are laden with colloquial expressions.[5]

In addition to bureaucratic terminology, the translator must understand historical references, allusions, and unusual expressions that occur throughout the anthology. Some pieces refer to specific historical events and personages, and a proper translation requires explication of all such references. For example, the "Yang Ching-chou lei" 楊荊州誄 by P'an Yüeh 潘岳 (247–300) is a dirge for Yang Chao 楊肇 (ob. 275), P'an Yüeh's father-in-law.[6] In one section the dirge recounts Yang Chao's genealogy and family background:

> In the distant past his remote ancestors
> Are descendant from the rulers of the Chou.
> The main line prospered and flourished;
> The collateral lines branched and forked.
> The clan originated with Po-ch'iao;
> The family hailed from the Marquis of Yang.
> For countless generations they were great and illustrious;
> Truly they followed the grand design.
> When Heaven became displeased with Han's virtue,
> And the battle of the dragons was unresolved,
> Our lord's father and grandfather
> Found themselves right in the midst of the conflict.
> Just as a bird selects a tree,
> The vassal also chooses his lord.
> They transferred their loyalty to the Wei court,
> Enlisted their names, and offered their lives.
> They eagerly leapt from the muck of the pool,
> To stride and soar on the wind and clouds.
> One led the Resolute Cavalry;
> Another was Commander of the Army.

> 邈矣遠祖，
> 系自有周。
> 昭穆繁昌，
> 枝庶分流。
> 祖始伯僑，
> 氏出楊侯。
> 奕世丕顯，
> 允迪大猷。
> 天厭漢德，
> 龍戰未分。
> 伊君族考，
> 方事之殷。
> 鳥則擇木，

臣亦簡君。
投心魏朝，
策名委身。
奮躍淵塗，
跨騰風雲。
或統驍騎，
或據領軍。

To explicate this passage, one must explain that the Yang clan to which Yang Chao belonged traced its origins to one Po-ch'iao 伯僑 of the early Chou. Later in the Chou period, the Yang-she 羊舌 family, which was one of the ducal clans of the state of Chin 晉, established the fief of Yang. After the fall of the Han, Yang Chao's grandfather Yang K'e 楊恪, served as General of Resolute Cavalry in the state of Wei. Yang Chao's father, Yang Chi 楊曁, held the post of General in Command of the Army.

Throughout the dirge there are similar references, mainly to events in Yang Chao's own life, all of which require elucidation. Thus P'an Yüeh relates how Yang Chao came to serve Ssu-ma Chao 司馬昭 (211–265), the first ruler of the Western Chin:

> His appointment was changed to the agricultural administration;
> This was at Yeh-wang.
> The granaries were full, the stacks numbered in the myriads.
> The state was rich and the army was strong.
> Bright and majestic was Lord Wen!
> Gradually advancing to the house of Chin.
> The late lord, in dual capacities,
> Assisted the army and served as aide.
> Thus was he granted a landed domain,
> And received this illustrious rank.

改授農政，
于彼野王。
倉盈庾億，
國富兵彊。
煌煌文后，
鴻漸晉室。
君以兼資，
參戎作弼。
用錫土宇，
膺茲顯秩。

To understand this passage, we need to know that at the end of the Wei period Yang Chao served as gentleman director of agriculture in Yeh-wang 野王 (modern Ch'in-yang, Honan). He later joined Ssu-ma Chao (here referred to as Lord Wen) as both a military and civilian official. As a reward for his meritorious service, Ssu-ma Chao conferred on Yang Chao the title of Viscount of Tung-wu 東武子. P'an Yüeh's entire piece requires detailed explication of this sort.

The *Wen hsüan* also contains a number of works that use unusual words or technical terms that must be properly understood before one can devise a translation for them. One example is P'an Yüeh's "She chih fu" 射雉賦 (Rhapsody on Pheasant Shooting), which employs a host of terms pertaining to crossbow shooting, pheasants, and hunting blinds. In this case we are fortunate to have a near contemporary commentary by Hsü Yüan 徐爰 (394–475), who provides clear explanations for most of these words. Thus we know that *yi* 翳 is a type of blind made of branches and leaves behind which hunters shot pheasants.[7] Hsü Yüan also explains that *ch'iu* 鞦 is a term for the plumes "inserted between the tail feathers."[8] Thus it probably is a term for the coverts. Hsü Yüan elsewhere provides a detailed description of the *pieh* 鷩, or golden pheasant, including information about its "ferocious" (*pieh* 憋, an obvious pun on its name) temperament.[9]

The *Wen hsüan* also requires familiarity with the writings, lives, and thought of a large number of writers. It contains the works of 130 writers, and for a proper understanding of an individual piece, one must determine not only the circumstances of composition but also how the piece relates to the author's entire oeuvre. I have devoted much time to reading almost the complete works of the writers represented in the *Wen hsüan*. In some cases the collections are rather small. However, such writers as Ts'ao Chih 曹植 (192–232), Lu Chi 陸機 (261–303), P'an Yüeh, Hsieh Ling-yün 謝靈運 (385–433), Pao Chao 鮑照 (ca. 414–466), Hsieh T'iao 謝朓 (464–499), Chiang Yen 江淹 (444–505), and Shen Yüeh 沈約 (441–512) have more substantial corpora that are not quickly mastered. Most of these writers have a large portion of their corpora in the *Wen hsüan*. To gain a comprehensive understanding of an author's work, I prepare translations of the entire *Wen hsüan* corpus of each writer as I come to him in the anthology. So far I have translated, at least in rough form, all of the pieces in the *Wen hsüan* by Pan Ku 班固 (32–92), Chang Heng 張衡 (78–139), Tso Ssu 左思 (ca. 250–ca. 305), Yang Hsiung 揚雄 (53 B.C.–A.D. 17), Ssu-ma Hsiang-ju 司馬相如 (179–117 B.C.), Wang Ts'an 王粲 (177–217), P'an Yüeh, Kuo P'u 郭璞 (276–324), and Pao Chao.

Familiarity with a writer's complete works can provide information that serves to elucidate a problematic passage. For example, the "San-yüeh san-jih ch'ü-shui shih hsü" 三月三日曲水詩序 (Preface to the Third Day of the Third Month Poems at the Winding Waterway) of Yen Yen-chih 顏延之 (384–456), written for the imperial celebration of the Lustration Festival on March 28, 434, has the following lines: 正體毓德於少陽　王宰宣哲於元輔 "The legitimate issue nurtures his virtue in Lesser Yang; / The royal chancellor displays wisdom to the arch-aides."[10] In a poem composed for this same celebration, Yen Yen-chih uses the term *wang-tsai* 王宰 (royal chancellor): 於赫王宰, 方旦居叔 "Oh majestic was the royal chancellor, / Like Tan he is the uncle."[11] Here Yen Yen-chih compares the royal chancellor to the Duke of Chou, who served as chancellor for his nephew King Ch'eng. Thus the *wang-tsai* to which Yen Yen-chih refers must be Liu Yi-K'ang 劉義康, Prince of P'eng-ch'eng 彭城 (409–451), who was the uncle of the heir-designate Liu Chün 劉駿, mentioned in the preceding line as "the legitimate issue." During this period he and Wang Hung jointly had charge of the court administration. However, because Hung was often ill, Liu Yi-k'ang made most of the decisions.[12] Although Yen Yen-chih forces the comparison with the Duke of Chou,[13] his use of the same term in both places helps to determine the identity of the *wang-tsai*.

Another challenge faced by the translator of the *Wen hsüan* is its difficult language. One-third of the collection is devoted to the *fu*, a genre renowned and often reviled for its use of rare words and unusual expressions. In addition, the *Wen hsüan* is a major collection of *p'ien-t'i wen* 駢體文, or parallel style prose, an ornate literary form that requires great learning simply to read, let alone to translate. The *Wen hsüan* also contains a large number of *shih* pieces that employ learned allusions and a substantial number of rare words. The language of such poets as Lu Chi, P'an Yüeh, Hsieh Ling-yün, and Hsieh T'iao is rarely easy to understand without the aid of several commentaries.

One obvious reason twentieth-century readers find the *Wen hsüan* so difficult is that the linguistic and cultural gulf that separates them from ancient and medieval Chinese literature is so vast. Modern Chinese students of the *Wen hsüan* have almost as much difficulty understanding and explicating the text as their non-Chinese counterparts. Professor Lu Tsung-ta 陸宗達, referring to the problem of translating the *Wen hsüan* into *pai-hua*, stated that "to annotate [the *Wen hsüan*] is not easy. To translate it probably is even more difficult. The thought and subtleties of writers from a thousand years ago are not easily grasped, and their unique qualities are even harder to express."[14] Even translators of contemporary works from languages very close to their own do not always have a perfect understanding of the language from which they are translating. For example, in his French translation of Edgar Allen Poe's "Gold-Bug," Baudelaire misconstrued the black dialect word "gose" (ghost) as "goose" (in the phrase "as white as a gose").[15] If the French translator of Poe could be misled by "gose," one wonders how many words of ancient and medieval Chinese we misread and mistranslate simply because we are so far removed from the culture and language of these periods.

To bridge this gulf one must learn as much as possible about both the language and the culture of ancient and medieval China. Linguistic knowledge alone is not sufficient in most cases for a proper understanding of the meaning of a text. Although one may know the literal sense of all the words in a line and be able to explain their grammatical function and even to reconstruct their putative ancient or medieval pronunciation, such knowledge may not produce a correct translation. For example, in translating the *fu* on the capitals, which occupy the first six *chüan* of the *Wen hsüan*, I spent much time reading historical and archaeological studies of Changan, Loyang, Chengtu, Chien-k'ang, and Yeh. I became intimately familiar with such works as *San-fu huang-t'u* 三輔黃圖, the reports on archaeological excavations, and studies of early Chinese architecture. The capital *fu* of Chang Heng and Pan Ku are replete with accounts of ritual, and it became necessary for me to acquire a thorough knowledge of the ritual classics *Li chi* 禮記 and *Chou li* 周禮 as well as the monographs in the *Hou Han shu* on ceremony and official dress. To translate the passages that describe the architectural features of ancient palaces and halls, I was forced to learn what I could about architecture and architectural terminology. The names of plants, animals, fish, stones, and stars occur frequently throughout the *Wen hsüan*, especially in the *fu* section, and I have had to explore words used in Chinese botany, zoology, icthyology, geology, and astronomy to determine Western-language equivalents.

Although the difficulties presented by the *Wen hsüan* itself are excuse enough for the slowness of my work, my approach to translation has contributed equally to the glacial pace at which my translation proceeds. My approach to translation is unabashedly philological, and I concur with Vladimir Nabokov's sage words that "the clumsiest literal translation is a thousand times more useful than the prettiest paraphrase."[16] Because the texts in the *Wen hsüan* all come from the ancient and medieval periods, the language is far removed from modern Chinese and even more remote from contemporary American English. As Edward H. Schafer aptly put it, one should not attempt to dress "medieval Chinese verse in twentieth-century American garb."[17] Although readability is an admirable ideal, the faithful translator of these ancient and medieval works should be willing to display what Roy Andrew Miller termed "lexical and linguistic courage."[18] One should not shrink from representing what the original text actually says, retaining the surprising metaphors and unusual (perhaps for us) expressions as much as possible in the English rendering. For example, the Western Chin poet Mu Hua 木華 (fl. ca. 290) in his "Hai fu" 海賦 (Rhapsody on the Sea) describes the floods that occurred in the time of Yao and Shun as 天綱浡潏.[19] The meaning can be paraphrased as "The Heaven-appointed waterways swelled and overflowed,"[20] or even "eine gewaltige Ueberschwemmung."[21] However, the Chinese original says nothing about "Heaven-appointed waterways" or "a mighty flood." The original uses the term *t'ien-kang* 天綱, "mainstays of Heaven," which are the cords that bind the heavenly bodies. The flood waters swelled so high they caused the mainstays of Heaven to "froth and foam" (the rhyming binome *po-yü* 浡潏 [*bət-kjiwət*] describes the seething waters in flood). Although the literal rendering results in a startling statement that challenges our conventional understanding of celestial phenomena ("the mainstays of Heaven frothed and foamed"), I prefer a direct translation of Mu Hua's wording to some bland paraphrase that excises from Mu Hua's line the rich and novel expression that it contains.

In my translation of the *Wen hsüan* I have preferred to err on the side of literality, which Nabokov equates with "absolute accuracy."[22] I also have opted to provide ample annotation and explication of the original. My method of translation—absolute accuracy cum a surfeit of annotation—in fact coincides precisely with the qualities Nabokov stipulated as basic to proper translation:

> I want translations with copious footnotes, footnotes reaching up like skyscrapers to the top of this or that page so as to leave only the gleam of one textual line between commentary and eternity. I want such footnotes and the absolutely literal sense, with no emasculation and no padding....[23]

I am aware, however, that absolute accuracy has its limits. Consider the opening lines of the "T'an shih fu" 歎逝賦 by Lu Chi:[24]

伊天地之運流，
紛升降而相襲。
日望空以駿驅，
節循虛而警立。

The general sense is clear enough: Heaven and Earth are in constant motion, the four seasons alternate, and time swiftly passes. However, putting these four lines into a comprehensible English version that does not sacrifice Lu Chi's rich language presents a great challenge to even the most gifted translator. The words themselves are rather plain and ordinary, and it is often the case that the most difficult passages to render into intelligible English are those that contain the most common words of literary Chinese. The difficulty comes from casting English sentences that represent the phrasing and structure of the Chinese as much as possible. What is the force of the initial *yi* 伊? Does one give full force to the *chih* in the first line? In the *fu* each line is a complete sentence, and thus one should ignore the *chih* and construe the basic meaning as *t'ien-ti yün-liu* 天地運流, "Heaven and Earth turn and flow." The initial particle *yi* may have a rhetorical force, but in this instance it seems untranslatable. It may have some emphatic force as in this line from Chang Heng's "Ssu hsüan fu" 思玄賦 (Pondering the Mystery): 伊中情之信脩, "Indeed, my inner feelings are truly good!"[25]

The second line presents more difficulty. How does one construe the adverb *fen* 紛 (which is one of the most troublesome words in ancient and medieval Chinese to render into English)? What is the subject of *sheng chiang* 升降? Li Shan says that the implied subject is the *ch'i* 氣 (*pneuma*) of Heaven and Earth.[26] He then cites a passage from the "Yüeh ling" 月令 of the *Li chi* 禮記 to illustrate his interpretation: in early spring the vapors of Heaven descend while the vapors of Earth rises; in early winter the process is reversed.[27] Although *ch'i* is not in the text, one could supply it for the sake of clarity: "Their *ch'i* thickly ascends and descends in mutual succession." However, is the translator justified in supplying a word that is not in the original text? Can one devise a rendering that preserves the economy of the original without the insertion of padding words such as *pneuma* that are awkward in an English line? My solution to this problem may not be ideal, but I suggest that if one must add a word, it should be to the first line, for it really is not Heaven and Earth that "turn and flow" but their *ch'i*. If the implied subject is *ch'i*, the verb *yün* here does not mean "turn" in the sense of "revolve" or "rotate" but rather "to move in a circular fashion," "to swirl." I suggest the following English rendering of the two lines:

> Oh, how the vapors of Heaven and Earth swirl and flow!
> Thickly they ascend and descend in continuous succession.

In my rendering I have supplied the word "vapors" to indicate that it is the *ch'i* (air, breath, vapor, vital force) that emanates from Heaven and Earth to propel the process of creation and growth. Although the word "vapors" does not fully convey the sense of the term *ch'i*, it matches well with "swirl and flow." To preserve the vapor image, I have rendered *fen* as "thickly." In a note I would explain that the rising and falling of the *ch'i* represent the cyclical changes in the cosmos. Finally, I have translated *hsiang-hsi* 相襲 as "continuous succession," a rendering with which I am not fully pleased. The literal sense, "following one upon another," does not work well in the English line. The meaning here clearly is that the process by which the cosmic *ch'i* rises and falls goes on unabated. The *ch'i* of Earth is replaced or followed (*hsi*) by the *ch'i* of Heaven and vice versa. Again, all of these implications must be spelled out in a note.

The last two lines of the "T'an shih fu" passage cited above are relatively straightforward. However, *ching li* 警立 in line 4 is a rather unusual expression that requires some attention. Li Shan explains that *ching* 警 is like *ching* 驚 "startling,"[28] presumably in the sense of startling swiftness. The usual translation of *li* "to stand" or "to establish" does not fit this context, and one must find another English equivalent. The subject of *li* is *chieh* 節 "season." The sense of *li* perhaps is "begin" or "set in." Since the two lines are parallel, one should attempt to produce nearly parallel English lines. My approximation is:

> Across the sky the sun drives like a racing courser;
> Out of the void the seasons set in with surprising swiftness.

If he knew Chinese, Nabokov might take exception to my rendering of *chün ch'ü* 駿驅, which literally means "rapidly race." However, the T'ang dynasty *Wen hsüan* commentator Lü Yen-chi 呂延濟 sees in the phrase the metaphor of a horse riding at full gallop 日行于空虛如駿馬之馳驅.[29]

The genre that offers the greatest linguistic challenge to the translator is the *fu*. Arthur Waley has characterized the *fu* as engaging in a kind of "word magic" that achieves its effect by "a purely sensuous intoxication of rhythm and language."[30] *Fu* poets such as Ssu-ma Hsiang-ju are well known for their long catalogues. For example, the "Tzu-hsü fu" 子虛賦 (Rhapsody of Sir Vacuous) contains the following rhymed list of names of minerals, precious stones, plants, water creatures, trees, birds, and animals:

> In their soil:
>> Cinnabar, azurite, ocher, white clay,
>> Orpiment, milky quartz,
>> Tin, prase, gold, and silver,
>> In manifold hues glisten and glitter,
>> Shining and sparkling like dragon scales.
> Of stones there are:
>> Red jade, rose stone,
>> Orbed jades, vulcan stone,
>> Aculith, dark polishing stone,
>> Quartz, and the warrior rock.
> To the east there is Basil Garden,
>> With wild ginger, thoroughwort, angelica, pollia,
>> Hemlock parsley, sweet flag,
>> Lovage, selinum,
>> Sugar cane, and mioga ginger.
>
> The high dry lands grow:
>> Wood sorrel, oats, twining snout, iris,
>> Cadweed, nutgrass, and green sedge.
> The low wet lands grow:
>> Fountain grass, marshgrass,
>> Smartweed, water bamboo,
>> Lotus, water oats, reeds,
>> Cottage thatch, and stink grass.
> So many things live here,
> They cannot be counted.
> To the west there are:
>> Bubbling springs and clear ponds,
>> Where surging waters ebb and flow.
>> On their surface bloom lotus and caltrop flowers;
>> Their depths conceal huge boulders and white sand.
> Within them there are:
>> The divine tortoise, crocodile, alligator,
>> Hawksbill, soft-shell, and trionyx.
> To the north there is a shady grove:
>> Its trees are elm, *nanmu*, camphor,

Cinnamon, pepper, magnolia,
Cork, wild pear, vermilion willow,
Hawthorn, pear, date plum, chestnut,
Tangerine and pomelo sweet and fragrant.
In the treetops there are:
The phoenix, peacock, simurgh,
Leaping gibbon, and tree-jackal.
Beneath them there are:
The white tiger, black panther,
The *Man-yen* and leopard cat.[31]

其土則丹青赭堊，
雌黃白坿，
錫碧金銀，
眾色炫耀，
照爛龍鱗。
其石則赤玉玫瑰，
琳瑉昆吾，
瑊玏玄厲，
瑌石碔砆。
其東則有蕙圃：
衡蘭芷若，
芎藭菖蒲，
茳蘺糜蕪，
諸柘巴且。

其高燥則生葳菥苞荔，
薛莎青薠；
其埤溼則生藏莨蒹葭，
東薔雕胡，
蓮藕觚蘆，
菴䕡軒于。
眾物居之，
不可勝圖。
其西則有湧泉清池，
激水推移，
外發芙蓉菱華，
內隱鉅石白沙；
其中則有神龜蛟鼉，
瑇瑁鱉黿。
其北則有陰林：
其樹楩柟豫章，
桂椒木蘭，
蘗離朱楊，
樝梨梬栗，
橘柚芬芳；
其上則有鵷鶵孔鸞，
騰遠射干；

其下則有白虎玄豹,
蟃蜒貙犴。

Although the identification of some of the items listed in Ssu-ma Hsiang-ju's catalogue is difficult, the task is made easier thanks to such sources as Bernard Read's translation of the terms in the *Pen-ts'ao kang-mu* 本草綱目,[32] the philological notes by Ch'ing dynasty *Wen hsüan* commentators such as Chang Yünao 張雲璈, Hu Shao-ying 胡紹煐 (1791–1860), and Chu Chien 朱珔 (1759–1850),[33] and various specialized works on botanical terms.[34] For those terms that cannot be precisely identified, I have invented my own English equivalents. For example, K'un-wu 昆吾 is a stone found in a famous volcanic peak that produced copper and gold.[35] I have thus given it the name "vulcan stone." I have no idea what *wu-fu* 碔砆 might be, so I have dubbed it "warrior stone" (ex 武夫). For most plant names, I provide the English common name or give a literal translation of the scientific name. For example, "twining snout" for *pao* 苞 is my English translation of the scientific name *Rhychosia volubilis*. In at least one instance where the authorities do not agree on the identification of the plant, I also coin my own term. Thus the foul-smelling *hsien-yü* 軒于 becomes stink grass.[36]

Names of mythological creatures always present special problems to the translator. There are established sinological conventions for the *feng* 鳳 (phoenix) and *luan* 鸞 (simurgh), but there are many creatures for which one must either romanize the name or create a new English term. The inventions include "roving simian" for *hsiao-yang* 梟羊, "flying chimera" for *fei-chü* 蜚遽, "canopy bird" for *yi niao* 翳鳥, and "blazing firebird" for *chiao-ming* 焦明.[37]

One problematical term is the word *Man-yen* 蟃蜒 of the last line in the passage translated above. Kuo P'u explains it as a large beast, eight hundred feet long, resembling a wildcat.[38] Some commentators have argued that the length Kuo P'u specifies for this creature is a gross exaggeration and that it actually was *eight* feet long.[39] However, since the *man-yen* clearly is an imaginary being, its precise length is of no consequence. Kuo P'u perhaps derived his explanation from Chang Heng, who refers to it in his "Hsi ching fu" 西京賦 (Western Metropolis Rhapsody) as the "giant beast eight hundred feet long" 巨獸百尋.[40]

Translators have provided various renderings for *man-yen*. Watson simply gives "leopard" with no explanation for his choice.[41] Yves Hervouet calls it a "loup long de cent mètres." In a detailed note discussing the name, he cites the *Shuo-wen* explanation of *man* 獌 as belonging to the wolf class.[42] However, this word refers to the animal known as *ch'u-man* 貙獌 or *ch'u-an* 貙犴, which is possibly the leopard cat.[43] In my own translation of this passage I was content simply to romanize the term.[44] Whatever manner of creature *man-yen* was, its name obviously is descriptive of its great length: "long and extended." (The name in fact also is written simply *man-yen* 曼延.) One could render it as "behemoth," but this name generally applies to the hippopotamus. Thus, lacking a better alternative, I have opted in this case to leave the word in romanization.

The most troublesome words of the *fu* are the binomial descriptives (*lien-mien tzu* 連綿字). I have written elsewhere about these expressions,[45] and I will provide only a brief discussion of the matter here. The binomial descriptives are either alliterative or rhyming binomes (*shuang-sheng* 雙聲 and *tieh-yün* 疊韻). They are common in such works as the *Shih ching* and *Ch'u tz'u* but are the stock language of the *fu*. The grand epideictic *fu* of such poets as Ssu-ma Hsiang-ju, Yang Hsiung, Pan Ku, Chang Heng, Tso Ssu, and Kuo P'u consist of long series of such expressions many of which were difficult to understand. Liu Hsieh comments on how hard it was even for learned men to read what he called these "precious words" (*wei tzu* 瑋字):

> Furthermore, when rhapsodizing on capitals and parks, most [*fu* writers of the Han period] used loan graphs and phonetic compounds. Thus the philology of the Former Han largely is concerned with precious words. This was not only because the expressions they created were unusual but also because they were difficult for most people to understand. By the Later Han, philology became neglected.... In the Wei dynasty, writers composed in elegant language, but graphs had a common standard. When they looked back on the Han writings, they found them difficult and abstruse. Thus Ts'ao Chih, in referring to the writings of Yang Hsiung and Ssu-ma Hsiang-ju, said that their aim was hidden and their import deep, but without a teacher the reader was unable to decipher their language, and without broad learning he cannot comprehend their meaning. This was not only because their talent was far-reaching, but also because the words they used were obscure.[46]

> 且賦京苑,假借形聲,是以前漢小學,率多瑋字。非獨制異,乃共曉難也....魏代綴藻,則字有常檢,追觀漢作,翻成阻奧。故陳思稱揚馬之作,趣幽旨深,讀者非師傅不能析其辭。豈直才懸,抑亦字隱。

If the learned scholars and writers of the Han and Six Dynasties period found the binomial descriptives difficult to understand, what of the hapless translator who attempts to render the less common of such words into English? One of course can consult the commentaries. However, the commentaries provide only limited assistance in understanding the precise meaning of these "precious words." First, they do not always gloss individual words but provide only the general sense of several words in a series. For example, Kuo P'u's "Chiang fu" 江賦 (Rhapsody on the Yangtze River) contains the following two lines consisting of a series of four binomes:

> 㶁湟潎泧,
> 滭沸澗瀹,

Li Shan explains that the two lines are descriptive of swift movement of water 皆水流漂急之貌。[47] Although helpful for understanding the general sense, his paraphrase does not provide any information about the meaning of each term. The Ch'ing philologists have made studies of some of these words, and their learned glosses often contain useful information about related words or variant ways of writing the same word. For example, Hu Shao-ying compares *yü-huang* 潏湟 (**gjiuet-guang*) with *lü-huang* 律皇 (**ljuet-guang*), which occurs in Yang Hsiung's "Yü lieh fu" 羽獵賦 (Plume Hunt Rhapsody) in the sense of "swiftly moving."[48]

Even if one obtains a gloss on a particular expression, either from an early glossographer or a later philological commentary, one still must decide how to render it into English. One solution simply is to provide a paraphrase of the entire line. This is the method generally used by von Zach. For example, he renders four lines of Kuo P'u's "Chiang fu" into one line of German: "Im Kampfe unter einander stürmen sie rasend dahin."[49]

潏湟忽泱，
潚洄瀾瀹，
漩澴濙濴，
溉灂濆瀑。

My method of translating these words is to endow each binome with an English meaning that conveys the sense, at least in context. I also have attempted to devise alliterative (or occasionally rhyming) equivalents that convey something of the euphonic effect these words have in the original. Thus my translation of these same lines reads:

> Dashing and darting, scurrying and scudding,
> Swiftly streaking, rapidly rushing,
> Whirling and swirling, twining and twisting,
> Peaked and piled, spurting and spouting.[50]

In my notes I attempt to explain why I translate each word as I do. For example, the alliterative binome *shu-shan* 潚洄 (**sjok-sjam*) perhaps is a synonym compound composed of *shu* (ex 倏) "sudden" and *shan* (ex 閃) "flashing"; thus, my "swiftly streaking." The rhyming binome *wei-lei* 溉灂 (**juei-ljuei*) may have for its signific *lei* (ex 累) "piled up"; hence, my "peaked and piled."

In this essay I have been able to touch on only a small number of the numerous problems that confront the translator of a work such as the *Wen hsüan*. What I hope I have demonstrated is the importance of the philological approach to understanding ancient and medieval texts. If we do not properly understand the language of our texts, we cannot hope to translate them correctly.

NOTES

1. David R. Knechtges, trans. *Wen xuan, or Selections of Refined Literature* (Princeton: Princeton University Press, 1981), xi.

2. *Wen hsüan* (Taipei: Cheng-chung shu-chü, 1971), 37.23a.

3. Michael C. Rogers, *The Chronicle of Fu Chien: A Case of Exemplar History* (Berkeley: University of California Press, 1968); Richard B. Mather, trans., *Shih-shuo Hsin-yü: A New Account of Tales of the World* (Minneapolis: University of Minnesota Press, 1976).

4. See Huang K'an 黃侃. "*Wen hsüan* tsou t'an Liu Cheng p'ing-tien" 《文選、奏彈劉整》評點. *Hsün-ku yen-chiu* 《訓詁研究》(Ed. Lu Tsung-da 陸宗達, Beijing Normal University Press, 1981) 15–18; Wu Shih-ch'ang 吳世昌 "Lo-yin shih tu-shu pi-chi" 羅音室讀書筆記, *Hsüeh-lin man-lu* 學林漫錄 5 (1982): 87–95.

5. See Liu Chien 劉堅, ed., *Chin-tai Han-yü tu-pen* 晋代漢語讀本 (Shanghai: Shanghai chiao-yü ch'u-pan-she, 1985), 9–14.

6. *Wen hsüan* 56.25a–29b.

7. *Wen hsüan* 9.8b.

8. *Wen hsüan* 9.11a.

9. *Wen hsüan* 9.11b.

10. *Wen hsüan* 46.6b.

11. Yen Yen-chih, "Ying-chao yen ch'ü-shui tso shih" 應詔讌曲水作詩 (Poem Composed in Response to Command for the Feast at the Winding Waterway), *Wen hsüan* 20.26a.

12. See *Sung shu* 宋書 (Peking: Chung-hua shu-chü, 1974), 68.1790.

13. When the Duke of Chou served as chancellor, his nephew King Cheng was already ruler. Liu Chün, however, would not become emperor for many more years.

14. Ch'en Hung-t'ien 陳宏天, Chao Fu-hai 趙福海, and Ch'en Fu-hsing 陳復興, eds., *Chao-ming wen-hsüan yi-chu* 昭明文選譯注 (Chang-chun: Chilin wen-shih ch'u-pan-she, 1987), 4.

15. See Stephen Peithman, ed., *The Annotated Tales of Edgar Allan Poe* (New York: Avenel Books, 1981), 267. The French version still reads "pâle comme une oie." See Charles Baudelaire, *Histoires extraordinaires par Edgar Poe*, Oeuvres complètes de Charles Baudelaire, Traductions (Paris: Louis Conard, 1932), 86.

16. Vladimir Nabokov, "Problems of Translation: 'Onegin' in English," *Partisan Review* 22 (1955): 496–512.

17. Edward H. Schafer, *Pacing the Void* (Berkeley: University of California Press, 1977), 4.

18. Roy Andrew Miller, *Nihongo: In Defence of Japanese* (London: Athlone Press, 1986), 219.

19. *Wen hsüan* 12.1b.

20. Burton Watson, *Chinese Rhyme-Prose: Poems in the Fu Form from the Han and Six Dynasties Periods* (New York: Columbia University Press, 1971), 72.

21. Erwin von Zach, trans., *Die Chinesische Anthologie* (Cambridge: Harvard University Press, 1958), vol. 1, 180.

22. Nabokov, "Problems of Translation," 510.

23. Nabokov, "Problems of Translation," 512.

24. *Wen hsüan* 16.14a.

25. *Wen hsüan* 15.1b.

26. 升降謂天地氣上下也. See *Wen hsüan* 16.14a.

27. *Li chi chu-shu* 禮記注疏, in *Shih-san ching chu-shu* 十三經注疏 (Kyoto: Chūbun shuppansha, 1972), 14.21b (2934) and 17.11b (2988).

28. *Wen hsüan* 16.14a.

29. *Liu-ch'en chu Wen hsüan* 六臣注文選, Ssu-pu Ts'ung-k'an (SPTK), 16.17b.

30. Arthur Waley, *The Temple and Other Poems* (New York: Knopf, 1923), 17.

31. *Wen hsüan* 7.18b–20a. Trans. from Knechtges, *Wen xuan*, vol. 2, 57–63.

32. Bernard Read, trans., *Chinese Materia Medica: Animal Drugs* (1931; rpt. Taipei: Southern Materials Center, 1977); *Chinese Materia Medica: Avian Drugs* (1932; rpt. Taipei: Southern Materials Center, 1977); *Chinese Materia Medica: Dragon and Snake Drugs* (1934; rpt. Taipei: Southern Materials Center, 1977); *Chinese Medicinal Plants from the Pen Ts'ao Kang Mu A.D. 1596* (1936; rpt. Taipei: Southern Materials Center, 1977); *Chinese Materia Medica: Turtle and Shellfish Drugs* (1937; rpt. Taipei: Southern Materials Center, 1977); *Chinese Materia Medica: Fish Drugs* (1939; rpt. Taipei: Southern Materials Center, 1977); *Chinese Materia Medica: Insect Drugs* (1941; rpt. Taipei: Southern Materials Center, 1977); with C. Pak, *Chinese Materia Medica: A Compendium of Minerals and Stones* (1928; 1936; rpt. Taipei: Southern Materials Center, 1977).

33. *Wen hsüan chiao-yen* 文選膠言 (1822; rpt. Taipei: Kuang-wen shu-chü, 1966); *Wen hsüan chien-cheng* 文選箋證 (preface dated 1858; rpt. Taipei: Kuang-wen shu-chü, 1966); *Wen hsüan chi-shih* 文選集釋 (1836; rpt. Taipei: Kuang-wen shu-chü, 1966).

34. Most helpful is Lu Wen-yü 陸文郁, *Shih ts'ao-mu chin-shih* 詩草木今釋 (Tientsin: T'ien-chin jen-min ch'u-pan-she, 1957) and the five-volume *Chung-kuo kao-teng chih-wu t'u-chien* 中國高等植物圖鑒 edited by the Chih-wu yen-chiu-so of the Chung-kuo k'o-hsüeh-yüan (Peking: K'o-hsüeh ch'u-pan-she, 1972–1976).

35. See *Wen hsüan* 15.7a, Li Shan's commentary.

36. The *hsien-yü* is another name for *yu-ts'ao* 蕕草, which is variously identified: *Digitaria sanguinalis* (crabgrass), *Caryopteris divaricata* (spreading bluebeard), or possibly a *Potamogeton*. See Read, *Chinese Medicinal Plants*, 36, no. 143.

37. See *Wen xuan*, vol. 2, 102, l. 329n, l. 330n, l. 334n, and l. 344n.

38. *Wen hsüan* 7.20a.

39. See the various commentaries cited by Kao Pu-ying 高步瀛, comp., Ts'ao Tao-heng 曹道衡 and Shen Yü-ch'eng 沈玉成, eds. *Wen hsüan Li chu yi-shu* 文選李注義疏 (Peking: Chung-hua shu-chü, 1985), 7.1660–1661.

40. *Wen hsüan* 2.25a.

41. Watson, *Chinese Rhyme-Prose*, 33.

42. Yves Hervouet, *Le Chapitre 117 du Che-ki*, 30.

43. See Hao Yi-hsing 郝懿行 (1757–1825), comm. *Erh-ya yi-shu* 爾雅義疏, SPPY, 6.6a.

44. *Wen xuan*, vol. 2, 63.

45. David R. Knechtges, "Problems of Translating Descriptive Binomes in the *Fu*," *Tamkang Review* 15 (Autumn 1984–Summer 1985): 329–347.

46. *Wen-hsin tiao-lung* 文心雕龍, SPPY, 8.10b.

47. *Wen hsüan* 12.11a.

48. See *Wen hsüan chien-cheng* 14.9a.

49. *Die Chinesische Anthologie* 1: 186.

50. *Wen xuan*, vol. 2, 327.

Translating Six Dynasties "Colloquialisms" into English

The *Shih-shuo hsin-yü*

RICHARD B. MATHER

It is with considerable fear and trembling that I approach this subject, for I realize that "colloquialisms" are not easy to identify in the first place, especially when they occur in a language other than one's own. And when they are embedded in a literary text some fifteen hundred years old, the problem is only the more compounded. Since no one ever tape-recorded the conversations that have been encoded in the relatively terse but nevertheless elegant Middle Chinese of the conversational portions of the anecdotal collection *Shih-shuo hsin-yü* 世說新語, compiled by the Liu-Sung prince Liu I-ch'ing 劉義慶 (403–444), we will never know exactly what was said in the first place, let alone how "colloquial" or "literary" the resulting text should be considered.

It is well known that classical (i.e., pre-Han) texts seem bare and almost abbreviated in comparison with later writings. The fourth-century B.C. *Tso-chuan* 左傳 commentary on the "Spring and Autumn Annals" (*Ch'un-ch'iu* 春秋) is a prime example of terseness, carried in some instances almost to the point of unintelligibility. The style of the *Shih-shuo*, on the other hand, marks the beginning of a trend toward greater subtlety in shades of meaning and feeling, through the addition of disyllabic expressions and new functional words and particles, including new meanings for old ones. One reason for the rise of this subtler style during the Six Dynasties (roughly A.D. 200–600), which has been suggested by the late Japanese sinologist Yoshikawa Kōjirō 吉川幸次郎, was the popularity among the leisured classes during this period of drawing-room debates on abstruse topics, an activity known at the time as "pure conversation" (*ch'ing-t'an* 清談). In these debates, two qualities were held in very high regard: rhetorical skill—the ability to make sententious statements in balanced cadences (which often resulted in phrases of four or six syllables)—and the ability to modulate one's speech to convey fine gradations of meaning or feeling. According to Yoshikawa, these practices resulted in an increase in disyllabic expressions to replace the staccato of monosyllables and a corresponding expansion in the use of function words.[1]

In this essay I shall attempt to illustrate some of these features, especially as they appear in the conversational portions of the *Shih-shuo*. The *Shih-shuo hsin-yü* is something of a pastiche, based on earlier written sources from the third and fourth centuries, most of which have been lost but fragments of which have been incorporated in Liu Chün's 劉峻 (462–521) commentary. In spite of this, it has its own consistent and recognizable style in which it records incidents and remarks attributed to historical persons who lived between about 150 and 430. The anecdotes are separated into thirty-six chapters, each illustrating a particular trait of character or style of life, progressing from the exemplary (the first eight chapters) to the cautionary (the last thirteen). I propose to cite a few pertinent passages illustrating various aspects of what I deem to be colloquial style in this rich source and to render them in what I hope to be appropriately colloquial English. At the same time I will discuss some of the problems involved in such an attempt.

Expressions Still Found in Colloquial Mandarin

Let us begin with the most obvious cases, namely, expressions that are still used colloquially in Mandarin in very much the same form they had in Middle Chinese. Since these expressions occur only in conversation and occasionally deviate from the standard literary style, it seems safe to conclude that they were indeed colloquial.

Take the familiar interrogative adverb *nǎ* 哪 of the Mandarin exclamation *Nǎ'rh-de huà* 哪儿的話, "Where [did you hear] that nonsense?" In the *Shih-shuo*, *nǎ* 那, used alone or in combination, as in *nǎ-té* 那得, or *nǎ-k'ě* 那可, introduces a rhetorical question meaning something like "How come?" "Why on earth ... ?"

The story is told of the Eastern Chin statesman Hsieh An 謝安 (320–385) that his wife, Madame Liu 劉夫人, once asked him, "*Why on earth* is it that I've *never even once* seen you instructing our sons (*Nǎ-té ch'ū-pū-chièn chūn chiāo-érh* 那得初不見君教兒)?"[2] With an air of injured innocence, Hsieh replied, "But I'm *always* naturally instructing our sons (我常自教兒)!" He meant, of course, that he was setting them a fine example and that nothing he said would speak louder than his actions. We might note in passing that in Madame Liu's question there was another Six Dynasties idiom, *ch'ū-pū* 初不 (literally, "from the start, not even once"), which is glossed in the revised *Tz'u-yüan* 辭源 of 1979 as *ī-tiĕn yĕh-pū* 一點也不, "not in the slightest."

Another familiar modern colloquial expression that crops up frequently in the *Shih-shuo* is the adverb *tou* 都, "altogether," "entirely." There is a curious story in the *Shih-shuo* involving the Kashmiri missionary Saṅghadeva (僧伽提婆), who came to Chien-k'ang (modern Nanking) in the year 397 and began a series of lectures on the Abhidharma (阿毗曇), or philosophical presuppositions, of the Sarvāstivāda School. The layman Wang Mi 王彌, after listening to the first lecture for a few minutes, got up from his seat and announced confidently, "I already understand it *completely (Toù ĭ-hsiăo* 都已曉)." Whereupon he marched out of the lecture hall with a few like-minded friends and in a separate room expounded everything in his own words. According to a monk who followed him out, his exposition was "essentially correct," give or take a few superficial details.[3]

Still another Six Dynasties expression, which appears to be a forerunner of the modern demonstrative pronoun *chè* 這, "this," was the disyllabic word *ā-chĕ* 阿堵, used where one might normally expect *tz'ŭ* 此 or *tzū* 玆. The story is told of the general Yin Hao 殷浩 (306–356), who, after a disastrous defeat in a failed attempt by the Eastern Chin to retake the north, was exiled to western Chekiang, where he became a devout student of the Buddhist scriptures. Once when he observed a sutra lying on a table he pointed to it and said, "The Truth must also be in *this (Lĭ ì yīng ā-chĕ shàng* 理亦應阿堵上)."[4]

Ā-chĕ was also used adjectivally, as the following story will demonstrate. The rather impractical and otherworldly grand marshal Wang Yen 王衍 (256–311), who is often blamed for the loss of North China to barbarian rule in the years following 311 when Lo-yang fell, was, appropriately, married to a very worldly-wise woman (some were unkind enough to call her "avaricious"), Madame Kuo 郭. Wang had once made a vow never to utter the sordid word "cash" (*ch'ién* 錢), so his wife decided to put him to the test. She had a slave girl surround his bed with cash while he was sleeping. When he awoke and saw what she had done, he immediately called in the slave girl and ordered her, "Pick up *this stuff* and get it out of here (*Chŭ-ch'üèh ā-chĕ wù* 舉郤阿堵物)!"[5]

I offer one more example of "proto-Mandarin" in the *Shih-shuo*, where *shih* 是, normally the demonstrative pronoun "this," is used as a copula in equational sentences. The poet K'ung Jung 孔融 (153–208), one of the "Seven Masters of the Chien-an Era," was only nine years old when he decided to pay a visit completely on his own to Li Ying 李膺, the commandant of the Eastern Han capital province, and arrived unaccompanied at the front gate of the latter's mansion in Lo-yang. No persons were ever granted entry unless they could demonstrate that they were blood relatives of the commandant or otherwise very prominent figures. K'ung Jung confidently announced to the gatekeeper, "*I am* a relative of Commandant Li (*Wŏ shìh Lǐ fŭ-chūn ch'īn* 我是李府君親)."

Since the remainder of the narrative is also of interest as an example of colloquial style, I shall continue the story. The gatekeeper was duly impressed by Jung's statement, and the boy was ushered into the presence of his host in a room full of very prestigious guests. Amused at Jung's temerity, Li Ying asked, "And what relation, pray, do you have with me?" (*Chūn yǔ p'ú yǔ hó-ch'īn* 君與僕有何親)?" Jung explained that his ancestor Confucius (K'ung Chung-ni 孔仲尼) had once studied the rites with Li's ancestor Lao-tzu (Li Po-yang 李伯陽). "*This means*," he continued, "that you and I have been close friends for generations (是僕與君奕世爲通好也)."

Naturally, Li and all those present thought that explanation was pretty clever for a nine-year-old, so when another guest arrived shortly afterward, someone reported K'ung Jung's *bon mot* to him. The new arrival snorted and said, "Just because he's clever when he's little doesn't necessarily mean he'll amount to anything when he grows up (小時了了,大未必佳)." K'ung Jung snapped right back, "I imagine when you were little, you must have been clever (想君小時,必當了了)!"[6]

If we were to add up the fragments of dialogue I have just quoted from this single anecdote from chapter II, the translation would come to some sixty English words, representing exactly thirty-eight Chinese characters. Of course, if these were turned into modern colloquial Chinese, the contrast would not be so striking. But one cannot help wondering how many words actually were spoken during the original incident—assuming, of course, that the whole story is not pure fiction.

Expressions No Longer Found in Colloquial Mandarin

Turning now from the expressions which have left faint echoes in contemporary speech, let us examine examples in the *Shih-shuo* which appear to have been early colloquialisms that have since dropped out of the spoken language. In this murky domain I feel even more insecure than before, but with the guidance of reputable scholars such as Yoshikawa Kōjirō of Japan and Hsü Shih-ying 許世瑛 and Chan Hsiu-hui 詹秀惠 of Taiwan,[7] I will cite a few cases that I believe qualify as such.

One of the most celebrated passages in the entire book is an expression of three words: *chiāng-wú t'úng* 將無同. The man who coined the phrase won instant fame as the "Three-word Aide" (*sān-yǔ yüàn* 三語掾). Perhaps the reason the expression is so celebrated is that it is quite ambiguous. At least interpreters over the years have differed drastically in clarifying what it meant. In the eleventh century the poet Su Shih 蘇軾 (1036–1101) explained it as *ch'ū-wú t'úng* 初無同, which is glossed in the *Tzu-yüan* as *kò-pū hsiāng-t'úng* 各不相同, "dissimilar in every respect," "altogether different." Four centuries later, the Ming scholar Yang Shen 楊慎 (1488–1559) said it meant *pì-chìng t'úng* 畢竟同, "in the last analysis similar," "basically the same." The *Tz'u-yüan's* own definition is itself ambiguous: *mò-pū-shìh hsiāng-t'úng* 莫不是相同. Since the double negative *mò-pū* 莫不, or *mò-fēi* 莫非, usually implies a strong affirmation ("there is no case where it is not …"), the statement *mò-pū-shìh hsiāng-t'úng* could mean either "They're exactly the same" or, possibly, "Aren't they the same?" The latter implies that the speaker believes they're the same but is not insisting on it. One could also translate it as "Perhaps they're the same."[8] To test the validity of the last interpretation (which I favor), I will first quote the complete context of the original story of the "Three-word Aide" and follow with other incidents in the *Shih-shuo* where the expression *chiāng-wú* occurs at the beginning of a statement, to see if this interpretation works in all cases. Here is the story of the "Three-word Aide."

> Since Juan Hsiu 阮修 (ca. 270–312, a nephew of Juan Chi 籍 of Bamboo Grove fame) had an excellent reputation, the grand marshal Wang Yen 王衍 (the same man who never let the word "cash" [*ch'ién*] pass his lips) called him in for an interview and asked, "The teachings of Lao-tzu and Chuang-tzu, and those of the Sage (Confucius)—are they the same or different?" (*t'úng-ì* 同異)
> Juan replied, *"Aren't they the same (Chiāng-wú t'úng)?"*
> The grand marshal liked his answer and appointed him his aide.[9]

If we were to accept the notion that Juan's three-word answer meant either "They're exactly the same" or "They're altogether different," there would be no clue as to why Wang Yen liked it. As a very vocal advocate of the current mode of "Mysterious Learning" (*hsüan-hsüeh* 玄學), Wang would have welcomed an ambiguous answer and shied away from one which would have bound him to any absolute position. "Yes, of course," he would be thinking, "they are *basically* the same—both the Taoist philosophers and Confucius believed in the Tao (the basic principle by which things are what they are), but while Confucius *embodied* the Tao, Lao-tzu and Chuang-tzu just talked about it. So, no, they aren't quite the same, either."[10]

Now let us compare this incident with other cases in the *Shih-shuo* where statements were introduced by the expression *chiāng-wú*.

> Wang Jung 王戎 (234–305, one of the "Seven Worthies of Bamboo Grove") once said, "Although Wang Hsiang 王祥 (185–269, known for his filial devotion to a cruel stepmother) lived during the Cheng-shih Era (240–249, which produced many famous conversationalists), he himself was never numbered among the able talkers. Yet whenever anyone conversed with him, his reasoning went right to the center of the Pure and Remote. *Wasn't this* a case of his

speech having been overshadowed by his virtue (*chiāng-wú ĭ-té yěn ch'í-yén* 將無以德掩其言)?"[11]

Here I think the implied answer is "Yes, you're right, he was more famous for his virtue than for his speech, but perhaps he himself didn't *want* to be known as a conversationalist." The same kind of ambiguity is present in the next example.

Hsieh An 謝安 (whom we met earlier defending his "wordless" instruction of his sons) was once enjoying an outing on a lake near his hermitage in K'uai-chi 會稽 (in Chekiang) with several of his friends. A sudden squall came up and the wind was beginning to whip up the waves to alarming levels. While his companions were scrambling about the boat in a panic, urging that they return to shore, Hsieh seemed utterly oblivious and was whistling and chanting poems as if nothing were amiss. The boatman, observing Hsieh's serenity, continued to row the boat farther out into the lake. Finally, Hsieh began to be aware of his companions' panic and said very calmly, "If things are like this, *perhaps we should* go back (*Jú-tz'ŭ, chiāng-wú kuēi* 如此, 將無歸)?"[12] The force of this remark was "If you fellows are so panicky, I guess we should go back, but isn't it too bad to end such a wonderful outing?"

The next example also involves Hsieh An, but under very different circumstances. It seems he was very fond of gambling, and soon after his arrival in Chien-k'ang after many years of idyllic hermitage in the hills of K'uai-chi, he found himself no match for the fast crowd in the capital and promptly lost both his ox and his carriage in a game of *chaupar* (*shū-p'ŭ* 樗浦), an Indian dicing game that was in fashion there. Hobbling home on foot, leaning on his staff, he happened to run into his brother-in-law, Liu T'an 劉惔 (ca. 311–347), who was riding in a carriage. When Liu recognized him, he called out in evident concern, "An-shih 安石 [Hsieh's courtesy-name], *are you all right* (*chiāng-wú shāng* 將無傷)?" Stated literally, the question would read, "*Have you been hurt?*" It is the ambiguity introduced by the *chiāng-wú* which conveys the sense of anxiety. Very relieved to see a friend, Hsieh climbed into Liu's carriage and rode back home with him. We are not told what he said to his wife when he got there.[13]

Some expressions carried over from classical times developed a slightly different function in the Six Dynasties. Such, for example, was the word *pièn* 便, which in Han texts usually meant "instantly." In the *Shih-shuo* it had become a very weak connective, meaning "and then," very much like modern *chiù* 就. In chapter IV there is an account of a *ch'īng-t'án* session, where a sizable group of "able talkers" had gathered at the home of Wang Meng 王濛 (309–347) for conversation. They had picked chapter 21 of the *Chuang-tzu;* "The Old Fisherman" (*Yü-fu* 漁父), as the focus of their discussion. The *Shih-shuo* text goes on to say:

Hsieh An looked at the title, *and then* had each in turn make an explication of it (*pièn kò shǐh ssù-tsò t'ūng* 便各使四坐通).[14]

Another case is the adverb *hsiāng* 相, which in older texts always implied some kind of mutuality or reciprocity. In the *Shih-shuo* it is often untranslatable and seems merely to imply that more than one person is involved. As an example, let us look at a story in chapter I concerning Hua Hsin 華歆 (mentioned earlier in connection with the abdication of the last Han emperor) and Wang Lang 王朗 (d. 228). In the year 190, as they were fleeing by boat from Lo-yang at the time of Tung Cho's 董卓 (d. 192) removal of the Eastern Han capital to Ch'ang-an (modern Xi'an), they were accosted by another refugee needing transportation. Wang insisted, over Hua's objections, on taking him on board. Later they were pursued by bandits, and Wang was all for getting rid of the extra passenger. Hua replied, "It was precisely for this reason that I hesitated in the first place. But since we've already acceded to his request, how can we now *abandon him* in an emergency (*níng-k'ǒ ǐ-chí hsiāng-ch'ì yéh* 寧可以急相棄邪)?"[15] In this case, one can't help feeling that the cadence of the six-word sentence demands an extra syllable before the verb, *ch'ì* 棄. The final interrogative particle, *yéh* 邪, serves merely as punctuation.

The same seems to be true for the adverb *fù* 復, which normally means, "again," or "once more." In the *Shih-shuo* it is, indeed, also used with this meaning. But there are many cases where it seems merely to be an untranslatable space filler. One such case is found in chapter III, where Chancellor Wang Tao 王導 (276–339) of the newly established Eastern Chin regime in Chien-k'ang (the old capital of the Wu Kingdom), in an effort to cement friendly relations with both the native Wu population and foreign visitors from the west, held a grand reception in his residence. Seeing a certain guest from Lin-hai 臨海 (in Chekiang) named Jen Yung 任顒 looking alone and uncomfortable, he came over and greeted him warmly: "When you came here to the capital, Lin-hai was then left *without any people* (*Chūn ch'ū, Lín-hǎi pièn wú-fù jén* 君出，臨海便無復人)!"[16] Besides the rather bad pun on the man's name, *Jèn* 任, and *jén* 人, "people," we find the word *fù* tucked between *wú* and *jén* in a grammatically anomalous function.

Another example of a seemingly superfluous *fù* can be found in the story cited above about the *ch'īng-t'án* discussion of "The Old Fisherman" chapter of *Chuang-tzu*. At the end of the discussion, after everyone had said his piece and felt satisfied that there wasn't anything more that could be said, Hsieh An raised a few "general objections" on the basis of which he went on to set forth his own interpretation in over ten thousand words.

[Afterwards, the monk] Chih Tun 支遁 (314–366) said to Hsieh, "You rushed ahead without stopping, *and so it was just* naturally superb, that's all (*kù-fù tzù-chiā ěrh* 故復自佳耳)!"[17]

Degrees of Intimacy and Social Level

One of the nuances preserved in most other Indo-European languages but lost in modern English is the degree of intimacy conveyed by the form of the second personal pronoun—the difference between *vous* and *tu* in French and *Sie* and *du* in German. Middle Chinese was equipped with similar distinctions, plus a good many more special pronominal substitutes suitable for particular situations. In the case of royalty vis-à-vis commoners, the distinctions were obvious, as in the following incident.

> When Emperor Wen of Wei (Ts'ao P'i 曹丕, r. 220–226) accepted the abdication of the last Han ruler (Emperor Hsien, r. 190–220), Ch'en Ch'ün 陳群 [who had served under the former dynasty] had a grieved expression on his face. The emperor said to him, "We (*chèn* 朕) received the mandate in response to Heaven. Why are you (*ch'īng* 卿) unhappy?"
>
> Ch'ün replied, "Your vassal (*ch'én* 臣) and Hua Hsin 華歆 [another Han loyalist] cherish the former dynasty in our hearts, and today, although we rejoice in [your] sage rule (*shèng-huà* 聖化), still the old loyalty shows in our faces."[18]

There were many terms for addressing the emperor. "Sage" (*shèng* 聖) may have been excessive; it was used in this case somewhat for sardonic effect. The most common address was *pì-hsià* 陛下, "Your Majesty" (literally, "[the ground] beneath the steps to your throne"—the highest point a suppliant dared raise his eyes in addressing the throne).

But we expect such conventions in formal court language. What distinctions were observed between ordinary people? *Chūn* 君, "my lord," "sir," was polite and deferential; *ch'īng* 卿, "you," was informal and familiar. *Ěrh* 爾 and *jǔ* 汝 were condescending, sometimes insulting. These were only a few of the possibilities. Chan Hsiu-hui 詹秀惠, following the lead of Hsü Shih-ying 許世英, has conveniently assembled all the pronouns and pronominal substitutes that occur in the *Shih-shuo* in the handbook *Shih-shuo hsin-yü yü-fa t'an-chiu* 世說新語語法探究 (Researches into the Grammar of the *Shih-shuo hsin-yü*). I list a few of these here, realizing that some appear only once and were appropriate only to a particular situation.

For the first person: *wú* 吾, *yú* 余 and *yǔ* 予, "I"; *chèn* 朕, "We" (royal); *shēn* 身, "myself"; *mín* 民, "this subject" (to a superior); *ch'én* 臣, "your vassal" (to a ruler); *p'ú* 僕, "your servant" (polite, to someone of comparable rank); *kū* 孤, "I, the Orphan" (royal, used by the successor); *kuǎ-jén* 寡人, "I, the Deficient" (royal, or facetious); *hsiǎo-jén* 小人, "this petty person" (humble); *chièn-mín* 賤民, "this humble subject" (to superiors); *hsià-kuān* 下官, "this lowly official" (to superiors); *tì-tzǔ* 弟子, "your disciple" (to Buddhist clergy); *p'ín-tào* 貧道, "this indigent monk" (to a layman); *hsīn-fù* 新婦, "this bride" (by a wife to her husband, or members of his family); *ch'ièh* 妾, "your concubine" (by a wife to her husband).

For the second person: *kung* 公, "your lordship" (to a superior); *tzu* 子, "you" (neutral); *tsūn* 尊. "honorable sir" (to a superior); *tsú-hsià* 足下, "your excellency" (to one of equally high status); *fŭ-chūn* 府君, "governor" (to a superior officer); *hsiēn-shēng* 先生, "prior-born" (to a teacher or religious leader); *fŭ-tzŭ* 夫子, "Master" (to a revered teacher); *tào-jén* 道人, "reverend" (to a monk); *ā-nú* 阿奴, "kid" (to a younger brother); *laŏ-tséi* 老賊, "you old rascal" (affectionate within the family); *hsiăo-láng* 小郎, "young master" (for young men of good families).[19]

Our English heritage provides us enough terms at least to approximate these subtle social distinctions, even though most Americans try to think that hierarchical class terms are archaic. But it is obvious even from the incomplete sampling I have given that a strain is being placed on the so-called English equivalents that are available.

I will close with two stories which illustrate rather nicely some of the gradations already mentioned. The first involves Wang Jung 王戎 (mentioned earlier as one of the "Seven Worthies of the Bamboo Grove") and his wife, whose name, alas, is not known.

Wang Jung's wife always addressed him with the familiar pronoun, "you" (*ch'īng* 卿). Wang said to her, "For a wife to address her husband as "you" is considered disrespectful in the rites. Hereafter, kindly do not do so again."

His wife replied, "But I'm intimate with *you* and I love *you*—so I *call you* '*you*'! If *I* didn't *call you* 'you,' who else would *call you* 'you' (親卿愛卿, 是以卿卿。我不卿卿, 誰當卿卿)?"

After that he always permitted it.[20]

As for the condescending terms *ěrh* 爾 and *jŭ* 汝, there is another story in the *Shih-shuo* about the last ruler of the Kingdom of Wu 吳 in the southeast, Sun Hao 孫浩 (r. 264–280). When the Chin Emperor Wu (Ssu-ma Yen 司馬炎, r. 265–290) conquered Wu in 280, in a playful attempt further to humiliate the vanquished king, he said to Sun Hao, "I hear you southerners like to sing 'Y'all songs' (*erh-ju ko* 爾汝歌). Could you sing one for us?"

Hao, who was just in the midst of drinking, raised his wine cup and toasted the emperor with the following song [in which he used the denigrating pronoun, *ju*, in every line]:

"Yesterday I was *y'all*'s neighbor;	昔與汝爲鄰
But today one of *y'all*'s underlings.	今與汝爲臣
I pledge *y'all* a cup of wine,	上汝一杯酒
And wish *y'all* ten thousand springs!"	令汝壽萬春

The emperor regretted having asked him.[21]

NOTES

1. See Yoshikawa Kōjirō 吉川幸次郎, *"Sesetsu shingo no bunshō"* 世說新語の文章 (The Style of the *Shih-shuo hsin-yü*), *Tōhō gakuhō* 東方學報 10.2 (1939), 86–109 (reprinted with revisions in *Chūgoku sambun ron* 中國散文論, Tokyo, 1949, 66–91); translated by Glen Baxter in *Harvard Journal of Asiatic Studies* 18 (1955), 124–141.

2. *Shih-shuo hsin-yü* 世說新語 (hereafter, *SSHY*) I, 36 (Yü Chia-hsi 余嘉錫, *SSHY chien-shu* 箋疏, Peking, 1983, 38 (hereafter, Yü); Richard Mather, trans., *SSHY: A New Account of Tales of the World* (Minneapolis, 1976), 18 (hereafter, Mather).

3. *SSHY* IV, 64 (Yü, 242; Mather, 125).

4. Ibid., IV, 23 (Yü, 214, Mather, 104).

5. Ibid., X, 9 (Yü, 557–558; Mather, 281).

6. Ibid., II, 3 (Yü, 56; Mather, 26).

7. Yoshikawa, op. cit.; Hsü Shih-ying 許世瑛, *"Chin-shih hsia-chi kuan-li tui shang-chi tzu-ch'eng yüeh 'min'"* 晋時下級官吏對上級自稱曰「民」 (On Low-ranking Officials Calling Themselves "This Subject" When Addressing Superiors), *Ta-lu tsa-chih* 大陸雜誌 27.9 (1963), 273–282; (same author), *"T'an-t'an SSHY 'chien'-tzu te t'e-shu yung-fa"* 談談世說新語「見」字的特殊用法 (On the Special Use of *chien* in the *SSHY*), *Ta-lu tsa-chih* 25.10 (1961), 297–303; (same author), *"SSHY-chung ti-i-shen ch'eng-tai-tz'u yen-chiu"* 世說新語中第一身稱代詞研究 (A Study of the First-personal Pronouns in the *SSHY*), *Tamkang Review* 淡江學報 2 (1963), 1–24; Chan Hsiu-hui 詹秀惠 *SSHY yü-fa t'an-chiu* 世說新語語法探究 (Researches into the Grammar of the *SSHY*), Taipei, 1972.

8. Chan Hsiu-hui, op. cit., 322–326.

9. *SSHY* IV, 18 (Yü, 207–209; Mather, 101).

10. See the similar conversation between Wang Pi 王弼 (226–249) and P'ei Hui 裴徽 (fl. 230–249) in *SSHY* IV, 8 (Yü, 199; Mather 96).

11. *SSHY* I, 19 (Yü, 22; Mather, 11).

12. Ibid., VI, 28 (Yü, 369; Mather, 190).

13. Ibid., XXIII, 40 (Yü, 753; Mather, 385).

14. Ibid., IV, 55 (Yü, 237; Mather, 120).

15. Ibid., I, 13 (Yü, 14; Mather, 8).

16. Ibid., III, 12 (Yü, 175; Mather, 86).

17. Ibid., IV, 55 (Yü, 237–238; Mather, 120–121).

18. Ibid., V, 3 (Yü, 281; Mather, 147).

19. Chan, op. cit., 1–104.

20. *SSHY* XXXV, 6 (Yü, 922; Mather, 488).

21. Ibid., XXV, 5 (Yü, 781; Mather, 402).

A Second Look at Li Wa chuan

GLEN DUDBRIDGE

Critical editors face the task of translation with some perplexity. They have put their best skills and efforts into restoring a literary text to the state in which its author left it. Their work, if done well, has cleaned away layers of transmitted corruption, smoothed out the distortions of less scrupulous editors, shown up the bright colors and clear lines of a true work of art. How can they now subvert the whole enterprise by dissolving the very words of the text into the language of another culture? There is no real answer to this question, but editors who work in a foreign literature must still respond to it.

Preparing a critical edition of the T'ang tale *Li Wa chuan* 李娃傳[1] proved complicated work in which establishing a text was only one step—even that not a simple or wholly successful one. But reading, interpreting, and glossing the text challenged the editor more subtly and fundamentally, even within a frankly traditional frame of reference. Following the pattern of the Arden Shakespeare—particularly of Frank Kermode's brilliant edition of *The Tempest*[2]—I tried to probe the text beyond the surface of its narrative, to seek out its resonances in Confucian scripture, in literary tradition, and in the usage of its own day. The rich promise and rewards of that inquiry were balanced at every point by problems of judgment. Here more than anywhere the plight of a foreign editor made itself felt. For while the act of translation might make redundant the hundreds of merely explanatory glosses which fill out the work of the Arden editors, resonance and allusion need more elaborate treatment. China's traditonal tool for this is commentary within the text; the foreign editor uses footnotes. But as his notes accumulated, they bring with them a risk. This was brought home to me in correspondence with a Chinese literary friend after the appearance of *The Tale of Li Wa*. He wrote:

> You are, of course, aware of the risk of over-annotating, that is, giving force to expressions that are conventional and jaded . . . , explanatory notes, if provided in the language of the original, will have a certain advantage of immediacy in that the cultural consciousness you want to bring in to bear does not have to travel through the language barrier.

These words go to the heart of the question, and the two points they raise set the agenda for this essay.

The second point, of course, offers the same bleak dilemma as the opening paragraph above. If translation will dissolve the integrity of a Chinese text, then the use of a foreign language to explore its literary roots must do similar damage. For Chinese readers this can only bring discomfort, even pain. But if foreign editors accept the task of interpreting Chinese literature to their own people, they must steel themselves to do their best in the circumstances. Inevitably the tension will remain: no compromise can ease it, nor discussion resolve it.

By contrast, the question of "over-annotation" begs unlimited debate, and what follows will aim to encourage and feed that debate. In practice most foreign editors would no doubt accept that they react to the nuances of Chinese cliché and stylistic commonplace less sensitively than those who have grown up within the tradition. They may well, as my correspondent suggested, place significance where Chinese readers would place none, write notes where Chinese readers would see no call for them. But is this not a matter of degree rather than of substance? For in a sense all annotation is over-annotation. A literary text in its original integrity speaks directly to readers within its parent culture, which we can define as the circle within which such direct communication prevails. Notes, even when written by the author[3] or the author's direct contemporaries,[4] by definition speak to readers outside that circle, for the very act of annotation implies failed communication. And it follows that those inside the circle will see annotations as clumsy intrusions, whose effect is to distort by over-emphasis a more delicate latent structure of hint and suggestion within the text. So even with the "advantage of immediacy" offered by "the language of the original," explanatory notes will always create a background climate of distortion. In these circumstances what concerns us is not over-annotation or distortion in principle but the pattern of relative values within that generally harsh environment. We might see the pattern as a series of ever-widening circles, each populated by readers who gratefully accept notes and glosses disdained by the inner circles, then in turn disdain notes and glosses addressed to the outer.

But "over-annotation" implies more than reaching out to distant zones of ignorance. It raises questions about what we have just called a "latent structure of hint and suggestion in the text." That structure is complex as well as delicate, and to attempt explanations brings risks of mishandling as well as distorting it. I recognized this problem in *The Tale of Li Wa*, and will take the liberty of quoting here the frame of reference sketched out in that book, which will once again shape the discussion of examples below:

> The author may use one phrase as a conscious and calculated scriptural reference, intending his readers to recognize it and register its scriptural force; he may use another as a familiar classical formula, recognized by author and reader but bearing no special weight; another as a phrase internalized and used unconsciously, when it surfaces in the mind to meet some inarticulate need; another as part of the common stock of current literary usage, familiar but long detached from its ancient source.[5]

These four assessments clearly stand as no more than markers along a continuous spectrum: a multitude of others could weave and blend among them. So an editor from another culture, and separated by 1,200 years, takes a desperate gamble each time he attempts a judgment between them. But I risked the attempt for two reasons. First, in China's own tradition of exegetical commentary the canons of judgment—as often implied as expressed—are subtle and even ambiguous; yet this is still not forbidden territory. The tradition is almost as old as the literature itself: it seemed legitimate to follow it. That in turn endorsed a second motive, which aimed "to stimulate a reading of the story in which depth of literary culture has a full part to play" (102). Faulty judgment here matter less than awakening a critical sense of the literary past alive beneath the narrative's two-dimensional surface. These points are easily illustrated.

Pu-hsieh 不諧 (*Li Wa*, line 37): The anonymous hero of the story, desperate for a liaison with Li Wa, declares himself ready to pay big money and adds: "My one concern is that things might not accord" (苟患其不諧). I offered a note summarizing the historical anecdote in which Sung Hung 宋弘 uttered the famous words: "the wife who has shared coarse food with you should never leave your side." And the Han emperor Kuang-wu ti, who had hoped to remarry Sung to his sister, commented: "The business will not accord!"[6] The note went on to suggest an ironic contrast in values between the two situations. And here, perhaps, arises a question about over-annotation. We must accept that the phrase *pu-hsieh* (out of harmony, in discord) had broader uses in ancient China. The *Tso chuan* gives a speech describing relations among the assembly of feudal lords: "Nine times the lords have come together in the course of eight years. Like music in harmony, there has been no discord (無所不諧)."[7] Later, the official biography of the Eastern Han official Chou Tse 周澤 describes an episode of A.D. 69, during his service as Director of Ceremonial: suffering sickness while observing formal ritual abstinence, he furiously disciplines his wife for breaking the ritual seclusion by coming to tend him. Public reaction speaks out in a rhyme:

> Born out of harmony (*pu-hsieh*),
> She became wife to the Director of Ceremonial:
> Of three hundred and sixty days in the year
> Three hundred and fifty nine go in abstinence,
> One day, abstinence-free, is for getting dead drunk.[8]

Might these examples not suggest that *pu-hsieh* should count merely as "part of the common stock of current literary usage, familiar but long detached from its ancient source"? And that it should not be asked to bear a burden of significance in relation to the narrative?

Yes it appears that the flavor of longed-for but questionable union clung to the phrase in later prose. In 802, as my original note pointed out, Po Chü-i used it in a sentence matching closely what we read in his brother's *Li Wa chuan*. One of the "judgments" (判) he wrote on specimen legal and ritual cases concerns a man who, though born the son of a concubine, aspires to become an imperial son-in-law. The judgment strongly disapproves: "Concealing his concubine stock, he cares only that accord might not come (唯慮其不諧). Craving to win favor and glory, he recks not that guilt might result."[9] This close contemporary parallel, in which the phrase expresses distaste at unseemly hunger for an unsuitable union, creates a sense that Li Wa's lover condemns himself with his own words. Centuries later P'u Sung-ling used the phrase in his *Liao-chai* story of Ying-ning 嬰寧, on the lips of the young man sent out to trace that seductive girl: "I have found her.... She is one of your mother's nieces, and not yet betrothed. Even though marriages with mother's kin meet with disapproval, if you tell them the truth there will be no dissent."[10] The nineteenth-century *Liao-chai* commentators stay silent on the background to this phrase—a sign that for them it has merged into the mainstream of the classical language. And I find Wang Meng-ou, in his annotated collection of T'ang fiction, equally silent at this point in *Li Wa chuan*.[11] Yet an editor from outside the culture perhaps still owes his readers the chance to glimpse what first gave that phrase its characteristic coloring, and to sense what intangible air of moral disapproval surrounds it. It was of phrases like this that I suggested (102): "To some indefinable extent they work in the prepared reader's mind and add value to meaning."

Hsiang shih erh hsiao 相視而笑 (*Li Wa*, line 115): As Li Wa and her lover return from their brief pilgrimage to the Spirit of the Bamboo Grove, they call upon a woman in Ch'ang-an described as Li Wa's aunt. When these two women meet they "look at one another with a smile." This is the opening move in the "switched houses trick," by which Li Wa will rid herself of the encumbrance of an impoverished lover. My note on the phrase drew attention to a story from *Tso chuan* in which a private smile was exchanged between two men who eventually went on to assassinate their liege-lord. I commented: "The confidential smile has menacing implications for Li Wa's lover too."[12]

But why place significance upon this particular locus? The phrase does appear elsewhere in ancient literature. Chuang-tzu's fable of the two men, Po-i 伯夷 and Shu-ch'i 叔齊, who go to inspect the regime of Wu-wang 武王, records that "The two men looked at one another with a smile and said: 'Oh, how very remarkable! This is not what *we* call the Way....'"[13] A totally different situation, in a later text, shows two practicing magicians of Han times agreeing to pool their skills to heal the sick. They begin by demonstrating their magic powers to one another. Then: "the two men looked at one another with a smile, and together put their arts to work."[14]

In neither case does the exchange of a private smile threaten a sequel of trickery, betrayal, or violence. The stories seem on the contrary to suggest that the phrase *hsiang shih erh hsiao* could work as flexibly and open-endedly as shared smiles in real human body language. In observing this I am one step away from confessing to an act of over-annotation in the first place. Certainly I cannot invoke with any confidence "a conscious and calculated scriptural reference" intended for the reader to recognize and register its scriptural force. Easier to describe it as "a familiar classical formula, recognized by author and reader but bearing no special weight"—in which case it should be enough for the editor to establish its familiarity with a few examples and pass on without comment.

But let us pause for thought at another point on the spectrum of resonance: "a phrase internalized and used unconsciously, when it surfaces in the mind to meet some inarticulate need." We must surely feel intense curiosity to know more intimately the workings of a creative mind in the remote world of medieval China, and may even choose to speculate on the matter. No need to spell out again how desperately hopeless the prospects will be if we try to establish any conclusions. But the work of annotation does at least challenge us to reflection.

As the second act of *Macbeth* portrays the murder of Duncan and the eschatological disarray that follows, images and echoes from the Geneva Bible sound fitfully through the spoken lines. But the third act brings a scene which in its very conception might echo the Old Testament: while Macbeth holds a feast at which he alone can see the threatening ghost of Banquo, it falls to his wife to take charge in her shaken husband's place. So, in the Book of Daniel (chap. V), did Belshazzar at his feast watch the fingers of a hand write menacing words upon the wall and depend on his queen to rally his troubled spirits. We can imagine what implications of divine judgment were sensed by an audience raised on such images from the

Old Testament, not only by their preachers but also through the folk tradition of miracle plays.

A systematic attempt to annotate the text of *Li Wa chuan* reveals similar processes at work there. The background presence of the canonical *Ch'un-ch'iu* commentaries, above all the *Tso chuan*, shows through in frequent glimpses—not only in the words of the text,[15] but betraying through more indirect clues some of the building blocks for incidents in the body of the narrative. The young man who deliberately drops his whip to the ground in order to remain in the bewitching presence of Li Wa is repeating a move made at the climax of a dramatic incident in the *Kung-yang chuan*: the words *chui ts'e* 墜策 (dropped his whip) give the clue.[16] And other words—*su kuei* 速歸 (hurry back home)—give a more delicate, almost imperceptible clue to an ancient act of deception dimly prefiguring the "switched houses trick," in which Li Wa uses her mother's pretended death to get rid of her unwanted lover.[17]

These examples hint at a firm grounding of scriptural knowledge which seems to underlie the surface texture of the narrative. Its tendency to supply implications of moral censure at points of misguided decision balances a rival scheme of sensuous, evocative language, resonating from the poetic world of the *Wen-hsüan*. The two fields of influence meet head on in this story: their thematic clash generates its shape and resolution,[18] and their unconscious promptings, so fresh in a young graduate's mind, will have offered the author the use of words tinged with moral or sensuous value.

Reflecting now once more on the words which signal the women's confidential smiles in line 115, I find no real cause to regret drawing attention to their ancient appearance in the *Tso chuan*. But I cannot articulate what mechanisms might have been at work in the author's mind. Over-interpretation would certainly begin there.

This discussion of over-analysis has shaped itself around certain specimens which might seem to beg the question. But we cannot really escape the ultimately subjective character of judgment on this or that allusive phrase. If editors are to defend themselves properly, they must be prepared to face questions raised by others on their annotations, not set up targets of their own and stage dummy attacks upon them. In the nature of things this debate will remain fluid, and many questions will remain open. What seems more fundamental is the continuing validity of this kind of inquiry: the conviction that we should react sensitively to the rhetoric deployed in the texts we read. In the end only one position would effectively break down the delicate structures we have been trying to explore: the argument that the language of classical narrative was a wholly sterile and neutral medium, bearing no coloring or reflected value from the literary past that gave it birth. Such a position would certainly make life simpler for editors. It would also leave us all very much poorer.

APPENDIX

A return to the text of *Li Wa chuan* gives a convenient and inviting chance to discuss certain points of translation, interpretation and annotation which have come up since my first attempt in 1983. In particular I gratefully acknowledge the material introduced by Wang Meng-ou in his book of the same year: here, as often before, I have learned much from Professor Wang and his wide experience of T'ang literature, which has enriched our reading of many other stories besides *Li Wa*. There are in that story, however, a small number of points that possibly repay an even closer look. Some notes on these now follow.

Fei lei pai wan 非累百萬

Bewitched by Li Wa, the young man seeks guidance from experienced men about town, who advise him that a huge quantity of cash will be needed to win her. I translated their words as "unless you put up a million" (line 35). The choice of "put up" for *lei* 累 (pile up, accumulate) was consciously ambiguous: it can certainly mean "to compound," but here would additionally suggest "to deposit" or "pay up." Wang Meng-ou (176, n. 16) comments on *lei* as follows: "no doubt a million is being used as the unit for reckoning accumulation." If I understand him correctly, he thinks the young man is being advised to pile up several of these units—i.e., several millions—not just one. But this reading is hard to reconcile with the young man's own immediate response: "I would certainly not grudge even a million" (雖百萬何[所]惜: line 37). He expresses willingness to part with the highest conceivable sum, and defines it as a single million—a sum which compares with 0.4 million paid for a girl in a ninth-century text (see my original note). It seems preferable, then, to understand the earlier *lei* in the sense of "build up," "get together," rather than "multiply."

Shang/hsiang 尚/向

Once formally married to her now successful lover, Li Wa (we read) "was treated with the greatest affection and esteem by her husband's family" (lines 337–338). The translation "affection and esteem" accepts a textual variant found in the Ming manuscript version of *T'ai-p'ing kuang-chi* associated with Shen Yü-wen 沈與文. Where the printed versions by T'an K'ai 談愷, Hsü Tzu-ch'ang 許自昌, and Huang Sheng 黃昇 give 眷向, Shen's text gives 眷尚. The effect, as Professor Wang rightly points out (185, n. 79), is to change the punctuation as well as the sense. 尚, "esteem," would belong with the previous sentence, as I translated it; 向 would go with the following phrase, which continues "several years after this" (後數歲). Wang favors the second course, on the grounds that T'ang verse and prose make wide use of *hsiang* as an expression of approximation. He cites examples from four poems and one prose narrative. And indeed, twice as many examples of this same *hsiang* appear in Chang Hsiang's standard glossary of medieval verse.[19] Yet not one of them presents a parallel in usage to the phrase *hsiang hou shu sui*: in every single case cited from T'ang literature the word *hsiang* is directly followed by a numeral, and that in turn most often by a unit of time. For Chang Hsiang this made *hsiang* equivalent in meaning to *k'o* 可 (roughly, about). But in the *Li Wa* context there is no numeral at all, and *hsiang* would come before the word *hou* 後 (later). It seems that there is no real parallel to give authority to the variant in the printed editions. As so often transpires, the variant in Shen Yü-wen's manuscript seems of superior quality.

T'a 榻 (couches)

The central part of the story mounts a lavish competition in equipment and performances between the master funeral-undertakers of Ch'ang-an. They each set up stages made of couches, and at this point in the text I offered a note with some contemporary references and illustrations.[20] This material can now be supplemented with a much fuller description of four tenth-century couches recovered from a tomb in Kiangsu. The tomb was excavated in 1975 and given a preliminary report in.1980.[21] A detailed study of the dimensions, material, and construction of the four pieces appeared in 1984.[22] This gives us perhaps our clearest available picture of what the story might represent.

I sui san hsiu 一穗三秀

When at the end of the story the young man's parents die, he mourns them with such exemplary grief that auspicious natural signs appear: a sacred fungus adorns his mourning hut, white swallows[23] nest in the rafters (lines 339–341). The characteristic growth pattern of the fungus appears in many variant forms among the different textual sources. They nearly all reflect confusion in detail about one general feature—the growth of several heads upon one stem. Historical sources certainly confirm that multiple growths on a single stem were reported as auspicious signs to the T'ang court, but these all seem to concern grain-bearing plants such as wheat.[24] I nonetheless accepted what the textual evidence seemed to require and reproduced modern illustrations of multiple growth on cultivated fungi, even though historical data were not forthcoming.

But in one text there is an exceptional variant: the Yüan (?) work *Tsui-weng t'an-lu* 醉翁談錄 by Lo Yeh 羅燁 here reads: 一歲三秀 (blooms thrice in one year). Although not a primary textual authority for this story, the work occupies an interesting and sometimes illuminating position in what I earlier called the synoptic tradition of textual versions.[25] A distinctive variant in this version might not in itself command acceptance, but it happens that its phrase describing the fungus growth echoes a scriptural source. The canonical glossary *Erh-ya* 爾雅 comes to us with an early commentary by Kuo P'u 郭璞 (276–324): its section on herbs lists two fungus terms, *ch'iu* 茵 and *chih* 芝, upon which Kuo P'u observes: "A *chih* fungus that blooms thrice in one year (一歲三華) is an Auspicious Herb (瑞草)."[26] This raises a strong temptation to accept the *Tsui-weng t'an-lu* variant—for in all other respects it would solve the problems surrounding this crux in the text. Not only should we no longer feel the awkward lack of supporting contextual material, but we might even see ways to explain the different variants found in *T'ai-p'ing kuang-chi* and *Lei-shuo*, the main textual sources for *Li Wa chuan*. *Sui* 歲 would have sounded close to *sui* 穗 in the ears of the post-Sung copyists who transmitted our text of *T'ai-p'ing kuang-chi*, and perhaps corrupted it.[27] And the graph 莖 might have been substituted for 歲 in the transmission of *Lei-shuo* by editors or copyists familiar with the terminology of multiple-eared auspicious grain.

NOTES

1. G. Dudbridge, *The Tale of Li Wa: Study and Critical Edition of a Chinese Story from the Ninth Century* (London, 1983).

2. Frank Kermode, ed., *The Tempest*, in the Arden Edition of the Works of William Shakespeare, 6th ed. (London, 1958).

3. A well-known and illuminating example is the long "Poem in One Hundred Rhymes, in Place of a Letter" written in 810 by Po Chü-i to his distant friend Yüan Chen, who replied with a verse composition echoing the first in every rhyme. Both long poems are transmitted with authors' annotations explaining personal and topical references in the text. The poets thus give these works a dual identity: they are intimate communications in which the correspondents share an entirely private discourse, but also literary performances consciously released to a public readership which has no access of its own to that discourse. See *Po Chü-i chi* 白居易集, ed. Ku Hsüeh-chieh 顧學頡 (Peking, 1979), 13.245–247; *Yüan Chen chi* 元稹集, ed. Chi Ch'in 冀勤 (Peking, 1982), 10.116–120; Dudbridge, *The Tale of Li Wa*, 21ff.

4. A more challenging example here is the celebrated group of *Rhapsodies on Three Capitals* 三都賦 by Tso Ssu 左思 (ca. 253–ca. 307), for which annotative commentaries were provided by several contemporary men of letters: *Chin shu* 晉書, ed. Chung-hua shu-chü (Peking, 1974), 92.2376; David R. Knechtges, trans., *Wen xuan, or Selections of Refined Literature*, vol. 1 (Princeton, 1982), 337–339 (note). The relationship of that kind of annotation to the text would need a more searching discussion, to acknowledge the characteristic aesthetic surrounding the *fu* rhapsodies, with their saturation of circumstance, lore, and verbal ornament; also the implication that commentaries (like prefaces) by distinguished contemporaries in themselves conferred ornament and prestige.

5. *The Tale of Li Wa*, 101–102.

6. *Hou Han shu* 後漢書, ed. Chung-hua shu-chü (Peking, 1965), 26.904–905. I have modified my original translation of *pu-hsieh* (will not work) to a more literal version: cf. *The Tale of Li Wa*, 115.

7. Hsiang/11/9: see *Ch'un-ch'iu Tso-chuan chu-shu* 春秋左傳注疏 31.21b–22a in *Ch'ung-k'an Sung-pen shih-san ching chu-shu* 重刊宋本十三經注疏, ed. Juan Yüan 阮元 (Nan-ch'ang, 1815–1816).

8. *Hou Han shu* 79B.2579. The final line is supplied from *Han kuan i* 漢官儀. For this reference I am indebted to William H. Nienhauser, Jr.

9. *Po Chü-i chi* 66.1397.

10. *Liao-chai chih-i hui-chiao hui-chu hui-p'ing pen* 聊齋志異會校會注會評本, ed. Chang Yu-ho (Peking, 1962), 2.148.

11. Wang Meng-ou 王夢鷗, *T'ang-jen hsiao-shuo chiao-shih* 唐人小說校釋, vol. 1, (Taipei, 1983), 166.

12. *The Tale of Li Wa*, 133.

13. Chapter 28, "Hsiang-wang," in *Chuang-tzu chi-shih* 莊子集釋, ed. Kuo Ch'ing-fan 郭慶藩 (repr. Peking, 1961), 9B.987–988. The same passage appears in *Lü-shih ch'un-ch'iu*: see *Lü-shih ch'un-ch'iu chiao-shih* 呂氏春秋校釋, ed. Ch'en Ch'i-yu 陳奇猷 (Shanghai, 1984), 12.633–634.

14. *Hou Han shu* 82B.2741. The short biographical notice is translated by Kenneth J. DeWoskin, in *Doctors, Diviners, and Magicians of Ancient China: Biographies*

of Fang-shih (New York, 1983), 76–77. I read the sentence translated above differently from Professor DeWoskin.

15. Wang Meng-ou's annotations of 1983 identify several of the same loci picked up in my own notes of the same year, but also add more—for example, the phrase *mo chih yü ching* 莫之與京 from *Tso chuan*, Chuang/22/Spring: see Wang, *T'ang-jen hsiao-shuo chiao-shih*, vol. 1, 186, n. 85.

16. *The Tale of Li Wa*, 112–113 (line 26).

17. *The Tale of Li Wa*, 134–135 (line 123).

18. This statement is documented in *The Tale of Li Wa*, Introduction, 37–80.

19. Chang Hsiang 張相, *Shih tz'u ch'ü yü-tz'u hui-shih* 詩詞曲語辭匯釋 (Peking, 1953), 372.

20. *The·Tale of Li Wa*, 147, line 183; cf. 190–191.

21. See the Yangchow Museum's report in *Wen-wu* 文物 1980/8, 41–51, with 42–43 on the couches.

22. Ch'en Tseng-pi 陳增弼, "Ch'ien-nien ku t'a" 千年古榻, *Wen-wu* 1984/6, 66–69.

23. Albino swallows, reported in the T'ang annals as my original note pointed out (181), are also reported as a rare phenomenon in modern times. On 5 August 1983 the *Times* of London carried a report from Reuter that one had nested in northern Bulgaria that week, adding that ornithologists expect them only once in fifty to seventy years. On 8 August a reader of the same newspaper wrote to report an earlier sighting in Kent, England, in 1911.

24. See references in *The Tale of Li Wa*, 181, to which can be added pre-T'ang entries listed in *Ch'u-hsüeh chi* 初學記, by Hsü Chien 徐堅 et al. (repr. Peking, 1963/1980), 27.663.

25. *The Tale of Li Wa*, 7–10.

26. *Erh-ya chu shu* 8.4b, in *Ch'ung-k'an Sung-pen shih-san ching chu-shu*.

27. See Hugh M. Stimson, *The Jongyuan in Yunn: A Guide to Old Mandarin Pronunciation* (New Haven, 1966), 95, nos. 0882 and 0884.

Two Tools for the Translation of San-ch'ü

JAMES I. CRUMP, JR.

I hold the conviction that translation is a highly individualized art form, and as such not much can be said to improve, alter, or lessen the personal artistry each translator brings to the work. However, having said this I must observe that, in another art form, gifted sculptors *may* be able to hack out an aesthetically pleasing shape using nothing more than a naturally sharp rock, but we have reason to expect that their genius might enjoy freer scope were they supplied with steel tools of great durability: at the very least they would spend less effort and time searching for the accidentally edged stone and more time modifying their ground-stuff with talent. In short, I am persuaded that furnishing artists (and in our context this means translators) with good tools and then letting them get on with their creations is the greatest kindness scholarship can bestow.

I have been involved with Yuan dynasty *san-ch'ü* for almost two decades —time enough to have watched interest in the genre grow almost exponentially. The publication of *Ch'uan Yuan San-ch'ü* (CYSC) came in 1964, and in 1967 the first book devoted to English translations of Yüan songs (*Fifty Songs from the Yuan*) appeared under UNESCO sponsorship. From that time on there has been a steady growth in publications from the United States, Taiwan, and the China mainland. It is my hope that the finding lists to be furnished here will put in the hands of Yuan *ch'ü* translators the best available tools to help them with their work.

A caveat goes with the finding lists: not all tools are equally sharp, and in the case of annotations and comments in Chinese works, the would-be translator must be aware of an underlying tendency in them all to varying degrees: for the sake of convenience I will call this phenomenon Mongol-bashing.

Chinese scholars can be just as restrained and objective as their Western counterparts so long as the subject is not one that has accumulated emotional freight—in this they do not differ greatly from their colleagues abroad. Foreign dynasties like those of the Yuan and the Ch'ing (and in some respects all of their works) are among the most difficult topics for Chinese scholars to maintain their objectivity about. For generations Chinese historians, with much more nationalistic fervor than critical acumen, have written about the Mongol dynasty as though it were an unrelieved, black, and bloody disaster from start to finish. They also have written as though the era were monolithic in its control, exclusion, and suppression of the native Chinese population.[1]

Let me cite a typical Chinese treatment of China and Chinese letters under the Mongols. What makes this paragraph so mordant is that it was written (back in 1957, to be sure) by Cheng Ch'ien, the Taiwan scholar most respected for his fair-mindedness and learning:

> There are two aspects of Yuan dynasty songs which are less than admirable: a tendency toward decadence on the one hand and vulgarity on the other—*these are entirely due to the age* [italics mine]. The Yuan dynasty suffered from control by a foreign race, racial inequality, ignorant and cruel rulers, and privileged and arrogant classes. It was a time when powerful ministers and unscrupulous clerks looked to their own profit and flouted the moral order. All of this contributed to a benighted government and a deformed society. So the literati of the day (as the saying goes) "*Eked out existence in an age of anarchy | Hobbled, with no hope of galloping free.*" Faced with this kind of society and government, they were depressed by a mixture of loathing, fear, and pessimism. They could neither bear nor escape their era.... they either turned to love and eroticism, or hid their tracks in the wilds; they either anesthetized themselves to or escaped from reality.

The force of Cheng's argument is seriously blunted by the simple fact that *many* eras in China's history suffered greatly from oppression by the mighty, subversion by the petty tyrant, and lawlessness and inequity in high places. Cheng's linking of eroticism with the presence of foreign rule, as most Chinese literary historians will admit, is contradicted by the fact that literature of the dynasty which *succeeded* the Mongols (the Ming dynasty, which could hardly have been more Chinese) is the age most characterized by celebration of and emphasis on love and eroticism. The Ming was the era of *Chin P'ing Mei*, *Jou Pu-t'uan*, *Mu-tan T'ing*, and numerous other works in which the central focus was *ch'ing*—love, emotion, or eroticism. That awkward historical fact obviously cannot be laid at the door of an invader dynasty. To Cheng Ch'ien, eroticism as a central theme in poetry counted as a weakness, and it is received opinion among Chinese scholars that the Mongol era manifested to the highest degree all the recognized weaknesses in Chinese history.

The reader may object that Cheng wrote his indictment thirty years ago and the last several decades of scholarship may have altered traditional historical stereotypes. Such a conclusion fails to take into account the power of scholarly continuity in a culture like that of China. Such continuity—master passing on his knowledge to disciple—*can* be very constructive; but when accompanied by misconceived worshipfulness, it eventually robs scholarship of all forward motion.

The very excellence of Cheng Ch'ien's credentials as a scholar is what makes his strictures so seemingly plausible, and his best students and intellectual heirs would find it very hard (nay, it would hardly occur to them) to take issue with their mentor on his evaluation of the Yuan dynasty. For example, in Tseng Yung-yi's *Meng-Yuan ti Hsin-shih: Yuan-jen San-ch'ü* (Taipei, 1981; a valuable tool which is analyzed in the finding list) he repeats almost verbatim his teacher's assessment of the era. On pages 401–403 he cites the three well-known satire-on-the-times songs, saying: "These verses, taken in conjunction with the material adduced in my opening chapter, make it only too clear what difficult and depressing lives the literati lived under the governance of an alien race." Yet in the subject-matter statistics he and a fellow worker put together on Yuan *san-ch'ü*, it appears that considerably less than one-tenth of 1 percent of the songs found in CYSC are concerned with social complaint.

I have singled out two Taiwan scholars because I know and admire their work, but the last thing I want to do is leave the impression that Mongol-bashing is somehow unique to Taiwan. Quite the contrary, many more and much graver scholarly offenses have been committed on the mainland, where this traditional view of the Mongol age has become entangled with Marxian historical dogma. Now it is one thing to become wearied by knee-jerk Mongol-bashing—one can, after all, compensate for this weakness and use the rest of the work for its strengths. It becomes something much more disturbing when you find the anti-Mongol mindset wrenching common sense, contributing to serious misinformation or disingenuous slanting of interpretation.

For example, in the introduction to *Yuan San-chü Hsüan-hsi* (Tientsin, 1982), which is by and large a helpful work, one can read the expected: "Since Yuan dynasty *san-chü* were for the most part written by literati, the majority of these compositions were written to express the depression and melancholy inflicted on them by the oppressive weight of Mongol feudalism." The remainder of the book, with its love songs, landscape and mood, and joys of retirement, does not bear this statement out, but the work can be utilized for helpful annotations and generally sensible analyses.

Compare, on the other hand, the treatment of the "Song of the Giant Butterfly" (CYSC 41.2) to be found in Wang Chi-ssu's *Yuan San-ch'ü Hsuan Chu* (Peking, 1981). I once translated this sprightly little piece as follows:

To the Giant Butterfly

This butterfly escaped, it seems,
From the chrysalis of Chuang Tzu's dreams,
Spread two great wings upon spring air
Then sucked three hundred gardens bare
Might not elegant creatures such as these
Shame to death our simple honey bees?
Or, giving their wings a tiny shake,
Blow our flower vendors in the lake?

But Wang Chi-ssu on page 17 of his *Hsuan Chu* solemnly assures me that

in early times the way of a butterfly with flowers was often used as an allusion for the way of a man with a maid. During the era of Mongol control in the capital cities of Pien-liang and Ta-tu, there were many instances of "forcible gratification of desires" in that "era of debauchery" [花花太歲] when the Mongols in the cities "Stole daughters and wives" ... who knows how many women were debauched then!? What kind of giant butterfly could "suck three hundred gardens bare"? This clearly is using the art of exaggeration to paint a picture of powerful men who could steal the women of the citizens at will ...

Here the tendency toward Mongol-bashing has led to distortion and the abandonment of common sense—not to mention complete neglect of an earlier commentary in *Ch'o Keng-lu* by T'ao Tsung-yi (who lived much closer to the times than Wang or any of the rest of us).

The composer Wang Ho-ch'ing is well known for other humorous verse so perhaps I can be forgiven for wondering what biting social satire Wang Chi-ssu might have discovered had he commented on an equally famous Wang Ho-ch'ing piece, "The Long-Haired Little Dog" (CYSC 46.1), which goes:

Ugly as a jackass
But the size of a pig.
This curious thing
Cannot be found in the *Shan-hai Ching*.
Head to toe and everywhere
Its body's completely covered with hair.
I think you're a wicked household sprite—
The Malevolent Dustmop with a bite!

Since their Mongolian cousins are no more hirsute than *Han* Chinese, it might be difficult to find hidden social complaint in that delightful little song.

For over a decade now, Western, to some degree Japanese, and even some Chinese scholarship on the Mongol era has pointed out that far from being a totally black page in the history of China (*hei-an shih-tai* is a much-favored characterization of the Yuan), some important enclaves governed by Chinese agents of the Mongol command remained for decades all but unaffected by the presence of those nomads "reeking of fermented mare's milk and wearing the skins of animals." Furthermore, an important opening up of the Middle Kingdom to the wide world took place, which, though often abrupt and brutal, ironically was in the long run beneficial in destroying China's insularity.

In any event, Chinese scholars need not have read foreign scholarship to be more sensible and very much more circumspect about asking ephemeral and entertainment literature such as *san-ch'ü*—or, indeed, *hsi-ch'ü*—to tell them anything directly about deep social discontents of the Yüan dynasty, or of any other age. Holding a commonsense view of what popular art can and should tell us surely should not be the monopoly of non-Chinese!

With these admonitions, I give those interested in the translation of Yuan dynasty *san-chü* my finding lists of English translations and Chinese annotations in the hope that they may make your labors easier and more fruitful. I fear there are still errors in them—I found it peculiarly difficult to completely master a computer program devoted to spraying numbers all over my pages—and I hope you will see fit to bring them to my attention.

NOTE

1. "... the innate and expansive pride of the sons of Han hardly permits an objective, let alone favorable, analysis and judgement of a time politically dominated by foreign barbarians." Sherman Lee and Wai-kam Ho, *Chinese Art under the Mongols: The Yüan Dynasty* (Cleveland: Cleveland Museum of Art, 1968).

Critical Bibliography on *San-ch'ü*

Works in this bibliography are listed in alphabetical order, not in the sequence of the finding lists.

In English

BIRCH = Cyril Birch, ed., *Anthology of Chinese Literature*, vol. 2. New York, 1972. The second volume of C. Birch's very useful anthology—sadly, both volumes now appear to be out of print—contains translations by Graham, Birch, and Schlepp (pp. 3–24) and in all probability more students were introduced to Yuan songs by this work than by any other.

SCHLEPP = W. Schlepp, *San-chü: Its Technique and Imagery*. University of Wisconsin Press, 1970. [Rev. *JAOS* 92, 4 (1972)]

In his introduction Schlepp says: "It is the aim of this book to attempt, through analysis, a description of the techniques and imagery that occur in *san-ch'ü*." One supposes he means formal techniques, in which case he unwisely uses as examples many pieces from the group of slightly bawdy songs (CYSC, pp. 1492–1493), which I believe were impromptu matching pieces saved from some kind of raffish party. It stands to reason that adherence to the usual formal requirements will take a bad second place to cleverness and mildly risqué wit in songs with that kind of subject matter or composed under such social conditions. Therefore these pieces constitute an unsatisfactory set of examples with which to examine form. Take, for instance, 1692.4, which Schlepp does not treat but which comes from the same cluster he uses:

ANON. (Hung Hsiu-hsieh)-667335

I choose a text,
Trim the silver lamp for light, and feign
To read. The woman, then, with arms like iron chain
Pins me to my chair.

I suggest she might
Brew us both a pot of tea,
Or, failing that, sew something she could wear.
She replies instead:
"First things first, let's go to bed."

The meter for almost every line is atypical, and we should logically expect their tonal melodies to be irregular as well. This set of songs (and other less-irregular samples) is analyzed by Schlepp for meter, rhyme, and tone-melody simultaneously. The results are inaccurate (which can happen to anyone) and confusing in the extreme. The latter condition could have been avoided—or greatly diminished—by treating each of these three formal considerations separately and using a wider sample of more regular pieces having more nearly typical subject matter. Schlepp's bibliography does not list *Fifty Songs from the Yuan*, though that work was published three years earlier. He does use songs from Ch'en Nai-ch'ien's *Yuan-jen Hsiao-ling Chi* (Peking, 1962). This curious work, which I have never seen, contains a number of *hsiao-ling* Sui Shu-sen did not see fit to include in CYSC. For a Chinese editor to include pieces written by himself "in the manner of" some form or another without apprising the reader of this fact has happened before. Schlepp's work is pioneering enough to be easily forgiven its shortcomings and used for its insights.

SEATON = J. P. Seaton, trans., *The Wine of Endless Life: Taoist Drinking Songs*. Ardis/Ann Arbor, 1978.

One hundred songs, all of which "deal in some way or another with drunkenness. In some the drunkenness is simply that; in others it serves as a metaphor for spiritual enlightenment." The translator says he has "attempted to mirror the modernity of the style in general" and succeeds rather well. In any event his translations show a well-articulated sense of poetry. This little book includes a section on "Allusions in the Poems: A Cast of Characters," which introduces the reader to the most famous and most frequently mentioned personalities found in Yuan songs. Seaton says, on the songs' use of *kuei ch'ü-lai* (return home) from T'ao Ch'ien's famous *tz'u-fu* of that name, that "the getting back" or "going home" may refer to actual retirement or, metaphorically, to getting back to the source, to simplicity and mystical enlightenment." Some of these songs Seaton had already translated for SUNFL. (q.v.)

SONGS1 = J. I. Crump, *Songs from Xanadu*. Michigan Monograph in Chinese Studies, no. 47, University of Michigan Center for Chinese Studies, Ann Arbor, 1983.
Chapters I and VI attempt to clarify the peculiarities of *san-ch'ü* prosody; meter, rhyme, and tonal melody are dealt with separately. The remainder of the book treats a variety of song types, song subjects, and song peculiarities. It contains something over 100 translations of *hsiao-ling* and *san-t'ao*. The work suffers from several mechanical glitches: on p. 47, for instance, 427.3 is accompanied by the characters for 427.2, and in the computer-generated chart on p. 163, the figures in square 8-B should appear in square 8-C. Likewise, on p. 166, the figures in square 7-B should appear in square 7-C. The finding list (pp. 207–222) is useful, but now outdated by the one featured in the present paper. One other change I would make simply for my own gratification: in the dedication, were I writing it today, I should add to my list of *doktor kinder* the name of my last one—Cindy Ning (Yi), currently with the University of Hawaii's East-West Center.

SONGS2 = J. I. Crump, *More Songs from Xanadu*. Michigan Monograph in Chinese Studies, University of Michigan Center for Chinese Studies, Spring 1991.
A sequel to SONGS1 but directed toward the nonspecialist. The introduction treats many of the unique features of Yüan *san-ch'ü* and supplies translations for them. Chapter 1 (by far the longest) explores love songs of all types and includes nearly fifty examples. Chapter 2 displays the songs' interest in derision and parody. Chapter 3 treats other favored topics, and the last chapter is devoted to seven songs by the eccentric composer Feng Tzu-chen.

SUNFL = Liu Wu-chi and Irving Lo, eds., *Sunflower Splendor: Three Thousand Years of Chinese Poetry*. Garden City, 1975.
Pages 411–455 are devoted to *san-ch'ü*. The *san-ch'ü* section (and, indeed the entire work) suffers from the very uneven quality of its translations. Soliciting translations by scholars whose cradle language is not English is to invite this kind of difficulty. A number of famous pieces, including CYSC 669–672, the long, dull, and sycophantic "To Commissioner Kao," appear in the collection, and on the whole it can be used—with discretion—to familiarize oneself with them. There is a list of translated tune titles (pp. 625–626) from which can be derived, with considerable difficulty, the romanized *ch'ü-p'ai* of the original. I feel the translation of "tune titles" is a lost cause: we don't understand many of the technical terms the musicians used and we add little to the reader's appreciation of the songs by doing it, since the *ch'ü-p'ai* seldom have any relationship to the verses one is reading. The bibliographical and biographical sections (pp. 523–621) are much more useful.

Y AND M = Richard F. S. Yang and Charles R. Metzger, eds., trans., *Fifty Songs from the Yüan: Poetry of 13th Century China*. London, 1967.
To the best of my knowledge, this is the earliest collection of Yuan *san-ch'ü* in English translation. The introduction to this pioneering work presents a traditional Chinese view of the songs as somehow being the outcome of the Mongol conquest.

Though somewhat less openly given to Mongol-bashing than is usual, the introduction also imputes a rise in Chinese alcoholism to Mongol oppression—I don't believe there are any statistics to support an increase in wine consumption during the Yuan dynasty. Yang Fu-sen, curiously, associates songs sets (*lien-t'ao*) with Japanese *tanka* instead of with the song sets which constitute acts of Yuan drama. The latter are certainly the direct ancestors (or, less likely, the immediate offspring) of *san-ch'ü* song sets. I consider the choice of one syllable in English for each Chinese syllable to indicate the metrics of the original song's line a very unfortunate choice of formal stricture. There are a number of reasons why this is undesirable, but the most important one for students of the genre is the resulting lack of clarity in the translations by Metzger. Fortunately, the word-for-word and literal translations by Yang (pp. 85–138) are quite accurate and perfectly comprehensible. The selection of *ch'ü* to translate was made by Cheng Ch'ien, and most of the genre favorites appear in this collection of fifty. The Index of First Lines, though traditional in poetry collections, appears in this book to be as useful as a fifth wheel.

In Chinese

CYSC = *Ch'üan-Yüan San-Ch'ü* [全元散曲], ed. Sui Shu-sen [隋樹森]. Peking, Chung-hua, 1964. Rep. Taipei, 1969.
A careful and thorough work arranged by the putative dates of the composers, each of whom has a brief biographical sketch (if anything is known): two hundred composers, 3,800 *hsiao-ling*, and more than 400 *lien-t'ao*. Each song is accompanied by variorum notes gleaned from a thorough bibliography of 117 works. A newly discovered six chapters of *Yang-ch'un Pai-hsueh* found in the Liaoning provincial library appears to contain twenty-five *lien-t'ao* not known when CYSC was compiled. (See *Tung-li Yueh-fu Ch'üan-chi*, Chü Chün, ed., Tientsin, 1990, p. 2.) Sui appears to have used his judgment in rejecting songs of questionable origins; e.g., Chu Lien-hsiu's purported reply to Lu Chih's song addressed to her and many of the *hsiao-ling* to be found only in Ch'en Nai-ch'ien's *Yuan-jen hsiao-ling Chi*. Serious work on Yuan *san-ch'ü* began with this edition, which contains indices of *ch'ü-p'ai* and composers. Most of the works analyzed in this paper follow the CYSC order.

HCLS = *Hsiao-ch'iao Liu-shui* [小橋流水], ed. Cheng Ch'ien et al. Taipei, 1965 and 1967.
The title comes from the first line of a song by Chang K'o-chiu (916.2), and the book consists of a selection of sixty *hsiao-ling* and two *lien-t'ao* (chosen by Cheng Ch'ien?). The songs are annotated, and attached to each is an "appreciation" by Liu Hsiang-fei [劉翔飛] or Ch'en Fang-ying [陳芳英]. These appreciations, though usually personal in nature, do contain substantive information and useful insights. Brief biographical sketches of the composers (pp. 208–212).

HSUANCHU = *Yuan San-chü Hsüan-chu* [元散曲選注], ed. Wang Chi-ssu [王季思] et al. Peking, 1981.
A depressingly doctrinaire volume. "If the contents [of a song] be reactionary, even though it definitely displays artistic value, we have not selected it, for that would serve the purposes of the reactionary classes" (p. 24). The "explications" are predictable and often annoying, but the vast majority of annotations are accurate and usable. The twenty-five-page introduction treats the contents and forms of *san-ch'ü*.

The use and effects of *ch'en-tzu*, though not done with any thoroughness, is described in enough detail to give the untutored reader some sense of their importance. With the first use of any *ch'ü-p'ai* the traditional syllable count for each line is given. Considerable time is spent on the difference between traditional *shih*, *tz'u* and Yuan *chü*. As is frequently the case with works from the mainland, the putative persona of the songs is taken to be the actual composer: "In the *san-ch'ü* we can see the courageous pursuit of love lives by young men and women (especially women)" (p. 14). All we actually see are the songwriters' views—shaped by what they thought their audience wanted.

HSUANHSI = *Yuan San-ch'ü hsüan-hsi* [元散曲選析], ed. Fu Cheng-yü [傅正谷] and Liu Wei-chün [劉維俊]. Tientsin, 1982.
The editors state that they "have chosen examples of the most important forms," but this is misleading, since a single example of a song containing some social complaint, for example, is unconsciously assumed by the reader to represent as many of its type as one love song does. The "analyses" for each song are somewhat naive and tend toward overkill (see, e.g., p. 19). Also, that determined old sinner in Kuan Han-ch'ing's "Pu Fu-lao" is "analyzed" as a valiant protester against "feudal Mongol overlords." However, the analyzers do show more common sense than some—see especially their final paragraph (p. 23) on Wang Ho-ch'ing's "Giant Butterfly." The annotations are unexceptionable and apparently aimed at middle-school readers—always an advantage for the foreign student of *san-ch'ü*!

LUHSUAN = *Yuan-jen Hsiao-ling Hsüan* [元人小令選], ed. Lu Jun-hsiang [盧潤祥]. Ssu-ch'uan Jen-min, 1981.
Contains notes and comments on 350 items, of which I can identify in CYSC only 340. I'm not certain where Lu's ten others come from, but I suspect the source is Ch'en Nai-ch'ien's *Yuan-jen Hsiao-ling Chi*. When a song does not have a traditional title, Lu gives it one of his own devising. The Yuan dynasty was a "socially ill dark age" (p. 136), and we are told that hedonism and alcoholism were caused by the presence of the invaders and that song 584.4, which expresses the fisherman's winter woes, "reveals Ch'iao Chi's sympathy for the working classes." While all this may be true, there is certainly no way of demonstrating it. In general, however, the explanations are less doctrinaire and more sensible than those in many other mainland works. There is a unique and appealing little piece titled "Romance" (1621.2) attributed to Lan Ch'u-fang, which goes:

> In everything I'm truly dense
> And she's as homely as an old mud fence.
> Let the face be ugly,
> Let the wit be dim,
> If he cares for her as she cares for him
> They'll be in heaven, if anywhere,
> This homely couple,
> This lackbrained pair.

Lu Jun-hsiang's explanation (see p. 227) says simply, "This piece tells of true love: in the eyes of these lovers, obtuse becomes smart and homely becomes handsome ...". Contrast this with the "100" *shuo-ming*, which says: "Such a liaison flies in the face of the feudal morality which is why the final line ... reads 'it will be found only in heaven'" (p. 103). The editor does not anchor his notes to the text by means of numbers, but they are useful and accurate.

TSENG = *Meng-Yuan te Hsin Shih—Yuan-jen San-ch'ü* [蒙元的新詩：元人散曲], ed. Tseng Yung-yi [曾永義]. Taipei, 1981.
This work is a primer for those who would know more about *san-ch'ü*. The first twenty pages are devoted to relationships between the society and the songs. The editor has collected a good deal of negative information about the Mongol era, but it never becomes clear why such events as he describes should have led to the composition of songs. The next section is a rather complete bibliography of collections which have preserved the songs for us. The following 100 pages treat their origins, types, and formal requirements; the most interesting parts are those in which he tries to match musical and linguistic "melodies." Tseng also does what few other writers have done: he treats the songs' playful forms (pp. 130–138). The last section—divided into early and late period composers—is devoted to helpful annotations and commentaries on some 100 *san-ch'ü*.

YANGCHU = *Yuan-jen San-ch'ü Hsüan* [元人散曲選], ed. Yang Ch'un-ch'iu [羊春秋]. Hunan, Ch'angsha, 1982.
The brief introduction concentrates on description of the landscape-and-mood songs and the association of these with withdrawal and retirement—truly the most frequent subject matter of this genre. Most of the annotations are devoted to the elucidation of allusions—sometimes giving the reader more information than is helpful (see p. 33, n. 3, and p. 323, n. 1). Though I suspect many of the 315 songs he explicates were chosen because they contained such allusions, this is not a drawback. The selection is quite representative, and his notes are helpful.

YJSCH = *Yuan-jen San-ch'ü Hsüan* [元人散曲選], ed. Liu Yi-sheng [劉逸生], notes by Lung Ch'ien-an [龍潛菴]. Hong Kong, 1979.
One hundred and seventy songs annotated with brief "explications" (*t'i-chieh*). Published in Hong Kong, it is done in traditional characters, which is curiously helpful since one does not have to guess which of several homophones was in the original. In general, notes are sensible and helpful, but from time to time the editor seems to grasp things by the wrong handle. The finding list's most annotated song (seven of the nine works have notes on it), Hsü Tsai-ssu's "Night Rain" (1056.1), has a line which reads "Under the dimmed lamp the scattered chessmen lie," which Lung construes as "the heavy rain sounds like the clatter of chessmen." But unlike most other annotators he sometimes gives several possible interpretations (see p. 96, n. 4) and points out when normal grammar has been wrenched for the sake of rhyme and "thimble phrasing," for which CYSC 1731.3 is famous. (See his n. 2, p. 181.)

"100" = *Yuan San-chü Yi-pai Shou* [元散曲一百首], ed. Hsiao Shan-yin [蕭善因], Shanghai, 1982.
One hundred six *hsiao-ling* and twelve *lien-t'ao*. So many of the "explanations" (*shuo-ming*) torture texts into a Marxian mold that they are often more an annoyance than a help. The pungent "Winterscene" (CYSC 648–9), by a composer who knew that some of us simply hate winter, is "explained" by the following—"For most of the Yuan the examinations were abolished ... most of the intellectuals had low social status and a hard life. How should they not cry out against hunger and cold?"

Much can be forgiven the editor because he has done more of his job than is usual—he has underlined proper names; only in the songs proper, but still ... First use of any *ch'ü-p'ai* is accompanied by comment on its metrical requirements. These are prescriptive, however, not descriptive. For example, his note on the opening song of "Winterscene," *Tou An-ch'un*, insists that "it uses *shang-sheng* rhymes, and the syllable before the rhyming one must be in *ch'ü-sheng*." One glance at "Winterscene" would have disabused the editor of that opinion.

"200" = *Yuan-jen Hsiao-ling Erh-pai Shou* [元人小令二百首], ed. Wang Ying [王鍈]. Kueichou, 1982.
"Because of the class limitations of the age, there are many dregs of feudalism left in the songs ... efforts to praise the virtue of the age and its false peace and security, praise of wealth, honor, good fortune and longevity; counsels on the nullity of human life and acceptance of the will of heaven, extreme pessimism and contempt for the age. Some illustrate naked lust or ridicule the lives of others—such songs should be criticized" (introduction, p. 5). Perhaps they should be criticized, but their existence is of great interest and to exclude them is knowingly to distort the era. A number of the editor's "précis" (*chien-shuo*) show greater-than-average exercise of common sense. CYSC 12.1 goes:

> Green stems bend
> Flexing in the wind.
> But the lotus leaves are sere.
> Some yellow added,
> Some fragrance lost
> In last night's heavy frost.
> How lonesome the river now that autumn's here.

Wang Ying's précis includes this: "Critics have claimed that this song mourns the inability of Southern Sung to resist the Mongols, but this is unlikely since [the composer] was a favored and important minister during the Yuan.... Here he is simply expressing a generalized melancholy over rise and decay."

Addenda

The above constitutes a selective bibliography, limited to those books I have actually used in my own work on *san-ch'ü* and which were made truly accessible by the creation of a finding list. In recent years there has been an encouraging expansion in publications of local and provincial presses on the mainland. Their contents being limited to the songs of a single composer, there was no need to analyze them in the finding list; however, I would like to call attention to two of these new publications which contain many helpful notes:

Tung-li Yueh-fu Ch'üan-chi [東籬樂府全集], ed. Chü Chün [瞿鈞]. Tientsin, 1990. Complete works annotated, including six previously unknown *lien-t'ao*.
Kuan Han-ch'ing San-ch'ü Chi [關漢卿散曲集], ed. Li Han-ch'iu [李漢秋] and Chou Wei-p'ei [周維培]. Shanghai, 1990. Twenty-eight pieces annotated; two appendices, the second of which is a collection of biographical statements about Kuan Han-ch'ing through the ages.

FINDING LISTS FOR *San-ch'ü*

English Translation Code

SONGS1 = J. I. Crump, *Songs from Xanadu*. Michigan Monograph in Chinese Studies, no. 47, University of Michigan Center for Chinese Studies, Ann Arbor, 1983.

SONGS2 = J. I. Crump, *More Songs from Xanadu*. Michigan Monograph in Chinese Studies, University of Michigan Center for Chinese Studies, 1991.

Y AND M = Richard F. S. Yang and Charles R. Metzger, eds., trans., *Fifty Songs from the Yüan: Poetry of 13th Century China*. London, 1967.

SEATON = J. P. Seaton, trans., *The Wine of Endless Life: Taoist Drinking Songs*. Ardis/Ann Arbor, 1978.

SCHLEPP = W. Schlepp, *San-chü: Its Technique and Imagery*. University of Wisconsin Press, 1970.

SUNFL = Liu Wu-chi and Irving Lo, eds., *Sunflower Splendor: Three Thousand Years of Chinese Poetry*. Garden City, 1975.

BIRCH = Cyril Birch, ed., *Anthology of Chinese Literature*, vol. 2. New York, 1972.

Chinese Code

CYSC = *Ch'üan-Yüan San-Ch'ü* [全元散曲], ed. Sui Shu-sen [隋樹森]. Peking, Chung-hua, 1964. Rep. Taipei, 1969.

YJSCH = *Yuan-jen San-ch'ü Hsüan* [元人散曲選], ed. Liu Yi-sheng [劉逸生], notes by Lung Ch'ien-an [龍潛菴]. Hong Kong, 1979.

HCLS = *Hsiao-ch'iao Liu-shui* [小橋流水], ed. Cheng Ch'ien et al. Taipei, 1965 and 1967.

TSENG = *Meng-Yuan te Hsin Shih—Yuan-jen San-ch'ü* [蒙元的新詩, 元人散曲] ed. Tseng Yung-yi [曾永義]. Taipei, 1981.

"100" = *Yuan San-chü Yi-pai Shou* [元散曲一百首], ed. Hsiao Shan-yin [蕭善因]. Shanghai, 1982.

"200" = *Yuan-jen Hsiao-ling Erh-pai shou* [元人小令二百首], ed. Wang Ying [王鍈]. Kueichou, 1982.

HSUANCHU = *Yuan San-chü Hsüan-chu* [元散曲選注], ed. Wang Chi-ssu [王季思] et al. Peking, 1981.

HSUANHSI = *Yuan San-ch'ü hsüan-hsi* [元散曲選析], ed. Fu Cheng-yü [傅正谷] and Liu Wei-chün [劉維俊]. Tientsin, 1982.

LUHSUAN = *Yuan-jen Hsiao-ling Hsüan* [元人小令選], ed. Lu Jun-hsiang [盧潤祥]. Ssu-ch'uan Jen-min, 1981.

YANGCHU = *Yuan-jen San-ch'ü Hsüan* [元人散曲選], ed. Yang Ch'un-ch'iu [羊春秋]. Hunan, Ch'angsha, 1982.

CHINESE

CYSC	YJSCH	HCLS	TSENG	"100"	"200"	HSUANCHU	HSUANHSI	YANGCHU	LUHSUAN
2.5						2			
3.1				3					
3.4						3			
6.2									28
6.3			298	4		6			28
7.1					1	6			
7.3					1				
7.5					1				
7.6			298						
9.2						8			
12.1					3	10			
13.3					3	11			
13.4						320			30
13.6				6					
31-32	1		204	111		12-13	97		
41.2	5		210		5	16	20		31
42.2				17					
42.3				18					
42.4									33
43.1		28							
45.1			212						
45.2	6			16	6	18			32
47.2			212						
53.1						20			
53.2					7				
53.3					8				
54.1			214						
55.6						19			
60.2			215						
62.5			300		9				
63.1				6					
64.2						21			33
64.4					9				33
67.2					10				
67.3					10				
67.4						23			
68.1				7		23			
69.2						24			
72.2			217						
75.1			219						
93.1					16				
94.1					16				
96.1			301	33		26			
96.2					12				
98.3					15				
98.4					15				35
98.5									35
103.1								64	39
109.2									40
110.3								68	
110.4	35				17	30			39
113.2						31			

CYSC	YJSCH	HCLS	TSENG	"100"	"200"	HSUANCHU	HSUANHSI	YANGCHU	LUHSUAN
113.3				41				65	
114.1								66	
114.3		43			20			67	37
114.4	21		305						
115.1	22		304	38		31			37
117.3								68	
118.1						33			
121.2			304						
123.3					18				
125.1				40					
125.3						34			
126.3				39					
127.1			306						
131.4	19			42	21			63	41
132.1								70	
132.4						35			
132.5						35			
133.2						35			
133.6						35			
134.2	20								
134.4						37		70	36
135.1								71	
138.1					23				
144.1					30				
145.5									43
147.3					39				
148.1									44
148.2					30				
148.3					39				
148.5					30				
149.2			226						
155.1					24				
155.2					24				
155.3					25				
155.4					25				46
156.1							36		
156.2			313					11	
156.5				8	26			2	48
157.3									47
157.4		13							
160.2				10					
161.2				11					
162.4								2	
163.1	8			12		42	41	3	48
163.2								4	
164.2								5	
164.3				13					
165.1									51
165.2					27				51
165.3				14					
165.4					27			6	
165.6								7	
166.1								8	

CYSC	YJSCH	HCLS	TSENG	"100"	"200"	HSUANCHU	HSUANHSI	YANGCHU	LUHSUAN
166.2	8							9	
166.3			314			42			
166.4								10	
167.2						43			49
167.3									49
167.4									49
170-71				115		44	45		
172-73				118-20		47	25		
180.1			326						
193.1	15	26	333	(59)	32	(116)	5	13	56
194.1							13	14	
194.2									55
194.3								15	55
194.4	16								
195.1								16	52
195.4					33	54	2	17	52
195.5								17	
196.3						55	8	18	
197.1							8		
197.2			335				9	19	
197.3							9		
199.1			335	21	34				53
199.2					34				
199.3					35				
200.1	17	20	333	22	35				
200.2								19	
201.1		23	330			56		20	
201.3			337						
203.2									54
203.2									54
203.4	18								
208.1						58		22	
209.1	32								
209.2			228	31	37				
209.3	23		230		38			23	57
210.1									57
210.2	24								57
210.3					38			24	57
210.4						60			
211.2		30	228			60		25	59
211.4								26	
212.2									59
212.3									59
212.4		30		32	39	59	18	27	60
212.5								27	
214.4			228						
217.1								32	
218.1									61
223.1								29	
223.2								30	
224.3			232						
226.1			233						
230.1					40				
232.3					40				
233.1					40				

CYSC	YJSCH	HCLS	TSENG	"100"	"200"	HSUANCHU	HSUANHSI	YANGCHU	LUHSUAN
233.2	26								
233.3								35	
234.1	27		238					36	
237.1								37	
237.2								37	69
238.1									69
238.2								38	
239.1	27		240						70
239.2			244					39	62
242.2	28	49		25	42	63	77	35	71
242.3	38								
243.1	39	59	245		48	63		42	
243.2	41								
244.1	41								
244.2						68			
244.3	41								
244.4	31			26	43				65
245.1	31			26	43			39	66
245.2	32								
245.3	32			27	44			40	67
246.1	32								67
246.2	33			27	44				68
246.3	33				44			40	
247.1	34			27					
247.3	34						72	42	64
247.4	35			28			72		64
247.5				29			72		
247.6							72		
247.7							72		64
247.8				29					
248.1	36								
248.3									64
248.8									64
249.1				123	45				
249.8					45				
249.9	36								
250.1	37								
250.2			248						
251.1		63							
252.1					46				
252.6	29					66			
253.1					46	67			
253.4	29					65			
253.6					46				63
254.2		46							
262.1	46								
263-64				123		69-70	81	47-49	
269-70						72-74	62	44-46	
285.1								50	
286.1				32	52				
291.1	54	67		18	49	76	55	73	45
299.3					53	78		52	
300.4					53				
301.1						79			

CYSC	YJSCH	HCLS	TSENG	"100"	"200"	HSUANCHU	HSUANHSI	YANGCHU	LUHSUAN
303.2			262			80		54	72
304.1		76			51		105		
319-21			266				170		
324.1								55	
330.1						82			
341.1			274			85		58	73
342.1	57				56	85		59	74
342.3			275						
342.4	58								75
344.2	58								75
344.3			275						
344.4								60	
345.1	59							61	
348.3	59								
353.1						86			
354.1				43		88		62	
357.1	70		279	50			153	75	76
357.2	71								
357.3			281						
358.2									81
359.2						91			
360.2									81
361.3								76	
363.3									78
363.5								77	77
365.2								78	
365.5								79	
366.2				52					
367.2					59				
368.2	73		282	52		93			
368.3						94			
369.3								80	
369.7									83
370.3					57				79
370.4					57			81	
371.2				59	59				
371.4				53					82
372.1					58	92			80
372.3	72		284	51					
372.4		78	284		60				
373.2						92			
374.2								82	
374.3	72			54					
376.2								79	
390.4					62				
391.1		87				95			
392.1						96			
395.1					61	97			
395.3						97			
399.2			263		50			83	
399.3	71								
401.1								100	
404.2			293		63	100			
405.1								101	
405.2								101	

CYSC	YJSCH	HCLS	TSENG	"100"	"200"	HSUANCHU	HSUANHSI	YANGCHU	LUHSUAN
406.2						100			
406.3									98
407.2	64							102	
407.3	64		290		64		89	103	95
408.1									93
408.2									94
408.3								104	
409.4								87	
410.1								87	
410.6						101			97
411.1		94		44		102			96
412.1				45					102
412.5								85	
412.6					65				100
413.1			294		65				
413.2			294						
413.3				40	66			86	100
413.4				46	66				100
413.6									100
414.3			290	47					
414.4			293						
415.1						103		88	
415.2								89	
417.2				47	67			90	85
417.5									86
418.1								90	
418.2									83
418.3					67	105			85
418.4			293						
419.1			290						
421.1								91	
421.2								92	
422.4								93	
423.1								94	
423.3						106			
424.1									102
424.2	65								
425.1			290					95	
425.2								96	
427.2	62							97	
428.5						106			
434.3								99	92
434.5				49					
436.1						107		98	
437.1			287						
437.3	63	92		48	68	108	92	97	
438.1						109			
438.3									90
439.2									99
441.1	66		295						99
442-3				130-1					
444.1				133		110			
447.1	63	92	288	35	54			56	
462.1								105	
462.2					69				

CYSC	YJSCH	HCLS	TSENG	"100"	"200"	HSUANCHU	HSUANHSI	YANGCHU	LUHSUAN
462.3								106	
463.1	74					112			
463.3				58		113			
467.1				59		116			
471.1				61				108	
474.2								109	
481.2				62		118		110	
481.3					70			111	
487.1					73				
493.1						120			
494.3					71				
497.2					72				
511.2						121			
523.4						124			
534-36						127-29			
537-38						130-32			
538-39						133-35			
544-45				134-5			137	113-115	
551.1					74			118	104
552.2									
552.4					73				
554.1								119	106
555.1					75				
556.1						142			
558.2								120	
558.3								120	105
569.1					76	144			106
575.1	81		342					122	107
575.4			346						
577.1						147			
579.4					77	148			
580.4		121			77	148			
581.2	82								
581.3	83								
581.6	83				78	149			
582.1						149			116
582.2									116
582.3					78				
583.2								124	109
583.3					80				
583.4		118			82				
584.1			342			150	126	124	
584.2	84			82		151			110
584.3	85								110
584.4	86								110
589.1		132							
590.2	87								
592.4					84				
592.5	88	134					132	125	
594.1	88								
594.2	89			74				126	
594.3			346					133	113
594.4									113
596.1								126	
596.2		124							

CYSC	YJSCH	HCLS	TSENG	"100"	"200"	HSUANCHU	HSUANHSI	YANGCHU	LUHSUAN
596.3			348	79					
597.3								131	
598.2	98		349		86	152		127	
598.3								128	
601.2					85			129	
601.3						153			
602.3	95	128	339						
605.1	96						129		
607.1	97		348	80		155	123		
608.3									115
611.2								130	114
611.3			342						
612.4						156			108
613.2			342			156			
613.3	99								
619.1			343						
619.3	91		339						
620.2				78		157			
622.3	92					158			
623.1	93								
626.1	93			75	81	160	134		
627.1	94			76		161			
629.2								134	
630.3								135	
631.3		130				162			118
632.1								132	112
633.1	86								
633.2	89				84				
633.3	90		348		83				
640.1				139					
641-42						163-64			
648-49				141-2		165-67			
650.2						168			
651.1								137	
651.4								138	
652.5								138	120
653.3								139	119
653.4								140	
654.3						169			
658.1	100	49							
659.1					87				
661.3	102								
662.3								142	123
664.1					89			141	
666.1								144	
667.3						170		143	
668.1									122
668.4				63	88				121
669-72				143-4		172	182	145-50	
680-81						179-81			
685.2								153	
685.3						183		154	
685.4								155	
686.1								156	
686.4					90				

CYSC	YJSCH	HCLS	TSENG	"100"	"200"	HSUANCHU	HSUANHSI	YANGCHU	LUHSUAN
686.5					92				129
688.1						185			
688.2	68								
689.1					93				
689.2								158	
693.1						187			
694.1					94				
701-02						190-92			
703.1		384			95			161	
704.1		384				194			
704.2					96				
704.3						195			
705.3						196			
705.7						197			
706.3						198			
706.6						199			
709.2									125
709.3	106							162	
709.4				96					
710.1				97					
711.2									124
712.3								163	
714.2									127
714.4						199		160	126
715.4								164	
716.3						200			
717.3			386						
717.4				97		201		165	
718.1				98					
718.2	109					202		168	
718.3				98					128
727.2			88						
740.3						203			
741.2								168	
741.3								169	
744.1			86		99	204		170	131
745.1									130
745.4					101				
746.1			86		100				
747.1		113	87		101				
749.1		115						174	
749.2						205		175	
751.2								171	132
752.1								173	
752.2									133
753.1			85						
756.1	101	137	358					177	
756.3	101								
757.1	102								156
757.3								178	
758.1			69						
758.2								179	
760.1									153
760.2	114								
760.3						208		180	

CYSC	YJSCH	HCLS	TSENG	"100"	"200"	HSUANCHU	HSUANHSI	YANGCHU	LUHSUAN
765.3				71					
766.1	117	153	366			209		181	146
766.3			366			209			
767.4			367						
770.2								182	
771.4						211			
772.1					107				
773.3									147
775.2								182	
775.3						212		183	
777.3								185	
779.1									157
779.2						213			
780.3								186	
782.3								187	
783.4								188	
784.2						214			
785.2						215			
787.4						216		189	
788.1			367						
788.3			353					190	
788.5			360						
789.3	118							191	
790.1	119								
790.4								191	
791.1	119				105				163
791.2								192	
791.4					106				
791.5							116	192	
792.1	158								
795.1								193	
795.2								194	
796.1			353					195	
796.3				64					143
797.1	107								
797.2	108							195	141
797.4	108							196	
798.2					106	217			142
798.3								197	
799.1	106							198	
799.4								198	
802.4								199	
803.1								200	
803.2									139
803.3									139
805.4						218			
806.3						218			
806.4								201	
807.2		147							
807.3								201	
809.3								202	
810.1			353						
810.5									140
810.8	104								
811.1	112				112				

CYSC	YJSCH	HCLS	TSENG	"100"	"200"	HSUANCHU	HSUANHSI	YANGCHU	LUHSUAN
811.2				67					
814.1						219			
814.3					110				
814.4				72					
817.1					112				
823.2									160
823.3					110				
826.1	110				108	220			
826.2	111						109	203	148
827.4						221		204	
828.1									149
828.3								205	164
830.2						222			
836.2					108				
840.3	107							212	
843.4	103				114		119	211	135
844.3								207	
845.1				72			114		
845.2	113								
846.2									138
852.3								207	
853.2	116								154
854.2	115								
855.2									152
857.2	113								154
859.2	118								
859.3	116								
860.1								208	144
863.1		156							
864.4									145
867.3						223			
871.4								209	150
872.1						224			151
882.1									
882.3									136
883.3				65					
884.1								210	
884.5			352						
885.5	111								
889.3			358						
892.1									134
894.4			353						
895.2	105								
904.4									162
909.1					111				
911.2		143							
912.2				19		225			
915.2									137
917.5									161
922.1		140							
923.3								211	
923.6			354		113				
925.3			354						
933.4	105		354						
934.3		150							

CYSC	YJSCH	HCLS	TSENG	"100"	"200"	HSUANCHU	HSUANHSI	YANGCHU	LUHSUAN
934.4	109								
938.1			366		103	226			
951.1			360						
954.1									155
954.4						227			
956.1			354						
967.2						228			
971.4	170								
975.1			355						
976.2				66					
982.4	104								158
985.2				68		229	112		162
986.1	115								
990-91	120					230-31			
1006.1								214	
1006.3								215	166
1007.1								216	167
1007.4					117			216	
1008.2								217	
1010.2								218	165
1012.1								219	
1012.5									169
1014.3						233			
1015.1								220	
1017.1				82	118				
1017.3				84					
1018.2						234			
1018.4					119			220	168
1018.6									168
1020.1					120			.	
1030-31						236-38			
1032.1			282		121				
1033.2								222	
1033.4								223	
1033.5								223	
1034.1								224	
1034.3	123							225	
1035.4								225	
1037.2			379						
1038.2						243			
1040.2						244			
1040.3						247			
1041.3					122	248		226	
1044.2									175
1045.2								227	
1045.3						249			
1045.4									175
1047.1									173
1047.2									174
1047.3				57		245			173
1048.1	124		379	54		249			170
1050.2						246			
1051.1			376		124	247		228	
1051.2								229	
1054.2								230	176

CYSC	YJSCH	HCLS	TSENG	"100"	"200"	HSUANCHU	HSUANHSI	YANGCHU	LUHSUAN
1056.1	125	161	376		123		157	230	171
1056.2		164							
1057.1			376						
1058.2									172
1059.1			382			251			
1059.2								231	
1059.5								232	
1062.1			387						
1062.2			388		125				228
1065.1						253			
1065.4			388						229
1070.1					126				
1070.2		168							
1071.1								233	177
1077.2						255			
1078.5						256			
1079.1								236	
1079.3								235	
1080.2				89	129			237	
1080.3				91	129	257		237	178
1082.1						258			
1096.1						260			
1117.1						261			179
1121-22					263	263-65			
1123.2					140			239	
1123.3								240	
1124.1									182
1126.1								240	
1126.3									180
1126.5								241	180
1127.3								242	
1144.1					130				183
1149.4						266			
1156.1					132			243	186
1156.2						268			187
1157.3		170							
1158.3				90	133				
1159.2									184
1161.1								244	
1162.1						267		245	
1162.2								246	
1164.2								248	
1166.1		172				270		249	
1166.2									188
1166.3						270		249	
1167.6									189
1169.2		175						250	190
1169.3									191
1171.5									191
1174.1		178							
1180.3						272			
1185-86						273-74			
1186.1									192
1195.1		181							
1197.1					140				193

CYSC	YJSCH	HCLS	TSENG	"100"	"200"	HSUANCHU	HSUANHSI	YANGCHU	LUHSUAN
1210-11						275-76			
1222.1						277			
1223.1						279			
1248.1									194
1248.3									196
1249.1						281		252	196
1249.3									195
1251.4								253	
1253.4									197
1254.2								253	198
1280.1								255	
1282.1			400					256	199
1282.2	126			92					
1282.3	127		401		134	283	165	257	200
1283.4					135				201
1291.2						283			
1292.1			404						
1292.2			404						
1293.1								259	
1293.2								260	
1293.3								260	
1294.2									203
1295.2	130			91	136				202
1295.4						287		261	
1296.2	129								
1296.4								262	
1297.1					137	288			
1299.2					138			266	204
1300.2						290			
1300.3								264	
1301.3						289			
1302.2					139			265	205
1302.3									206
1303.1								267	
1313.1					141				
1321.3						291			
1334.1				93					
1334.3		186	390				161		
1334.1	133		390		142			268	209
1334.3									208
1335.1					143	293		269	210
1335.3				94		294			
1336.2	131							271	
1336.3	131			96				271	207
1336.4	132				144			272	207
1337.1	132								
1337.2				96					
1341.3								274	
1342.1						295			211
1351.1						297			217
1351.2					146	297			
1351.3	135			97		297			218
1352.2								276	
1359.1									216
1360.2					140				

CYSC	YJSCH	HCLS	TSENG	"100"	"200"	HSUANCHU	HSUANHSI	YANGCHU	LUHSUAN
1361.2						299			
1362.4								274	214
1362.5								274	214
1363.4								275	
1363.5								275	
1364.4					148				
1369.2			98						
1370.2									212
1371-73	136-42					301(abr.)		278-84	
1375.1						303			
1377.1	170								
1377.2					150			284	231
1377.3	171								233
1379.4									231
1379.7								285	
1380.2								286	
1380.6					151				
1381.5								287	
1381.6									233
1382.2									233
1383.3								288	230
1383.6	171								
1385.3								289	
1392.1								290	
1392.2								291	
1409.1			406						
1412.1			406						
1415-16						305-7			
1418.1					152			292	233
1418.2						310			233
1419.2				90	153	311			
1419.4				101	153				222
1420.1				100	154			293	221
1421.1								295	
1421.3								294	
1430.1						313			
1430.2					155	313			219
1431.3						312			
1431.4									219
1434.1					156				
1441-42						315-16			
1453.1								297	
1453.2								298	
1462.1								299	
1462.2								300	
1559.1								302	224
1566.2								304	
1571.3								306	
1573.1								305	
1580.3									225
1583.3								307	
1604.2								303	226
1610.1								309	
1621.2				102		318			227

CYSC	YJSCH	HCLS	TSENG	"100"	"200"	HSUANCHU	HSUANHSI	YANGCHU	LUHSUAN
1623.3									228
1660.2			408					317	
1661.3								318	
1662.1			410					320	10
1662.2			410					319	
1662.3			411						
1663.1								320	9
1663.3			411						
1664.2	173				157	321		310	1
1664.3				104	158	322		311	2
1665.1									3
1668.1				105					
1668.1								320	
1668.2								321	
1669.4			411						
1670.2			412						
1670.3									22
1670.5			412						
1674.4			412						
1678.3						323			
1680.2						324			
1680.3	175								
1683.3						325			
1688.1			403			326		312	
1688.2			403			326			23
1688.3									23
1691.2						327			
1695.1									14
1695.4								323	
1697.1						328		323	
1697.3									17
1699.3	179								
1699.4	179								
1701.2	176								
1701.3	177								
1701.4	177								
1701.2	178								
1703.4	179								
1707.3									13
1708.1									13
1711.1					159				
1711.3						329			
1715.1								324	24
1715.2								325	
1716.3						331			
1717.1					162				
1717.3	180				163				
1720.4						331			
1726.3								313	
1726.4						332			10
1727.1									11
1729.3								314	
1731.3	181				160	333			
1733.3	181								

CYSC	YJSCH	HCLS	TSENG	"100"	"200"	HSUANCHU	HSUANHSI	YANGCHU	LUHSUAN
1736.2				106		334			
1736.3						334			
1737.3						335			
1737.6									20
1740.1									18
1740.4									19
1741.1	182								
1742.5					164				
1743.4	182								
1751.1									17
1751.6									6
1754.3						337			
1754.5									4
1754.6						338			
1754.8								315	
1755.1								316	
1755.4								317	
1756.6						338			
1757.1						339			
1775.1								313	
1777.2					165				
1809-10						340-41			

ENGLISH

CYSC	SONGS1	SONGS2	Y AND M	SEATON	SCHLEPP	SUNFL	BIRCH
3.1		16					
6.3			23				
7.5			24				
12.1		16					
13.4		17					
13.6							
25.1	196						
31.1	113						
40.1	38						
41.1					56		
41.2	13						
42.3		13					
42.4		12					
43.1		9					
43.2		27					
44.1		66					
45.2		80					
46.1	14						
47.2	180	44			121		
54.1		84					
62.2			25				
62.3		53					
62.5		53					
63.1		52					
66.1			26				
68.1		114					15
69.1	104						
69.2	104						
72.2		90					
98.4			61				
109.2						418	
110.2	15						
110.3			49				
110.4						418	
110.5				7			
113.4				7	54		
114.3	42						
115.1						419	
131.4		35					
131.5	39						
134.4				8		419	
134.5				8			
135.2				9			
144.2				29			
145.1				29			
145.3				30			
145.4				30			
145.5		5		31			
145.6				31			
147.4				31			
148.1				32			
148.3				33			
149.4				33			
155.1		70					

CYSC	SONGS1	SONGS2	Y AND M	SEATON	SCHLEPP	SUNFL	BIRCH
155.5		71					
156.1							6
156.2		12					7
156.3							7
156.4		11					7
156.5			19		112		
157.1				15		412	
157.2				15		412	
157.3				15		412	
157.4				15		412	
163.1					62	412	
163.2						412	
164.2						413	
164.4						413	
165.3						412	
165.4				16		413	
165.6						414	
166.2					82		
166.3							
167.5						414	
168.1				16		415	
169.2			68				
172-3					37	415-17	8-10
188-9							11-13
193.1			20				
193.2	35						
194.1				27			
194.3				27			
194.4				28			
195.1		26					
195.4		34					
196.3							23
197.1							23
200.1			22				
200.2		10					
201.1	95		21				
204.1			72				
209.2		103					
209.3			27				
211.2			28				
212.6	14						
213.3	141		39				
233.2		95		22			
233.3				22			
233.4		95		22		420	
234.1		95	50	21			
237.3				21			
237.5				20			
238.1				21			
238.2		91					
239.1							
242.2			29		124	420	17
243.4				23			
244.4			38				
246.1					63		16

CYSC	SONGS1	SONGS2	Y AND M	SEATON	SCHLEPP	SUNFL	BIRCH
246.2		107					
246.2n		107					
247.4					81		16
247.6		112					
247.7		113					
247.8		25					
249.1						421	
253.4		90	51				
254.2				20			
255.2					115		
262.1						421	
262.2						421	
262.3						422	
263.1	27						
268.1			78				
269-70	25-6						
273.4				20			
298.3				17			
300.2				17			
303.2					33		18
303.3	41				65		
304.1					34		18
324.1					90		
339.1		99		4	106		
339.3		99		4			
341.1		132		10			
341.2		129		10			
342.1		126					36
342.4		126	17				
343.1		127					
344.2		128					
348.3		130					
349.1		131					
357.1			35				
363.5					100		
365.1						446	
367.2						446	
368.3		14					
368.4		14					
369.6				5			
369.8				5			
370.1					111		
370.3					116		
370.4	37						
370.5	18						
371.4							
372.1						446	
372.4		93					
372.5				5			
374.3			62				
378-80						447-49	
390.2				14			
399.2			36			427	
402.1	66			36		427	

CYSC	SONGS1	SONGS2	Y AND M	SEATON	SCHLEPP	SUNFL	BIRCH
402.3	64						
402.5				36			
403.2	61			37			
405.2	67,128						
407.2						427	
408.2	61						
409.1	72						
409.8	72						
410.6				46			
411.2		69					
413.2	74						
413.3	74	6					
415.2	71						
415.4	71						
415.5	72						
416.1	70						
416.2	142						
417.5	57						
418.1	57						
418.3	57						
418.4			34				
420.2	63						
420.3	64						
421.5			30	37			
422.4	77						
425.2	66						
427.3	47						
427.4	60		31				
428.2	64						
428.4	73						
432.3	62						
437.1	57						
437.3	59				123		18
441.1	75						
447.1	147	121	37		123		
463.1							
472.3				11			
473.1		46					
475.2				11			
476.1		43					
488.3		44					
492.2					89		
493.2		8				428	
493.4		114					
552.1				34			
552.2				34			
552.4					73		22
575.1		93				437	
575.3	37				110		
584.3						438	
585.1				24			
585.2				24			
585.3				24			

CYSC	SONGS1	SONGS2	Y AND M	SEATON	SCHLEPP	SUNFL	BIRCH
592.5					72		
594.1	199						
594.5	196						
595.1	199						
602.3			60				
607.1	130						
613.2		15					
619.3			59				
626.1		19			118		23
630.1					54		
630.6		100					
648-9	22-3						
651.2				19			
657.4				19			
659.3		38					
660.1		39					
668.4			43				
669-72						139-44	
704.2			44				
709.3		92					
714.2			45				
717.4			40				
718.2	16		41		115		
727.2		4					
734.2		98					
734.3				26			
734.4				26			
745.3	194						
756.3						425	
761.1			53		76		
788.5	127						
791.1		94					
791.5			57				
797.3			55			425	
798.2	129				107		24
800.2					93		
808.1						426	
817.1	140						
838.4				13			
853.2		102					
857.2		103					
871.4			58				
872.1	43						
881.4	196						
882.1	127						
912.2						426	
919.4	195						
920.2			52				
929.1		97					
929.2		97					
929.3		97					
930.3			56				
832.2		74					
936.2	42						

CYSC	SONGS1	SONGS2	Y AND M	SEATON	SCHLEPP	SUNFL	BIRCH
987.1		108					
1010.4			46				
1015.1			47				
1033.1			54				
1033.3	96						
1040.2					96		
1041.3		49					
1051.1					96		
1053.5	129						
1054.2						432	
1062.3	89						
1067.1			64				
1128.1		59					
1128.2		57					
1128.3		28					
1128.4		59					
1128.5		62					
1129.1		62					
1129.2		62					
1129.3		63					
1149.1		28					
1157.2	34						
1162.1			48				
1179.2		105					
1185.1		76					
1237.2	(35)				60		
1248.1			32				
1254.2					69		
1282.3		81					
1300.1					39		
1301.1	97						
1303.2	173						
1315.3	39						
1334.1	195						
1352.2			66				
1361.4				39			
1362.6				39			
1362.7				40			
1363.1				40			
1371-73						433-6	
1382.1	98						
1383.4	98						
1384.5	98						
1409.1		33					
1425.2		51			57		
1575.2		30					
1580.3	134	40					
1581.1	134						
1602.3		7					
1603.3	131						
1604.3	87						
1605.2	87						
1610.1	130						
1660.2					94		
1664.3		72					

CYSC	SONGS1	SONGS2	Y AND M	SEATON	SCHLEPP	SUNFL	BIRCH
1667.5				35			
1668.2			33				
1674.6				41			
1675.2	35	25					
1676.1					71		5
1678.2	41						
1683.2	13				53		
1687.3		74					
1688.1		82					
1688.2		82					
1692.2		67			23(abr)		
1692.3		68			24		
1692.4		67					
1692.5		69					
1692.6		68					
1693.1		68					
1693.2		69					
1694.3			32				
1694.4		88					
1695.1		89					
1695.4					108		
1704.2					98		
1719.1	44						
1723.2					50		
1723.4		45					
1726.4		72					
1728.4		22					
1732.3	11						
1732.5	11						
1733.2	10						
1740.6	142						
1742.4			63				
1744.3		5					
1748.2	179	42					
1753.1					79		
1756.1					48		
1764.1		13					
1847.2					92		
1883.1				42			
1883.2				42		451	
1884.1				43		451	
1884.3	125			44			
1884.4				44			
1884.5				44			
1885.1				45			
1885.2				45			
1885.3				46			
1885.4				46			
1885.5				46			
1885.6				· 47			
1886.1				47			
1886.2				47		451	
1886.3				48		452	
1886.4				48		452	
1886.5				48		452	

CYSC	SONGS1	SONGS2	Y AND M	SEATON	SCHLEPP	BIRCH
1887.1				49		
1887.2				49		
1887.3				50		
1887.4				50		
1887.5				50		
1887.6				51		
1888.1				51		
1888.2				51		

	Y.L. YIP Tam.Rev.6-1
113.3	43
157.2	42
166.3	41
209.1	47
242.2	44
243.2	46
245.1	45
437.3	48
658.1	49
788.5	52
925.2	50
933.4	51
	KU-TAI HAN-YÜ
31-32	1518
195.4	1510
242.2	1511
269-70	1516
437.3	1512
826.2	1513
1282.3	1514
1352.1	1515
	RENDITIONS 21-22(1984)
131.4	224
156.2	225
156.5	227
243.2	221
247.4	222
368.2	228
437.3	220
613.2	217
894.1	215
1009.1	219
1054.2	218
1661.1	226
1704.2	216
1883.2	229

On Translating Chen Shou's San guo zhi

Bringing Him Back Alive

ROBERT JOE CUTTER AND
WILLIAM G. CROWELL

This essay is in a sense the coming out of a pair of closet translators.[1] A few years ago, we began discussing the possibility of translating the *San guo zhi* 三國誌 (Records of the Three States) of Chen Shou 陳壽 (233–297), along with Pei Songzhi's 裴松之 (372–451) equally famous commentary. Since then, we have done drafts of a number of sections, as well as a complete and fully annotated translation of the text and commentary to the chapters on the empresses and consorts of each of the three states. We are now writing an introduction to these three chapters. This annotated translation and its prolegomena will, we hope, find a place as a monograph. At the same time, it will serve as a proving ground for the envisioned translation of the entire history, allowing us to test our approaches to various problems presented by the text.

The *San guo zhi* and Its Commentary

Following the abdication of the last Han emperor in A.D. 220, China split into the states of Wei 魏 (220–265), Wu 吳 (222–280), and Shu 蜀 (221–263). The *San guo zhi*, one of the twenty-five officially sanctioned standard histories (*zheng shi* 正史), deals with these three contending realms. Chen

Shou, author of the work, was from the state of Shu.[2] In his youth, he studied with the historian Qiao Zhou 譙周, learning the *Shang shu* 尚書 (Hallowed Documents) and the three commentaries to the *Chun qiu* 春秋 (Spring and Autumn Annals), and concentrating particularly on the *Shi ji* 史記 (Records of the Grand Historian) and the *Han shu* 漢書 (Han History).[3] Later, he served as an official in the Shu government.[4] Shu was conquered by Wei in 263, by which time affairs in Wei were controlled by the Sima 司馬 family. In 265 Sima Yan 司馬炎 (236–290) abolished Wei and ascended the throne as first emperor of the Jin 晉 dynasty (265–317). Chen Shou was recommended by the influential official and literatus Zhang Hua 張華 (232–300) and so came to serve the Jin. He was charged with editing the *Zhuge Liang ji* 諸葛亮集 (Collected Works of Zhuge Liang) and completed the task in 274.[5] Done a mere forty years after Zhuge's death, this earliest collection of that famous statesman-strategist's works was in all likelihood quite comprehensive and reliable; however, it was lost before the Song 宋 dynasty (960–1279).[6]

With Jin's conquest of Wu in 280, Chen began work on his history of the three defunct states.[7] He used a variety of sources to compile a history quite different from many of the standard histories;[8] the *San guo zhi* does not adhere to the format established by the *Shi ji* and the *Han shu*, since it lacks *zhi* 志 (or *shu* 書, treatises) and *biao* 表 (tables), consisting instead only of *ji* 紀 (annals) and *zhuan* 傳 (biographies).[9] From the outset, by referring to the Wei rulers as emperors and calling his accounts of them "annals", Chen makes Wei the legitimate successor of Han, placing Shu and Wu, whose rulers are merely accorded "biographies," in a lesser light. This viewpoint is also reflected in the amount of space allotted to each of the states, for of the sixty-five *juan* that make up the work, thirty are devoted to Wei, fifteen to Shu, and twenty to Wu. Wei's legitimacy is conveyed by other means as well. For example, Chen is silent in the "Wei shu" section about Liu Bei 劉備 (161–223) of Shu and Sun Quan 孫權 (182–252) of Wu being proclaimed emperors, and in the "Shu shu" section he gives coronation dates according to Wei reign years.[10] Chen has been criticized for this, but it is hard to see how he could have done differently. He was, after all, a Jin official, and Jin claimed succession from Wei. As the *Siku quanshu zongmu* 四庫全書總目 (General Catalogue of the Imperial Library) entry on the *San guo zhi* observes, to make Wei a usurper would have been tantamount to calling Jin a usurper.[11]

It is not known when Chen Shou completed his manuscript,[12] but drafts of the *San guo zhi* received the kind of reception writers dream of. Zhang Hua, for instance, likened him to Sima Qian 司馬遷 (145–ca. 86 B.C.) and Ban Gu 班固 (32–92), the authors of the *Shi ji* and the *Han shu*, respectively. Comparison to these quintessential historians of the past was high praise, indeed. It must have seemed that Chen had written the last word on the Three States period, for Xiahou Zhan 夏侯湛 (243–291), who was then writing his own *Wei shu*, gave up and destroyed his work.[13] Two hundred years later, the great literary critic and theorist Liu Xie 劉勰 (ca., 465–ca. 522) added his voice to the chorus acclaiming Chen and his history.[14] Let us note, however, that the *San guo zhi* was not originally officially sponsored. Official copies were not made until after Chen's death.

In short, given his political and intellectual environment and the materials he had to work with, Chen produced a kind of masterpiece. That is not to say it was perfect. Criticisms have been leveled at the work over time.[15] The first important criticism was that it was too brief and omitted too much. The complaint of brevity has some merit and is still heard.[16] As Carl Leban explains,

> despite Ch'en Shou's position and the availability of contemporary source material, great gaps still existed in certain parts of the record, most particularly with regard to Shu, but also evident in the sometimes overly terse reports on the activities of individual personalities and the vagueness with which events are dated both in the annalistic chapters and the biographies. The very excitement generated by the original *SKC* accounts further engenders a thirst for greater detail, frustration which must have been felt even by early readers.[17]

In about 426, enthusiasm for the text joined with frustration with its succinctness and led Emperor Wen 文帝 of the Liu Song 劉宋 dynasty (420–479) to order Pei Songzhi to write a commentary to it. Pei submitted the completed commentary to the throne in 429, and the emperor, with considerable foresight, deemed it an imperishable contribution.[18] This work with which the emperor was so taken differs substantially from commentaries associated with other histories, notably those to the *Shi ji* and the *Han shu*. The commentaries to those histories are primarily of the *xungu* 訓故, or glossatorial, type. But from the commentary itself and from Pei's memorial submitting it to the throne, it is obvious that his goal was different.[19] The task Pei set for himself was that of making the work better by supplementing Chen's accounts with whatever records were still extant. Despite the criticism leveled at the commentary by Ye Shi (1150–1223),[20] Pei does not seem to have simply gathered up material that had already been seen and rejected by Chen, for much of what is found in the commentary is contemporary to Chen or later and would not have been available to him.[21] The commentary is over three times the length of the *San guo zhi*[22] itself and cites more than 150 works, not including classical texts and Pei's own comments. It preserves a large amount of material from texts since lost.[23]

The base text used for our translation is the Zhonghua shuju edition, first published in Beijing in 1959. This is a modern punctuated edition containing useful collation notes.[24] The text of the *San guo zhi* has been remarkably well preserved.[25] The oldest printed edition of the text dates from the Xianping 咸平 period (998–1003) of the Northern Song (960–1126). A photograph of a page of this text was included at the front of the 1959 Zhonghua shuju edition published in Beijing but is not found in the 1973 revised reprint. The Xianping edition was not the only Song edition. In the Southern Song (1126–1279) there were several printings, and the commonly used Bona edition 百衲本 is a photolithographic composite of Shaoxing 紹興 (1131–1162) and Shaoxi 紹熙 (1190–1194) editions.[26] At least three important editions of the text appeared in Ming 明 times (1368–1644) and three during the Qing.[27]

Much work was done on the *San guo zhi* by pre–twentieth century scholars, but aside from the Zhonghua shuju recension, the most valuable single edition of the *San guo zhi* is the *San guo zhi ji jie* 三國志集解 (Collected Explanations to *San guo zhi*), completed by Lu Bi 盧弼 (1876–1967) in 1936.[28]

On the Translation of Chinese Texts

If permitted a translator's note, an introduction, or a preface, a translator will almost always give some indication of the value of the original text and, therefore, of the translation. Burton Watson calls the *Shi ji* a "monumental" work "widely and affectionately read" by "educated Chinese" and "men of learning in Korea and Japan"—a work of "incalculable influence" on the literatures of these three lands.[29] Homer H. Dubs, on the other hand, is strangely reticent on this point regarding the *Han shu*, perhaps because his translation, as the inclusion of a Chinese text and detailed notes shows, was intended for a more academic audience, one which could be presumed to know the significance of the work without being told. Even so, Dubs's omission is surprising. Even as scholarly a translator as David Knechtges quotes the Song saying *Wen xuan lan, xiucai ban* 文選爛秀才半 ("The *Wen xuan* thoroughly done, / Half a licentiate won"), pointing out that Xiao Tong's 蕭統 (501–531) anthology "was one of the primary sources of literary knowledge for educated Chinese in the premodern period, and it still is the *vade mecum* for specialists in pre-Tang literature."[30]

There can be no question of the importance of the *San guo zhi*. The Chinese consider it one of the most important of the dynastic histories, for in its pages are chronicled the ideas, events, and documents of one of the most exciting periods in Chinese history. This was a time of tremendous social, economic, and political changes as well as outstanding literary achievements, and the *San guo zhi* is crucial for an understanding of all of them. It is also an essential repository of information on personalities and topics such as Daoism and Daoist movements, medicine, and the customs of foreign peoples. As a moment's reflection will show, the book has exerted a powerful effect in the popular milieu on Chinese of all ages and been a "pervasive influence in fiction, drama, and popular religion,"[31] not to mention history and historiography. In Taiwan alone there must be scores of temples decorated with scenes from the *San guo zhi* as sifted through popular lore and fiction. The canonization of Guan Yu 關羽 and the widespread devotions to him today are a good example of this influence.[32] That the *San guo zhi* has long been referred to, along with Sima Qian's *Shi ji*, Ban Gu's *Han shu*, and Fan Ye's 范曄 (398–445) *Hou Han shu* 後漢書 (Later Han History), which was actually written later than the *San guo zhi*, as one of the Four Histories (Si shi 四史) is indicative of the high regard in which it has been held.

There is no Western-language translation of the *San guo zhi*. Books, articles, and dissertations sometimes contain translations of passages or sections, but they almost never include the relevant parts of Pei's commentary, and the total amount in translation is minuscule. Perhaps the translator who has sampled most broadly from the text is the redoubtable Achilles Fang.[33] Fang, of course, was translating the *Zi zhi tong jian* 資治通鑑 (Comprehensive Mirror for Aid in Governing), not the *San guo zhi*; it is only when the two texts overlap and in certain notes that he can be said to be dealing with the *San guo zhi* proper.[34]

If the *San guo zhi* is, as just suggested, an important Chinese text deserving an English translation, the question then becomes, what kind of translation? The answer has to do with the nature of translation itself. As a practical matter, there are three crucial and interrelated factors in the translation equation: translator, original text, and audience. With regard to the first of these, at least as far as translation from Chinese is concerned, we are much our mentors' children. This phenomenon is what makes it possible for people to speak of the Boodbergian influence, for example. It is not as hard to change one's approach to translation as it is for a leopard to change its spots, but it is no easy thing, either, for mostly we have no desire to do so. The nature of a given translation from Chinese is, therefore, frequently determined more by who does it than by cogitation on the art and craft of translation.

This is not to say that translators from Chinese are inflexible. Everyone tries to improve and adapt. We may even bone up on certain styles and genres of literature in English in order to adjust to the needs of particular Chinese texts. A translator of early medieval Chinese literature for scholarly publications certainly will not use exactly the same approach when called upon to provide an unannotated translation of a Tang tale for a general anthology of Chinese literature or render a modern Taiwanese short story into English. But insofar as Chinese is concerned, it is probably true that many translators prefer to stick to the way of doing things that they have developed under the influence of their teachers and others in the field whom they admire.

When a translator does alter his or her approach, it is rarely an act of apostasy. Rather, it has to do with one or both of the other elements of the

equation: the text or the audience. One of the advantages of being an academic translator is that one has a certain freedom to select one's material.
This means that such translators can choose to work almost exclusively on
texts more or less congenial to their style, background, and interests. This,
in turn, means that they have a good idea of their audience and its expectations. But most translators, perhaps, occasionally find themselves wandering
beyond their usual periodic or generic confines. And when they do, they
may decide that different kinds of texts call for different kinds of translations. Thus a person who normally deals with early texts in classical Chinese
and uses a fairly literal style when translating them may see that style as
inappropriate for modern fiction. The decision to switch approaches may be
inspired by the translator's beliefs about the different natures of the texts
and their relationship to modern man. But it may also be determined by the
intended audience of the translation.

Audience is a notoriously difficult problem when speaking about studies
and translations of Chinese.[35] In some cases, the audience is not much in
doubt. Although Burton Watson was thinking of specialists as well, he
makes it clear that his *Records of the Grand Historian* was done with a general
audience in mind.[36] At one point he writes:

> I am aware that some of these practices may render the translation unsatisfac-
> tory to specialists who are interested in the *Shih chi* as a source for historical
> data, rather than as a unified work of literature. Yet any attempt to please
> all readers, specialists and non-specialists alike, would almost certainly end by
> pleasing none. Michael Grant, in the introduction to his translation of Tacitus'
> *Annals*, states his opinion that "except as a mere crib, an unreadable translation
> is useless." Though the wording is perhaps a bit drastic, I fully agree with this
> dictum in principle, and ask the reader to keep it in mind in judging what
> follows.[37]

It is hard to disagree with the notion that an unreadable translation is
useless. But if it is truly unreadable, it is not even useful as a crib, so what
Grant and Watson have in mind is something else, not something totally
unreadable. Grant is rejecting outdated English and translatorese.[38] No one
is in favor of these, of course. Who today would translate like Legge, admirable though his work is for its time? But the question of readability is not so
simply settled. As Grant writes, "it remains a real issue, though one could
and should refine it by asking, readable *to whom*, an investigation which, in
regard to translations, has still hardly begun."[39] Thus we are thrown back
to the question of audience.

Eugene Eoyang tackled this problem as regards Chinese translation in an
illuminating paper entitled "Waley or Pound? The Dynamics of Genre in
Translation."[40] He posits three types of translations: co-eval, surrogate, and
contingent.[41] Coeval and surrogate translations are both self-sufficient, for
the former subsumes the original as a reference for an audience familiar

with it and effectively captures its spirit and meaning, while the latter assumes a readership totally unfamiliar with the original and must stand by
itself.[42] A contingent translation, on the other hand, is not self-sufficient, for
it presumes the presence of the original text and is meant to be read with it.
Such a translation is what might otherwise be referred to as a literal translation (whatever that means), and Eoyang argues that it is not for bilingual
readers, who have no need for such a literal rendering, or for general readers, for whom it would have no appeal. Contingent translations are essentially student trots for those neither wholly ignorant of nor wholly familiar
with the language.[43] Of such works he writes:

> Texts and editions for this readership have proliferated in recent generations.
> These versions, with their accompanying linguistic apparatus and the density of
> their annotation and exegesis, will often bewilder the general reader. They are
> sometimes presented in a "metalanguage" comprehensible neither to the speak-
> er of the original language nor to the native speaker of the target language
> untrained in the specialized discourse. In the case of Chinese, these may be
> familiar as "sinological" translations.[44]

Once again, one has to agree that translations "in a 'metalanguage'
comprehensible neither to the speaker of the original language [presumably
meaning one also well-educated in the target language] nor to the native
speaker of the target language [presumably meaning an educated reader
willing to expend some effort to enter a world which may be partly alien]"
are to be avoided at all costs. And Eoyang himself points out that his tripar-
tite generic categories are far from rigid.[45] Still, one regrets slightly the tone
of the statement and the seemingly pejorative use of the hoary word "sinological."

Now, one dictionary says that sinology means "the study of things Chinese," and a sinologist or sinologue is "one versed in the Chinese language,
or in the customs and history of China."[46] While these definitions are not
incorrect, they are unlikely to satisfy most scholars. Some might go so far as
to deny the validity of any field called sinology, while others, especially
those who think of themselves as sinologists, might feel that the above definitions do not really explain what they do. For them, sinology is in large
measure akin to philology. That is, it involves bringing knowledge of many
kinds to bear on the study of Chinese written materials, especially (but not
exclusively) literary texts, in order to answer various kinds of questions
about them. As such, sinology has to do with methods and approaches, and
while these may influence the final translation of a text, they do not perforce damn that translation to unreadability and ultimate failure.

While it is true that some translations by sinologists are tough going and
inelegant, some can serve all of the hypothetical audiences mentioned
above, provided we qualify the notion of general readership.[47] The likeli-

hood of any translation of classical Chinese literature attracting a truly general readership, however, has grown remote. Thus, while there should be a continuing need for anthologies for the classroom, the main audience for scholarship and translation of traditional Chinese texts is "our fellow specialists and the serious young students ... attracted to the field."[48] Translators of classical Chinese cannot reject a larger audience by making ridiculous translations, but they cannot count on that audience, either. Our goal, then, is to produce an accurate, philologically sound translation that avoids both excessive "'naturalization' of the foreign, which erases the unique character of the original," and "exploitation of the exotic, which exaggerates differences."[49]

On Translating the *San guo zhi*

The problems translators of the *San guo zhi* face are not much different from those faced by translators of other early dynastic histories and of old Chinese texts in general. The language of the text and commentary is usually fairly straightforward, but many terms and proper nouns require research and explanation. And the language does grow considerably more complex and difficult in quoted material, including memorials, letters, edicts, some sections of Pei's commentary, and other, still earlier texts such as the *Yi jing* 易經 and Han apocrypha.

Honorifics and official titles present a special problem. In the text they are frequently applied anachronistically. For example, in the Wei section, Cao Cao is regularly referred to by his posthumous title of *taizu* 太祖 (Grand Progenitor), and empresses are called *hou* 后 (empress), even in accounts of events before their assumption of the title and after their assumption of some other title, such as *tai hou* 太后 (empress dowager). These special usages occur not only in the descriptive and narrative parts of the material but also in ostensible reports of direct speech as well. In our translation, such honorifics are sometimes replaced by pronouns or the person's name, but they are often retained. To ensure clarity, they are sometimes followed by the person's full name set in apposition. This is especially useful for reminding the reader who's who at the beginning of a new *juan* 卷. For example, when Liu Bei's honorific *Xian zhu* (Former Ruler) first appears in the biography of Zhuge Liang, for 時先主屯新野 we may write "At the time, the Former Ruler, Liu Bei, was garrisoned at Xinye."[50]

Any translator of traditional Chinese historical or literary texts knows that there are a thousand such nuts-and-bolts questions involved in translating any substantial work. The *San guo zhi* does, however, present one unique problem—the relationship between the text and the commentary. The envisioned translation is of both Chen Shou's text and Pei Songzhi's commentary because it is unthinkable to do the text alone. The relationship between text and commentary is closer in the case of this history than any other, the closest analogue being perhaps the *Chunqiu* 春秋 (Spring and Autumn Annals) and the *Zuo zhuan* 左傳 (Zuo's Commentary). Furthermore, as already observed, the nature of the commentary is rather special. Certainly, no one would want to read *Han shu* without the commentaries of Yan Shigu 顏師古 (583–645) and others. But while those commentaries are read primarily as explanations or elucidations of the text, Pei's commentary is read as a supplement to the text, even as a rival work.

Pei's preservation of texts otherwise lost to us and his presentation of additional and alternative information does not come without a cost. In perhaps no other history is the prose of the original so broken up by long passages of commentary.[51] It is possible to skip over the commentary, but no serious reader is likely to do so, and the existence of any other kind of reader is unlikely. In most cases the interruption, though apparent, is not significant. An example is the following:[52]

Empress Zhen, consort of Emperor Wen and canonized Brilliant, was a woman of Wuji in Zhongshan, the mother of Emperor Ming and a descendant of Grand Guardian Zhen Han of Han times.[53] The family had been officials for generations at two thousand piculs.[54] Her father Yi was prefect of Shangcai.[55] She lost her father when she was three.

At this point, Pei Songzhi quotes *Wei shu* (History of the Wei) to supplement the information in the *San guo zhi*:

Wei shu says: Yi married a woman named Zhang from Changshan, and she gave birth to three boys and five girls.[56] The eldest son Yu died young. Next was Yan, who was recommended as filially pious and incorrupt, was a division head under the regent, and was magistrate of Quliang.[57] Next was Yao, recommended as filially pious and incorrupt. The eldest daughter was Jiang, followed in order by Tuo, Dao, Rong, and the empress. The empress was born during the Han on a *dingyou* day in the twelfth month of Guanghe 5 [January 26, 183]. Every time she went to sleep, her family seemed to see something like a person bringing a jade garment to cover her, and they often marveled over it together. When Yi died, whatever it was joined in the wailing for the deceased, and those within and without the family found it even stranger. Later, when the physiognomist Liu Liang examined the empress and the other children, he pointed to her and said, "This girl will be inexpressibly noble."

From the time she was small until she was grown, the empress never cared for frivolity. When she was eight, someone performed outside by riding standing up on a horse. The people in the household and all of her older sisters went up to the gallery to watch. Only the empress did not go. All of her older sisters thought this was odd and asked her why. She replied, "A woman should not watch such things." When she was nine, she enjoyed writing, and anytime she saw a character, she always knew it. She often used her elder brothers' brushes and inkstones, and they said to her, "You should stick to women's work. You don't think all of this writing and study will make a woman erudite of you, do you?" The empress replied, "I have heard that of all the worthy women of antiquity, there was never one who did not study the successes and failures of former times in order to admonish herself. If one does not understand writing, how can one examine these?"

Here Chen Shou's account resumes:

Later, when the armies of the empire rebelled and there was also famine, the people all sold their precious objects of gold, silver, pearls, and jade.[58] At that time, the empress's family had a great deal of stored grain, and they used a large amount to buy these objects. The empress was ten or so and said to her mother, "Now, while the world is in turmoil, we are buying a lot of precious objects. 'Though a man may have done nothing illegal, his cherishing his jade is a crime.'[59] Furthermore, all about everyone is starving and in want. It would be better to give our grain as relief to kinsmen and neighboring villages and to practice benevolence and charity on a broad scale." The whole family agreed it was a good idea and followed her advice.

The commentary once again interjects:

Wei lüe [Wei Epitome] says: When the empress was fourteen, she lost her middle elder brother Yan, and her sorrow continued beyond the stipulated mourning period. She served her widowed sister-in-law humbly and respectfully. She took care of all her duties and solicitously cared for Yan's children, and her affection and love were very great. The empress's mother was by nature stern and had treated all of her daughters-in-law in set ways. The empress often remonstrated with her mother, saying, "My elder brother unfortunately died young. Sister-in-law is young to be a celibate widow and has been left with but a single child. Speaking in terms of moral obligations, you ought to treat her like a daughter-in-law, and you should love her like a daughter." Her mother was moved by the empress's words and shed tears. She then ordered the empress and her sister-in-law to live together. Whether sleeping or resting, sitting or rising, they were always together, and their mutual affection grew deeper and deeper.

Chen's account then resumes with "In the Jian'an period, Yuan Shao obtained her for his middle son Xi...." It is obvious that the commentarial insertions at once retard Chen's narrative and provide additional information regarding Empress Zhen's special qualities.

The supplemental information provided by Pei is not always so innocuous. A few years ago one of us studied a particular event in the life of Cao Zhi 曹植 (192–232) in which the commentary had a mischievous effect on later scholars.[60] The passage in question reads:

Cao Zhi once rode his carriage down the speedway, opened the major's gate, and went out. Cao Cao was incensed, and the prefect of [the majors in charge of] official carriages was sentenced to death. Thenceforth, he added to the restrictions on the marquises, and his favoritism towards Cao Zhi declined daily.[61]

To flesh out the account in Chen's narrative, Pei Songzhi chose a passage from Guo Ban's 郭頒 *Wei Jin shi yu* 魏晉世語 (Conversations of the Wei and Jin Eras):

> Cao Cao dispatched the heir apparent Cao Pi and Cao Zhi each to go out one of the gates of Ye, but secretly ordered the gate that they were not to go out in order to see what his sons would do. When the heir apparent Cao Pi arrived at his gate, he was not allowed out and returned. Yang Xiu had previously cautioned Cao Zhi, "Since you have received a royal command, if the gate should not let you out, you may kill the gatekeeper." Cao Zhi followed his advice.[62]

This *Shi yu* version, as stated in Cutter's earlier article, is extremely suspect. Even Pei Songzhi himself was careful to point out that *Shi yu* is quite unreliable,[63] but later scholars have not always been as discerning. Guo Moruo, for instance, accepted the story in building an indictment of Cao Zhi.[64]

Unreliable, anecdotal material can always influence the interpretation of historical events, whether found in a contiguous commentary or not. Still, the basic fact is that here and elsewhere Pei's commentary interrupts Chen's original text and often offers conflicting information in a seductively convenient format. Interruptions are most frequent in an edition like Lu Bi's *San guo zhi ji jie*, but even the Zhonghua shuju edition, which uses note numbers, intersperses chunks of Pei's commentary between blocks of Chen's text. One way of minimizing this effect in the translation might be to place the translations of the text and of the commentary on facing pages, thus using page format to attempt to reintegrate Chen's narrative.

Chen Shou has been unfortunate in two ways. First, his work has had to compete with its own commentary, and second, *San guo zhi* has been overshadowed in the popular mind, at least, by *San guo yanyi* 三國演義. This important novel has greatly affected the popular perception of persons and events in the *San guo zhi*, in many instances placing historical figures in quite a different light. So pervasive is its influence that for many people around the world the title *San guo zhi* calls to mind the fictional work rather than Chen Shou's history. The primacy of *San guo yan yi* in popular lore is an understandable and immutable fact of life. The relationship between *San guo zhi* and Pei's commentary, on the other hand, is amenable to a slight, but more than cosmetic, modification. Thus one of our goals, in addition to that of producing an accurate and philologically sound rendering understandable to the educated Western nonsinologist, is to "restore" *San guo zhi* as an integrated narrative; one supplemented, not broken up, by Pei's commentary.

NOTES

We would like to take this opportunity to express our gratitude to Professor Miao Yue 繆鉞, a great scholar of the *San guo zhi* and a kind and considerate man.

1. The subtitle is borrowed from the title of Oliver Taplin's review of Homer, *The Iliad*, trans. Robert Fagles, intro. and notes by Bernard Knox (New York: Viking, 1990), which appeared in the *New York Times*, 7 October 1990. The significance of the subtitle has to do with "restoring" Chen Shou's narrative, a goal discussed at the end of the paper.

2. He was from Anhan 安漢 Prefecture in Ba 巴 Commandery. A biography of Chen appears in Chang Qu's 常璩 (fl. ca. 347) *Huayang guo zhi* 華陽國志 (Records of the Kingdom South of Mount Hua). See Liu Lin 劉琳, ed., *Huayang guo zhi jiao zhu* 華陽國志校注 (*Records of the Kingdom South of Mount Hua* Collated and Annotated) (Chengdu: Ba Shu shushe, 1984), 11.849–852.

3. Liu, *Huayang guo zhi jiao zhu*, 11.849; Miao Yue, "Chen Shou yu *San guo zhi*" 陳壽與三國志 (Chen Shou and *Records of the Three Kingdoms*), in *Zhongguo shixueshi lun ji* 中國史學史論集 (Essays in the History of Chinese Historiography), ed. Wu Ze 吳澤 and Yuan Yingguang 遠英光 (Shanghai: Renmin chubanshe, 1980), 315.

4. See Liu, *Huayang guo zhi jiao zhu*, 849; *Jin shu* 晉書 (Jin History), comp. Fang Xuanling 房玄齡 (578–648) et al. (Beijing: Zhonghua shuju, 1974), 82.2137; Miao, "Chen Shou yu *San guo zhi*," 313, 314n.

5. Miao, "Chen Shou yu *San guo zhi*," 313; Wen Xuchu 聞旭初, "Bian jiao shuoming" 編校說明 (Editorial Explanation), 1, in Duan Xizhong 段熙仲 and Wen Xuchu, eds., *Zhuge Liang ji* (Beijing: Zhonghua shuju, 1972).

6. Wen, "Bian jiao shuoming," 1.

7. Note that *San guo zhi* was not Chen's only work of a historical nature. He also authored *Yibu qijiu zhuan* 益部耆舊傳 (Accounts of the Elders of Yi Region) and *Gu guo zhi* 古國志 (Records of Ancient States), both now lost.

8. The sources potentially available to him are discussed in Carl Leban, "Ts'ao Ts'ao and the Rise of Wei: The Early Years" (Ph.D. dissertation, Columbia University, 1971), 3–19.

9. Miao, "Chen Shou yu *San guo zhi*," 321, suggests that the absence of the treatises found in other standard histories was due to insufficient data. While this may well be true, Leban suggests that a further reason for Chen's format is that at the time Chen wrote *San guo zhi*, the great histories of Sima Qian and Ban Gu notwithstanding, "the forms of historical writing were still in a state of experimental flux"; Leban, "Ts'ao Ts'ao and the Rise of Wei," 19. Many Qing dynasty (1644–1911) works attempt to supply *zhi* and *biao* for *San guo zhi*. Such works include those found in volumes 2 and 3 of *Ershiwu shi bu bian* 二十五史補編, 6 vols. (1936; Taibei: Kaiming shudian, 1959).

10. Miao, "Chen Shou yu *San guo zhi*," 317. See also Luo Hongzeng 羅宏曾, *Wei Jin Nanbeichao wenhua shi* 魏晋南北朝文化史 (A Cultural History of Wei, Jin, and the Northern and Southern Dynasties) (Chengdu: Sichuan Renmin chubanshe, 1988), 433. Cf. Leban, "Ts'ao Ts'ao and the Rise of Wei," 21–22.

11. Ji Yun 紀昀 (1724–1805) et al., comps., *Siku quanshu zongmu tiyao* 四庫全書總目提要, in *Heyin Siku quanshu zongmu tiyao ji Siku weishou shumu Jin hui shumu* 合印四庫全書總目提要及四庫未收書目禁燬書目 (Combined Printing of *Siku quanshu zongmu tiyao*, *Siku weishou shumu*, and *Jin hui shumu*) (Taibei: Shangwu yinshuguan,

1971), 10.17. See also Miao, "Chen Shou yu *San guo zhi*," 317–18; Leban, "Ts'ao Ts'ao and the Rise of Wei," 21. This criticism that Chen treated Wei rather than Shu Han as the legitimate successor of the Han perhaps says more about those making the accusation than it does about Chen's scholarship or integrity. Those who take this stance have usually been supporters of regimes such as the Eastern Jin 東晉 (317–420) and the Southern Song (1127–1270), whose situations were similar to those of Shu. See Miao, *San guo zhi dao du*, 7–8. There is some evidence that Chen may simply have seen Wei as *primus inter pares*. A related criticism is that Chen glossed over many incidents that place the Wei or the Sima family in an unfavorable light. See, for example, Zhao Yi's 趙翼 (1727–1814) *Nianer shi zhaji* 廿二史劄記 (Beijing: Zhongguo shudian, 1987), 74–76. Chen did have to show the Sima family in a good light, so any translation of the *San guo zhi* must include explanatory notes informing the reader of any discrepancy between the facts of an event and Chen's treatment of it.

12. Leban, "Ts'ao Ts'ao and the Rise of Wei," 1.

13. *Jin shu*, 82.2137; Miao, "Chen Shou yu *San guo zhi*," 315–316.

14. See Fan Wenlan 范文瀾, ed., *Wenxin diaolong zhu* 文心雕龍註 (Commentary to *Embellishments on the Heart of Literature*) (Beijing: Renmin wenxue chubanshe, 1978), 4.285; Vincent Yu-chung Shih, trans., *The Literary Mind and the Carving of Dragons*, bilingual ed. (Taipei: Chung Hwa, 1970), 122. For other accolades, see Luo, *Wei Jin nanbeichao wenhua shi*, 433.

15. One charge is that Chen omitted biographies of certain individuals for personal reasons. His biography in the *Jin shu* says that according to some people, he had offered to include biographies of Ding Yi 丁儀 (d. 220) and Ding Yi 丁廙 (d. 220) if their sons would pay him one thousand *hu* of grain. The account goes on to say that the grain was not paid and the biographies were not included. A number of scholars have questioned this story. Arguments on both sides are summarized by Miao Yue in the preface to his *San guo zhi xuan zhu* 三國志選注 (Beijing: Zhonghua shuju, 1984), 4–6.

16. One yearns to know, for example, what really transpired when Cao Pi 曹丕 (187–226; reigned as Emperor Wen of Wei 魏文帝, 220–226) had Empress Zhen 甄后 put to death (*San guo zhi*, 5.160). Chen says only that he was irate because she became fractious and discouraged over the favor he was showing to others, but this was probably not the whole story. Another omission of great concern, particularly since the *San guo zhi* has no treatises, is its lack of detail in describing the creation of the *tun tian* 屯田 system by Cao Cao 曹操 (155–220) and of the new method of levying land tax based on the amount of land held rather than according to the yield. Both were extremely important administrative changes and were the antecedents of major fiscal institutions in later dynasties, most notably the Tang. Chen mentions the first only in passing (*San guo zhi*, 1.14, 16.489) and the second not at all. Were it not for Pei's commentary and the *Hou Han shu*, we might completely misunderstand the origins of these two important institutions. On the other hand, the terseness of the *San guo zhi* may have contributed to its suitability for adaptation as fiction.

17. Leban, "Ts'ao Ts'ao and the Rise of Wei," 30.

18. *Song shu* 宋書 (Song History), comp. Shen Yue 沈約 (441–513) (Beijing: Zhonghua shuju, 1974), 64.1701. See also Miao, "Chen Shou yu *San guo zhi*," 321.

19. See Pei's "Shang *San guo zhi zhu* biao" 上三國志注表 (Memorial Presenting

the Commentary to *San guo zhi*), in *San guo zhi*, comp. Chen Shou (Beijing: Zhonghua shuju, 1959), 1471–1472. It is translated in Leban, "Ts'ao Ts'ao and the Rise of Wei," 30–32.

20. See Ma Duanlin 馬端臨 (ca. 1250–1325), *Wenxian tongkao* 文獻通考 (Comprehensive Examination of Documents), 191.1623, in *Shi tong* 十通 (The Ten Comprehensive Works) (Taibei: Xinxing shuju, 1965).

21. Miao, "Chen Shou yu *San guo zhi*," 322.

22. There are approximately 200,000 graphs in the text itself and around 540,000 in the commentary, according to Miao Yue, *San guo zhi daodu* 三國志導讀 (Directed Readings in the *San guo zhi*) (Chengdu: Ba Shu shushe, 1987), 30.

23. See also Leban, "Ts'ao Ts'ao and the Rise of Wei," 33–34. It is sometimes suggested that the presence of this material in Pei's commentary may have contributed to the disappearance of the originals, but this is far from certain.

24. This is not to say that the punctuation of the edition is entirely consistent, reliable, and free from error. See, for example, Fang Beichen 方北辰, "*San guo zhi* biaodian shangque" 三國志標點商榷 (On the Punctuation of *San guo zhi*), *Sichuan daxue xuebao* 四川大學學報 1987, no. 1: 90–97.

25. Leban, "Ts'ao Ts'ao and the Rise of Wei," 41–44, contains a survey of the publication history of *San guo zhi*.

26. See also Leban, "Ts'ao Ts'ao and the Rise of Wei," 42. The Bona editions of the twenty-four histories were published 1927–1937 by Shangwu yinshuguan (Commercial Press) in Shanghai. On standard histories and editions, see Yamane Yukio 山根幸夫, "Zong lun (san)" 總論(三) (General Discussion, Part Three), trans. Gao Mingshi 高明士, in Gao Mingshi, ed., *Zhongguo shi yanjiu zhinan* 中國史研究指南 (Research Guide to Chinese History), 4 vols. (Taibei: Lianjing chuban shiye gongsi, 1990), 1: 64–66.

27. See Leban, "Ts'ao Ts'ao and the Rise of Wei," 42–43. In the tally just given, Mao Jin's 毛晉 (1599–1659) Jigu ge 汲古閣 edition of *Shiqi shi* 十七史 (The Seventeen Histories) is counted twice. Printing was begun in 1628, then the works were reprinted in 1660 using reconditioned woodblocks. See Arthur Hummel, ed., *Eminent Chinese of the Ch'ing Period* (1943; Taibei: Ch'eng Wen Publishing Co., 1972), 565.

28. Lu was a disciple of Yang Shoujing 楊守敬 (1839–1915), on whom see Hummel, *Eminent Chinese of the Ch'ing Period*, 484. Other valuable contributions to our understanding of the language of the *San guo zhi* have been made by Qing scholars such as Gu Yanwu 顧炎武 (1613–1682), Yu Zhengxie 俞正燮 (1775–1840), and Zhao Yi, and the modern scholar Zhou Yiliang 周一良. See also Miao, *San guo zhi dao du*, 44.

29. Burton Watson, trans., *Records of the Grand Historian of China: Translated from the* Shi ji *of Ssu-ma Ch'ien*, 2 vols. (New York: Columbia University Press, 1961), 1:3, 6.

30. David R. Knechtges, trans., *Wen xuan, or Selections of Refined Literature*, vol. 1, *Rhapsodies on Metropolises and Capitals* (Princeton: Princeton University Press, 1982), 1.

31. Leban, "Ts'ao Ts'ao and the Rise of Wei," 30. Virtually every Chinese knows the main protagonists of the *San guo zhi*. Popularly held notions of what these historical personages were like may not conform to the contents of the text itself, but they are pervasive: Cao Cao was crafty, clever, and often brutal; Liu Bei was highly principled, gracious, but not sufficiently ruthless; Zhuge Liang (181–234) was a

master strategist and politician far cleverer than any of his opponents; and Sun Quan was vain and ambitious. Nothing reveals the hold exercised by these characterizations on the Chinese so much as the debate that led to the "rehabilitation" of Cao Cao in 1959. It began with a pair of articles published in January by Guo Moruo 郭沫若 and Jian Bozan 翦伯贊 reevaluating Cao Cao and his role in history. By the end of July, some 130 articles had been published on the subject. A number of China's preeminent historians participated in the debate, and the articles appeared in major national and provincial papers. Thirty-seven of the articles were collected in the anthology *Cao Cao lun ji* 曹操論集 (Collected Discussions on Cao Cao) (Beijing: Joint Publishing, 1960). The blurb on the jacket of the 1979 reprint of the book gives some sense of the issue: "In people's minds Cao Cao has always been considered the archetype of a treacherous minister and a traitor—a villainous bastard."

32. On Guan Yu, see Cai Xianghui 蔡相煇, *Taiwan de siji yu zongjiao* 台灣的祠祀與宗教 (Taiwanese Sacrifices and Religions) (Taibei: Taiyuan chubanshe, 1989), 107–12, and Prasenjit Duara, "Superscribing Symbols: The Myth of Guandi, Chinese God of War," *Journal of Asian Studies* 47, no. 4 (November 1988): 778–795.

33. Achilles Fang, trans., *The Chronicle of the Three Kingdoms (220–265): Chapters 69–78 from the Tzu chih t'ung chien* 資治通鑑 *of Ssu-ma Kuang* 司馬光 *(1019–1086)*, ed. Glen W. Baxter, 2 vols. (Cambridge: Harvard University Press, 1965).

34. On translations from *San guo zhi*, see Hans H. Frankel, *Catalogue of Translations from the Chinese Dynastic Histories for the Period 220–960*, Chinese Dynastic Histories Translations Supplement No. 1 (Berkeley: University of California Press, 1957), 11–55. Although over thirty pages of listings may seem like a lot, note that Frankel catalogues passages as short as twenty-five graphs, less than one full line on one page of the 1,510-page Zhonghua shuju edition. A fair amount has been done since Frankel compiled his catalogue. Several dissertations include blocks of the text, but even these constitute small fragments of the whole. Examples include Leban, "Ts'ao Ts'ao and the Rise of Wei"; Paul W. Kroll, "Portraits of Ts'ao Ts'ao: Literary Studies on the Man and the Myth" (Ph.D. dissertation, University of Michigan, 1976); Ronald C. Miao, "A Critical Study of the Life and Poetry of Wang Chung-hsüan" (Ph.D. dissertation, University of California at Berkeley, 1969); and Robert Joe Cutter, "Cao Zhi (192–232) and His Poetry" (Ph.D. dissertation, University of Washington, 1983). Miao's dissertation was later revised and published as *Early Medieval Chinese Poetry: The Life and Verse of Wang Ts'an (A.D. 177–217)* (Wiesbaden: Franz Steiner Verlag, 1982). There is a complete Japanese translation of the text and commentary: Imataka Makoto 今鷹眞 et al., trans., *Sangokushi* 三國志, Seikai koten bungaku zenshū 世界古典文學全集 no. 24a–c, 3 vols. (Tokyo: Chikuma shobō, 1984–1989. Wang Jingzhi 王靜芝 et al., trans., *Baihua San guo zhi* 白話三國志 (*Record of the Three Kingdoms* in Vernacular Chinese) (Taibei: He Luo tushu chubanshe, 1970) does not include Pei's commentary.

35. See James J. Y. Liu, *The Interlingual Critic: Interpreting Chinese Poetry* (Bloomington: Indiana University Press, 1982), ix–x, 17–20. Liu is not writing specifically about translation, but there is a connection. Some of his remarks will no doubt strike many readers as slightly imperious and sinocentric.

36. Watson, *Records of the Grand Historian*, 1:6–9.

37. Watson, *Records of the Grand Historian*, 1:8. Watson is quoting Grant's *Tacitus on Imperial Rome*. But Grant makes the same point about "unreadable" translations elsewhere. See Michael Grant, "Translating Latin Prose," in *The Translator's Art:*

Essays in Honour of Betty Radice, ed. William Radice and Barbara Reynolds (Harmondsworth: Penguin, 1987), 82–83.

38. Grant, "Translating Latin Prose," 83.

39. Grant, "Translating Latin Prose," 84.

40. Eugene Eoyang, "Waley or Pound? The Dynamics of Genre in Translation," *Tamkang Review* 19, nos. 1–4 (Autumn 1988–Summer 1989): 441–465.

41. Eoyang originally suggested these terms in his essay "Translation as Excommunication: Notes toward an Interworldly Poetics," presented at the first Sino-American Symposium on Comparative Literature. It now constitutes chapters 6–9 of his *Transparent Eye: Reflections on Translation, Chinese Literature, and Comparative Poetics* (Honolulu: University of Hawaii Press, 1993), 111–168.

42. Eoyang, "Waley or Pound?" 442–443. When dealing with old Chinese texts, the question of whether there is such a thing as a native reader arises; see Liu, *The Interlingual Critic*, 17–18.

43. Eoyang, "Waley or Pound?" 442–443.

44. Eoyang, "Waley or Pound?" 443.

45. Eoyang, "Waley or Pound?" 445. He has also spoken approvingly of sound philology, which I discuss below. See Eugene Eoyang, "The Maladjusted Messenger: *Rezeptionsästhetik* in Translation," *CLEAR* 10, no. 1–2 (July 1988): 66.

46. *The Shorter Oxford English Dictionary*, s.v. "Sino-." The modern media tend to use the word *sinologist* in a very broad fashion. It seems to be the equivalent of "China hand" and "China watcher."

47. David Knechtges's translations are a good example. They are highly accurate *and* literate renderings which reflect the spirit of the originals. C. T. Hsia has written:

> When the *Wen xuan* is completed, Professor Knechtges will have accomplished a work of unprecedented importance in the study of pre-T'ang literature. It is virtually the only anthology of "refined literature" that all scholars of the T'ang and after should know by heart to be truly educated in literature. The rhapsodies of the first two volumes are notoriously difficult to read and understand in the original; now even leading scholars in China, Japan, and Korea, if they read English, will find much to profit them in reading Knechtges' renditions of these compositions, along with the copious notes.

See C. T. Hsia, "Classical Chinese Literature: Its Reception Today as a Product of Traditional Culture," *CLEAR* 10, no. 1–2 (July 1988): 139. Other skillful translators having a strong sinological bent include Stephen West and Paul Kroll.

48. See Hsia, "Classical Chinese Literature," 133–140. He also writes (140), "The study of classical Chinese literature, insofar as it is a product of a traditional culture becoming increasingly remote from us, must be in part historical and philological to maintain its challenge and excitement."

49. Eoyang, "The Maladjusted Messenger," 75.

50. *San guo zhi*, 35.912.

51. Only in more recent compilations, such as Wang Xianqian's 王先謙 (1842–1918) collected commentaries on the Han histories and Takigawa Kametarō's 瀧川龜太郎 *Shiki kaichū kōshō* 史記會注考證, do we get such lengthy interruptions of the text. But even these do not appear to contain blocks of commentary as extensive as Lu Bi's *Collected Explanations to Records of the Three Kingdoms*. See Wang Xianqian, ed., *Han shu buzhu* 漢書補注 (Supplemental Notes to Han History) (1900; Taibei: Yiwen yinshuguan, 1956), and *Hou Han shu ji jie* 後漢書集解 (Collected Explana-

tions to *Later Han History*) (1915; Taibei: Yiwen yinshu guan, n.d.); Takigawa Kametarō, *Shiki kaichū kōshō* (Study of *Records of the Grand Historian* and Assembled Commentaries) (1932–1934; Taibei: Hongye shuju, 1987).

52. *San guo zhi*, 5.159–160.

53. Wuji 無極, in the Han kingdom of Zhongshan 中山, was in the vicinity of modern Zhengding 正定, Hebei. Zhen Han 甄邯 was the son-in-law of Grand Minister of the Masses Kong Guang 孔光, a supporter of Wang Mang 王莽 (45 B.C.–A.D. 23). Both Zhen and Kong played a role in Wang's consolidation of his power, and Zhen became a member of his circle of advisers and one of his most important officials. See Homer H. Dubs, trans., *The History of the Former Han Dynasty*, 3 vols. (Baltimore: Waverly Press, 1938, 1944, 1955), 3:137–138, 140, 142–145, 167, 181, 200, 225, 234, 236–237, 263, 319.

54. In Han times, officials were ranked in terms of *shi* 石, or piculs of grain, although this method of ranking had lost any direct connection with salary in kind. The highest officials had ranks of ten thousand bushels. Two thousand bushels marked the next level of the bureaucracy, with other ranks ranging down to one hundred bushels and less. See Hans Bielenstein, *The Bureaucracy of Han Times* (Cambridge: Cambridge University Press, 1980), 4–5; Charles O. Hucker, *A Dictionary of Official Titles in Imperial China* (Stanford: Stanford University Press, 1985), 16.

55. Shangcai 上蔡, in the Han commandery of Ru'nan 汝南, was located near modern Shangcai in Henan Province.

56. Changshan 常山 was a Han commandery with its seat located in modern Yuanshi 元氏 County, Hebei. Its name was changed from Hengshan 恆山 to avoid the personal name of Emperor Wen of Han (r. 180–157 B.C.), Liu Heng 劉恆.

57. Filially pious and incorrupt (*xiao lian* 孝廉) was a category of men recommended for service in the central government by the commanderies and kingdoms. See Bielenstein, *The Bureaucracy of Han Times*, 134–36, and Hucker, *A Dictionary of Official Titles in Imperial China*, no. 2418. *Da jiangjun* 大將軍 (general-in-chief) is here translated as "regent" to convey the function and significance of the office. See Bielenstein, *The Bureaucracy of Han Times*, 124. Quliang 曲梁 was a Han prefecture in the area of modern Yongnian 永年, Hebei.

58. This is apparently a reference to the turmoil of the 190s, when the Han was dissolving into pieces controlled by military leaders, rebels, and powerful regional administrators. See B. J. Mansvelt Beck, "The Fall of Han," in *The Cambridge History of China*, vol. 1, *The Ch'in and Han Empires, 221 B.C.–A.D. 220*, ed. Denis Twitchett and Michael Loewe (Cambridge: Cambridge University Press, 1987), 349.

59. This is a Zhou proverb found in *Zuo zhuan*. Cf. *Zuo zhuan*, Huan 10.

60. Robert Joe Cutter, "The Incident at the Gate: Cao Zhi, the Succession, and Literary Fame," *T'oung Pao* 71 (1985): 228–262, esp. 233–240.

61. *San guo zhi*, 19.558. Cf. Cutter, "The Incident at the Gate," 229.

62. *San guo zhi*, 19.561. See also Cutter, "The Incident at the Gate," 233–234; Hugh A. Dunn, *Ts'ao Chih: The Life of a Princely Chinese Poet*, new ed. (Beijing: New World Press, 1983), 59.

63. See also Leban, "Ts'ao Ts'ao and the Rise of Wei," 37. Although Leban does not give a locus for Pei's criticisms, they can be found in *San guo zhi*, 4.133.

64. Guo Moruo, "Lun Cao Zhi" 論曹植 (On Cao Zhi), in *Lishi renwu* 歷史人物 (Historical Personages) (Shanghai: Haiyan, 1947), 17.

Translation as Research

Is There an Audience in the House?

STEPHEN H. WEST

Writing about translation provides a unique opportunity for self-reflection, self-definition, and, some might say, self-delusion, for it provides occasion to critique not only the field but one's own work as well. It also allows us, who are primarily scholars, to draw a line between our work and that of professional translators and dilettantes. Most scholarly debates in the West that take as their topic the issue of translation, and with which I am familiar—I do not claim to have read exhaustively in this area—seem to me to come at the issue mostly from the standpoint of comparative literature; attention is riveted on questions of literary sensibilities; discussion takes form in countless words on what translates best: imagery, symbolism, allegory, meter, rhyme, or rhythm. But this debate skips what is to me a prior question, seldom put and seldom answered except in the stuffy pages of philological journals, about proper aims and proper audience. The exact role of scholarly translation is ill-defined despite the largess of government foundations, and ill-definition is abetted by scholarly journals in the West that, until recently, reviewed all translations of Chinese literature as if they were documents of equal value. This is a legacy of the early and middle twentieth century, when any document that purported to translate or render a Chinese word, phrase, sentence, paragraph, drama, poem, or novel into an intelligible Western tongue was greeted with joy by scholar and student alike. In Chinese literature courses I grew up on Witter Bynner and Arthur Waley, on old Giles and Rexroth; only by diligent curiosity did I find

Couvreur and Legge and Von Zach—in the world of the late sixties and seventies they were thought by many of my teachers to be stodgy and old-fashioned, put out of the sensible mind by Waley's work on the *Analects* and the *Book of Odes* or Burton Watson's on the *Records of the Historian* and early Chinese literature. Yet today, when I send my own students in search of a translation, those stodgy old works are their destination. Why? Because I want them to know that the *Shih ching* is more than a set of pretty little poems all dressed up in Bloomsbury garb or canting along to the Poundian beat; I want them to know that these are intellectually significant documents, texts that shine like diamonds in a matrix of commentary and culture.

The direction of my essay is set, then, by these predilections and by the knowledge that although I do translate Chinese literature, I am not very gifted in its art; perhaps as compensation for this lack of literary sensitivity and sensibility, I have chosen to use translation as a tool, a way to understand a text, a method to organize its various levels of meaning and significance into an integral and rational whole in my own mind. I am always somewhat surprised when someone reads a translation that I, or my partner in crime, Wilt Idema, and I have done together; I am, or the two of us are, my first audience. Neither of us, I believe, would make any claim to art; what we, and I, have always tried to do is to provide some semblance of accuracy as well as a context that would make the work useful not just to laymen but also to scholars and intelligent readers—readers of Johnson, Boswell, Bacon, Boas, or Steiner rather than *Time, USA Today*, Rod McKuen, or pulp fiction. In short, I believe that translation is an exercise in criticism of both a philological and a literary sort, a convenient way to organize a complex agenda of study and research.

This will naturally bias the case for selection of works to translate. Problems are immediately apparent. The question is not so much whether the translator should pick canonical or noncanonical texts (itself a daunting question in the modern world), but rather whether one is going to proceed with a cultural or literary translation. This is a somewhat fine distinction that is apparent more in the treatment of a work than in its intrinsic value. But at the root, one must entertain the question whether one is going to pick a culturally significant or simply an entertaining document. One can quite rightly argue that any piece of real literature is manifestly both; I am suggesting that *not all texts that are culturally significant translate as self-sufficient literary texts*, apprehendable without a large body of commentary. A choice here is linked directly to the demands one can make on a reader, and further to the issue of audience. There is, I argue, a radically different process involved in giving the Western world yet another translation of Wang Wei and in rendering into a different tongue a difficult classical Chinese text, freighted with hundreds of years, even millennia, of commentary, and still under debate by scholars. While Wang Wei's nature poetry, for example, may be taken into English without notes and be perfectly intelligible, the weight of the intelligibility will naturally fall more upon the quality of the English verse than upon the relationship of the translation to its mother text. A translation of Wang Wei's poetry deepened by consideration of its place in a cultural and intellectual context, the complexity of which is difficult to recover even for the native reader, is quite a different thing and brings to the intelligent and caring consumer both literature and culture at the same time.[1]

Since I have had the most experience with Yüan drama, I would like to use this genre—specifically two plays, *The Story of the Western Wing* (*Hsi-hsiang chi* 西廂記)[2] and *The Wrongs of Beauty Tou* (*Tou E Yüan* 竇娥冤)[3]—as case studies to suggest that the same rules that govern any form of serious study of literature also govern translation and that translation is, in fact, a serious form of commentary. I cannot cover every facet of translation and so would like to limit my discussion mostly to the issue of editions and language. It is safe to say that most translations of Yüan dramas in the West have used as their basis the editions of the *One Hundred Yüan Plays* (*Yüan-ch'ü hsüan* 元曲選) by Tsang Mao-hsün 臧懋循 (1550–1620), a literatus of no mean abilities.[4] This text has essentially been canonized since the seventeenth century, and has driven all other editions into relative obscurity by virtue of its literary brilliance. A similar phenomenon of textual obeisance exists for *The Story of the Western Wing*.[5] To quote myself and Idema on the subject of the popularity of Chin Sheng-t'an's revised version of the seventeenth century, which virtually eclipsed all earlier editions and upon which all Western-language translations of *The Story of the Western Wing* (prior to 1990) have been based:

> Jin Shengtan's edition of *The Story of the Western Wing* adheres to basically the same format as his earlier venture into vernacular criticism.[6] The main text is preceded by two prefaces and two general essays, each act is preceded by its own critical introduction, and the body of the text itself is accompanied by an extensive interlinear commentary. [The] wording of the text occasionally has been changed to fit the commentary. Because metrical requirements keep most of the songs inviolate, the prose dialogue suffers all the more. One of Jin Shengtan's major concerns is to safeguard Oriole from any accusation of indecency. He attempts this by proving that she remains chaste under all circumstances—even when she gives herself to the student Zhang Gong (in Jin's opinion she simply enacts the promise of marriage her mother has retracted). Accordingly, he makes many small changes throughout the text, once more supposedly on the authority of an otherwise unspecified "ancient edition"; in the process the text is thoroughly bowdlerized. As in the case of his edition of *Water Margin*, Jin Shengtan's textual changes may well have enhanced the readability of the text and increased its general acceptability by downplaying its morally offensive aspects. The breadth and wit of his commentary, moreover, remain an attraction to readers even to the present day.[7]

Part of the reason for the success of Chin Sheng-t'an's and Tsang Mao-hsün's editions is simply that by the time that they were editing and writing, drama had been thoroughly and completely appropriated by the literati classes of China as a minor form of art.[8] Since this same class governed the preservation and publication of dramatic texts—producing ever finer editions, often with attached commentary—it is to be expected that what survives as text should be governed by their literary and cultural orthodoxy. This can be demonstrated fairly easily: first Yüan drama, then in sequence, *ch'uan-ch'i* 傳奇, *k'un-ch'ü* 昆曲, and finally *ching-hsi* 京戲 have assumed the proportions of national drama and have been identified (in their extant—not original—forms) almost solely with landed, educated, well-positioned scholarly gentlemen. Their origins as popular forms have largely been forgotten. Yet they were originally what is now called "regional drama"; this regional drama, in turn, has maintained a strong and healthy tradition from at least the thirteenth century until the present, but has been subject to collection and analysis as a popular art form (or popular text) *only* after the folklore movements of the late nineteenth and early twentieth centuries.

One can, of course, say that these refined Ming editions provide the best literary texts; they are rationalized, seek uniformity in their literary expression, and sometimes (as in the case of Tsang Mao-hsün) show rather sophisticated and integrated philological and phonological scholarship. What I object to is their traditional and modern acceptance as documents of an urban and mercantile culture that is both distinct from and alien to that of the editors.[9] Historical evidence indicates that the textual tradition of drama (as distinct from its performing tradition) had its roots in the urban pleasure worlds (the so-called *wa-she* 瓦舍 of Pien-liang and Hangchow), and its first texts, the thirty so-called *Yüan-k'an tsa-chü san-shih-chung* 元刊 雜劇三十種, are marked in twenty-nine instances as texts produced in either Hangchow or Ta-tu (the Yüan capital in what is now Peking).[10] Literati culture is largely grounded on a mental and literary foundation of agricultural ethics, the values of which are often antagonistic to those of an urban experience.[11] It is only logical that such a fundamental conflict should appear in textual recensions.

Except for those cases in which we have at hand actual Yüan editions, however, we can *only* use Ming recensions. This necessitates a further step in decision making; not all Ming editions are created equal. The problem is extraordinarily complex in the case of *The Story of the Western Wing*. We have nearly forty extant Ming editions, the earliest of which we have in our hands only as a few fragmentary leaves.

In 1980 a few fragments of a very early printed edition of *The Story of the Western Wing* came to light. These fragments preserve the text of the final segment of the fourth act of the first play and the opening lines of the second play.

The character of their layout suggests that the fragments may derive from an edition printed in either the final years of the Yüan or the early decades of the Ming dynasty. In contrast to other preserved Yüan dynasty printings of *zaju*, which include only arias and the barest of stage directions and prompt lines from the dialogue, this edition of *The Story of the Western Wing* includes full stage directions and dialogue as well as full-page illustrations. The fragments suggest that the text was not accompanied by any explanatory annotations.[12]

When Idema and I decided to translate the *Hsi-hsiang-chi*, we picked the earliest extant edition, the *hung-chih* edition of 1498.[13] All translations to this point had used the Chin Sheng-t'an version, which was excessively bowdlerized; all modern annotations used either the Chin Sheng-t'an edition or that of Ling Meng-ch'u 凌濛初 (1580–1644).[14] We postulated that the Ling edition may have been based on the earlier *hung-chih* text and consequently we felt satisfied that we had traced our text back to its earliest complete edition.[15] The decision to use this edition was supported by the fact that in practically every instance the singer of each aria is identified, indicating in some instances that later traditions have assigned some arias to the wrong person.[16] The edition also has some value in that it is truly a commercial edition. While the overall quality of the work is very high and its woodblocks show the marks of craftsmen imported from the Suchow area, the low level of learning as exemplified in the annotations suggests that at least this part of the text was the product of someone who was not well educated in traditional Chinese cultural lore. That is, the annotator was not educated in historical or literary texts; the annotations, of course, may represent a substantial and consensual oral tradition.

The value of finding such a commentary in an otherwise quite elaborate edition should be useful for explaining the text's reception in a world of well-to-do urbanites who were not the traditional literati elite of Chinese culture. Indeed, when Wang Chi-te 王驥德 (ca. 1560–1623) compiled his recension (one of the masterpieces of *Hsi-hsiang chi* scholarship) in 1614, he took careful pains to account for and then dismiss what he called such "vulgar commentaries" as that found in the *hung-chih* edition.[17] Such scholarly fastidiousness is quite useful for the modern translator on several counts, but its major value lies in the fact that it begins to discriminate how the text was received and understood by different audiences in China. In some cases Wang Chi-te has been quite active in refuting commentary on passages that are clearly erotic or sexually suggestive; such disputation would culminate in the later seventeenth century bowdlerization of the text by Chin Sheng-t'an. Since Idema and I feel that one of the major subthemes of the play is that of sexual allegory, our choice of edition allowed us not only to explore that level of the drama but also to try and bring it out through translation. This avenue would have been quite closed to us if we had opted for another edition or had not been able to compare other editions and their appended commentaries. Conversely, the large amount of "negative" commentary—i.e., that "such-and-such a phrase" did not have an erotic or taboo meaning—opened up paths of investigation. In modern mainland Chinese society, the strength of negation or disavowal often is inversely proportional to the actual existence of the object or phenomenon of criticism.

The problem of editions is less complex but more compelling in the case of *Tou E Yüan*.[18] Three editions of this play are extant; they are, in chronological order:

1. *Ku ming-chia* 古名家 edition of 1588 (hereafter, KMC), produced over decades (1573–1620) by the Hsiung family of Lung-feng 熊龍峯(家). There are two collections, each said to be compiled by *Yü-yang hsien-shih* 玉陽仙史. The first is entitled 古名家雜劇, comprising eight collections and forty plays; the other is the 新續古名家雜劇, which contains four collections and twenty plays.[19]

2. *Yüan-ch'ü hsüan* (hereafter YCH), edited by Tsang Mao-hsün and also known as *Tiao-ch'ung kuan Yüan-jen pai-chung-ch'ü* 雕蟲館元人百種曲 after the name of his studio. Contains 100 of the 162 datable Yüan and early Ming plays. Of the 100 plays, forty do not exist in other editions that can be reliably dated before the *Yüan-ch'ü hsüan* was compiled.[20]

3. Meng Ch'eng-shun, *Ku-chin ming-chü he-hsüan* 古今名劇合選. Meng Ch'eng-shun's preface is dated 1633, making this the latest of the Ming editions of Yüan drama. There are two collections, each of thirty plays. Those devoted to "windy blossoms and snowy moons, misty flowers and powder and kohl" are found in the *Liu-chih chi* 柳枝集 and those about "spiritual transcendents and transformations of the Way, brandished blades and raised clubs, courtroom cases, and iron cavalry" (including *Tou E Yüan*), are found in the *Lei-chiang chi* 酹江集. Twenty of the sixty plays are Ming creations (including four by Meng himself), leaving only forty that are actually Yüan. Meng sometimes notes in the "eyebrow" register the provenance and rationale for his changes. Sometimes he also cites passages from other texts that he does not adopt.

Meng's collection represents a refinement of the *Yüan-ch'ü hsüan* tradition, since it primarily adopts the changes made by Tsang Mao-hsün, and so we are here faced with a choice, in fact, between only two basic texts. Tsang made several changes to the KMC edition, the most important of which are the following:

1. There is no demi-act or "wedge" (*hsieh-tzu* 楔子) in the KMC edition; both the YCH and the *Lei-chiang chi* (hereafter LCC) versions have added a wedge.

2. KMC has incorrectly split the second act and put half of the dialogue and arias in the third act. YCH and LCC both correctly restore that portion of the play to the second act.
3. YCH has altered the plot (*kuan-mu* 關目) and has changed the dialogue significantly (except for the first act), and has made the dialogue much more specific and detailed, especially in act four, where he has Tou E's ghost appear to confront the villains.
4. YCH has added arias to acts one, three, and four. These are clearly Tsang's own compositions. As Cheng Ch'ien remarks, although these are excellent compositions in their own right, when placed alongside the simpler and more natural lines of the earlier edition (KMC), they stand out as inappropriate changes.
5. The *t'i-mu* 題目 (title) and *cheng-ming* 正名 (name) have been changed. In the KMC edition they are very specific:

題目　復嫁婆婆忒心偏
　　　守志烈女意自堅
正名　湯風冒雪沒頭鬼
　　　感天動地竇娥冤

Title:　An old lady who remarries is too partial to her own desires,[21]
　　　A resolute girl guards her integrity and strengthens her own will;
Name:　Braving the wind and defying snow, a ghost without a head,
　　　Moving heaven and shaking earth, the injustice to Tou E.

while it has been reduced to a single couplet in YCH and LCC:

題目　秉鑑持衡廉訪法
正名　感天動地竇娥冤

Title:　Holding a mirror and grasping a balance: the laws of the Surveillance Commissioner
Name:　Moving heaven and shaking earth, the injustice to Tou E.[22]

The changes that Tsang wrought in the text systematically winnowed out certain features. As I remarked elsewhere,

Zang Maoxun's recensions of Yüan drama mark a new era in the history of *zaju* texts. They rationalize both the language and format of a large number of texts on the basis on a single set of editorial and linguistic criteria. In his appropriation of popular texts to high culture, he radically changes the master metaphors of earlier commercial texts—reciprocity, commodification, and economic transaction—to the myths of the relational ethics of orthodox Confucianism that dominate polite literature.

In the case of Tou E, specifically, he revised out of the play sexuality, commodification, and subversive comments on the judicial system. In the

KMC edition, which I understand as a purely commercial text that had a wide circulation in the bookstalls of urban China, metaphors of the mercantile world are rampant. The whole focus of the play is indeed indebtedness and the results of indebtedness. Madame Ts'ai's loan to Scholar Tou is repaid by Tou E, who is virtually sold into marriage; the old woman's loan to the physician by attempted murder and near death. Madame Ts'ai becomes indebted to the two Changs, who coerce her into marriage (she acquiesces so quickly in the KMC version that it leaves the actual amount of coercion unresolved). Indebtedness sets the play in motion.

Tou E's actions in the KMC edition are also harsher. She openly criticizes her mother-in-law, abusing her with the term *p'o-niang* (婆娘)[23] because of the old lady's flagrant disregard of her indebtedness to her deceased husband. Tou E is consistent in her sarcastic remarks about Ts'ai P'o-p'o's willing capitulation to the demands of Old Chang. Her decision to die for her mother in the KMC edition is also clearly a method for her to fulfill her own debts—the debt of karma that accounts for her miserable existence and the debt to her husband that she incurred at marriage. In the KMC version, her sudden capitulation to force is *not* filiality or love for her mother-in-law—who is otherwise the object of her considerable scorn—but a move *to repay a promise* made to her husband to keep *his* mother from harm.[24]

The power of sexuality is much more clearly writ in the KMC version, as well. Madame Ts'ai's speedy acquiescence to Codger Chang for marriage, the constant theme of "forgetting old favor to welcome the new," and the intense lust of Donkey Chang is considerably softened in Tsang Mao-hsün's rewriting of the text. Indeed, sexuality as a motive for action is diminished in Tsang's work to a minor chord, whereas in the KMC version it palpitates with immediacy.

Finally, Tsang considerably expanded the third and fourth acts of the earlier version, adding whole sets of arias. This radically changes the specific gravity of the play and was done, I suspect, to counter the subversiveness of the KMC edition:

> Zang Maoxun ... shifts the focus of the play to the gravity of the crime and the subsequent elicitation of Heaven's response. He does this by altering the specific gravity of the play, weighting it toward the third and fourth acts. He keeps enough of the issue of *karma* alive to account for Dou E's actions but still has to account for the fact that such an unjust death rends the delicate net of relationships that exist between the individual and the natural system of ethics that is envisioned by the Confucianist. He must also confront the fact that Dou E's death reveals a yawning gap between the flagrant abuse of the law and its supposed moral absolutism. Zang's expansion of the fourth act, in which Dou E confronts each participant in the actions leading to her father-in-law's murder, tidies up the issues of retribution and justice and reinforces the value of belief in a system of justice by moral law. The scenes of Dou E's torture may openly

criticise corrupt officials; but the same institution of justice that empowers them also empowers the agent of right. It can therefore not be held accountable for injustices perpetrated by its agents. By expanding this scene, Zang can affirm the judicial system both as an institution and as the proper executor of justice. By deploying the standard values of Confucian orthodoxy, Zang has effectively turned what are evil deeds that are as palpable as life in the KMC edition into a non-subversive didacticism that, if it does not give hope to others who suffer in this terrestrial drama, does preach that justice itself will, in the end, prevail.[25]

By resolving the basic conflict between individually centered values of reciprocity, karma, debt and repayment, Tsang Mao-hsün radically altered the operative metaphors of the original text:

> The cultural energies that are empowered in the KMC edition of *Dou E* show the domination of the values of the commercial world. The master metaphor of, at least the first part of, the drama is that of transaction. It begins with pure economics, but soon expands to the network of human relations, and then beyond the human world into the process of rebirth. An emphasis is placed on the value of keeping one's word and living up to one's responsibilities within a set of personal obligations—an important factor in a commercial society.[26] In-debtedness, whether in the form of owing money, of owing obligations in human relations, or living out the karmic debt of a past life, is an important feature of the text.
>
> The motive of sexuality is also clearer in the earlier text, and, in the metaphor of transaction, women are clearly considered to be commodities that are to be exchanged or bartered between men. The corollary to this proposition is that, no matter what economic power women may wield in the real world, that power is not enough to protect them from men or from the process of commodification. Zang Maoxun has gone to great lengths to defuse the issue of remarriage and sexuality as an organizing principle of dramatic literature fades into the discrete silence of literati discourse on filiality. The portrait of a sexually deprived, bitter young woman who must stand by and watch her beliefs in personal loyalty flagrantly flaunted by the woman she has sworn to honor and protect is softened into that of a devoted and filial daughter-in-law who acts out of righteousness.[27]

When such major changes take place in an edition, I submit that as translators, we cannot simply pick an edition because it is popular, because it is readily available in punctuated and annotated editions, or because it has been accepted by others. In the case of Tsang Mao-hsün, for instance, his editions were of such fine quality, so rationalized in terms of format and in terms of his own literary language, so attuned to the scholarly ear, that they simply drove all other editions of drama into a kind of limbo. In effect, he canonized the 100 Yüan plays that he revised. But since they are no longer connected to the world that produced them, to translate them is to translate a vastly different cultural document from the earlier versions. I would make the argument that the KMC version, for instance, represents the values of the commercial, mercantile world and that those values are antagonistic to the basic premises of traditional literati thought. I think one may argue about whether they represent a *performing* tradition, whether they were a conscious act of artists or writers to subvert or challenge the dominant order, or whether they were an attempt to create a literature consciously distinct from that of the literati—but they are different and that difference has to be taken in consideration when choosing a text for translation.

Another issue is central to the issues of editions and language: that drama is a collective literature. As I have written, "As scripts, dramatic texts are fair game for anyone. Drama as performance is essentially public property and subject to free interpretation and reinterpretation on stage." The play *Tou E Yüan*, for instance, exists as an abstract entity "that is tied to one or to several texts but is independent of all written sources, except as those sources are adapted for oral presentation."[28] No text is the equal of any one play and in changes of time and place texts may show the influence of actors' delivery, of audience's reception, or of writer's memory. "This process of change between texts may, in fact, not be primarily literary but one dictated by intellectual interests or the needs of stagecraft. While the notion of 'the play' may endure through time as a loosely circumscribed set of themes and tropes that can be assembled or revised according to different sets of criteria (i.e., the troupe's or the writer's) the text themselves—as transitional objects between author/culture, stage/actor, or audience/reader—are not subject to the same rigor and principles of textual transmission associated with more orthodox forms of publications; as literary artifacts of a decidedly secondary status, the texts of drama are not ossified into any canonical form."[29] It is well known, for instance, that the themes of drama are often repetitive and that there are a set of collective exchanges between drama and other forms of popular literature.[30] The same holds true for its language. In his excellent short piece on the language of prosimetric forms, Wang Chi-ssu, an eminent authority on the language of drama, made this point in isolating three characteristics of middle vernacular: that it is colloquial, that—in contrast to classical literature—it is explicit and discursive, and that it is a nonunified and complex mode of expression that is extremely dynamic and unstable. Because of this, he suggests, it will not generally reflect individual style.[31] Cheng Ch'ien made a similar comment about the contents and language of *Tou E Yüan*:

Comedy (*tsa-chü* 雜劇) was a popular art that circulated through society and among the people in the Yüan dynasty. It was not the canonical, formal writing of the classics of the sages or the biographies of worthy men. No one knows what it means to say, "respect the original text and maintain its true features."

Moreover, changes were unavoidable over time since texts passed through a long period of performance by actors. Therefore, I fear that Yüan comedy simply has no so-called, "true and original texts," and so we can only look for comparatively close approximations. And all changes that are wrought therein cannot be attributed to a single text or a single author.[32]

While I think it safe to say that Yüan drama utilizes a highly ritualized vocabulary, I think it a more problematical statement that a single edition will not reflect individual differences. I suspect that when Wang and Cheng talk about a "play," they have in mind an aggregate of texts (i.e., different editions of the same drama) that share linguistic and formal characteristics. More to the point for the current essay is that such texts are unstable until committed to paper and they reflect a language that hinges on oral-aural keys—that of spoken literature. Such a language creates its own set of problems in lexicon, phonetics, and grammar. One major problem is orthography. For instance, the oral phrase pronounced tşi-ui or tsï-ui or tsai-ui ("just because") can be represented by various orthographic conventions: 只爲, 子爲, 則爲, 祇爲, 止爲, the phrase p'uŋ-suŋ ("hair a'tangle") can variously be written as 蓬松, 鬖鬆, 髼鬆, 鬉松, etc.[33] Orthographically, these phrases are often rationalized by set rules; for instance, radicals may be added to make the meaning clearer or remove ambiguities (蓬松 > 鬖鬆 to show that it had something to do with hair). In some cases, radicals are also added to longer written forms that had been shortened to save block-cutting expenses. For instance, the word t'iəŋ 聽 was shortened to 丁; then to stabilize the word a mouth radical was added to the shortened form of t'iəŋ 聽 > 厅, resulting in 听.

A second major feature of the language was the addition of head or tail adjuncts for emphasis. In some cases, this was a simple replacement of more classical forms with particles still common in the modern language; in other cases it involved vocative phrases used for emphasis or as metrical fillers in songs: iɛ-mua-kɔ 也麼哥, iɛ-puɔ-kɔ 也波哥, or iɛ-puɔ 也波, for instance.

Orthographic changes such as this may provide useful indices of change between editions; indeed, it is probably the study of language that will, in the end, help us sort out the complicated history of Yüan dramatic texts. Earlier attempts, such as Hsü Wei's 徐渭 *Nan-tz'u hsü-lu* 南詞叙錄 and Chai Hao's 翟灝 *T'ung-su pien* 通俗編, are not reliable. Mao Ch'i-ling's commentary on the *Hsi-hsiang chi* and Tsang Mao-hsün's on the 100 Yüan plays both have phonological and explanatory notes, but they are also sometimes mistaken.[34] Modern dictionaries present a more comprehensive lexicon, yet they are still primarily descriptive. As Wang Chi-ssu remarked, we now have a better picture of what something means, but not why. He proposes three major steps toward improving our knowledge of vernacular lexicon and grammar. First he suggests the investigation of sources. By this he means not only historical linguistic sources, but also the language of dialects and even the argot of social, work, and minority groups as well. Second, he suggests that the evidence be extracted directly from the works on the model of the great Ch'ing philologists Wang Yin-chih and Yü Yüeh. Finally, he wisely proposes that the study of Sung and Yüan texts be placed in the larger context of the development of works *written in* northern dialects.[35]

Wang's proposal to resurrect social, professional, and dialect registers in the text offer us, I think, a sounder approach to understanding the text as a whole and is echoed in the posthumous writings of Hsü Cheng-yang, who also proposed a study of the vocabulary of drama, based on several strata of lexicography. Hsü disputes the categorization of the language of Yüan drama as "dialect and colloquial" (*fang-yen su-yü* 方言俗語), a term that he claims was fabricated by early Ming scholars:

It is extremely inappropriate that generations have called the vocabulary of Yüan drama "dialect and colloquial." Dialect is the language of one particular area; colloquial is the oral language of customary speech and is always spoken of in distinction to "book language" (*shu-mien yü* 書面語). Both terms imply limitations of either place or level. But the vocabulary of Yüan drama is not like this. For one thing, it is not limited to a single area; it is a generalized form of language that spread as far as Ta-tu (the area of modern Pei-ching) and as far as Hangchow. Even though the home registry of playwrights was either northern or southern, there was no difference in their use of the language. So, to call it dialect is simply a product of imagination. On the other hand this was not a truly colloquial language because it did not exist in contradistinction to any book language. For instance, *yü-t'u hu* 玉兔鶻 means a waist wrap and *p'en-tiao* 盆吊 means a way of torturing a convict to death, whether in written or in oral form—it simply appears to be colloquial.[36]

In his unfinished proposal[37] for a methodology for studying the language of Yüan drama ("how to find a road to solving difficult lexical problems" as he called it)[38] Hsü suggested five directions of inquiry:

1. Dialect and Yüan colloquial (language specific to Yüan dramatic texts 所謂方言俗語).
2. Professional and secret language (of professions, crafts, vagabonds, and secret societies 市語, 行語, 術語, 隱語, 點語, 江湖, 切語).
3. Mongol and Jurchen language 蒙古語, 女貞語.
4. Institutions and names of things 名物制度.

This somewhat broader investigation of sources takes into account dialect, foreign words, and the communicative language of work and secret societies. The last of these three sections, secret language, has also been the subject of a short article by Ch'ien Nan-yang, who has traced the use of such language as far back as the T'ang.[39] Both of these works have excellent bibliographies of traditional works attached to them that can be consulted at will.

While some may argue that a dictionary definition is a fine enough distinction for translation, can it really prepare the way for understanding, for instance, degrees of register in a character's speech? Since speech is linked intimately to characterization, a better understanding of the nuance of dramatic language will lead directly to a clearer presentation of character in text. Idema and I encountered this problem in the characterization of Student Chang in the *Hsi-hsiang chi*. For the most part, his language oscillates between prudish and pedantic on the one hand and lustful and vulgar on the other—depending largely on the ratio and intimacy of contact with Oriole. Between these two poles is a wide band of spoken language: some playful, some mournful, some satiric. To quote a good example, we can turn to the opening suite of songs sung by the student when he first visits the Monastery of Universal Salvation and encounters Oriole:

> Stunning knockouts—I've seen a million;
> But a lovely face like this is rarely seen!
> It dazzles a man's eyes, stuns him speechless,
> And makes his soul fly away into the heavens.
> She there, without a thought of teasing, fragrant shoulders bare,
> Simply twirls the flower, smiling.[40]

As we remarked in *The Moon and the Zither*,

> He begins this song with a very colloquial interjection, *dianbula*, which has been variously understood as "frivolous or nonsensical," "unrestrained or romantic," "absolutely first-rate," although here it clearly means something like "fantastic" or "stunning." The colloquial tone of the song gradually degenerates into the kind of lascivious yearning that critics have traditionally labeled "extremely vulgar" (*shuli* 殊俚).[41]

In this case, we were fortunate to have a long note on the word by the eminent *Western Wing* scholars Chiang Hsing-yü and Wang Chi-ssu, on the meaning of the word tien-pu-la 顛不剌, which clearly pointed to its colloquial overtones in describing a woman of physical beauty.[42] In other cases, especially those that reflect sexual innuendo, we are at more of a loss, since the puritanical traditions of neo-Confucian philosophy and communist ideology do not allow for frank scholarly discussion of that level of language.

In the case of *The Wrongs of Tou E*, the issue of level and register also figure prominently in decisions about which text to translate. In his recension of the text, Tsang Mao-hsün has consistently softened the language of the Beauty Tou, turning her from an embittered and somewhat sarcastic young widow into something more closely resembling the Confucian ideal of a daughter-in-law in loving service of her mother-in-law. This agenda is carried on throughout the text in a subtle but cumulative way. To give an example, when Tou E is commanded to make the fateful ragout that causes Old Chang's death, she sings two quite different arias in the two editions:

KMC

【隔尾】
你說道少鹽欠醋無滋味
加料添椒纔脆美
但願娘親蚤痊濟
飲湯一盃勝甘露灌體
您三口兒團圓到大來喜

【賀新郎】
一箇道你爺先喫
一箇道你娘喫
這言語我聽也難聽
我可是氣也不氣
新婚的姻眷偏歡喜
不想那舊日夫妻道理
常好是百從千隨
這婆娘心如風刮絮
那里肯身化做望夫石
舊恩情到不比新佳配
他則待百年爲婚眷
那里肯千里送寒衣

YCH

【隔尾】
你說道少鹽欠醋無滋味
加料添椒纔脆美
但願娘親蚤痊濟
飲湯一盃勝甘露灌體
得一個身子平安倒大來喜

【賀新郎】
一箇道你請喫
一箇道婆先喫
這言語我聽也難聽
我可是氣也不氣
想他家與咱家有甚的親和戚
怎不記舊日夫妻情意
曾有百縱千隨
婆婆也你莫不爲黃金浮世寶
白髮故人稀
因此上把舊恩情全不比新知契
則待要百年同穴
那里肯千里送寒衣

KMC
"Separated Coda"
You say
It lacks salt, is missing vinegar, has
   no taste at all,
And that I must add some seasoning,
   put in some pepper before it is
   smacking good.
I just want my mother to heal
   swiftly—
Drinking a cup of ragout
Is better than sweet dew pouring
   over the body.
   You
Three can still rejoice over your
   happy union!

"Congratulating the Bridegroom"
   One says
"Old master, you eat first,"
   One says
"Oh, madam, you first,"
   This language I
Have a hard time listening to—
   Even if I try
I can't stop getting angry!

YCH
"Separated Coda"
You say
It lacks salt, is missing vinegar, has
   no taste at all,
And that I must add some seasoning,
   put in some pepper before it is
   smacking good.
I just want my mother to heal
   swiftly—
Drinking a cup of ragout
Is better than sweet dew pouring
   over the body.
   If her
Whole body becomes well again,
   then I will greatly rejoice!

"Congratulating the Bridegroom"
   One says
"Please eat,"
   One says
"Oh, madam, you eat first."
   This language I
Have a hard time listening to—
   Even if I try
I can't stop getting angry!

These new relations by marriage are all happiness,
And never think about the principled way of husband and wife of olden days
Who truly were together always.
This rotten woman's
Heart is like floss tossed by the wind
Would she be willing to
Turn into a "husband-longing stone?"[43]
Old
Favor can never come up to this new happy match!

What kith or kin exists between our family and his?
Doesn't she remember the principled way of husband and wife of olden days
When they were together always?
Oh, mother,
Do you think yellow gold only a treasure of this floating world
And old friends so rare in white-haired age?
And because of this think
Old favor can never match newfound intimacy?

Tsang's changes won the acclaim of Meng Ch'eng-shun, who remarked on the opening lines of the aria "Congratulating the Bridegroom": "Superb. Superb. The tone of speaking of a true-to-life ardently filial young girl" 妙妙逼真烈孝女口氣.[44] He also applauded the changes that Tsang made in the second half of the couplet with the commentary,

> The lines in the original text, "This rotten woman's heart is like willow floss tossed by the wind, / Would she be willing to turn into a 'Husband-longing Stone'?" are not the kind of words a daughter-in-law should say to her mother-in-law (非媳婦說阿婆語). I have followed the Wuxing edition here.[45]

Now, it is apparent that such changes in language are not made randomly. But the question of why they were made is elusive. I had earlier suggested that they were made in this drama because it was dominated in the earlier edition by the metaphors of the commercial world. In terms of the larger agenda, I still believe that to be true. But I also now suggest that we cannot know, at the present level of investigation, whether the registers of language that Tsang Mao-hsün winnowed out are indicative of a unique characterization that needed to be changed or whether they simply violated the etiquette of discourse in polite literature.

Furthermore, we must also attempt to identify what is acceptable sociolect; that is, we must attempt to identify what are registers within a particular social level of characterization. This can be accomplished in special cases by paying attention to the so-called market language, a form of argot often used as a secret language to confuse and eventually bamboozle unwary hicks from the country or people who did not speak the standard local dialect.[46] We are fortunate to have a short passage from one of Chu Yutun's plays which exemplifies two points wonderfully. First is that it shows how this secret language of the guild can be used to confuse the unwary, but secondly it shows how little trust we can place in the relationship between the language of a text and its author. In this case we can positively identify the author, and since he was a royal prince we can be absolutely sure about his identity and his status. That he was able to reproduce such a passage in his own works testifies to the point that we must, above all, realize that the language of drama is *not* the speech of the author:

〔末云〕　且住再聽他說箇甚麼
〔淨云〕　大嫂你收了銀子了將前日落了人的一箇旗兒兩搭兒荒資把那膏資載一張
　　荒資荷葉了壓重處潛垛著休那著老婆子見
〔貼淨云〕　你的嗽我鼻涕了便去潛垛也
〔末云〕　小鬼他說的甚麼言語我不省的
〔小鬼云〕　他說旗兒是絹子荒資是紙膏資是刀兒荷葉了是包裹了壓重是櫃子潛垛
　　是藏了他說教他老婆將那落的人的絹子紙用刀兒截一張紙包裹了櫃子里藏了不
　　要他娘見那婦人說鼻涕了是省得了便去藏也
〔末云〕　他的市語聲嗽我也不省得你如何省得
〔小鬼云〕　小鬼自生時也是箇表背匠

Male lead speaks: Stop a minute! Listen to what she is saying again.

Clown speaks: Sister, have you got the silver yet? Take the flag that fell into our hands and the two loads of weed stuff, with our green stuff cut up a piece of weed stuff. After you lotus leaf it, sink it into a pile in a heavy place. Don't let the old lady see it.

Added clown speaks: My nose drips when I hear your sniffle. I'll go and sink it away.

Male lead speaks: Sprite—what did he say, I can't comprehend it.

Sprite speaks: The "flag" he talked about is silk, the "weed stuff" is paper, "green stuff" is a knife, "lotus leafing" is packing it away, a "heavy place" is a cabinet, and "to sink it away" is to hide it. He told that old woman to take that silk and paper that fell into their hands, then cut a piece of paper with a knife to wrap it up, and then to hide it in a cabinet, so that his wife doesn't see it. What the woman meant when she said "my nose drips" was that she understood him, and then she went and hid it.

Male lead speaks: I don't know what this kind of market talk means; how do you know?

Sprite speaks: When I was alive, I was a craftsman who mounted paintings.[47]

Another way to solve this problem of register and provenance of language is to place the language of drama within a larger framework of the development of northern language as the written medium of fiction and drama. As far as I know, the most impressive advances in this field have been made by Chang Hui-ying, whose fieldwork in dialects and textual work in the *Chin P'ing Mei* have helped solve some of the problems of language use. In her work on *The Story of the Western Wing*,[48] she has made several important discoveries by comparing the use of words in the Tung Chieh-yüan All Keys and Modes version, Wang Shih-fu's version, and the *Chin P'ing Mei*. Among several examples, she has pointed out the use of a set of homophones (or close homophones) meaning the male organ, but used as a curse word: t'úi 頹, t'úi 飈, and t'ŭi 腿.

老夫人說著長老喚太醫來看我我這頹證候非是太醫所治的則除是那小姐美甘甘香噴噴涼滲滲嬌滴滴一點唾津兒嚥下去這 • 病便可.⁴⁹

Idema and I translated it as:

The madam tells me that the abbot has called a physician to examine me. But these shitty conditions can't be cured by just any physician. If only I could swallow down one drop of my missy's sweetly, sweetly delicious, aromatically, aromatically perfumed, piercingly, piercingly cool, dripping, dropping, lovable spittle, then this fucking illness would be over.⁵⁰

Chang Hsiang, in his groundbreaking work on the vocabulary of poetry and drama, could only deduce that the word meant more than "wilting" or "emaciated." He referred to its use in the *san-ch'ü* suite "A Country Bumpkin Knows Naught of the Theater" 莊家不識枸欄, where it occurs in the phrase *lü-t'ui* 驢頹, which he correctly surmised meant the penis of a donkey. But his conclusion leaves some doubt: "Is it that the word *t'ui* originally meant something vile or base that it was used to signify the penis of a donkey or a horse? Or was it that it first meant the penis of a donkey or horse and then was construed to mean vile or base?"⁵¹ Wang Chi-ssu, in his notes, correctly identifies the word *t'ui* as a dialect word (still in use) that means penis.⁵² Chang Hui-ying carries the investigation further to the *Chin P'ing Mei*, where she elicits nine passages in which the word used is t'ŭi 腿 rather than one of the two true homophones. This, in turn, solves a problem with understanding the following lines from the Yüan play *Sending the Wrong Person the Mandarin Duck Covers at the Convent of Jade Clarity*:

【張瑞卿云】 若是小生負了心呵小姑頭上生碗來大疔瘡干我甚麼腿事⁵³

Chang Jui-ch'ing speaks: If I am ungrateful and carbuncles as big as bowls grow on your head, what fucking affair is it of mine?

While other dictionaries have improved on Chang Hsiang⁵⁴ and have come to the same conclusions as Chang Hui-ying, they lack the kind of substantial fieldwork in dialects—in this case Wenchow, Shanghai, Ch'ung-ming Island, and Fuchien—that offers more than conjecture and provides solid evidence.

The fact that many of the curse words, maledicta, and taboo vocabulary of Yüan drama are also found in fiction that is clearly the product of Suchow writers and that so much of it is also still extant in other dialects (mainly southern) leads to some interesting conclusions. How much of "northern drama" is actually the product of southerners? Does the same hold true for drama as for fiction—is it actually a form that is supposed to be written in northern dialect, but into which the taboo vocabulary of its southern authors creeps? I am not aware of any single study that tests the phonology of the so-called Yüan editions against that of the KMC or the YCH texts. How far will a careful phonological analysis, tested against the ideal patterns of the *Chung-yüan yin-yün*, carry us, for instance, into discovering not only regional differences but also levels of language in the plays?

Such detailed knowledge of a period's language, while difficult to obtain, is essential if we are to spot what is conventional and enduring in a single text and what is original. We cannot deduce "the play." As I have remarked about *Tou E Yüan*,

> Drama as performance is essentially public property and subject to free interpretation and reinterpretation on stage. As a play, *Tou E Yüan* exists as an abstract entity that can be tied to one or to several texts but is independent of all written sources, except as those sources are adapted for oral presentation. No text is the equal of any one play—being only a portion of its staging—and in changes of time and place texts may show the influence of actors' delivery, of audience's reception, or of writer's memory.

When Idema and I decided to accentuate, without bringing to center stage, the level of sexual punning that runs like a minor chord through *The Story of the Western Wing*, or when I chose to translate *The Wrongs to Beauty Tou*, using the *Ku-ming-chia* edition, those choices were made on the notion that we, or I, could deduce a consistency in language choice and usage that was specific to a single editon. A further assumption is that this specificity will reflect the values of the culture that gave it life.

Chin Sheng-t'an's, Tsang Mao-hsün's, and especially Meng Ch'eng-shun's recensions are superb reading dramas. They offer the reader a sophisticated and elegant rendition of *The Story of the Western Wing* or of *Tou E Yüan*. If we are honest with our audience we tell them that these are Ming or Ch'ing plays, heavily redacted for reading pleasure, edited by a literatus intent on imposing his view of the text or of the northern tradition of drama on his contemporaries,[55] rewritten to make their diction more palatable to literati readers. While I do not claim to have discovered a performing text in the case of *Tou E Yüan*, for instance, I do believe that it will reflect the values of its urban consumers, who were also probably the audience of the urban theater. If we are interested in giving our own readership a cultural document closer to the values of those who might have seen that complex of events—both oral and kinetic—that we call "the play" on stage, then we must attempt to isolate the linguistic and representational structures of the earlier texts. We must decide whether the language of those texts represents a sociolect that is distinct from the literati version; we also must determine if the values it represents are the shared values of the commercial world that breathed life into the public stage and whether they are antagonistic to or subversive of high culture. And, if so, if they are in a broadly accepted but little understood or consciously and artistically created contradistinction to the values of that culture.

Even shorn of the issue of editions or the level of culture that an edition and its language might reflect, the very act of embodying in another language a complex text is enormously knotty, and in the end not helped much by what I might have to say. But as the literary genre most closely tied to the values of a social group and most enmeshed in the process of collective negotiation between producer and consumer, drama challenges us as translators. If we skip the initial step of decoding the context and linguistic structure of each edition that confronts us and of linking it to its provenance, we risk misleading our own readership. While we may provide them with a good literary work, interesting to read in isolation, we will have failed to give them a full document from a rich, varied, and interconnected world of language and culture that is associated with early drama's rise. And having failed that, we commit even grosser errors when we use these Ming and Ch'ing recensions—without considering their provenance—as documents to resurrect the literary, cultural, or stage life of a far earlier period.

NOTES

1. What I have in mind here is the difference between simply one more popular translation of a vintage nature poet like Wang Wei brought out in a popular paperback series and something of the quality and extensiveness of David Knechtges's work on the *Wen xuan*.

2. See Stephen H. West and Wilt L. Idema, *The Moon and the Zither; Wang Shifu's Story of the Western Wing* (Berkeley: University of California Press, 1990).

3. See Stephen H. West, "A Study in Appropriation: Zang Maoxun's Injustice to Dou E," *Journal of the American Oriental Society*, 111, no. 2 (April–June 1991), 283–302.

4. On Tsang Mao-hsün and his literary works, see Hsü Shuo-fang 徐朔方, "Tsang Mao-hsün he t'a-te *Yüan-ch'ü hsüan*" 臧懋循和他的元曲選, in *Chung-kuo ku-tien hsiao-shuo hsi-ch'ü lun-chi* 中國古典小說戲曲論集, ed. Chao Ching-shen 趙景深 (Shanghai: Shang-hai ku-chi ch'u-pan-she, 1985), 51–82, and his "Tsang Mao-hsün nien-p'u" 臧懋循年譜, in *Ku-chi cheng-li yü yen-chiu* 古籍整理與研究 (Peking: Chung-hua shu-chü, 1989), vol. 4, 185–208; Hsü Fu-ming 徐扶明, "Tsang Mao-hsün yu *Yüan-ch'ü hsüan*" 臧懋循與元曲選, in *Yüan tsa-chü lun-chi* 元雜劇論集 (T'ien-chin: Pai-hua wen-i ch'u-pan-she, 1985), 142–149 (originally published December 2, 1956, in *Kuang-ming jih-pao* 光明日報); Cheng Ch'ien 鄭騫, "Tsang Mao-hsün kai-ting Yüan tsa-chü p'ing-i" 臧懋循改訂元雜劇評議, *Wen-shih-che hsüeh-pao* 文史哲學報 10 (1961); see also Chang Hui-ying 張惠英, "*Chin P'ing Mei* ti yü-yen yü tso-che" 金瓶梅的語言與作者, *Hsü-chou chiao-yü hsüeh-yüan hsüeh-pao* 徐州教育學院學報 2 (1989): 38–41, on Tsang's possible editorship of the *Chin P'ing Mei*.

5. As West and Idema, *The Story of the Western Wing*, pp. 24–25, state:

The earliest translation [of *The Story of the Western Wing*] into a European language is the French version by the eminent sinologue Stanislas Julien, which first appeared in 1872 in the pages of the periodical *Atsume Gusa* and was reissued in 1880 in book form as *Si-siang-ki; ou, L'histoire du pavillon d'occident, comédie en seize actes.* From the very start of his career, Julien had been a student and translator of Yüan drama. In 1839 he translated Ji Junxiang's *Orphan of Zhao* (*Zhaoshi gu'er*) in an attempt to redress the eighteenth-century prejudices against Chinese drama that stemmed from Prémare's earlier rendition, and his translation of Li Xingdao's *Chalk Circle (Huilan ji)* indirectly influenced Bertolt Brecht in his conception of *Der kaukasische Kreidekreis.* Julien's *Si-siang-ki* was the crowning achievement of a lifelong involvement with Chinese vernacular literature. The next Western-language translation to appear was the German rendition of all five plays by Vincenz Hundhausen in 1926, entitled *Das Westzimmer, Ein chinesisches Singspiel aus dem dreizehnten Jahrhundert.* This is a very free adaptation in the German tradition of *Nachdichtung*, or "re-creation," which allows the translator a very wide leeway in superimposing his own thoughts and fancies on the text of his choice. Nevertheless, it caused quite a scandal upon its appearance: Hundhausen was accused by one reviewer of having plagiarized Julien's translation and in response sued the reviewer for libel. One way or another, many members of the German sinological community became involved in the imbroglio. In the midthirties, two English-language versions of *The Story of the Western Wing* appeared almost simultaneously. In 1936 Stanford University Press published Henry H. Hart's *The West Chamber, A Medieval Drama.* Hart limits himself to a translation of the first four plays and even omits the final act of the fourth play since "it is an anticlimax and adds nothing to the interest of the play." In his preface Hart chides Hundhausen for casting his rendition of the arias into rhymed couplets, calling it "an effort which more often than not distorts the sense of the original." Hart accordingly presents the arias as free verse. Ironically, Hart's version has been "poeticized" by Henry W. Wells, who published an adaptation of Hart's translation in 1972 in which all prose passages have been recast into blank verse and all arias have been rhymed. Hart's rendition was preceded a year earlier by the publication of another, soon-to-become-standard translation, S. I. Hsiung's *Romance of the Western Chamber*, which includes all five plays. It was reissued as late as 1968 by Columbia University Press with a new introduction by C. T. Hsia, who regrets that the translator relies on the Jin Shengtan edition rather than one of the earlier Ming editions. Although Hsia credits Hsiung with having done "a conscientious job of reproducing in English the paraphrasable meaning of his adopted text," he makes it abundantly clear that in his opinion the translator has failed to do justice to the stylistic variety of his original. We should not forget, however, that whatever the modern view may be, for their times and for the sources then available these earlier translations constitute quite creditable, even excellent, achievements.

See also Wang Li-na 王麗娜, "*Hsi-hsiang-chi* ti wai-wen i-pen he Man Meng wen i-pen" 西廂記的外文譯本和滿蒙文譯本, *Wen-hsüeh i-ch'an* 文學遺產, 1981, no. 3, 148–154; and Chiang Hsing-yü 蔣星煜, "*Hsi-hsiang-chi* ti jih-wen i-pen" 西廂記的日文譯本, *Wen-hsüeh i-ch'an* 文學遺產, 1982, no. 3, 32. On translations into Western languages, see Erich Haenisch, "Review of Vincenz Hundhausen, *Das Westzimmer, Ein chinesisches Singspiel in deutscher Sprache*," *Asia Major* 8 (1932): 278–282. See Wang Shih-fu 王實甫, *The Romance of the Western Chamber*, trans. S. I. Hsiung, with a critical introduction by C. T. Hsia (New York: Columbia University Press), 1968; *Si-siang-ki; ou, L'histoire du pavillon d'occident, comédie en seize actes,* trans. Stanislas Julien (Geneva: H. Georg.–Th. Mueller), 1872–1880; *The West Chamber, A Medieval Drama,* trans. Henry H. Hart (Stanford: Stanford University Press), 1936; *The West Chamber (Hsi-hsiang chi),* rendered into English verse by Henry W. Wells, in *Four Classical Asian Plays in Modern Translation,* ed. Vera Rushforth Irwin, 95–230; *Das Westzimmer, Ein chinesisches Singspiel aus dem dreizehnten Jahrhundert,* trans. Vincenz Hundhausen (Eisenach: Erich Roth Verlag, 1926). Hundhausen went on to produce a *Nachdichtung* of Tang Xianzu's famous sentimental melodrama, *The Peony Pavilion,* in 1933.

6. John Ching-yu Wang, *Chin Sheng-t'an,* provides a succinct but lucid survey of Jin's life and criticism.

7. At least three recent typeset editions of Chin Shengtan's version of the play are available: Chin Sheng-t'an 金聖嘆, *Kuan-hua-t'ang ti-liu ts'ai-tzu shu Hsi-hsiang chi* 貫華堂第六才子書西廂記, annotated by Ts'ao Fang-jen 曹方人 (Nanking: Chiang-su ku-chi ch'u-pan-she, 1986); *Kuan-hua-t'ang ti-liu ts'ai-tzu shu Hsi-hsiang chi,* annotated by Fu Hsiao-hang 傅曉航 (Lanchow: Kan-su jen-min ch'u-pan-she, 1985); *Chin Sheng-t'an p'i-pen Hsi-hsiang chi* 金聖嘆批本西廂記, collated by Chang Kuo-kuang 張國光 (Shanghai: Shang-hai ku-chi ch'u-pan-she, 1986).

8. See Stephen H. West, "Mongol Influence in the Rise of Northern Drama," in *China under Mongol Rule,* ed. J. D. Langlois (Princeton: Princeton University Press, 1980).

9. The two most influential works on the history of Yüan drama, Wang Kuo-wei's *Sung Yüan hsi-ch'ü k'ao* 宋元戲曲考 and Yoshikawa Kōjirō's 吉川幸次郎 (*Gen zatsugeki kenkyū* 元雜劇研究, are written entirely on the basis of material presented in Tsang's anthology. Wang cannot really be faulted, since he did not have the 200-odd plays from the *Mo-wang kuan* collection available to him, but Yoshikawa simply chose to follow Tsang's texts in preference to others. Yoshikawa's many judgments about what are and what are not characteristics of Yüan drama should therefore be highly suspect, as should be virtually all Western-language works on drama that exclusively use the editions of *Yüan-ch'ü hsüan* as a basis for textual or literary analysis of Yüan popular texts.

10. For the texts of these early plays, see Cheng Ch'ien (collator and annotator), *Chiao-ting Yüan-k'an tsa-chü san-shih-chung* 校訂元刊雜劇三十種 (Taipei: Shih-chieh shu-chü, 1962); Hsü Ch'in-chün 徐沁君 (collator and annotator), *Hsin-chiao Yüan-k'an tsa-chü san-shih-chung* 新校元刊雜劇三十種, 2 vols. (Peking: Chung-kuo hsi-chü ch'u-pan-she, 1980); and Ning Hsi-yüan 寧希元 (collator and annotator), *Yüan-k'an tsa-chü san-shih-chung hsin-chiao* 元刊雜劇三十種新校, vol. 1 (Lan-chou ta-hsüeh ku-chi cheng-li ts'ung-k'an 蘭州大學古籍整理叢刊) (Lan-chou: Lan-chou ta-hsüeh ch'u-pan-she, 1988).

11. On the close relationship of customs and language in rural and urban life in China, see Ch'ü Yan-pin 曲彥斌, "Min-su yü-yen hsüeh ti hsiang-ts'un yü-yen yü ch'eng-shih yü-yen" 民俗語言學的鄉村語言與城市語言, *Min-su wen-i hsüeh-k'an* 民俗文藝學刊 3 (1987): 117–131.

12. West and Idema, *The Moon and the Zither,* 11. For discussions of these late Yüan–early Ming fragments, see, e.g., Tuan Mi-heng 段洣恆, "Hsin-pien chiao-cheng *Hsi-hsiang chi* ts'an-yeh ti fa-hsien" 新編校正西廂記殘頁的發現, *Hsi-chü yen-chiu* 戲曲研究 7 (1982): 261–268, which includes transcriptions and reproductions

of these fragments; Chiang Hsing-yü, "Hsin fa-hsien ti tsui-tsao *Hsi-hsiang chi* ts'an-yeh" 新發現的最早的西廂記殘頁, *Ming k'an-pen Hsi-hsiang chi yen-chiu* 明刊本西廂記研究 (Peking: Chung-kuo hsi-chü ch'u-pan-she, 1982) 20–25; Chou Hsü-keng 周續庚. "T'an *Hsin-pien chiao-cheng Hsi-hsiang chi* ts'an-yeh ti chia-chih" 談新編校正西廂記殘頁的價值, *Wen-hsüeh yi-ch'an* 文學遺產 1984, no. 1, 108–114.

13. West and Idema, *The Moon and the Zither*, 12:

The Hongzhi edition of Wang Shifu's work is preserved only in a single copy, unknown to the scholarly world until the late 1940s, when it was acquired by Yanjing University, from which it passed into the holdings of the Beijing University library. This very handsome edition was produced by a commercial publishing firm, the Yue family of Jintai, Beijing. The upper register of each page of the main text is graced by a continuous set of illustrations that occupy two-fifths of each page. These illustrations are of a fine quality, especially when compared to those in other Ming editions, and by themselves provide an interesting interpretative commentary on the text. It is clear from the publisher's advertisement that the illustrations are meant to provide visual clues to famous scenes onstage, but it is also clear that they represent the story itself and not any one performance.

See also the publisher's advertisement in Wang Shifu, *Hsin-k'an ch'i-miao ch'üan hsiang chu-shih Hsi-hsiang chi*, 161b, translated in West and Idema, *The Moon and the Zither*, 414–415.

14. There are several modern annotations, including Wang Chi-ssu's 王季思 masterpiece of modern philology, *Chi-p'ing chiao-chu Hsi-hsiang chi* 集評校注西廂記, annotated by Wang Chi-ssu and compiled by Chang Jen-he 張人和 (Shanghai: Shang-hai ku-chi ch'u-pan-she, 1987). Others include *Hsi-hsiang chi* 西廂記, annotated by Wu Hsiao-ling 吳曉鈴 (Peking: Tso-chia ch'u-pan-she, 1954); *Hsi-hsiang chi t'ung-su chu-shih* 西廂記通俗注釋 (Kunming: Yun-nan jen-min ch'u-pan-she, 1983); *Hsi-hsiang chi hsin-chu* 西廂記新注; annotated by Chang Yen-chin 張燕瑾 and Mi Sung-i 禰松頤 (Nan-chang: Chiang-hsi jen-min ch'u-pan-she, 1980).

15. West and Idema, *The Moon and the Zither*, 15:

Ling Mengchu (1580–1644) ... claims that his edition is based on an earlier one published by Zhu Youdun. Although this assertion may be just a sales pitch to assure buyers of a reliable and authentic text, the edition is indeed remarkable among late Ming printings for its close similarity in places to the Hongzhi edition—a text that, in turn, appears to imitate the editorial practices employed in Zhu Youdun's private printings of his own *zaju*. So Ling Mengchu might have based his edition on a copy of the Hongzhi edition—one missing the vulnerable final leaf of the second volume that carries the publisher's colophon, that is—and he might have concluded, on the evidence of similarities in editorial convention, that this edition was indeed prepared by Zhu Youdun.

16. West and Idema, *The Moon and the Zither*, 73: "the editor of the Hongzhi edition has sensibly noted the singer's name or role type after the tune title of each song. (At times the editor even provides instructions on *how* the song is to be delivered.)"

17. Wang Shifu 王實甫, *Hui-t'u hsin chiao-chu ku-pen Hsi-hsiang chi* 繪圖新校注古本西廂記, annotated and collated by Wang Chi-te 王驥德 (rpt. of 1614 woodblock ed., Peking: Fu-chien shu-she, Tung-lai-ke shu-tian, 1927).

18. On the issue of editions for Yüan drama generally, see Cheng Ch'ien, "Yüan Ming ch'ao k'e pen Yüan-jen tsa-ch'ü chiu-chung t'i-yao" 元明鈔刻本元人雜劇九種提要, *Ch'ing-hua hsüeh-pao* 清華學報 New Series 7 (1969): 145–155.

19. Of these sixty, forty-four are authentically those of Yüan writers. An older tradition, first mooted by Wang Kuo-wei 王國維, attributes the texts to Ch'en Yü-chiao 陳與郊. In recent years, however, the *Ku-ch'ü chai* 顧曲齋 editions were discovered; they bear a preface by *Yü-yang hsien-shih* and two seals that can be positively identified as those belonging to Wang Chi-te 王驥德 (i.e., those of his name and his studio's name, *pai-hsüeh chai* 白雪齊), show that *Yü-yang hsien-shih* was simply another studio name for Wang Chi-te. While others have been led to ascribe the KMC texts to Wang on the basis of this discovery, Cheng Ch'ien has concluded that based on the quality of the editions—the plays are sloppily edited and cut in an amateur manner, unlike the fine quality that marks Wang's other editions—these are really second-rate commercial texts that were attributed to Wang Chi-te simply to enhance the value of the texts on the market. (That is, in respect to the physical quality of the edition.) Fifty-five of the plays are found in the *Mo-wang kuan ch'ao-chiao pen Ku Chin tsa-chü* 脈望館鈔校本古今雜劇. Extant editions in the Nanking and Peking libraries together total sixty-five plays, but thirteen other plays mentioned in the table of contents are completely missing. These plays are most easily available in *Ku-pen hsi-ch'ü ts'ung-k'an* 古本戲曲叢刊 4th ser., vols. 9–92.

20. Tsang Mao-hsün, *Yüan-ch'ü hsüan*, 4 vols. (Peking: Chung-hua shu-chü, 1979 [reprint of 1958 ed.]) is the usual edition of citation.

21. While the term *p'ien-hsin* 偏心 in modern Chinese means "partial" or "biased," the meaning of this term here is clearly something like "to follow the dictates of one's own mind-heart." It is probably somewhat analogous to the use of *hsin-chieh* 心趄, which means to be fickle or insincere or to be changeable of mind; see *Tung Chieh-yüan Hsi-hsiang chi chu-kung-tiao* 董解元西廂記諸宮調 (Master Tung's *Story of the Western Wing* in all keys and modes), where it occurs in the phrase, 一向志誠不道他心趄 ("She has always been sincere in her ambition; don't say that she is fickle"). See Ling Ching-yen 凌景埏, annotator, *Tung Chieh-yüan Hsi-hsiang chi* (Peking: Chung-hua shu-chü, 1962), 153 n. 36.

22. For information on these changes and collations of editions, see Cheng Ch'ien 鄭騫, "Tsang Mao-hsün kai-ting Yüan tsa-chü p'ing-i" 臧懋循改訂元雜劇評議, *Wen-shih-che hsüeh-pao* 文史哲學報 10 (1961): 2–12. See also Liang P'ei-chin 梁沛錦 and Hatano Tarō 波多野太郎, *Kuan Han-ch'ing hsien-ts'un tsa-chü yen-chiu* 關漢卿現存雜劇研究, in *Yokohama Shiritsu daigaku kiyō* 橫濱私立大學紀要 2 (1971); and Cheng Ch'ien, "Kuan Han-ch'ing *Tou E Yüan* tsa-chü i-pen pi-chiao" 關漢卿竇娥冤雜劇異本比較, *Ta-lu tsa-chi* 大陸雜誌 29, nos. 10 and 11 (1964): 105–110. For collations and a study of the text, see *Pei-ching ta-hsüeh chung-wen-hsi Kuan Han-ch'ing hsi-chü chi pien-chiao hsiao-tsu* 北京大學中文系關漢卿戲劇集編校小組, ed., *Kuan Han-ch'ing hsi-ch'ü chi* 關漢卿戲劇集 (Peking: Jen-min wen-hsüeh ch'u-pan-she, 1975); Shih Chung-wen, *Injustice to Tou ó (Tou ó Yüan); A Study and Translation* (Cambridge: University Press, 1972); Wu Hsiao-ling 吳曉鈴 et al., *Kuan Han-ch'ing hsi-ch'ü chi* 關漢卿戲劇集 (Peking: Chung-hua shu-chü, 1956); Tseng Yung-i 曹永義, ed., *Kan-t'ian tung-ti Tou E yüan* 感天動地竇娥冤, *Ku-chin wen-hsüan* 古今文選, New Series 372 (1976): 2147–2154; 374 (1976): 2163–2170; 378 (1976): 2195–2202; 400 (1977): 2371–2378. Each act is followed by the appropriate section from Cheng Ch'ien's collation as found in "*Kuan Han-ch'ing Tou E yüan* tsa-chü i-pen p'i-chiao

關漢卿竇娥冤雜劇異本比較," *Ta-lu tsa-chi* 大陸雜誌 29, nos. 10 and 11 (1964): 105–110.

23. According to T'ao Tsung-i 陶宗儀, *Nan-ts'un cho-keng lu* 南村輟耕錄 (Peking: Chung-hua shu-chü, 1958), 14, in the section entitled "Married Women are Called *Niang* 婦女曰娘," this was a term for low-class married women: "Low status married women are called such-and-such *niang*, or such-and-such-a-number *niang*. To really denigrate them, they are called *p'o-niang* 謂婦人之卑賤者曰某娘曰幾娘鄙之曰婆娘." There is obviously a homophonic play on the phrase *p'o-niang* 潑娘, which is also a vile term for women.

24. See Perng Ching-hsi, *Double Jeopardy: A Critique of Seven Yüan Courtroom Dramas* (Ann Arbor: University of Michigan Center for Chinese Studies, 1978), 119–120, and West, "A Study in Appropriation: Zang Maoxun's Injustice to Dou E."

25. West, "A Study in Appropriation: Zang Maoxun's Injustice to Dou E."

26. This value reappears, for instance, in the *Mulian* play, where the real crime of Madame Liu, is above all else her failure to keep her word to her son. The issue of commodification also stamps all of the courtesan sing-song plays of the Yüan and Ming period, and even the great drama *The Story of the Western Wing*, where Oriole laments her status as "goods to be sold at a loss."

27. West, "A Study in Appropriation: Zang Maoxun's Injustice to Dou E."

28. Ibid.

29. Ibid.; see also Cheng Ch'ien, "Tsang Mao-hsün kai-ting Yüan tsa-chü p'ing-i," 2.

30. For instance, see Chao Ching-shen 趙景深, "Yüan-ch'ü ti erh-pen," 元曲的二本., in *Chung-kuo hsi-ch'ü ch'u-t'an* 中國戲曲初探 (*Chung-kuo ku-tai li-lun ts'ung-shu*), ed. Wang Hung-lu 王鴻盧 (Loyang: Chung-chou shu-hua-she, 1983), 87–90. This was also a theme in Tseng Yong-yih's early work; see esp. *Chung-kuo hsi-chü lun-wen chi* 中國戲劇論文集 (Taipei: Lien-ching chu-p'an-she, 1975).

31. Wang Chi-ssu 王季思, "Sung Yüan chiang-ch'ang wen-hsüeh ti t'e-shu yung-yü" 宋元講唱文學的特殊用語, in *Ku-tai wen-hsüeh li-lun yen-chiu ts'ung-k'an* 古代文學理論研究叢刊 (Shanghai: Ku-chi ch'u-pan-she, 1981), 265.

32. Cheng Ch'ien, "Tsang Mao-hsün kai-ting Yüan tsa-chü p'ing-i," 2.

33. Reconstructions based on Ning Chi-fu 寧繼福, *Chung-yüan yin-yün piao-kao* 中原音韻表稿, 1982.

34. Wang Chi-ssu, "Sung Yüan chiang-ch'ang wen-hsüeh ti t'e-shu yung-yü," 267.

35. Ibid., 268. As Chang Hui-ying has suggested in her work on the *Chin P'ing Mei*, we should keep in mind that many works are authored by speakers of southern dialects but are written in the dialect of the areas in which the novels are placed. In such cases, the intrusion of the author's local dialect is unavoidable. While her evidence derives mainly from the *Chin P'ing Mei*, Tsang Mao-hsün, though an ardent supporter of northern dialect and drama, also made decisions about the language of the *Yüan-ch'ü hsüan* based on the principles of his local dialect.

36. The quotation is from Huang K'o 黃克 (compiler, from notes he took in Hsü's class on Yüan drama), in "Yüan-ch'ü yü-shih yen-chiu ts'an-k'ao shu-mu" 元曲語釋研究參考書目, *Hsü Cheng-yang wen-ts'un* 徐政語文存, ed. Chou Ju-ch'ang 周汝昌 (Peking: Chung-hua shu-chü, 1984), 132; on *p'en-tiao* as torture, see Hsü's own notes in "Sung Yüan hsiao-shuo hsi-ch'ü yü-shih (I)," 宋元小說戲曲語釋, in ibid., 10.

37. Hsü was a victim of the Cultural Revolution. According to the preface written by his good friend Chou Ju-ch'ang, he was hounded to death by the Red Guards and the Gang of Four. The act that finally broke his spirit was the destruction of over 10,000 cards that Hsü had accumulated from reading Sung and Yüan texts in preparation for a fully annotated version of the *Tung-ching meng Hua lu*.

38. Ibid., 131.

39. See his "Shih-yü hui-ch'ao," in *Han-shang i-wen ts'un* 漢上遺文宧存 (Shanghai: Wen-i ch'u-pan-she, 1980), 117–150. (This book's title and several pages were misprinted as *Han-shang-huan wen-ts'un* 漢上宧文存.)

40. Wang Shih-fu, *Hsin-k'an ch'i-miao ch'üan-hsiang chu-shih Hsi-hsiang chi* 新刊奇妙全相註釋西廂記 (rpt. of 1498 woodblock ed., Shanghai: Shang-wu yin-shu-kuan, 1955). (Title on inside leaf: *Hsin-k'an ta-tzu k'uei-pen ch'üan-hsiang ts'an-tseng ch'i-miao chu-shih Hsi-hsiang chi* 新刊大字魁本全相參增奇妙註釋西廂記; reprinted as *Hsin-k'an ch'i-miao ch'üan-hsiang chu-shih Hsi-hsiang chi* 新刊奇妙全相註釋西廂記 in *Ku-pen hsi-ch'ü ts'ung-k'an* 古本戲曲叢刊, lst ser., vols, 1–2, in both texts, I.1.36a.)

41. Wang Chi-te, quoting Hsü Shih-fan 徐士範 in Wang Shih-fu, *Hui-t'u hsin chiao-chu ku-pen Hsi-hsiang chi*, 1.7b.

42. See Wang Chi-ssu's note in *Chi-p'ing chiao-chu Hsi-hsiang chi* 集評校注西廂記, annotated by Wang Chi-ssu 王季思 and compiled by Chang Jen-he 張人和 (Shanghai: Shang-hai ku-chi ch'u-pan-she, 1987), 13, and Chiang Hsing-yü, "'Tian-pu-la' wei mei-yü mei-nü k'ao 顛不剌爲美玉美女考," *Hsi-hsiang chi k'ao-cheng* 西廂記考證 (Shanghai: Shang-hai ku-chi ch'u-pan-she, 1988), 173–180.

43. From the story of a woman who watched so intently from a hilltop for her husband's return that she was turned to stone.

44. Meng Chengshun 孟稱舜, *Tou E yüan* 竇娥寃, Lei-chiang chi 酹江集, *Ku-chin ming-chü he-hsüan* 古今名劇合選 (*Ku-pen hsi-ch'ü ts'ung-k'an* ed.) ser. 4, 15a.

45. Ibid., 15b.

46. Ch'ien's article accumulates several quotes about Hangchow guild members using such language to deceive people from other places. See esp. 132–133, where he cites two works copied from T'ien Ju-ch'eng's 田汝成 *Hsi-hu yu-lan chih yü* 西湖游覽志語, the *Li-yüan shih-yü* 梨園市語 and the *Ssu-p'ing shih-yü* 四平市語, which in turn quotes from T'ao Tsung-i's *Cho-keng lu*.

47. See Chu Yu-tun 朱有燉, *Ch'iao-tuan kuei* 喬斷鬼, in *Ch'eng-chai yüeh-fu* 誠齋樂府 (She-mo-t'a shih ch'ü-ts'ung ed.), vol. 2, cited in Ch'ien Nan-yang, "Shih-yü hui-ch'ao," 134–135.

48. Unpublished manuscript, *Hsi-hsiang su-yü li-shih* 西廂俗語例釋.

49. 108b.

50. West and Idema, *The Moon and the Zither*, 317.

51. Chang Hsiang 張相, *Shih tz'u ch'ü yü-tz'u hui-shih* 詩詞曲語辭匯釋, 2d ed. (Hong Kong: Chung-hua shu-ch'ü, 1973), 528–529.

52. Wang Shih-fu, *Chi-p'ing chiao-chu Hsi-hsiang chi*, 123.

53. Tsang Mao-hsün, ed., *Yü-ch'ing an ts'uo-sung yüan-yang pei* 玉清菴錯送鴛鴦被, in *Yüan-ch'ü hsüan* 元曲選 (Peking: Chung-hua shu-chü, 1958), vol. 1, 60.

54. For instance, the *Sung Yüan tz'u-tien* 宋元辭典 (Shanghai: Shang-wu yin-shu-kuan, 1984) also identifies *t'ui* as the penis and goes on to remark on its use as an expletive or curse word; see 942.

55. See esp. Tsang's prefaces to the *Yüan-ch'ü hsüan*.

Translating Ming Plays

Lumudan (The Green Peony)

CYRIL BIRCH

One of the practical issues that I raised in my keynote address to this conference (see "Reflections of a Working Translator" in this volume) was the question of partial translation or abridgment. As a test case I put forward some of those long, rambling, and often quite uneven *chuanqi* plays of the late Ming–early Qing period. While it may be reasonable to expect a superb masterpiece like Tang Xianzu's *Mudanting* or Hong Sheng's *Changshengdian* to prove attractive to the Anglophone reader, there are simply too many plays of the second rank that would surely turn out to be, as I suggested, oppressively pedantic, repetitious, and boring. Yet the delights to be found among these works should not be allowed to stay hidden forever. Perhaps the day will come when the entire oeuvre of a dramatist such as Wu Bing will be available in English translation to a public which has acquired sufficient familiarity with the life and culture of traditional China to enjoy them. But I believe this day is not yet here, and meanwhile I propose the translation of selected scenes as a worthwhile stopgap solution.

In the later part of my "Reflections" I briefly described two of Wu Bing's five plays. *Xiyuanji* (The West Garden) is, I believe, of a nature and quality to merit complete translation, the sooner the better; *Lumudan* (The Green Peony) is a different matter. It contains much wit and beauty and some scenes of hilarious comedy both high and low; but it is, in my view, too specifically aimed at a particular feature of late Ming life, the abuse of the examination system of official selection, to be enjoyable to readers who have not to some degree specialized in the study of Chinese history and literature. What I propose would be to translate a single scene or a selection of scenes and to attempt to make this small sampling of the play intelligible and enjoyable for the general reader by providing the appropriate kind of introductory material. This essay presents a draft translation of one scene from *The Green Peony* (Scene 18, "Alcove Quiz") preceded by the kind of introductory comments I believe to be needed for its enjoyment.

The first requirement is to define the mode of the play. This is in fact about the last decision critics make, since it relies on their conception of the entire play and a process of comparison with various other plays known to them. They get little help from traditional criticism in this regard, since Chinese plays were usually categorized either by theme type or by (subjectively determined) lyrical quality. In defining *The Green Peony* as a stylish romantic comedy with a strong component of satire, I draw on a rough comparison with the nearest play in English, *Much Ado about Nothing*. Parallels among the comic devices used are interesting but not nearly as illuminating as the total dissimilarity in the nature of the villains. The clownish "villains" of *The Green Peony* are in fact the butts of the satire; they reveal the author's underlying purpose to be the attack on abuses of the examination system.

To introduce an extract, a synopsis of the action of the whole play is no doubt helpful, but since this is also the most boring thing one can do, it should be done as briefly as possible. The new Chinese Encyclopedia (*Zhongguo Da Baike Quanshu*; Beijing and Shanghai, 1983) contains an excellent brief synopsis, and this I borrow, modifying my translation by identifying the role types of the dramatis personae. This permits me then to exhibit the overall structure of the action as a pattern of pairs and triangles, a kind of complicated minuet in which the leading characters evolve from three pairs of friends into two triangles of potential marital partners.

Wit, as in *Much Ado*, is the prime criterion for the pairing of the lovers of *The Green Peony*, but the preoccupation with examination prowess means that wit must be defined here as poetic ability. One of the outstanding literary features of the play is indeed the way in which the poems composed by the protagonists stand as surrogates for these young people, who, under the kind of segregation common to late Ming households, have never set eyes on each other. The importance of these poems to the pattern of action and to the total impact of the play requires that they be translated and analyzed in detail, even for the purpose of introducing a single scene in which the only poem to appear is a piece of almost senseless doggerel.

The ideal introduction would include some trenchant comments on the traditional examination system itself; for the present purpose I substitute a brief reference to Wu Bing's own experience of and concern with this dominant feature of his society.

To begin, then, with our brief synopsis: Shen Zhong (*wai*, or FATHER), scholar of the Hanlin Academy, forms a literary club in order to select a husband for his daughter Wan'e (*xiaodan*, or COMPANION). In a club meeting held in the format of a literary examination, each member composes a quatrain on the set topic, "the green peony." Liu Wuliu (*jing*, or VILLAIN) deputes his resident tutor, Xie Ying (*sheng*, or HERO), to supply his poem for him, while Che Shanggong (*chou*, or CLOWN) asks his sister Jingfang (*dan*, or HEROINE) to ghostwrite his; only Gu Can (*xiaosheng*, or FRIEND) composes his own poem. HERO and HEROINE fall in love upon reading each other's poems, but for much of the action HEROINE confuses the identities of HERO and VILLAIN. After viva voce examination, the machinations of VILLAIN and CLOWN are exposed. HERO and FRIEND pass high on the list of the official examinations, and in the finale HERO and HEROINE, FRIEND and COMPANION are joined in marriage.

This simple synopsis shows us seven principals. If we exclude the FATHER we are left with six young people who in the course of the action perform an elaborate minuet of groupings. There are, first of all, three pairings in terms of the traditional role types of Chinese opera. HERO (juvenile lead) and FRIEND (secondary male character) are *sheng* and *xiaosheng*, HEROINE and COMPANION are *dan* and *xiaodan*, and VILLAIN and CLOWN are *jing* and *chou*. In each of these pairs the person listed first takes the leading position. HERO must mate ultimately with HEROINE, FRIEND with COMPANION; and in the machinations of the negative characters the initiative is taken always by VILLAIN while CLOWN plays the sidekick part. In this way we get two new pairings, of the marital kind, while the VILLAIN–CLOWN combination remains unchanged and unloved through to the end of the play, which finds them appropriately dishonored and discomfited.

The six young people form also, it will readily be seen, two triangles. The VILLAIN, as chief negative character, has set his sights on the female lead, the HEROINE, so that we have a triangle of HERO–HEROINE–VILLAIN. The CLOWN, since the HEROINE is his own sister, must center his desires on the secondary female figure, the heroine's COMPANION, which gives us a second triangle of FRIEND–COMPANION–CLOWN. We may diagram the pattern of these groupings as follows:

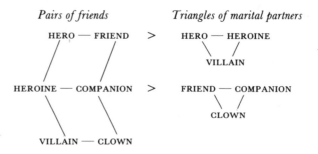

| *Pairs of friends* | *Triangles of marital partners* |

At this point we may look more closely at the boy-girl pairings. The matches of the lovers are made on the basis of the quality of their wit, as displayed in poetic composition. Significantly, their status as wits, and therefore as lovers, is exactly the reverse of the social position they occupy at the beginning of the play. HERO Xie Ying might in fact be described as a refugee, the scion of a family displaced from the Northern Song capital of Bianjing (modern Kaifeng) by the "crossing to the south" when the dynasty retreated to Linan (Hangzhou), yielding up most of the lands north of the Yangzi to the Jin dynasty of the Jurchen invaders. Xie Ying now occupies the unenviable position of a poor dependent tutor in the household of the rich wastrel Liu Wuliu (VILLAIN). Our HERO is thus on a distinctly inferior social level to that of his FRIEND, Gu Can. This young literatus is associated with Xie Ying only by virtue of shared interest in fine writing, but he is an old family friend of the distinguished Hanlin academician Shen Zhong (FATHER in our schema).

As with the men, so with the young women. HEROINE Che Jingfang is presented to us merely as the improbably talented sister of the CLOWN Che Shanggong. Their parents are deceased, and although Che Shanggong is evidently rich enough to keep up with Liu Wuliu, his companion, in the classic pursuits of drinking, gambling, and whoring, Liu himself reflects (in a monologue early in Scene 16) that Che Jingfang would not compare with COMPANION Shen Wan'e as a marital catch. Again, the supreme social ranking is that of FATHER Shen Zhong. Like the HERO, our HEROINE Che Jingfang also must rely on superior literary skill rather than social status to justify her leading part in the action of the play.

Since the exercise of wit in poetic composition is the determining factor in the pairing of these lovers, it is clear that anyone wishing to present this play to English readers would have to be very careful in translating the poems composed by the lead characters. I should like now to give my translation of a few brief extracts from the play to illustrate my point.

A series of poems carries the identities of the principals, acting as it were as surrogates for them when social proprieties prevent them, boy and girl, from meeting in person. The first of these poems is composed at her father's request by the *xiaodan*, Shen Wan'e, as follows:

SHEN ZHONG: Since you are so enamored of it, why not dash off a little verse, in the manner of Xie Daoyun hymning the snow?

WAN'E: (Tune: Yu baodu)

>Dust gathers on brush and inkstone
>lax for so long to prepare silk for writing.

(Aside):

>Concerned lest verse composed at this moment of spring's approach
>should tease my idle heart to the brink of sorrow;

> yet how today should both remain silent,
>> fair bloom and seductive maid, no word from either?
> Then must I perforce
>> study the hawk-cuckoo and bewail the spring!

SHEN ZHONG: Have you finished your poem?

WAN'E (recites her composition):

> A sip of wine among the flowers,
>> choice lines press their claim,
> But impatience yields to shame, to lack
>> the gifts of the poetess Xie.
> Springtime blouse declines
>> to compete with flowers' finery
> Green sleeves henceforth
>> will show a special cut.

SHEN ZHONG: Distinction in the aspect of the flower, distinction in the feeling of the verse; no verse but this could match this flower, no flower but this could inspire this verse. Delightful! Phoenix, another cup of wine!

As is normal in Chinese verse, no pronoun, whether "it" or "she," appears in Wan'e's quatrain. Obviously the first couplet relates to the poet herself; it is she who is drinking and she who laments the inferiority of her own talent to that of the third-century poetess Xie Daoyun (the Xie of the scene's title, Xie yong, "Ode in the Xie Manner": it is part of the playwright's feminist ploy, surely, that the HERO Xie Ying shares the surname of one of the most celebrated women poets in China's history). But the light spring blouse, with its green sleeves, of lines three and four is both the dress Wan'e herself is wearing or will wear and a metonymy for the peony which is her subject. The woman who is composing the poem becomes the green peony itself, which cannot match the reds and yellows for gorgeousness but has its own "special cut."

Though not quite the equal of the supremely talented HEROINE Che Jingfang, Shen Wan'e here demonstrates her gift for composition, just as later, in Scene 6, "Clandestine Critique," she shows herself a discerning judge of poetry. It is this latter scene that sets before the audience the hard evidence for ranking HERO Xie Ying and HEROINE Che Jingfang as the prime pair of lovers, with FRIEND Gu Can and COMPANION Shen Wan'e herself subordinated to them. The contest has taken place, the ghostwriters have made their contributions, and FATHER Shen Zhong has ranked the three entries. Now Shen Wan'e reads out the poems of the three contestants which she has found on her father's desk:

WAN'E (reads out Liu Wuliu's poem [which is actually the work of Xie Ying]):

> Profusion of blooms from the hands of Yao and Wei
> > vie to be first to open,
> But this is sought in vain
> > in the Temple of Mercy gardens.
> Roll up the blind when the rain stops
> > to enjoy the clearing sky—
> Surely it is the freshness of moss
> > reflected in this flower!

[Several varieties of peony took their names from their cultivators, the Yao and Wei families of the city of Luoyang, which was famous for its flowers. The Temple of Mercy, Ci'ensi, was founded in the Tang capital of Chang'an. Though its gardens contained both the earliest- and the latest-blooming varieties, the green peony, as the poem indicates, was not to be found there.]

This is the most wonderful verse-making in the world; no wonder my father ranked it number one.

(She reads out Che Shanggong's poem [which is actually the work of Che's sister Jingfang]):

> If not the scion of prized blooms
> > that grow on Tianpeng Mountain
> Would it challenge the red and purple
> > in contests of the fragrant?
> In vase of slender neck
> > the color of rain-washed sky
> A single stem might well suit
> > a coiffure of "green clouds."

No less charming than the previous piece, this can only be placed second.

(She reads out Gu Can's poem):

> Jade-green as the light sea-swell,
> > emerald as mountain mist,
> A flower that wears so fair a face
> > must know how it is loved,
> As if the name it bears
> > should still be remembered
> Though Li Bo, the "Green Lotus Master,"
> > chose the wrong hues to praise!

[Syntactic inversion in the fourth line does not make this poem any easier to read. Gu Can alludes to the same story already cited by Shen Wan'e in Scene 3, quoted above, of Li Bo's composition on imperial command. Li's verses praised red, purple and white peonies but missed the green, even though his own cognomen was "Master of Green Lotus."]

Powerful in concept, evidently an expert literary talent, an injustice to relegate him to third place....

> (Tune: Yi chun le)

> Making clandestine judgment
> Silently I ponder:

The line about the "freshness of the moss reflecting in the flower" seems to soar in such a natural way—how could I ever match that?

> Women, you must graciously accept defeat!

The line in my own poem, "Green sleeves henceforth will show a special cut," is authentically feminine; but the line in the second-place poem, "A single stem that well might suit a 'coiffure of green clouds'"—this too smacks a little of paint and powder!

> If not a dweller in maiden's chamber
> how came so subtle a conceit to tease this poet?
> First the image of emerald sleeves' new mode
> and then, to match, "green clouds" of woman's hair!

(She laughs:)

> Smart scholar,
> filching a line from the boudoir
> for his own skillful use.

And I do not think the third-place poet is in any way less gifted than the other two!

> (Tune: Xueshi jie cheng)

> A scatter of bright pearls flung in the face—
> no easy task to find a match!

The first two answers

> by chance won favor with my connoisseur father—
> yet you should not be bringing up the rear!
> Willing to be placed third
> when ranking is so difficult
> you'll stay for now in lowly state.

We have reached only the sixth of the thirty scenes of the play, not one of the four young people has yet set eyes on his or her future partner, and yet the love affinities are already crystal clear. Two facts strike us at once. First, no matter who claims to have authored the poems (and, of course, a major part of the fun of the play arises from the business of ghostwriting, as hero and heroine stand in for villain and clown at examination time), two of the four are obviously of feminine origin. When in Scene 7 the academician Shen Zhong claims Wan'e's quatrain as his own work, Gu Can immediately protests that the author must be female—and young. The self-comparison with the "poetess Xie (Daoyun)" and the self-identification with flower in green-sleeved blouse make the case clear. Turning to the second of the three poems recited in Scene 6, there is a feminine air to the phrase "contests of the fragrant" (which could refer to competition between pretty women as well as flowers), and boudoir touches in the images of the slender-necked vase and the cloud-styled coiffure (each suggestive of the allure of the poet herself).

The second obvious fact is the close affinity between the first and second poems of Scene 6, which are indeed the quatrains by HERO and HEROINE respectively. Each of the two quatrains opens with a couplet proclaiming the rare quality of its subject, the green peony not to be found even in the gardens, famous for their peony collection, of the Temple of Mercy in Chang'an, but surely descended from the green variety listed by the Song poet Lu You in his catalogue of peonies at Tianpeng Mountain in the southwestern province of Sichuan. By this time we should be receptive to the notion that in each poem the flower that is the topic stands for the poet's own self, put forward as a rare prize in the marital stakes. But the truly remarkable correspondence between the first- and second-ranked poems is in the identical comparison of the flower's color with the pale turquoise green of the sky after rain. Though the color is the same, the two poets use different phrasing to define it and pursue different associations from it. The male poet, the HERO Xie Ying, looks upward and outward from his study window to "enjoy the clearing sky": his action and attitude are evidently symbolic of his aspirations for his career, which in the old cliché will place his feet above the clouds once examination success has secured a place for him in the official world. The woman who composes the second poem, the HEROINE Che Jingfang, in contrast looks downward and inward to the vase in her boudoir. She in her imagination sees the flower as cut, placed in a vase or at the temple of a beautiful woman, an indoor bloom: hers is the claustrophobic feminine view, not the sweep of vision which in the brilliantly original figure of the first poem sees the moss of the path reflected from the sky upon the petals of the green peony, the subject image which unifies the whole quatrain.

The one poem we have not yet considered, the quatrain by the FRIEND Gu Can which is placed third in the ranking in Scene 6, is more contrived than the first two, more far-fetched and at the same time less original in its imagery. The images are undoubtedly appropriate to a male poet, outdoor visions of sea waves and mountain mists, and the poet's aspiration is daring enough as he summons up the revered figure of Li Bo in the last line. Gu Can, like the two women poets, personifies the flower as a beautiful woman in his second line, but he does not identify himself with it; rather, he may be seen as delicately suggesting his own readiness to attach his affections to the flowerlike authoress of the poem originally set as model for the contest, the work of the COMPANION Shen Wan'e who will be his choice as bride.

As mentioned, if one were looking for a possible parallel to *Lumudan* from English dramatic literature one might settle on *Much Ado about Nothing*. But why should one be looking for anything of the kind? My answer would be that the comparative perspective can be helpful to critical evaluation. Even in a crude kind of analogue study like the one I am suggesting now between totally unrelated works, I at least find it a comfort to be able to move in on a new and unfamiliar play from the vantage point of another piece that I have known well for a long time and that shows a number of similar features and devices.

And just as an incidental comment: Shakespeare provides a handy resource for this kind of purpose. He has so many advantages: close in historical time, protean in the range of his art, analyzed through the centuries with microscopic care, performed all the time everywhere so that one can consider his plays from the aspect of stage as well as study. Better drama criticism has flowed from Shakespeare studies, no doubt, than from any other area; and criticism is important to the translator, because the nature of a translation, from its overall tone down to the specific choices the translator will make at given points of the text, will be affected by the estimate originally made of the work's generic type.

So we will consider *Lumudan* as a comedy of wit along the lines of *Much Ado*, noticing first the clear parallel in the matter of the pairing of lovers. Gu Can and Shen Wan'e, more elevated in social standing but with distinctly inferior poetic gifts, parallel the rather colorless couple Claudio and Hero, while Che Jingfang and Xie Ying are the Beatrice and Benedict of *The Green Peony*. This is why Jingfang and Xie Ying fill the type roles of heroine and hero, dominating the action just as Beatrice and Benedict dominate *Much Ado* (which has at times, indeed, been known by their names rather than by the title Shakespeare gave it).

Then, as we turn from the successful lovers to the would-be gallants, villain and clown, we become more and more aware of correspondences in the comic structure of the two plays. Liu and Che, negative characters, in their fruitless pursuit of the gifted and beautiful young ladies, must present themselves as scholarly men of outstanding merit. The means they choose to perpetrate this swindle are the classic devices of comedy; we are in the world of mistaken identities, impostures, and deliberate falsifications familiar to us from *Much Ado* and the whole tradition of Italian comedy from which it stems.

We may list in short order some noticeable parallels: both plays being comedies of wit, the negative characters among their dramatis personae will by definition include specimens of witlessness to offset the principals. In *Much Ado* these include the celebrated manglers of words, the pre-Malaprop perpetrators of malapropisms, Dogberry and Verges; in *The Green Peony*, the negative characters, Liu Wuliu and Che Shanggong, are themselves the prize ignoramuses, whose first display of verbal incompetence is the gross misreading of the topic set for the poetry contest (in Scene 2).

As for impersonation, in Scene 9, "Seeking the Handsome One," the go-between nurse Qian puts some pointed questions to Xie Ying under the misapprehension that he is Liu Wuliu. Xie, amused by the woman's evident matchmaking intent, for no apparent reason allows the error to stand, which of course leads to further complications. Similarly, in *Much Ado* Don Pedro's undertaking to impersonate Claudio is weakly motivated in terms of rationale, but useful to the dramatist for comic plotting purposes; again, where Shakespeare inserts a masked ball into his action to facilitate a whole series of mistaken identities, Wu Bing has his characters attach false names to their literary compositions, with similar consequences in terms of comic misunderstanding; one result of such misunderstandings is the kind of talk at cross purposes which runs all through the masked ball scene, and is found in *The Green Peony* in Scene 18, when Liu Wuliu insists that he is truly the author of the atrocious doggerel that Xie Ying has cooked up for him. As examples of deliberate misinformation, we could cite from *Much Ado* the Friar's plan to announce the death of Hero and from *The Green Peony* the false report of examination results engineered by Liu and Che in Scene 29.

But when we look more closely at Liu and Che we see them as quite different in kind from the negative characters, Don John and Borrachio and the others, of *Much Ado*. Though we have used the term *villain* for Liu Wuliu, we must stress that this is only a coarse, general translation for the role type *jing*, which more precisely indicates something like "leading character of the pair *jing-chou*, often negative, possibly violent, occasionally villainous." Liu Wuliu is certainly not a villain in the sense of Don John, the very type of the Shakespearean bastard consumed with envy of those more fairly favored. Liu and Che are more fools than knaves. Nothing in *The Green Peony* comes close to melodrama; there is no parallel to the vile traducement of Hero, the threat of Hero's death, or the order Beatrice gives Benedict to assassinate his friend.

For now we must stress the fundamental difference in intent of Wu Bing's comedy. Wu Bing is not writing of love threatened by spiteful envy, nor of love denied by scornful wits who by the end of the play will have their eyes opened even as their pride is humbled. For Wu Bing's characters, love means the recognition and reward of talent; but the real purpose of his writing is not so much to celebrate love as to castigate the self-love of foolish impostors. Where for Shakespeare satire constitutes merely one element, the substance of the Beatrice and Benedict subplot, for Wu Bing satire is the fundamental justification of his play. The primary and specific target of the satire is the abuse of the examination system by shallow men with deep pockets, men who could afford to bribe examiners, to pay surrogates, to buy their way into the ranks of the scholar-officials who ran the country and monopolized social prestige.

Even the briefest consideration of Wu Bing's life history will explain this concern. He is honored by Chinese scholars as a Ming loyalist. He was styled Wu Shiqu, "Stone Gully," and used the pen name Canhua zhuren, "Bright Flower Master." He was born in Yixing in the east coast province of Jiangsu in 1595, developed poetic skills as a boy, and passed the third-degree examination of *jinshi* at the age of twenty-four. For twenty-five years he served as a Ming official, rising at one time to the important position of superintendent of schools for Jiangxi province. Evidently his knowledge of examination procedures and their abuse was the fruit of years of experience. He wrote five major plays, of which the best known is not *The Green Peony* but a romantic comedy, *Xiyuanji* (The West Garden), whose ghostly lovers owe much to Tang Xianzu's *Peony Pavilion*. When Wu Bing was close to fifty, in 1644, the Manchu invasion reduced the Ming dynasty to abortive attempts at revival in the south and west of the country. Wu Bing continued his service to the dynasty at the court of the prince Yongming in the south, taking the rank of secretary of the Board of War and scholar of the Eastern Cabinet. He was taken prisoner in a mop-up operation by the Manchus in 1647, and the following year he died of starvation, supposed to have been self-imposed in demonstration of his unshaken loyalty to the native dynasty.

It is a far cry from the light satirical comedy of *The Green Peony* to the loyalist martyr's suicide, and we should do wrong to take Wu Bing's "villains" too seriously. Still, it is clear that for much of his life Wu Bing watched his beloved Ming imperial order being undermined by worthless and corrupt place seekers and pseudoscholars until it was shaky enough to collapse at a push from the new Manchu power. In *The Green Peony* he works his revenge on a breed of rich idlers with absurd pretensions to learning and taste. As models for such men he establishes Liu Wuliu and Che Shanggong as his *jing-chou*, or villain-clown combination. Of these two, Liu is the more cunning rogue, Che the slow-witted hanger-on; both are vain, self-indulgent, and fundamentally stupid. They dominate the major comic scenes, which follow their adventures as candidates for examination in pursuit of the hand of the heiress Shen Wan'e. And here I come at long last to my point in all this, which is that precisely the problem with the play for a modern English reader is the monotonously reiterated satire of this whole series of examination scenes.

I will end my comments on the play with a brief mention of three scenes, strategically placed through the action, which are basic to the characterization of Liu and Che and in this way central to Wu Bing's satiric purpose. All are examination scenes. Ostensibly they depict friendly literary contests held under club rules in a domestic setting; in fact the audience is perfectly aware of the parallel with the official halls of examination, in the provincial or national capital, where the prize will be not the hand of a local beauty but entrance into the imperial bureaucracy with its open avenues to wealth and fame.

Scene 5, "Club Meeting," sets the pattern for the chicanery of Liu Wuliu and Che Shanggong, as their servants smuggle into the examination room the poems their surrogates have composed for them. Scene 25, "Examination by the Rules," is essentially a repeat performance, with the difference that on this occasion the rules against leaving the room or communicating with outsiders are strictly enforced.

Scene 18, "Alcove Quiz," is the central major comic scene in which the essential stupidity of Liu and Che is exposed, and this is the single scene I would choose to present in translation to the English reader as representative of the entire play. The scene turns poor Liu Wuliu inside out. He is onstage throughout, most of the time seated at his examination desk, where he shows every sign of embarrassment and discomfort. He is a rich idler, overfed and overdressed, ill fitted to the confines of the scholar's desk. Being totally incapable of literary composition, he can only stretch and yawn, drum his fingers, and pretend to be humming his lines over; in fact he is dividing his time between waiting for his crony to bring him the answer Xie has promised to write for him and trying to crane his neck round the curtain to catch a glimpse of the delectable Che Jingfang, his examiner and intended bride.

Behind the curtain Miss Che is accompanied by her old nurse. Miss Che, as is only proper, never leaves the privacy of her alcove, but the nurse emerges from time to time to bully poor Liu, especially at the point where he is strutting and mincing round his half of the stage in the absurd attempt to impress the young lady with his elephantine "elegance."

The comings and goings from the alcove to the "examination hall" proper are complicated also by Miss Che's brother, Che Shanggong, the clown who is Liu's crony. He serves as a sort of go-between in this scene, smuggling in the crib to the hapless examinee, skulking onstage and off in the attempt to avoid detection, and finally entering the alcove to plead, in vain, the virtues of Liu's ghosted poem before his sister. By the end of the scene even Che Shanggong has given up on Liu, who is left alone on stage completely discomfited.

All in all, the construction of the alcove scene is a fine example of Chinese dramaturgy, where, in the absence of sets and scenery of any kind beyond a couple of poles supporting a simple curtain, the groupings and movements on stage are skillfully orchestrated for maximum comic effect, until in the climactic concluding lines of the scene the heroine Che Jingfang finally condescends to read out loud the absurd "poem" which the hero has conned the hapless villain into submitting as his own work.

Lumudan, SCENE 18: THE ALCOVE QUIZ

(An examination desk is set up onstage).

LIU WULIU (enters):

> "Were't not for bone-piercing cold
> How could the plum's scent reach our senses?"

[Some varieties of plum, or more properly Chinese apricot, bloom so early in the year that snow may still cover the branches—constituting a popular subject for painters, with its suggestion of triumph over hardship. The lines Liu is quoting are from the final scene of the classic southern play *The Lute*.]

Poor Liu Wuliu, nothing I can do but submit myself for examination if I plan to wed Miss Che. She has set "green peony" as topic, and I've passed this on to my servant with instructions to get the answer from young Xie. I'm only afraid that Miss Che's a sharp one, nothing to stop those sparkling clear-as-autumn-stream eyes of hers from looking round the curtain, not like last time when the old boy was in charge and I could fool around as I wished. If I try to have my man smuggle in the answer again, won't that just blow the whole thing? Best to ask brother Che to do it for me this time; his sister will never suspect him. Good scheme, good scheme! (He shouts:) Brother Che!

CHE SHANGGONG (enters in response):

> If whoever wants to marry has to face an oral quiz
> I'm happy to live a bachelor, thank you very much!

Why don't you just write your piece, what are you calling me for?

LIU: Something I want you to do. Very shortly my man will be along with a paper, and I'd like you to pass it to me on the quiet.

CHE (laughs): Smuggling in the answer, eh?

LIU: Not so loud, your sister will hear!

CHE: She isn't here yet.

LIU: I've no alternative, I must ask you to do this for me, but if we can bring it off I swear I'll give up my engagement to Miss Shen in your favor!

CHE (laughs): Well, all right then, I'll back you up just this once.

LIU (peers across): Some shadow moved behind the curtain; I think your sister's here.

(CHE scuttles offstage)

CHE JINGFANG (enters followed by NURSE QIAN): A novel phenomenon to-day—

[The musical structure of this scene is unusual and effective. "Northern" and "southern" tunes alternate, which is not in itself so uncommon; what is special to this scene is that the more virile and vigorous northern melodies are given to the heroine, who is performing a strictly male function as examiner, whilst the man in the scene, the absurd fop Liu Wuliu, is given the more langorous, flute-accompanied southern music, presumably to accentuate his wimpy nature, until his final comic ditty of the scene.]

(Tune: Northern Xinshuiling)

> Raise the crimson curtain on a woman examiner
> seated in high hall, gilt hair-ornaments a-quiver.
> Young lady placed in charge
> old nurse must serve as proctor.
> Here where lowered curtain sways
> you see our Halls of Examination, blossom-bowered.

LIU: Oh, with her

(Tune: Southern Bubujiao)

> pearls and feathers and wisps of scent
> here so close beside me—
> puts me beside myself—what can I do?

(He takes a peek around the curtain)

> She's stealing glances beneath her fan!

(He rises to his feet)

I'll take an elegant pace or two

> with mincing gait and twisting waist
> how debonair can one get!

NURSE QIAN (steps out from behind the curtain and bawls at him): Hey, mister scholar! Leaving your seat like this, wandering off for a little stroll, aren't you afraid the lookout will grab you for breaking the rules?

LIU (rushes back to his seat): Here! Here I am—

> would I dare disregard the rules?
> Please, honored tutor,
> lenient treatment for a first offense!

NURSE QIAN: Pay attention to your composition, sir.

LIU: I will.

(As NURSE QIAN retires behind the curtain again, LIU sets himself to intoning in a loud mumble)

JINGFANG: (Tune: Northern Zheguiling)

> Buzzing his misbegotten lines like a swarm of mosquitoes at dusk—

(She laughs): Nurse, look there at his shadow in the sunlight,

> sun shines on fuzzy whiskers
> as his shadow dances.

NURSE QIAN (laughs): He really is a funny sight, just like a sheep munching grass.

(LIU rubs his eyes, pummels his waist, strokes his belly and shows every sign of weariness)

JINGFANG: Why does he

> thrust his knuckles deep into his eyes
> pretend his waistband is a winnowing sieve
> lightly pat his tremendous paunch?

NURSE QIAN: From the looks of it, he's ready for a snooze.

JINGFANG:

> Don't think to win a bride by lying abed—
> nothing for you but a dream of anthills!

[Two well-known allusions here, the first to the story of a young man who succeeded as suitor because of the nonchalance he displayed by taking a nap in the east room or guest room, which gave the origin to the expression "eastern bed" for son-in-law; the second to the famous "dream of Nanke," in which a man found a microcosm of the world with all its successes and failures in the busy affairs of an anthill.]

(LIU falls asleep and begins to snore.)

> What is this sound of breathing?
> Can young Jiang's magic writing-brush
> be furnished him in his dream?

[Allusion to the story of a youth who dreamed that the poet Guo Pu bestowed a multi-colored brush on him in his dream. On waking he was able to compose fine lines, but inspiration deserted him later in life, after Guo Pu in a second dream visit retrieved his magic brush.]

(NURSE QIAN comes out again and pounds on LIU's desk.)

LIU (waking with a start): Servant, has Mr. Xie finished that crib yet?

NURSE QIAN (in a loud shout): Mr. Liu, no more sleeping, wake up and write your piece!

LIU: I wasn't asleep, I was meditating on the inner significance of the topic!

(Tune: Southern Jiang'ershui)

> Propped at table, lost in pursuit of thought,
> d'you think I had pillowed my head to lure the demon slumber?

I tell you, mum, it's not that my

> inspiration's flagging for the moment,

it's more like

> palpitation of a lover's heart—

how can I be sure to understand when her

> lute's vibration sounds a secret message?

[Allusion to the ancient lovers Sima Xiangru and Zhuo Wenjun, who communicated via the cryptic "language of the lute." Each of these three lines of the aria uses the word *xin*, "heart/mind," in the sense of "thoughts" in the phrases "literary thoughts," "spring (i.e., lascivious) thoughts," and "lute(-borne) thoughts."]

NURSE QIAN: Hurry up and finish!

LIU: Oh, I'll be sure to

> hand in my today's exercise
> at clang of warning gong
> to save you the bother of pressing me for it.

SERVANT (enters):

> Answer composed, we hasten its transcription
> but keep transaction secret from maiden in alcove.

I've solicited the answer from Master Xie, and now I have to pass it in to the examination room.

NURSE QIAN: Orders to the gatekeeper: no one admitted without authorization. (She disappears behind the curtain again).

SERVANT: What to do?

CHE SHANGGONG (enters and beckons to SERVANT): Over here! Your master and I have settled it, I'm to pass the answer to him.

SERVANT: That's the best way. The author says to tell you that no matter how they interrogate my master, he must insist that this is his own work. (He passes the poem to CHE).

> "Eyes see banner of victory,
> ears hear news of joy."   (Exit)

CHE (comes down to LIU's desk): Feeling satisfied, brother Liu?

LIU: I've got it all composed here in my belly, I just haven't written it down yet.

(They exchange knowing winks)

JINGFANG: (Tune: Northern Yan'erluo with Deshengling)

> Why these meaning glances?

(LIU and CHE whisper in each other's ears)

> Why this junction of lip and ear?

(CHE stands by LIU's side and slips the crib to him)

> Why this interest so intense he's leaning on him?

(LIU, as he takes the crib, looks in the direction of the alcove)

> And why this sudden concern about me?

CHE (stands away from LIU and pretends to study a draft answer): What a marvelous beginning, the very first word of this draft.

(LIU makes gestures of modest deprecation)

JINGFANG: Nurse, the way those two are mumbling to each other, I suspect a crib is being smuggled in.

NURSE QIAN (draws aside the curtain and yells): The young lady says someone is smuggling a crib!

(CHE scurries offstage)

LIU: Who could that be? That was your young master just now, coming to read my composition.

NURSE QIAN: Miss, you don't think it could be the young master passing a crib to him?

JINGFANG:

> It's not my own brother worries me
> but the thought that he's working for someone else.

Nurse, I'd like you to go out there and search him—but please don't think me

> an over-cautious overseer:

it's just that I can't stand

> tricks played in front of my very face,
> so don't imagine, slippery sir,
> you can slide so smoothly through the needle's eye.

NURSE QIAN: How can I be so bold as to search him?

JINGFANG: Now, nurse,

> no muttering, or
> reluctance to inspect puts you at fault,
> reluctance to inspect puts you at fault!

NURSE QIAN (emerges from behind the curtain): Master Liu, it really did look as though there was some cheating going on just then.

LIU: If you think I was cheating, why don't you search me?

(He makes a show of displaying an empty sleeve and opening the front of his gown)

NURSE QIAN: I can't see there's anything there. (She reports back at the top of her voice): Search completed, no one's cheated. (She returns to the alcove)

JINGFANG: It was perfectly obvious there was cheating going on, but since we found nothing when we searched him, let's have a look at his poem. If it really is a good one, we'll have to examine him some more.

LIU (sings to himself as he surreptitiously copies out the poem):

(Tune: Southern Jiaojiaoling)

Let the man of honor strive as he will
the crafty trickster gets the better of him—
and how to convict when no loot is found?

See how fast

my writing brush "scatters a thousand troops"
my writing brush "scatters a thousand troops."

(He finishes writing and yells):

Candidate submits answer!

CHE SHANGGONG (enters): Have you finished your distinguished composition? (He reads it and expresses admiration)

LIU (complacently): I myself feel that I haven't completely disgraced myself this time, but I fear it is unworthy of your honored sister's perusal.

CHE: Let me take it in and show her.

LIU: With reverently folded hands I await her disposition.

(CHE presents the poem to JINGFANG, who reads it and bursts out laughing)

JINGFANG: (Tune: Northern Shou Jiangnan)

Oh dear! Now I see how exquisite it is,
such a display of skill was worth the lengthy wait!

CHE: It took a lot of effort.

JINGFANG: And to his credit

so beautifully copied, not a word wrongly written!

CHE: Nicely copied, really.

JINGFANG: Compared with last time

> a far superior composition.

CHE: He placed first last time—this time there should be a special category.

JINGFANG: But good as it is, I'm only afraid it isn't his own work.

CHE: You supervised the examination yourself, sister—did you see anyone smuggle anything in to him?

JINGFANG:

> Ask him the truth
> ask him the truth—
> who was it ghosted this doggerel for him?

CHE (emerges from behind the curtain): All my sister did when she read your poem was laugh out loud.

LIU: She must have enjoyed it. Did she say it was good?

CHE: She laughed, and then she said it was even better than the last time.

LIU: So she really likes it?

CHE: The only thing is, she suspects you got someone else to write it.

LIU: With a talent like mine, it's bad enough that other people don't ask me to write things for them, but that I should ask others to write for me . . . !

JINGFANG (laughs): He believes I really meant to praise it and insists that it's his own work! Nurse, go out again and ask him about it.

NURSE (emerges from alcove): Master Liu, if you didn't write it yourself you should come right out and say so.

LIU: Three of you standing there, six eyes watching me, you've even searched me, are you telling me a composition could fly in here out of thin air?

CHE: If you didn't cheat, why not swear an oath?

LIU: I'll swear. (He lowers his head and raises his folded hands in a gesture of oath-taking). Ha, I know what's happening!

> (Tune: Southern Yuanlin hao)

> False accusation, blame without cause
> groundless excuse to back out of the betrothal!

I'll tell you this, mum, you're not going to break off this marriage agreement!

NURSE QIAN: Master Liu, you mustn't get so upset.

LIU: I didn't offer myself for examination; it was your young mistress invited me. If the poem's no good, that's an end of it, but

since my modest offering has been accepted,

why now do you

use it to drag me into all this fuss,
use it to drag me into all this fuss?

CHE: I'll go in again and plead your case.

(With NURSE QIAN, he returns behind the curtain)

NURSE QIAN: Did you hear how he was acting up?

JINGFANG (laughs):   (Tune: Northern Gu meijiu with Taiping ling)

Convinced his lines are precious gold
his scale's too wobbly to weigh their worth.
Mixing up his words absurd
he reduces all present to helpless hoots—
has he really no clue what his poem means?

CHE: From what you say it can't be very good. What is it really like, sister?

JINGFANG (laughs): His ghostwriter has been playing tricks on him—

making him hop like a monkey on a string
puppet-master working him at every chance.

The victim of the trick

too foolish to show any judgment;

the perpetrator

too clever by half to escape all blame!

NURSE QIAN: If you merely tell him it's all a joke, miss, I'm afraid he won't accept that. Best to explain what's behind the joke to our young master so that he can go respond to him.

JINGFANG (recites the poem, laughing as she does so):

"This peony flower

has a color all its own . . ."

CHE: That's good and clear.

JINGFANG:

"Not red or purple,

not yellow or white . . ."

CHE: It's neither red nor purple nor is it yellow or white, precisely because it's green. On the mark, on the mark!

JINGFANG: The last two lines are the funniest of all, they go

> "A green-haired turtle
>> crawled up the stem,
> But I guess the young lady
>> can't tell what it is"—

obviously this means he's calling himself a turtle!

(CHE and NURSE QIAN join in her laughter)

> True or false
> he says it himself!
> Better for him, if he'd only think,
> to admit he had someone else write it!

(JINGFANG and NURSE QIAN exit, and CHE SHANGGONG comes out from behind the curtain again)

LIU: I suppose your sister didn't have much to say about it?

CHE (laughs): Just let me ask you—how do you interpret the meaning of this poem?

LIU: There's no disputing it's a superb work; what's the need for interpretation?

CHE: My sister says you've been made a fool of, being called a turtle right there in the poem.

LIU: How can that be?

CHE: Just now I listened to my sister reading it aloud and so I still have some notion of it. Let's try reading it together.

(They read it aloud together, and CHE bursts out laughing)

From now on I'll just call you Turtle Liu! This paper is your own handwritten admission; I'm going to keep it right here.

(LIU grabs the paper and tears it up)

I've wasted a lot of thought and effort on this marriage agreement, acting as go-between for you, and then helping you out today by smuggling in the answer for you; I thought we had it made. Who told you to go copying out this poem and wreck your own chances? It's not just you that have lost face; I've lost face as well. Excuse me, I'm off! Like they say, "bring me every drop of water the West River holds, it can't wash clean the shame I feel today." (He exits)

LIU: That beast young Xie, eats my rice, takes my fees, then turns right round and tricks me! I'll send him packing on the spot! I was so full of beans when I presented myself for this quiz this morning, and now I feel so flat, how can I just turn round and go back home? Let's have a song, cheer things up a bit:

(Tune: Northern Qingjiang yin)

Pretty maid claims to judge poesy
quizzing a single examinee;
boasts of discrimination, nice as can be,
puts on an act of authority—
but what a mistake to flunk a beau like me!

"Pieces of Eight"

Reflections on Translating *The Story of the Stone*

JOHN MINFORD

The Island

In that never-never land of the mind which some translators (and their readers) inhabit, the language and symbols of one culture, the shapes, sounds, and sensations of one time and space, the structures of one consciousness merge with those of another, as in a dream. I picture this land as an island in the midst of a Hundun Sea (Sea of Primordial Undifferentiated Chaos), its shores washed by the tides of the Collective Unconscious. If we may extend the scope of Lu Ji's *Rhymeprose on Literature* to include translators, we can perhaps imagine strange islanders, to use his words,

> distilling drops afresh from a sea of words since time out of mind ... now blithe as swimmers borne on celestial waters, now sinking like divers into a secret world, lost in subterranean currents.... Those arduously sought expressions, hitherto evasive and hidden, like stray fishes from the deepest ocean bed arise on the angler's "hook."[1]

The difference on *this* island is that the words are lowered down in one language and fished out in another.

I should like to journey to this translators' Atlantis and examine the sort of sea-change that *The Story of the Stone*, beloved of Chinese readers in its original shape and form for over two hundred years, has undergone. The island's Chinese name would surely be *Hua-jing* 化境, that Realm of

Change, to which (as Qian Zhongshu said) all translations aspire. I shall look at a few examples of what happens in this process of change. But before setting sail, I think it would be wise to heed the following warning, a gale warning, as it were, issued by a great German scholar, E. R. Curtius, to all readers of Literature in Translation:

> Spiritual treasures cannot be converted to the standard of a common currency. The best that the great classics hold in store for you will not pass into translation.... The message of the poet must be heard in his own tongue. If people are not prepared to do so, then they must do without the Pearl of Great Price.[2]

Having broadcast the warning, I still urge intending passengers to take heart; it may be possible, with a certain amount of diving, to come home from the island with a reflection at least of the luster of a lesser pearl and—who knows—perhaps an inkling of what the Great One looks like?

Greensickness Peak

ROOT OF LOVE

On the first page of volume one of *The Story of the Stone*, we read:

> Long ago, when the goddess Nü-wa was repairing the sky, she melted down a great quantity of rock and, on the Incredible Crags of the Great Fable Mountains, moulded the amalgam into thirty-six thousand, five hundred and one large building blocks, each measuring seventy-two feet by a hundred and forty-four feet square. She used thirty-six thousand five hundred of these blocks in the course of her building operations, leaving a single odd block unused, which lay, all on its own, at the foot of Greensickness Peak in the aforementioned mountains.

Greensickness Peak might at first sight seem an odd way to translate the name of the place where the stone "rejected by the builder" first lay. The Chinese expression 青埂峰 literally means Blue (or Green) Ridge Peak, and this is indeed how Yang Xianyi and Gladys Yang translate it. Where does sickness come into it?

Listen carefully to the opening words of the novel:

> Gentle Reader,
> What, you may ask, was the origin of this book? Though the answer to this question may at first sight seem to border on the absurd, reflection will show that there is a good deal more in it than meets the eye.

While a few pages further on, the author describes his work as

> Pages full of idle words,
> Penned with hot and bitter tears:
> All men call the author fool;
> None his secret message hears.

What is this "secret message"? Probably no two readers will ever agree; but we are lucky to have some clues in the annotations written by various members of the author's family and included in the early handwritten copies of the novel. Sometimes the secret remains a secret, as when the notes merely say, "Ah what a marvellous likeness!" But sometimes we are actually told what the secret is.

Our friendly annotator, in this case the most prolific one, a relative with the pen name Red Inkstone, tell us that *qing-geng* (Green Ridge) is one of the many puns used by the author of *The Story of the Stone*, Cao Xue-qin, to hint at his message. It is homophonous with the expression *qing-gen* 情根 meaning literally Root of Love.[3] And because the Stone contained this Root of Love (we would more naturally say Seed of Love, I think) it was found unfit to repair the sky. Root of Love is an expression rather like *bing-gen* 病根 Root of Illness, which figuratively means Cause of Trouble; or *nie-gen* 孽根 Root of Retribution, often used of children. And indeed Love causes a great deal of the trouble in the novel, and children bring much of the Karmic retribution.

But Love is also portrayed as a path to Enlightenment. In this sense the Root of Love is a Positive Root, like the Pancendriyani, or Five Roots of Moral Strength in Buddhism: the Roots of Faith, Energy, Memory, Meditation and Wisdom.

The novel is the personal testimony of the Loves, Disenchantment, and final Illumination of the Stone's earthly incarnation.

> Found unfit to repair the azure sky
> Long years a foolish mortal man was I.
> My life in both worlds on this stone is writ:
> Pray who will copy out and publish it?

Vanitas the Taoist and copyist was so affected by this aspect of the story that he changed his own name to Brother Amor or the Passionate Monk, and changed the title of the book from *The Story of the Stone* to *The Tale of Brother Amor*. He had rediscovered Truth by way of Love. Starting off in the Void (which is Truth)—as a monk should—he came to the contemplation of Form (which is Illusion)—the Illusion or Fiction so lovingly depicted in the Inscription on the Stone; this Form engendered Love; and by communicating Love he entered again into Form; and from Form awoke once more to the Void, which is Truth. There is yet a third possible level of meaning in *qing-gen*. Coming as it does after the Incredible Crags of the Great Fable

Mountains[4] *qing-gen* may have the further meaning of Real Basis of the Plot—taking *qing* in the sense of *qing-jie* 情節 and *gen* as in *wugenzhici* 無根之辭. In other words, although the whole mythical introduction in chapter 1 is Incredible, Fantastic, a Great Fable, an Invention for the Purposes of Fiction, it is also an allegorical representation of the True Origin of the Events, their psychological kernel in myth-form.

Green Ridge/Root of Love is in Chinese a pun with a riddling ring to it, as are many of the expressions in this first chapter. It is a play on words, but a play that indicates a key, a meaning. Greensickness has a similar ring. It is not a word in late twentieth century usage. But in order to recreate through translation the intricate fabric of this riddling first chapter, the translator has delved below the surface of everyday English, to angle for those "stray fish that rise from the ocean bed." He, like the author, is playing his line.

Chlorosis, or Greensickness, is (so any curious reader can discover) an old-fashioned word for an old-fashioned condition: an anemic disease which affects mostly young people, usually young ladies, at the age of puberty, and which gives a pale or greenish tinge to the complexion. Dr. Robert Hooper, in his *Dictionary of Medicine and the Various Branches of Natural Philosophy Connected With It*, published at the beginning of the nineteenth century, tells us that this condition is characterized by "a heaviness, listlessness, fatigue on the least exercise, palpitations of the heart, pains in the back, loins and hips, and a peculiar craving for chalk, lime and various other absorbents, together with many dyspeptic symptoms. As it advances in its progress, the face becomes pale or assumes a yellowish hue ... the pulse is quick but small ... and the person is apt to be affected with many of the symptoms of hysteria." Not a bad description of the Ailing Naiad, Lin Dai-yu.

Greensickness, in other words, is a form of Lovesickness. Robert Louis Stevenson, in *Virginibus Puerisque* (1881, p. 104), writes: "There is some meaning in the old theory of Wild Oats; and a man who has not had his Greensickness and got done with it for good is as little to be depended on as an unvaccinated infant." Earlier in the seventeenth century, Thomas Brooks (a Puritan divine) used the expression figuratively, in his *Golden Keys to Open Hidden Treasures* (1867 edition, vol. V, p. 142): "Curiosity," he said, "is that greensickness of the soul, whereby it longs for novelties: and loathes sound and wholesome truths."

Greensickness, while meaning lovesickness, has the great advantage, for the translator of the Chinese pun *qing-gen*, of not directly mentioning the word Love. Instead it preserves the surface Green of the original and sends the modern reader diving for a deeper meaning.

Incidentally, the treatment given for this ailment by Dr. Hooper is "to increase the tone of the system by a generous nutritive diet, with the moderate use of wine, by gentle daily exercise, particularly on horseback, by agreeable company, to amuse and quiet the mind, and by tonic medicines, especially the preparations of iron joined with myrrh." *The Stone's* views on the cure are perhaps most succinctly put in the saying quoted in chapter 90:

> No remedy but love
> Can make the lovesick well;
> Only the hand that tied the knot
> Can loose the tiger's bell.

REINCARNATION

Root of Love not only implies a constitutional flaw in Bao-yu's character (what is elsewhere referred to as his *ai-hong-bing* 愛紅病); it also refers to the karma which binds together the main characters in the story. As the Buddhist Mahasattva Impervioso somewhat flippantly puts it in Chapter One, "There is a batch of lovesick souls awaiting incarnation in the world below." To which his jokey sidekick, the Taoist Mysterioso, replies: "Well, well, so another lot of these amorous wretches is about to enter the vale of tears.... How did all this begin?" Impervioso goes on to tell him about the Stone's attachment to the Crimson Pearl Flower, "for which he conceived such a fancy that he took to watering her every day with sweet dew, thereby conferring on her the gift of life." The flower assumed the form of a girl, and this fairy girl wandered about outside the Realm of Separation, eating the Secret Passion Fruit when she was hungry and drinking from the Pool of Sadness when she was thirsty (Alice in Wonderland and the Pool of Tears?). The thought that she owed the Stone something for his kindness in watering her began to prey on her mind and ended by becoming an obsession. "I have no sweet dew here that I can repay him with," she would say to herself. "The only way in which I could perhaps repay him would be with the tears shed during the whole of a mortal lifetime, if he and I were ever to be reborn as humans in the world below."

When Stone and Flower first meet in human form, as Bao-yu and Dai-yu, Bao-yu says with a laugh: "I have seen this cousin before!" "Nonsense," says his grandmother. "How could you possibly have met!" "Well," replies Bao-yu, "perhaps not; but her face seems so familiar that I have the impression of meeting her again after a long separation."

Although reincarnation is a characteristically Eastern belief, it has not been without its adherents in the West. Plato inherited it from the Orphic tradition. In the Phaedrus he explains the experience of love in this way:

> It is the past history of men in the other world that accounts for their destinies here, and also for the effect upon them of beauty. At the sight of it men fall in love. For it is a "copy" of the original beauty they saw elsewhere.... Whenever one who is fresh from those mysteries, who saw much of that heavenly vision, beholds in any godlike face or form a successful copy of original beauty, he first

of all feels a shuddering chill, and terror creeps over him. . . . Afterwards follow the natural results of his chill—a sudden change, a sweating and glow of unwonted heat. For he has received through his eyes the emanation of beauty, and has been warmed thereby, and his native plumage is watered.

A French critic, Charles Commeaux, has described Cao Xue-qin as one of the great theoreticians of Platonic Love.[5] I think he meant Platonic in the broad sense of spiritual; I would go further. Plato and Cao share a concept of Love that is based on reincarnation. Love for Cao is karmic debt. In the payment of it (which may take many incarnations) lovers are drawn together as irresistibly as enemies at war. The process must continue until it is broken off by the force of Enlightenment, and the elimination of desire.

AFFINITY

The bond between Bao-yu and his cousin Bao-chai is commonly referred to as the Affinity of Gold and Jade—Bao-chai's golden locket matches Bao-yu's Jade Talisman—while the bond between Bao-yu and Dai-yu is called the Bond of Old by Stone and Flower Made. These elemental affinities have a close parallel in Western astrology and in the Elective Affinities of the Western alchemical tradition. I am not qualified to pursue this parallel in greater depth. I mention it as a further reason for my belief that to do full justice to a work such as *The Story of the Stone*, which represents the last flowering of Chinese culture in its entirety, we need, as translators, not only to immerse ourselves in Chinese culture but also to continue imbibing our own great European tradition, of which alchemy and astrology were intrinsic parts. To put it another way, the "island" should not be moored just off the South China coast: it should be somewhere, or nowhere, equidistant from both East and West.

UNIVERSAL CULTURE

The translator from the Chinese must, at least during the process of translating, suspend any belief that East is East and West is West. He or she must somehow believe in the universality of the human spirit and the possibility of a universal culture. I once dreamed that I was standing in a Byzantine church, with shafts of colored light illuminating vivid little patches in an otherwise dark and claustrophobic interior. The air was heavy with incense and the scent of candles, The shadows had a purplish tinge. The overall effect was suffocating, and I felt a compelling need to escape. When I pushed open the great west door, I found myself at once bathed in light, and looking around me saw a square with on either side palaces built in a Moorish style out of golden stone. I was, I suppose, in Saint Mark's Square in Venice (although I have only seen it on postcards). Straight ahead of me, however, was no Venetian palace but a long, low-lying Chinese mansion, all airiness and light, grace and delicacy, in contrast to the Byzantine labyrinth I had just come from. It was predominantly a pale gray-blue, with touches of red and green. There were steps leading up to the main entrance, and walking down the steps toward me was a tall elderly gentleman with white goatee and scholar's gown. He smiled at me, took me by the hand, and led me up the steps. As we walked together toward the entrance he introduced himself as Mr. Ito.

Ito Sohei, whom I have never had the pleasure of meeting, is the Japanese translator of *The Stone* and the possessor of one of the rare old manuscript transcriptions of the novel. But to me the enduring interest of this dream lies in the fact that Venice is one of the historical meeting places of East and West. Another is Macau. It is only a faith that such places also exist in the mind that can justify and sustain the attempts of translators, their endeavors to create a never-never land where Chinese aristocrats converse in the Queen's English, Latin and French, while their servants swear in Cockney.

Sometimes, it is true, the material for this alchemy has been lost nearly beyond recovery. As the result of the scientific, industrial, and electronic revolutions, the West has become over the past two hundred years more and more cut off from its own heritage. And this heritage is the translator's own Sea of Words, without which his endeavor will run aground.

CONCLUSION

Let me end this ramble by returning to Greensickness Peak, and by recalling in the shade of that ominous crag a short extract from *Romeo and Juliet*, one of the great tragedies of star-crossed love.

Juliet's mother, in Act 3, scene 5, has come to tell Juliet that she is to be married to Paris. Juliet replies:

> I pray you tell my lord and father, madam,
> I will not marry yet, and when I do, I swear
> It shall be Romeo, whom you know I hate,
> Rather than Paris.

When her father arrives and is told of her refusal to comply with his plans, he starts to get into a rage:

> How, will she none? Doth she not give us thanks?
> Is she not proud? Doth she not count her blessed,
> Unworthy as she is, that we have wrought
> So worthy a gentleman to be her bride?

Juliet replies:

> Not proud you have, but thankful that you have.
> Proud can I never be of what I hate,
> But thankful even for hate, that is meant love.

And Capulet replies:

> How, how, how, how, chopt logic ... What is this?
> "Proud" and "I thank you" and "I thank you no,"
> And yet "not proud" ... Mistress minion you,
> Thank me no thankings, nor proud me no prouds,
> But fettle your fine joints 'gainst Thursday next,
> To go with Paris to Saint Peter's Church,
> Or I will drag thee on a hurdle thither.
> Out you greensickness carrion, out you baggage,
> You tallow-face!

"You greensickness Carrion" is a rather strong way of saying "you anemic, unmarried lovesick corpse." Greensickness is that aspect of love that "unmakes" the lover. It seems to me a nearly perfect way to translate *qinggeng*, hinting at some of the deeper meaning, the secret message, of the name of that Peak, where the Stone lay, and in whose shadow the story's theme of Love, Disenchantment, and Enlightenment was born.

In ploys such as this, where verbal wit combines with literary allusion and philosophical depth, author and translator are as one.

Gem-like Ecstasy

Milestones

The Story of the Stone is, among other things, the story of the inner transformation of the stone's incarnation, Jia Bao-yu. It shows us the psychological progress of an aristocratic boy through adolescence.

One of the signposts used to mark the stages in this inner journey is the *dream*. It is in a grand dream (chapter 5) that Bao-yu is initiated into sexual love; it is in a dream (chapter 116) that he finally receives illumination. The riddles shown him in the first dream are only understood by him in the last.

Other milestones are the *books* that he reads. For example, in chapter 21 we see him "setting down to a volume of Zhuang-zi." He finds that the words of Zhuang-zi wonderfully suit his mood, and even dabbles in a little amateur Taoist composition of his own. In chapter 22, a few days later, he still has Zhuang-zi's words ringing in his head, and this time tries his hand at writing poetry with a Zen flavor. For both of these premature "excursions into the void" he is mercilessly teased by his cousins.

In chapter 23, when the young people of the family are allowed to move into Prospect Garden, we are told that life for Bao-yu "became utterly and completely satisfying. Every day was spent in the company of his maids and cousins in the most amiable and delightful occupations, such as reading, practicing calligraphy, strumming on the *qin*, playing Go, painting, composing verses, etc. He was blissfully happy." And yet, we read a few pages further on, "quite suddenly, in the midst of this placid, agreeable existence, he was discontented. He got up one day feeling out of sorts. Nothing he did brought any relief. Whether he stayed indoors or went out into the garden, he remained bored and miserable. The garden's female population were mostly still in that age of innocence when freedom from inhibition is the fruit of ignorance. Waking and sleeping they surrounded him, and their mindless giggling was constantly in his ears. How could *they* understand the restless feelings that now consumed him? In his present mood of discontent he was bored with the garden and its inmates; yet his attempts to find distraction outside it ended in the same emptiness and ennui."

In the end, the only thing that lifts him out of this state is the gift his page boy Tealeaf brings him, a parcel of novels and plays he has managed to buy from the bookstalls and smuggle in. We are given a short list of them, and watch Bao-yu exploring the world of Chinese fiction and drama—and especially the long Yuan dynasty play *The Western Chamber*, which he and Dai-yu discover together. Only a few lines from the play are quoted, but they are enough to make the point that their love is no longer a playful affair between children.

For the "middle part" of the novel, Bao-yu settles down to an idyllic exploration of the world of poetry, together with the other members of the Crab-flower Poetry Club. His own noms de plume reveal something of the spirit of this hothouse for literary blooms: Lord of the Flowers, Lucky Lounger, and Green Boy.

And again in chapter 36, he reads lyric drama, this time Tang Xianzu's haunting masterpiece *The Peony Pavilion*, or *The Return of the Soul*: "a day arrived when Bao-yu seemed to have exhausted the Garden's possibilities, and its charms were beginning to weary him. *The Return of the Soul* was very much on his mind at this time. He had read it through twice without in any way abating his appetite for more...."

The Other Half of the Garden

By the beginning of volume 4, this idyllic world is already crumbling around Bao-yu. Harsh reality is breaking through the delicate protective structure of the Garden, and he gradually has to bring his perceptions to bear not just on art and literature and idealistic love but on the seamier side of life. One of his cousins, Ying-chun, has been married to Sun Shao-zu, a callous brute, who mistreats her appallingly. The marriage was arranged by her father, Jia She, an unpleasant character throughout the novel, as payment for some of his debts. When Bao-yu learns of her suffering he is profoundly disturbed. In chapter 81, he goes to see his mother and pleads with her to mount a rescue operation. Surely an edict from Grandmother Jia will enable them to bring Ying-chun home again to the sanctuary of the Garden? Lady Wang predictably tells him to stop being so silly, and he leaves her apartment with his hopes dashed. He goes straight to see Dai-yu and pours his heart out to her.

"*Why is it that the minute they're grown up girls are married off and have to suffer so?*[6] When I think of the happy times we all had together when we first started the Crab-flower Club, always inviting each other round for parties and holding poetry contests—there seemed no end of wonderful things to do. And now? *Bao-chai has already moved out, which means Caltrop can't come over either, and with Ying gone as well,* our band of kindred spirits is being broken up, everything is being spoiled!

"I had thought of a plan, to get Grannie on our side and rescue Ying. But when I told Mother, she just called me naive *and silly. So I had to give up the idea.*"

Wang Xilian: . . . captures to perfection the way a pampered young aristocrat, gone a bit soft in the head, *would* speak![7]

"You only have to look around you! Our Garden's altered so much in such a short time. What could become of it in the next few years just doesn't bear thinking about. Now do you see what I mean, and why I can't help despairing?"

Wang Xilian: This tearful speech of Bao-yu's about the decline of the Garden etc., touches Dai-yu to the quick (it is so close to her own preoccupations). The whole scene develops a central theme of the novel, an organic link connecting and reflecting at a distance previous and subsequent strands in the plot (與前後文遙遙照應, 通皆血脈貫通).

As she listened to all that he was saying, Dai-yu *very slowly bowed her head and moved back almost imperceptibly onto the kang.* She did not say a word, but only sighed and curled up facing the wall.

Yao Xie: How could she express her feelings by more than a sigh?

Later that same day, after his afternoon nap, he awakes in a mood of intense ennui. Aroma advises him to go out into the Garden to shake it off. In the first draft of this section, Bao-yu simply gets up and walks out into the Garden—where sure enough he finds a little respite, a brief afterglow of the old joie de vivre, in the form of a ladies' fishing excursion. But in the final draft, there is a short passage—205 characters long—inserted between his waking up and his walk in the Garden.

In the afternoon, when he woke from his sleep, he felt very bored, *and picked up a book to read. Aroma hurried off to make tea, eager to sustain him in his studies. He had chanced upon an anthology of early verse, and as he turned its pages found himself reading a stanza by Cao Cao:*

> Come drink with me and sing,
> For life's a fleeting thing.
> Full many a day has fled
> Like the morning dew . . .

Far from distracting him, this only served to increase his ennui, and he put the book down and picked up another. This time it was The Gathering at Orchid Pavilion and other Prose Selections from the Jin Dynasty. *After a page or two he suddenly closed it, and when Aroma returned with his tea, she found him sitting there, head propped on hand, looking his most dazed and distant.*

Yao Xie: What a vivid touch! What can he have come across this time?

"Why have you given up so soon?" she asked.
Bao-yu took his tea without a word of reply, drank a sip, then mechanically replaced the cup. Aroma was out of her depth and could do nothing but stand there dumbly looking on. Suddenly he stood up, and muttered sarcastically: "Oh gemlike ecstasy . . ."

Yao: He already seems close to enlightenment.... *Very* Zen! So it was the *Orchid Pavilion Preface!* Come across an expression like this in a mood of depression, and the more you understand it the more it compounds your depression.

The intention of this editorial insertion is clear. Indeed, this is one of those cases where the translator (the close reader par excellence) can gain a great deal from looking at the (often complicated) process of textual change. The purpose of the inserted passage is to indicate, obliquely, by an almost casual reference to two well-known pieces of literature, the nature of Bao-yu's depression. Of the two quotations, the first is less problematic to the translator, as two lines from the original poem by Cao Cao are quoted, and by a slight extension of the quotation it is possible to convey to the English reader some of the theme of the poem, the evanescence of human life, and to suggest why it touched Bao-yu to the quick. The second reference is more difficult to deal with.

The piece Bao-yu was reading, and from which he quotes a phrase, was the famous *Orchid Pavilion Preface* by Wang Xi-zhi, though it is not mentioned by name—the book is merely described as *Jin-wen*, Jin prose. In this short prose idyll Bao-yu finds an echo of the Garden way of life, the "communion of kindred spirits" whose dispersal he had been lamenting only that morning in the Naiad's House. The gathering at Orchid Pavilion was the prototype of the scholars' picnic, a carefree, convivial gathering of sensitive souls. But for Bao-yu the halcyon days of picnics and innocent artistic pursuits are over. He is witnessing the disintegration of the Garden world; he hasn't the time any longer, and even if he had, he no longer has the inclination, to spend his days in the old way. He is being forced to spend hours every day studying the classics and preparing for his exams.

Let me quote the *Orchid Pavilion Preface* at slightly greater length (in a revised version of Lin Yutang's translation):

Here, mid lofty mountain ranges and majestic peaks, among trees with thick foliage and tall bamboos, with clear streams and gurgling rapids catching the eye on both sides, we sit by the waterside. Our cup floats down the meandering stream and we drink in turn. And though we have no strings and flutes to fill the air with music, yet with singing and drinking we can while away the hours in quiet intimate conversation. The sky is clear, and the air fresh; a mild breeze blows. How fine it is to contemplate the mighty firmament and all creation's wonders, letting our eyes wander over the landscape, while our hearts roam at will. When people are gathered together, some like to sit and talk and unburden their thoughts in the intimacy of a room; others overcome by a sentiment, soar forth into a realm of ecstasy.

And then this:

All that is actual in it (this world of impressions) is a single moment, gone while we are trying to apprehend it, of which it may ever be more truly said that it has ceased to be than that it is. To such a tremulous wisp constantly reforming itself on the stream, to a single sharp impression, with a sense in it, a relic more or less fleeting of such moments gone by, what is *real* in our life fines itself down. It is with the movement, the passage and dissolution of impressions, images, sensations, that analysis leaves off—that continual vanishing away, that strange perpetual weaving and unweaving of ourselves.

A counted number of pulses only is given to us of a variegated, dramatic life. How may we see in them all that is to be seen in them with the finest senses? To burn always with this hard gem-like flame, to maintain this ecstasy, is success in life. Failure is to form habits; for habit is relative to a stereotyped world.... We are all condamnés, as Victor Hugo says, condemned to death with an indefinitely suspended sentence. We have an interval and then our place knows us no more. Some spend this interval in listlessness, some in high passions, the wisest in art and song.

This famous (in fact notorious) passage is from the conclusion to Walter Pater's *Studies in the History of the Renaissance*, published in 1873. The short pieces in this collection were prose idylls rather than critical essays in the conventional sense. Their theme was "art for art's sake" and the cult of the dilettante, in the strict sense of "one who delights in the arts and the things of the mind for their own sake." The phrase "to burn with a hard gem-like flame" became the motto of the late nineteenth-century aesthetic movement in England. Pater the inspirer of aesthetic youth was anathema to the Victorian establishment with its belief in "moral fiber" and muscular Christianity. He was often condemned as the spokesman of hedonism, self-indulgence, and sexual perversion. His writings retain some of their power today, and it has been said that no one who comes under Pater's influence before the age of twenty will ever be content to remain gross and ignorant.

The phrase "gem-like ecstasy" refers, then, by way of its Pateresque echoes, to a world somewhat similar to that of the Orchid Pavilion, and the eccentric aesthetes of Jin times.[8] But the crucial point here (in terms of the novel's development) is that Bao-yu is beginning to see all this picnicking not with nostalgia but with disenchantment. No number of sessions of the Poetry Club, no amount of gemlike ecstasy, can alleviate the suffering of real people like his poor Cousin Ying-chun. Nor can Grandmother Jia be called upon any longer, to conjure up magic solutions to the complexities of adult life, however much she may have been able to protect her grandchildren in the past.

Walter Pater has been portrayed in his early fifties as prematurely decrepit (burning with a faltering flame), a creature of habit (and therefore in his own terms a failure), addicted to lying in bed till noon reading not lyric verse but a dictionary. And Oscar Wilde, his most flamboyant disciple, describes in *De Profundis*, written late in his life from Reading Gaol, how he became disenchanted with Pater's philosophy:

> Once I knew [how to be happy], or I thought I knew it, by instinct. It was always springtime once in my heart. My temperament was akin to joy. I filled my life to the very brim with pleasure, as one might fill a cup to the very brim with wine. Now I am approaching life from a completely new standpoint, and even to conceive happiness is often extremely difficult for me. I remember during my first term at Oxford reading Pater's Renaissance—that book which has had such strange influence over my life.... I don't regret for a single moment having lived for pleasure. I did it to the full, as one should do everything that one does. There was no pleasure I did not experience. I threw the pearl of my soul into a cup of wine. I went down the primrose path to the sound of flutes. I lived on honeycomb. But to have continued the same life would have been wrong because it would have been limiting. I had to pass on. The other half of the garden had its secrets for me also....
>
> For the artistic life is simply self-development. Humility in the artist is his frank acceptance of all experiences, just as love in the artist is simply the sense of beauty that reveals to the world its body and soul. In *Marius the Epicurean* Pater seeks to reconcile the artistic life with the life of religion, in the deep, sweet and austere sense of the word. But Marius is little more than a spectator; an ideal spectator indeed, and one to whom it is given "to contemplate the spectacle of life with appropriate emotions," which Wordsworth defines as the poet's true aim; yet a spectator merely, and perhaps a little too preoccupied with the comeliness of the benches of the sanctuary to notice that it is the sanctuary of sorrow that he is gazing at.

In other words, the phrase "gem-like ecstasy" hopes (perhaps in vain) to evoke in its English echoes not only the aesthetic creed of Pater, but also the inadequacy of that creed. Bao-yu has reached just such a turning point. He is beginning to see through his own shallow aestheticism, while his father and teacher offer him only the cold comfort of Neo-Confucian philosophy. Rejecting both to follow the compass of his own experience, he is ultimately drawn toward his authentic spiritual goal.

Holy Pretentious Woffle

On the evening of the day we have just been reading about, Bao-yu's father and mother are talking in their private apartment, and the subject of Bao-yu's education comes up.

"Bao-yu's present state of idleness is thoroughly unsatisfactory, and in my opinion the best solution would be for him to resume his studies at the Family School."

"I agree with you entirely," said Lady Wang. *"Since your last posting he has been constantly ill, and what with one thing and another has fallen a long way behind with his studies. I think the routine of going to school would do him good."*

Jia Zheng nodded, and they continued chatting for a while longer.

Little time was lost. The very next day, as soon as Bao-yu was up and had finished washing and combing his hair, a deputation of pages arrived and sent in the message: "Sir Zheng wishes to see Master Bao." Hurriedly tidying his clothes, Bao-yu went straight over to his father's study. He paid his morning respects *and stood to attention.*

"Tell me," Jia Zheng began, "what you have been doing recently in the way of work? A fair amount, were you going to say? A very *magnum opus* of your worthless doodling, no doubt.... *I have observed you of late. Your idleness goes from strength to strength. I am also constantly hearing of some new ailment of yours, or shall we rather say ingenious pretext to play truant. I trust I find you fully recovered?*

"Another thing: I gather you spend the greater part of your time fooling around with your cousins in the garden, and that even the maidservants are permitted to participate in your infantile antics. Isn't it time you grew up and acquired a little self-esteem? You must understand that those verses you write are not going to impress anyone. The only thing the examiners are interested in is a well-written composition. *And the effort you have expended in that direction has so far been nonexistent.*[9]

> Yao Xie: Jia Zheng's exhortation to Bao-yu to study the Octopartite is a preparation for his subsequent success in the examination: without such a detailed section describing Bao-yu's efforts at composition, his later success would be quite implausible. It is the general rule with this book that in its structural organization there is never a superfluous word, and never a word left out.

"Now listen carefully to what I have to say. From today, I want you to forget all about your verses and couplets. You are to concentrate exclusively on Octopartite Compositions. I will give you twelve months' grace. If by the end of that time you are still in your present unregenerate state, you may as well give up altogether, and I for my part shall have to think again about owning a creature like you as my son."

He summoned Li Gui. "Inform Tealeaf that he is to take Bao-yu first thing tomorrow morning to collect the required textbooks, and then bring them here for my inspection. I shall be accompanying him to school myself."

Turning to Bao-yu: "Off with you!" he trumpeted. "I shall expect you early tomorrow morning."

Bao-yu returned to Green Delights, where Aroma was anxiously awaiting him. The pleasure with which she received the news of his renewed course of study contrasted strangely with the incredulous horror *that had rendered him speechless while in Jia Zheng's presence, and that now prompted him to send an urgent message through to Grandmother Jia, begging her to intervene. She sent for him at once and said: "You should give it a try, my darling. You don't want to anger your father. Don't worry. Remember, I shall always be here if you need me."*

There was nothing for it but to go back and give the maids their instructions. "Wake me at the crack of dawn, as Father will be waiting to take me to school." Aroma and Musk, took it in turns to stay awake that night.

Yao Xie: If Skybright had still been alive, she too would have had a sleep-less night.

In the morning Aroma woke Bao-yu punctually, helped him wash, comb his hair *and dress*, and sent *a junior maid out with* instructions for Tealeaf to wait with the books *at the inner gate. She had to spur him on a couple of times before finally he left and* made his way toward the study. On his way he stopped to inquire if Sir Zheng had arrived yet, and was informed by a *page from the study* that *one of the literary gentlemen had just called, but had been kept waiting outside as,* the Master was still in his dressing room. This calmed Bao-yu's nerves a little, and he proceeded on to the inner sanctum. As luck would have it, a servant was at that very moment coming out on his way to fetch him, so he went straight in. After another brief homily, Jia Zheng led the way and father and son took a carriage to the school, *Tealeaf following with the books.*

A lookout had been posted, and Dai-ru *had been alerted and* was standing in readiness for the party's arrival. *Before the old man could come forward to greet him, however,* Jia Zheng walked into the schoolroom and paid his respects. Dai-ru *took him by the hand and* inquired politely after Lady Jia. Bao-yu then went up and paid his respects. *Jia Zheng remained standing throughout, and insisted on waiting until Dai-ru was seated before sitting down himself.*

"I have come here today," he began "*because I felt the need to entrust my son to you personally, and with a few words of instruction.* He is no longer a child, and if he is to shoulder his responsibilities and earn a place in the world, it is high time he applied himself conscientiously to preparing for his exams. At home, unfortunately, he spends all his time idling about *in the company of children.* His verses, the only field in which he has acquired any competence, are for the most part turgid juvenilia, at their best romantic trifles devoid of substance."

Yao Xie: A salutary warning to all parents blinded by fondness for their children. Jia Zheng is not just mouthing high-sounding platitudes.

"And he looks such a fine lad," interposed Dai-ru. "He seems so intelligent. Why this refusal to study, this perverse streak of hedonism? *Not that one should entirely neglect poetic composition. But there is surely time enough for that later on in one's career.*"

Yao Xie: It is his intelligence that enables him to take the Octopartites in his stride. Dai-ru's approach is rather broader than Jia Zheng's.

"Precisely," said Jia Zheng. "For the present I would humbly suggest a course of reading and exegesis of primary scriptural texts, and plenty of compositions. If he should show the least sign of being a recalcitrant pupil, I earnestly beseech you to take him in hand, and in so doing to save him from a shallow and wasted life."

On this note he rose, and with a bow and a few parting remarks took his leave. Dai-ru accompanied him to the door.

"Please convey my respects to Lady Jia." "I will," said Jia Zheng, and climbed into his carriage.

When Dai-ru returned to the classroom, *Bao-yu was already sitting at a small rosewood desk in the south-west corner of the room, by the window. He had two sets of texts and a meager-looking volume of model compositions stacked in a pile on his right. Tealeaf was instructed to put his paper, ink, brush, and inkstone away in the drawer of the desk.*

Yao Xie: The monkey has been locked up.

"I understand you have been ill, Bao-yu," said Dai-ru. "I hope you are quite recovered?" Bao-yu rose to his feet. "Quite recovered, thank you sir." "We must see to it that you apply yourself with zeal from now on. Your father is most insistent that you should do well. Start by revising the texts you have already memorized. Your timetable will be as follows: *Pre-prandium*—General Revision; *Post-prandium*—Calligraphy; *Meridianum*—Exegesis. And conclude the day's work by reciting quietly to yourself a few model compositions. That should do for the time being."

"Yes, sir."[10]

The author might have been content to leave it at that, and we would then have only a vague idea of what these dreadful Octopartite Compositions were like. But Gao E (if we continue to make the assumption that he edited the last forty chapters) goes to considerable trouble to show us exactly what Bao-yu had to put up with, and writes two further scenes, describing the Octopartite experience in great detail.[11] In the first, the Preceptor supervises Bao-yu's oral exegesis of the classics, while in the second his father inspects some of his written work.

This part of the novel seems to me of great interest. After all, the Chinese intelligentsia went through much this kind of training for over five hundred years. And yet, so violent has been the reaction against Octopartites that very few modern writers acknowledge their existence except to say how sterile and stifling they were, and Gao E has been labeled a reactionary for dwelling on them at such length. Cao Xue-qin, it is argued, would never have compromised himself in this way.

Let me try to give both sides of the picture. At one end of the spectrum is Gu Yan-wu's well-known view that the insistence on Octopartites in public examinations did more harm to Chinese culture than the Burning of the Books. The eighteenth-century poet Yuan Mei had a great natural aversion to them; but when he saw that his only chance of getting a job lay in passing the second- and third-degree exams, he worked at Octopartites furiously for two years, almost abandoning general study and reading, and did indeed become a master in this rather ignoble art. A collection of his model compositions, known as *Academician Yuan's Drafts*, became a standard textbook for candidates. The great seventeenth-century critic Jin Sheng-tan wrote that "in spite of its stifling effects on the intellectual life of China ... when viewed simply as a piece of literary composition, the Octopartite has at least the following two merits to recommend it: first, it teaches the writer how to write tightly woven compositions, in which each segment contributes substantially to the whole; second, it forces the writer to write economically by presenting his main point without bringing in any unnecessary words." Surely these are words that twentieth-century writers of *baihua* prose should take to heart? In his own literary criticism, indeed, Jin used Octopartite technical terms. And the final "witness for the defense" is James Legge's collaborator Wang Tao, speaking in the mid-nineteenth century. "It is very common," he said, "nowadays to show how cultivated you are by attacking the style of writing demanded in the official examinations, and by sneering at those who cultivate it as a lot of pedants. Actually, the examination style is a definite kind of prose style, and cannot be dismissed lightly. Among the works of the best writers of it you will find pieces equal to anything in classical literature and worthy to be mentioned, in their own way, side by side with Tang poetry and Yuan drama."

My first attempt at translating the Octopartite scenes was in terms of my own experience. Like many people, I have memories of having suffered at the hands of pedantic old schoolteachers. The parallel seemed a hopeful starting point. It would be quite a business to translate the *wen-yan* into Latin, but if it would give a real feeling of the dreariness of a classical education to a young mind, while at the same time hinting that there were one or two good things buried beneath it all somewhere; it would be worth doing. Of course, I would have to make allowances for modern readers with no Latin: that meant, in effect, double-translating certain passages. And I provided one or two helpful tips, in the form of commentary. Here is how the "oral exegesis" scene turned out.

> "Help!" cried Bao-yu. "I'm late!" He quickly washed and combed his hair, completed his round of morning duties and set off for school. The Preceptor's *severe expression* as he walked into the schoolroom did not bode well. "Tardy, boy, tardy! What is the meaning of this? Small wonder that you have incurred your father's displeasure and caused him to call you his prodigal son, if this is the way you think you can behave on your second day."
>
> Bao-yu told him of his fever the night before, then crossed over to his desk and sat down to his work.
>
> It was late in the afternoon when he was called forward. "Bao-yu, step up here. Oral Exposition of this text." Bao-yu walked up. On inspection, he found to his relief that it was a rubric he knew. *Analects*, chapter IX, verse XXII: *Maxima Debetur Puero Reverentia*—RESPECT DUE TO YOUTH. "What a

stroke of luck!" he thought to himself. "Thank goodness it's not from the *Mag* or the *Med!*" (Young scholars of that time were wont to use these affectionate abbreviations to refer to those two other venerable texts of Scripture, the *Magna Scientia*, or Great Learning, and the *Medium Immutabile*, or Doctrine of the Mean.)

Yao Xie: People writing compositions nowadays are scared of the Great Learning and the Doctrine of the Mean.

"How do you wish me to begin, sir?"

"*Amplificatio Totius*, boy. Give the substance of the passage carefully in your own words."

Bao-yu first recited the original chapter, in the prescribed sing-song intonation, and then began: "In this verse we have the Sage's Exhortation to Youth to Seize the Hour and Strive with Zeal, lest they end up becoming ..."

Bao-yu looked up at Dai-ru. The Preceptor sensed what was coming and tried to conceal his embarrassment with a short laugh: "Come on, boy, come on. What is holding you back? Are you afraid of using a non-licet expression up to books? Remember: Scriptural Exegesis is exempt from the normal rules of Verbal Prohibition. Liber Rituum, Book I: 'In Canonicorum Classicorumque Librorum Studiis Nomenclationum cessat Prohibitio.' What may they end up becoming?"

"Complete Failures, sir," said Bao-yu, barely suppressing a mischievous smile. "In the first Segment, *Sunt Verendi*, the Sage is Spurring Youth on to Moral Endeavor in the Present, while the last Segment, *Non Sunt Digni Quos Verearis*, contains his Caution for the Future." *He looked up again at Dai-ru.*

Yao Xie: A lifelike stroke.

"That will do. *Interpretatio Partium.*"

Bao-yu began again: "Confucius saith: 'For the Duration of Youth each Spiritual and Mental Talent must be held in Due Esteem. For how can we ever Predict with Certainty another's Ultimate Station in Life? But if a man, by Drifting and Wasting his Days, should reach the Age of Forty or Fifty and still be Unsuccessful and Obscure, then it can fairly be said that his Youthful Promise was an Empty One. He will have Forfeited Forever the Esteem of his Fellow Men.'"

"Your *Amplificatio Totius* was passably clear," commented Dai-ru *with a dry smile.*

Yao Xie: Dai-ru's homily is a serious study of the teacher, not just any old pedantic claptrap.

"But I am afraid your *Interpretatio Partium* showed a good deal of immaturity. In the phrase *sine Nomine, Nomen* refers not to Success in the Worldly Sense but rather to an Individual's Achievement in the Moral and Intellectual Spheres. In this sense it by no means implies Official Rank. On the contrary, many of the Great Sages of Antiquity were Obscure Figures who Withdrew from the World; and yet we hold them in the Highest Esteem, do we not? *Nonne sunt Digni Quos Vereamur?*"

"You construe the last sentence incorrectly," he droned on. "Here it is not the element of Esteem but the Irreconcilable Nature of the Judgment of his

Fellow Men that is being contrasted with their Tentative Appraisal of him as a Youth (see second sentence of your text). This emphasis is central to a Correct Elucidation of the passage. Do you follow me?"

Yao Xie: Nice speech!

"Yes, sir."
"Good. Here is another."
Dai-ru turned back a few pages and pointed out a passage to Bao-yu. It was Analects *again, this time chapter IX, verse XVIII:* Ego nondum vidi qui amet Virtutem sicut amat Pulchram Speciem—*THE RARITY OF A SINCERE LOVE OF VIR-TUE. Bao-yu scented danger ahead and said with his most ingenuous smile:*

Yao Xie: Struck to the quick!

"I'm afraid I can't think of anything to say, sir."

Yao Xie: Bao-yu has plenty of ideas on the love of Beauty. It's a question of where to start, and how to say it in a penetrating, pithy way. Old Fuddy-duddy scolds him for talking nonsense, and completely fails to understand how pupil differs from teacher.

"Nonsense, my boy! Is that what you would write if it turned up as a Thema *in your paper?"*

Yao Xie: Good point!

Reluctantly Bao-yu set the wheels in motion. "Confucius saith: 'Men will not love Virtue, and yet they Fall Down and Worship Sensual Beauty at First Sight. The Reason for this Disaffection is that they are Blind to the Intrinsicality of Virtue. Beauty is an Intrinsic Quality too, and as such Loved by All, but it belongs to the Realm of Human Desire, whereas Virtue is a Natural Principle. How can Principle hope to Compete with Desire for the Affections of men? Confucius is both Lamenting the State of the World and Hoping for a Change of Heart. The Love of Virtue he has observed has been for the most part a Shallow and Short-lived Affair. How Fine it would be if only men would feel for Virtue the Devotion they feel towards Beauty ..."

"Thank you, that will do," said Dai-ru. "I have but one question to put to you. If you understand the words of Confucius so well, why is it that you transgress these very two Precepts? I am only an outsider, but *without need of explanation from your Father* I can identify your Moral Shortcomings. One cannot hope to become a Man except by dint of Constant Self-Improvement. You are at present a Youth of Promise, or as our text has it, *Puer Verendus.* Whether or not you Fulfill this Promise depends entirely on your own efforts. Are you to be a Man of Merit, *Vir Nominis,* or are you to be a Man no Longer Esteemed by his Fellow Men, *Vir Non Iam Verendus?*

"I shall allow you an initial period of one month in which to revise your old texts thoroughly, and a further month in which to study models of Octopartite Composition. At the end of the second month I intend to set you your Maiden Theme. If I detect any sign of slackness on your part, you need not expect me to be lenient. As the saying goes, 'Perfection comes through ceaseless effort; effortless ease brings but perdition.' Be sure to bear in mind all that I have said."

"Yes, sir."

Wang Xilian: The Preceptor's texts are most aptly chosen, a perfect remedy for Bao-yu's defects, calculated to bring our young fop into the paths of Virtue.

While working on this scene in the early 1970s in the Bodleian Library (an institution whose connection with China goes back at least to the seventeenth century), I came across *Cursus Litteraturae Sinicae* by Father Angelo Zottoli of the Jesuit Mission at Zikawei. This extraordinary work, in five hefty tomes, covers the entire corpus of Chinese literature systematically, starting with spoken Mandarin, then treating the Classics, the Four Books, Poetry, Prose, and Octopartite Composition. The whole thing is translated and copiously annotated in Latin and took fifteen years to complete. The final volume was published in 1893. For me the most interesting thing about it was the effortless ease with which the Octopartite section (the fifth and most advanced volume) went into Latin. It dawned on me that Father Zottoli was drawing on a far older tradition than my schoolboy Latin prose composition. He was applying to the Octopartite his knowledge of traditional Latin rhetoric, in which as a Jesuit he had been strictly trained in Naples. The Jesuit textbook of rhetoric, the *Ars Dicendi* of Joseph Kleutgen, was still being reprinted as late as 1928. In other words, the Society of Jesus preserved intact a discipline that elsewhere had been extinct for more than a hundred years.

I decided to take the parallel one stage further back and to imagine Bao-yu more as an aristocratic schoolboy in the sixteenth, seventeenth, or eighteenth century, when fluency in Latin was still taken for granted. Here is part of the scene in chapter 84, when Jia Zheng decides to take a look at his son's academic progress.

Jia Zheng was waiting for him in the inner study. Bao-yu entered, made his bow and stood attentively to one side.

"As you know," Jia Zheng began, "I have been rather preoccupied recently and have not had an opportunity to question you on the progress of your studies. Let me see, I recall that the Preceptor had set you a month for revision, after which time he was to give you your Maiden Theme. That must have been at least two months ago. You should have made a start by now, I think."

"I have, sir," replied Bao-yu. "I have written three compositions. I have been waiting for my work to improve before venturing to trouble you with any specimens of it. Those were the Preceptor's instructions, sir."

"What were your first three Themes?"

"The first was from Analects, sir, Book Two," replied Bao-yu. "'*Annos Quindecim natus:* The Sage Bent upon Learning in his Fifteenth Year.' The second was also from Analects, Book One: '*Obscuritatem Aequo Animo Toleratam:* Lack of Acclaim Borne with Equanimity.' And the third was from Mencius, Book Three, Part Two: '*Tunc Accedunt Micium:* They Succumb to the Mician Heresy.'"

"And have you kept your draft versions?" asked Jia Zheng.

"I have fair copies of all three, sir, with the Preceptor's emendations."

"Are they at home, or in the schoolroom?" "In the schoolroom, sir." "Then have someone go and fetch them at once. I should like to see them."

Bao-yu sent an "express" message through to Tealeaf: "Go to the schoolroom; in the drawer of my desk is a thin bamboo-paper copybook with *Tasks* written on the cover. Bring it here, quickly!"

In a short while Tealeaf returned with the book, which he handed to Bao-yu, who presented it to his father. Jia Zheng opened it at the first page and began reading the first of the eight "legs" of Bao-yu's Maiden Task.

AMPLICATIO PRIMA
THEMA: ANNOS QUINDECIM NATUS
CRUS PRIMUM: APERTURA
Sapiens perfectusque Vir
a puero quidem
se ad Philosophiam applicavit.

Jia Zheng glanced at the emendation and asked Bao-yu to construe his Apertura orally. Bao-yu began: "The Sage, while still a boy ... forsooth ... was wholly Bent upon Learning."

Jia Zheng looked up. "Your use of *puer* betrays an inadequate comprehension of the Theme. I see the Preceptor has substituted the *annos quindecim natus* of the original. Good. *Pueritia*, you see, covers the whole span of boyhood up to and including the age of sixteen, whereas here the Sage is alluding to specific milestones in his own life. We must echo the numbers he uses, if we are to preserve the correct sequence of his moral and intellectual development." Jia Zheng continued with the second "leg."

CRUS SECUNDUM: CONTINUATIO
Tantam autem Applicationem
Rarissimam esse confiteor.

"And what," he asked with a shake of the head, "do you mean by this?"

"That the Sage's application," replied Bao-yu, "is a thing ordinary mortals scarcely ever achieve."

"Childish nonsense, my boy! It only shows what a creature of indolence you are. I am glad to see that the Preceptor has rewritten the entire *Continuatio* for you. Kindly construe, from *romnibus enim*."

Bao-yu obliged: "For many are those who aspire to Learning. But how few alas possess the application necessary for the fulfillment of his Aspiration. Does not the Sage's achievement testify to the strength of his Moral Convictions in his Fifteenth Year?"

"I thank you. I trust you understand the emendation?" "Yes sir."

Jia Zheng passed on to the second Theme: "Lack of Acclaim Borne with Equanimity." (It may be helpful at this point to provide some idea of the pedagogic principles that guided Dai-ru in his selection of Themes for his young pupil. His plan was roughly speaking as follows: First Theme—reiterate need for Youthful Zeal; Second Theme—clarify point raised during second day's oral exegesis, viz., Worldly Success versus Moral Achievement; Third Theme—Orthodoxy versus Heresy). Jia Zheng read the Preceptor's emended version, translating to himself as he went along: "If a man is able to view Worldly Acclaim with Equanimity, nothing can affect his Pleasure and Delight." He screwed up his eyes to decipher Bao-yu's original: "What's all this? 'Equanimity is the Essence of Scholarship.' You have completely failed to treat the first element in your Theme, *Obscuritas*, and have embarked prematurely on a discussion of *Nobilitas*, which should be kept for a later section. Your Preceptor's emendation shows a correct *Dispositio*. I hope you notice the way in which he uses *Amoenitatem Delectationemque Animi* to allude to the passage in Analects immediately preceding the rubric? Do you recall? *Nonne quidem amoenum? Nonne quidem delectabile?* You must study this sort of thing carefully."

"Yes sir."

Jia Zheng went on to read Bao-yu's *Continuatio*. There was another reference here to the Essence of Scholarship, which had once again been emended by the Preceptor to Pleasure and Delight. "The same fault as in your *Apertura*," commented Jia Zheng. "The emendation is tolerable. Not particularly stylish, but clear."

He moved on to the third and last Theme: "The Mician Heresy." As he recollected the provenance of the quotation, he looked up in surprise and after a moment's thought asked Bao-yu: "Have you reached this far in Mencius?"

"Yes sir," Bao-yu hastened to assure him. "The Preceptor decided to go through Mencius with me first, as it is the easiest of the Four Books. We finished the whole of Mencius three days ago, and now we are doing Analects Part One."

Jia Zheng continued reading. By the time Bao-yu had come to write this third composition, he had more or less mastered the "ignoble art of the Octopartite," and had learned to handle the necessary rhetorical constructions with a certain glib dexterity. Jia Zheng studied the first two "legs" and observed that in this case the Preceptor had paid the young essayist the compliment of a total suspension of the corrective brush. The *Apertura* lamented the fact that those who rejected the Hedonist Doctrine of Yanxius (*Yanxianam illam Voluptatis Doctrinam*) were still unable to find the True Path of Confucian Orthodoxy (*Orthodoxiae Confucianae Veram Viam*), but were instead blindly drawn into the fold of that prevalent (and deplorable) Mician Heresy of Universal Love (*Micianam illam Caritatis Universae Heterodoxiam*).

"Nicely put," Jia Zheng commented, and continued reading. A little further on he paused. "Tell me," he asked, evidently impressed by what he read, "did you write this unaided?" "Yes, sir." He nodded pensively. "Nothing brilliant about it, of course, but for a first attempt not at all bad, I must say. Ah, Mencius! I recall how during my tour of duty as an examiner I had occasion to set as one of my Themes '*Soli Nobilitatis Sapentiaeque Alumni sunt potis.*' All the first-degree candidates, I regret to say, had their heads crammed full of the standard compositions on the Theme, and not a single one of them could come up with anything original. All plagiarisms. Are you familiar with the quotation?" "Yes, sir. Mencius, Book One, Part Two: 'Only Good Breeding and a Heritage of Culture have the power to sustain a man in the face of Adversity.'" "Good," replied Jia Zheng. "I should like you to show me what you can do. Something of your own, please, not another feat of memorization. An *Apertura* will do."

Bao-yu lowered his head in concentration and began racking his brains for a pithy opening phrase, while Jia Zheng stood thoughtfully in the doorway, hands clasped behind his back. Just at that moment, a diminutive page boy went flashing past. As he caught sight of the Master in the doorway, he froze, his body slightly inclined, his arms hanging limp at his side. "What is your errand, boy?" asked Jia Zheng brusquely. "Please, sir, Mrs. Xue has just arrived at Her Old Ladyship's and Mrs. Lian has sent me with special instructions to the kitchen, sir," jabbered the unfortunate boy. Jia Zheng made no reply, and he fled.

Now Bao-yu assumed that if Aunt Xue had come over for a visit, then Bao-chai (whom he had greatly missed since her departure from the Garden) was sure to have come with her. His excitement at the thought of seeing her again spurred him on. "Sir," he ventured, "I have a draft *Apertura* for your approval." "Go ahead." Bao-yu intoned his opening sentence: "*Non amnes Sapientiae Alumni sunt, neque possunt carere Stabili Patrimonio.*" Jia Zheng nodded. "Thank you. That will do for today. In future, please bear in mind these two Golden Rules for Composition. Before raising your brush, always be certain of the sequence of your *Dispositio* and the clarity of your *Inventio*. Tell me, was your grandmother aware that I sent for you?" "Yes sir." "Off you go then. You had better go over and see her now." "Sir!" Bao-yu maneuvered his way backwards out of the study and set off along the covered way, imitating to perfection the scholar's leisurely gait. As soon as he reached the moon-gate, however, and had placed its large protective screen between himself and the study, he broke into a run and raced ahead toward Grandmother Jia's apartment. "Careful you don't trip!" Tealeaf shouted after him. "The Master's coming."

We have only to compare this with the following account of the sixteenth-century learning of rhetoric in Europe:

In their reading as in their own writing they were taught to observe the larger processes of rhetoric (the five parts of an oration, the three styles, how to write using a formulary system) and to know the name, definition and use of a large number of figures of speech. In the fourth year (at the age of about ten) they would use that seminal work Erasmus's *De Copia* "On the Copy (i.e., amplification) of Words and Things" and in the fifth form they would graduate to the list of figures in Susenbrotus's popular collection or in *Ad Herennium*, Book Four. What pupils actually did when confronted with these compilations may be expressed in quite a bald way: "first learn the figures, secondly identify them in whatever you read, thirdly use them yourself. . . . In the last stage (that of the pupil using the figures himself), the pupil when given the topic for his theme, should first take his notebook, look up everything that might be useful, sketch the argument, and then put it into the five-part form, endeavouring to use the formulae "proper to each part, so as to bring their matter into handsome and plain order." (From T. W. Baldwin, *William Shakespeare's Small Latine & Lesse Greeke*)

And for a detailed example, we can do no better than Edward VI:

... the teaching of royalty was of sufficient importance for the notebooks of King Edward VI to have been preserved. The king had the best humanist teacher in England, Sir John Cheke (who was to have such an enormous influence on Cambridge), and one can trace the progress of instruction in his pupil's exercise-book. In 1547–8 he was taught the figures and the parts of an oration from the *Ad Herennium* (the King's own copy of this has also survived and is well thumbed, especially in the relevant parts) and he simply memorized them like everyone else. We can trace too the next stage, rhetorical analysis of the works studied. In 1548 he was reading the most popular book of moral philosophy in the Renaissance, Cicero's *offices*, extracting *sententiae* and phrases from it, then making an analysis of its structure. More interesting is the evidence that on 28 January 1549 he made a rhetorical analysis of Cicero's famous first speech against Catiline, noting the "figures and phrases" used in it. Of the celebrated direct opening "Quousque tamen abutere Catilina patientia nostra" ("In heaven's name, Catiline, how long will you abuse our patience?") he wrote *Exclamatio*; of another passage repeating "nihil" at the beginning of 6 succeeding clauses he wrote *conduplicatio* ... It is a formal enough exercise but at least as good as that performed by a modern historian of rhetoric. The third stage of the schoolboy's absorption of rhetoric can also be seen here, for in 1549 the young King Edward wrote a Latin composition on the theme "Love is a greater cause of obedience than fear," an especially interesting topic for a ruler. First he collected all his main arguments (*inventio*), also listing similes and examples which he intended to use; then he divided the material up in the form of the five parts of a speech (*dispositio*); lastly he wrote the whole thing out, neatly using up all his quotations.

King Edward VI may have had more individual supervision than other Renaissance schoolboys, but the teaching system and its dominance by rhetoric was the same for him or for Queen Elizabeth as for thousands of other pupils including all the great writers of this period. (From Vickers, *Classical Rhetoric in English Poetry*)

Father Zottoli's Latin translation of the terminology of Octopartite rhetoric is startlingly effortless. No wonder the Jesuits made such good Mandarins! Here are a few examples:

Structure of Octopartite Composition
1. Apertura 破題   2. Continuatio 承題   3. Exordium 起講
4. Transitio 提股   5. Adventitia 虛股   6. Medium Crus 中股
7. Extremum crus 後股   8. Conclusio 收題

Compare *Ad Herrenium*
1. Exordium   2. Narratio   3. Divisio
4. Confirmatio   5. Confutatio   6. Conclusio

Types of Apertura
1. Evidens 明   2. Obtecta 暗   3. Directa 順   4. Inversa 逆
5. A Recto 正   6. A Contrario 反   7. A Parallelo 對   8. Distributa 分

Faults of Style
1. Si continuat praecedentia 連上文   2. Si invadit subsequentia 犯下文
3. Si fiat manca, ita ut necessaria thematis verba non exponantur. 漏題

Envoi

Having dumped Jia Zheng into the sea and fished up Father Zottoli, it is
probably high time to leave the island, or else its heady alchemy will turn
our heads altogether. And yet that is what makes translating a great work
of the imagination, such fun, such an adventure. The island is alive with
magic, it is peopled with Ariels and Calibans. It was after all Chapman, the
translator, not Homer, the blind bard, who caused Keats to feel like "some
watcher of the skies, when a new planet swims into his ken." Translating
is an exciting creative endeavor, even though at times the island (like
Treasure Island) does seem accursed, and (in Robert Louis Stevenson's
immortal words) "the worst dreams that ever I have are when I hear
the surf booming about its coasts, or start upright in bed, with the sharp
voice of Captain Flint still ringing in my ears: 'Pieces of eight! Pieces of
eight!'"

NOTES

1. Ch'en Shih-hsiang's translation, from Birch's *Anthology*.
2. See his *Medieval Bases of Western Thought*.
3. Cf. Inferno, Canto V, ll. 124–25: "Yet, if so dear desire thy heart possess / To
know that root of love which wrought our fall" (Sayers translation).
4. I should like to pay tribute to C. C. Wang's "Nonesuch Bluff," one of his
inspired strokes in that early version, which was all we had for so many years. The
double entendre in *Bluff* and the teasing nomenclature of *nonesuch* are wonderful.
5. In *La Vie quotidienne en Chine sous les Mandchous*.
6. In this and following quotations, passages in italics are editorial additions or
changes in the so-called Gao Draft manuscript. I believe a study of these changes to
be of huge benefit to the translator searching for innuendo, or the "secret message."
I have used Pan Chong-gui's excellent black and red edition.
7. I occasionally add the comments of two nineteenth-century commentators,
Wang Xilian and Yao Xie, again because I find them helpful in interpreting the
"subtext."
8. Bao-yu's quip also refers to Zhuang-zi, and it is fascinating in this context
to note that Oscar Wilde was greatly taken with Herbert Giles's translation of
Zhuang-zi, describing it in 1890 as "the most caustic criticism of modern life I have
met with for some time."
9. Passages in italics and underlined are even later editorial additions, i.e., they

are nowhere to be found in the Gao Draft but are present in the Cheng/Gao printed text.

10. I give these passages in full, since it may not be easy to refer to the published text.

11. In so doing he put to good use his own considerable expertise in this field. Extracts from two of his own collections of model Octopartites are included in the 1955 *Gao Lanshu ji*.

Anthologizing

The Parting of the Ways

Anthologies of Early Modern Chinese Poetry in English Translation

DOMINIC CHEUNG

Harold Acton was an Englishman who taught Shakespeare and English poetry at National Peking University in the 1930s. When teaching at Pei-ta, he had the opportunity to become acquainted with many students and faculty members who had returned from abroad. In his *Memoirs of An Aesthete*,[1] an anecdotal account of his stay in northern China, Acton remembered the Western Languages and Literature Department at Peking University as an abode of young intellectuals well read in Western literature. This group included Liang Tsung-tai, Chu Kuang-ch'ien, and Liang Shih-ch'iu, who were on the faculty, and Pien Chih-lin and Ch'en Shih-hsiang, who were students at the time (Pien graduated a few years ahead of Ch'en).

Feng Chih left for Germany in 1930 for five years and, in 1936, when he returned to China, he made his home in Shanghai instead of Peking. By the time Feng finally returned to Peking after the Sino-Japanese War, Acton had already left. Acton and Feng might have never met; perhaps that was the reason why Feng is not mentioned in the memoirs.

However, finding himself without any language barrier among these people, Acton had a terrific time interacting with various scholars and poets. In describing his friendship with Liang Tsung-tai, who impressed Acton with his "elastic and slangy" English, he observed that "Liang had evidently been much petted in Paris: he seemed to have been brought up on the *Nouvelle Revue Française*; he swore by Stendhal, Racine, and Valéry, but he had never heard of Donne. Valéry had written a flattering preface to his French translations of T'ao Yuan-ming, and in consequence Valéry stood supreme in his eyes. He had returned to China with a determination to introduce Valéry to his countrymen. Valéry's difficulties only added fuel to his ardor. He was already translating *Le Cimetière Marin*."[2]

The Englishman soon found himself in hot debate with a Francophile. He recalled that "Liang enjoyed drawing everyone into argument, and so contemptuous was he of English literature that I found myself hotly defending Shakespeare and the Elizabethans against Racine and the Pléiade, and his bilberry eyes sparkled as he tried to get a rise out of me. We quoted English against French couplets, and as I secretly had no exclusive preferences, but could find room for both Shakespeare and Racine, the Pléiade and the Elizabethans—for me they belonged to one family—I could enjoy the fireworks of his enthusiasm, excessive though they were."[3]

Questioning Valéry's hopelessness that there would be any survival of personal consciousness after death in *Le Cimetière Marin*, Acton insisted with his characteristic Western conviction that the ultimate victory of human actions affirmed the dignity of life, however transient it might be. As far as Liang's respect for Valéry is concerned, Acton overlooked the convergence of metaphysics between these two poets. In his Chinese translation of Valéry's *Fragments du Narcisse*, Liang remembered an early morning in 1927 in France when he promenaded with his mentor in Bois de Boulonge in a chilly drizzle. After Valéry had explained to him the second half of the third stanza of the *Fragments du Narcisse*, he wrote back to Valéry in the same evening expressing his feelings of the *"présence pensive."*[4] It was indeed Liang's submergence in the Taoist empathy with nature that converged with Valéry's "epiphany." The same experience can also be traced regarding the influence of Rilke's mysticism on Feng Chih's sonnets.

Both Feng Chih and Liang Tsung-tai, however, were left out of Acton's anthology *Modern Chinese Poetry*,[5] which resulted from collaboration between Acton and Ch'en Shih-hsiang, who was still a junior at the time. This omission could have been due to Feng's long absence from Peking or to the fact that his famous sonnets were not written until his return from Germany. With Liang, however, while his mind was imbued with the poetics of Goethe, Rilke, and Valéry, his poetry couldn't match their sophistication and complexity.

Even with such regrettable omissions, *Modern Chinese Poetry* remains the most representative early anthology of modern Chinese poems in the 1930s. It is also an epitome of a unique friendship between a teacher and his student. Acton admits in his memoirs that he is indebted to Ch'en for whatever knowledge he possesses of modern Chinese literature, and that it is chiefly on Ch'en's account that he continues to teach at Pei-ta.

He recalls that he first scarcely knew Ch'en until the summer of 1933, when Japanese soldiers swarmed through the streets of Peking as if the old capital already belonged to them. Pei-ta had to cancel all classes because of the disturbances. Many students were dispersed back to their home villages. He received many touching letters of farewell from these students, and one of them was written in the form of a prose-poem by Ch'en Shih-hsiang, whose style reminded him of a letter of Po Chu-i.

A month later, the political tension began easing and the university was planning to reopen in the fall. Acton proposed that Ch'en return to stay with him. It was in early July when Ch'en rejoined his teacher, who was celebrating his birthday with some students at the time. After dinner they sat in the garden and Ch'en played the flute. The thrill of ancient melodies on that sultry summer night reminded Acton of the enchanted singing of the solitary reaper in Wordsworth's poem. He recalled passionately that "on a sudden I realized in every fibre of my being that I was in the China of all my reveries, as a passionate Hellenist might realize he was in Greece."[6]

Acton didn't read Chinese; nor could he assess the individual talent of Chinese poets from firsthand experience. It must have been Ch'en who did the initial selection and prepared the first draft of necessary literal translations before handing them over to Acton for reworking and polishing. When the translations began to pile up on the desk, Acton noted that "it was amusing but sometimes discouraging to contrast them with the originals. Poems of extreme simplicity often proved the most difficult...."[7]

They were more fortunate, however, in translating Pien Chih-lin, because Pien himself was often at their elbows. Pien's poem "The Grass on the Wall" was singled out by Acton, with transliterations, as a satisfactory example of their rendition:

> *Wu-tien-chung t'ieh i-chiao hsieh-yang*
> *Liu-tien-chung kua pan-lun teng-kuang.*
> *Hsiang yu jen ba so-yu-ti jih-tzu*
> *Chiu kuo-tsai, tso-tso meng, k'an-k'an ch'iang*
> *Ch'iang-t'ou ts'ao ch'ang-liao, yu huang-liao.*

> Sticking a patch of setting sun at five o'clock,
> Hanging a halo of lamplight at six o'clock,
> Maybe somebody passes all his days
> Dreamily watching the wall
> While on the wall grass grows and withers dry.[8]

> 五點鐘貼一角夕陽
> 六點鐘掛半輪燈光
> 想有人把所有的日子
> 就過在做做夢，看看牆
> 牆頭草長了又黃了。

Despite its stylistic fluency, Acton and Ch'en's translation fails to bring out the linguistic nuances of the first couplet—"Sticking a patch of setting sun ..." and "Hanging a halo of lamplight ..." As we know, *i-chiao* and *pan-lun* are "measure words" in Chinese and lack English equivalents. Such words not only convey a quantitative sense; they also serve as "geometrical metaphors" to indicate shapes of objects. For example, *I-chiao* implies a corner of the square, and *pan-lun* conjures up the semicircular shape of the lamp shadow. Readers who know Chinese will no doubt find the above translation rather inadequate.

When he comes to the translation of Tai Wang-shu's symbolist poems, Acton openly admits that the difficulties are insuperable. A version of Tai's poem reads as follows:

A Little Walk
Let us go round the wooden hedge
And sit on a chair by the river.
Wavelets forever nibble at the bank
And from your foot outstretched and white
Your tight lips tremble.
Here the *feng*-tree wood
Is red and silent as your lips.
Though autumn's withering wind has not yet come,
From your very silence
I have felt its chill.[9]

款步二
答應我繞過這些木柵
去坐在江邊的遊椅上。
嚙着沙岸的永遠的波浪，
總會從你投出着的素足
撼動你抿緊的嘴唇的。
而這裏，鮮紅並寂靜得
與你底嘴唇一樣的楓林間，
雖然殘秋的風還未來到，
但我已經從你的緘默裏，
覺出了它的寒冷。

Acton tells his readers that in strict order, lines four and five should run:

Must from your outstretched white foot
Tremble your tight-closed lips.[10]

Instead of rendering them as conjunctives, Acton separates the foot from the lips and insists that "even if we took out a surrealistic licence it is doubtful whether they would reach any closer affinity to poetry in English." However, he continues to offer the following explanations:

We might, of course, take liberties; lengthen the lines to explain that first the tender foot of the damsel (with all the Freudian connotations of feminine feet in

China) was frigid, then the chill shot upwards through the veins, penetrating her whole anatomy, so that her pursed lips trembled, however self-controlled (and in China women are admirably self-controlled). But apart from the awkward result of such an explanation, by previous downright mention of the sensitive girl's swift premonition of autumn, the delicate effect of the last two lines, in which the chill comes as climax, would be ruined. [11]

No matter which way the translation goes, the Chinese original remains as run-on lines starting with the nibbling wavelets in the third line, rather than the outstretched white foot of the fourth line, as the subject of the sentence. Thus it is wrong to assume that the trembling lips are caused by the outstretching of the white foot. And the problem is further complicated by the translator's male-chauvinistic Freudian association of the chilly weather preying on the fragile body of the lady. In fact, it is simply the forever persisting wavelets, a symbol of the poet's constancy toward his love, that eventually "move" (*han-tung*) the girl's tight-closed lips.

In translating the Chinese for maple trees, Acton raises the question whether to retain the transliteration *fêng* as a touch of exoticism or simply to substitute the English word "maple" and be satisfied with such a makeshift. He insists that like most Chinese trees, the *fêng-shu* has a definite individuality and fits its Chinese context perfectly. Acton did not use the botanical name *Liquidambar Formosana* because he feared, rightly, that it would be too pedantic and affected, in such a short poem. Obviously, none of these reasons will explain why the English word "maple" cannot be a satisfactory makeshift.

Another poem by Tai, "Dreams in Autumn," also caused problems to the translators. The poem goes as follows:

> The bell of the distant shepherdess
> Shakes the light leaves down.
>
> In autumn dreams are light;
> They are the love of a shepherdess.
>
> Then my dream comes silently,
> Sustained by old and heavy days.
>
> O, now I feel a touch of cold,
> A touch of cold and a touch of sadness. [12]

> 秋天的夢
> 迢遙的牧女的羊鈴,
> 搖落了輕的樹葉。
>
> 秋天的夢是輕的,
> 那是窈窕的牧女之戀。
>
> 於是我的夢是靜靜地來了,
> 但却載着沈重的昔日。

唔,現在,我是有一些寒冷,
一些寒冷,和一些憂鬱。

Acton complains that the mood indicator "O," abrupt and physical when
the poem is read aloud in Chinese, melts into banality in English. No doubt
a clarification is needed here. In fact, the Chinese original reads as *ng* (唔),
wu in Mandarin, which is more of a low-pitched subdued interjection than
of an obtrusive exclamation of an "O."

The overabundance of mood indicators or exclamations in the Chinese
language often causes frustration to translators, who try in vain to come up
with the exact equivalents in English. In fact, only a handful of such words
exist in the English poetic vocabulary, such as *oh* or *aye*.

Besides mood indicators, classical words with internal rhymes are also
hard to manage. Such is the case with the line "They are the love of a
shepherdess." The original has the internal-rhymed word *yao-t'iao* ("graceful" is the translation suggested by James Liu in discussing the art of Chinese poetry) inserted right before "shepherdess," thus effectively conveying
the theme of a feather-light mood. Acton simply ignored this crucial word
in his translation. Since he had insisted on using the transliteration *fêng* for
"maples," consistency might have dictated something like "the love of a
yao t'iao shepherdess."

Fifteen poets are included in Acton's anthology. The number of poems
selected from each poet varies from one to nineteen. To be sure, the quantity of the poems chosen does not necessarily correlate with the quality. But
the very fact that some poets have a larger presence than their peers in
the anthology may indicate the editors' personal preference in the selecting
process.

The following is a list of poets and the total number of their poems
translated:

Lin Keng: 19
Pien Chih-lin: 14
Ho Ch'i-fang: 10
Hsu Chih-mo: 10
Tai Wang-shu: 10
Ch'en Meng-chia: 7
Wen I-to: 5
Feng Fei-ming: 4
Chou Tso-jen: 4
Li Kuang-t'ien: 4
Kuo Mo-jo: 3
Yu Ping-po: 2
Shao Hsun-mei: 2
Shen Ts'ung-wen: 1
Sun Ta-yu: 1

The list reveals the editors' preference for a strong lyrical bend as represented by the poetry of Pien Chih-lin, Ho Ch'i-fang, Lin Keng, Hsu Chih-mo, and others.

Acton humbly states in his preface that it is not for a Westerner to predict along what lines Chinese poetry must develop in the future. Meanwhile, he argues that apart from European influences, a modern Chinese poet also needs to draw on the legacy of the great poets from China's glorious past in order to develop a modern poetic style and sensibility. He is, in fact, hinting in a Poundian or Eliotian modernist manner that a poet depends on his tradition as much as on his individual talent.

When *Modern Chinese Poetry* was published in London in 1936, it was the first comprehensive anthology of modern Chinese lyrics in English. What Acton and Ch'en may have overlooked in their anthology was a concurrent trend of realistic poetry that was to be taken as a direct result of China's unstable political situation and the subsequent war of resistance against the Japanese invasion. It was a time of great change, not just for the Chinese people in general but for poets as well. They began to awake from their ivory tower of locked-in egos to a more realistic social consciousness. Kuo Mo-jo was one of the early voices, but he was jeered by Acton for turning to the communists.

Eleven years after the publication of Acton's anthology, Robert Payne's *Contemporary Chinese Poetry* confirmed the emergence of the realistic trend in modern Chinese poetry.[13] He selected nine poets, ranging from Hsu Chih-mo to T'ien Ch'ien. The list of poets and number of poems runs as follows:

Hsu Chih-mo: 8
Wen I-to: 14
Ho Ch'i-fang: 8
Feng Chih: 15
Pien Chih-lin: 16
Yu Ming-chuan: 11
Tsang K'e-chia: 12
Ai Ch'ing: 8
T'ien Ch'ien: 12

If we compare this list with Acton's, we can see that the survival rate for the lyricists is high. Hsu Chih-mo, Wen I-to, Pien Chih-lin, Ho Ch'i-fang appear in both anthologies; and with Feng Chih added to Payne's anthology, we come to sense a strong continuity of the lyrical trend. Upon close inspection, however, the works included in Payne's anthology are quite different from those in the previous anthology. There is an apparent change in style and subject matter.

Take Ho Ch'i-fang, whom Acton once considered an auspicious omen for classical retention in modern poetry: his lyrics such as "Wash Not Away the Red," "Moonlight in Frontier Mountains," "A Wreath," "Seasonal

Ailment," "Old City," and "A Night Scene," mostly from his *Han Garden Collections*, are jewels glistening in Acton's anthology. In Payne's anthology, Ho is a totally different person, who, firmly committed to the progress of socialism, wrote such outspoken poems as "The Stream" and "Night Songs."

Since poets are capable of drastic changes and these changes are often their reactions to changing times, it is natural that a poetry anthology should not simply introduce poets and discuss the artistry of their works but should also bear witness to the changing of history through the voice of the poet. The life and work of Wen I-to are a good example: his assassination dramatized the tragic fate of China in the Republican era. He was selected by both Acton and Payne.

Five poems from Wen I-to's *Dead Water* collection, published by the Crescent Press in 1928, were translated by Acton: "Dead Water," "The Deserted Village," "The Laundryman's Song," "A Night Song," and "The Last Day." Payne, in honoring Wen I-to's tragic death and patriotism and dedicating his anthology to the memory of Wen, took more poems from *Dead Water*, adding to them early poems from the *Red Candles*, published in 1922. Except for "The Last Day," "Dead Water," and "The Deserted Village," most of Wen's poems chosen by Payne appeared in English for the first time. Poems such as "The Confession," "Perhaps," "The Heart Beats" (later retitled "A Silent Night"), "I Come, I Shout ..." (originally titled "Discovery"), "A Vassal," "Death," "Early Summer Night," and "Autumn Beauty" fairly well represent Wen's life and poetic career.

In June 1946, Payne showed Wen the introduction which the anthologist had written about him. One paragraph runs as follows:

> He was born in 1889 in the province of Hupeh. Graduating in Tsinghua University, he studied painting at the Chicago Art Institute and the Art Students' League of New York. He confesses that he was not a good painter, but developed a love of colour which has remained throughout his life.... He has since experimented in satiric poetry, but with the failure of the Great Revolution (1927–1929) and his self-imposed withdrawal from creative literature, it is unlikely that he will return to the field of his first love. He remains the scholar, perhaps the greatest and most representative, and certainly the most beloved in modern China, with a scholar's ferocious desire for clarification. It is not for nothing that the greatest influences on his poetry have been French.[14]

According to Payne, Wen smiled and felt a little dazed by the claims made for him. He humbly told Payne that he was the least of Chinese poets, but if he were to write again, he would again write only with devastating satire. Six weeks later, on July 15, he was assassinated.

Payne wrote in his preface that as early as 1926, a group of young poets had gathered in Peking, vowing to find a new path for modern Chinese poetry. But over the next several years, some of them met tragic deaths. Hsu Chih-mo died in an airplane crash, Chu Hsiang drowned himself in the Yangtze, and Wen I-to was assassinated by soldiers. The meeting in 1926 was apparently a gathering of the Crescent School poets, which was to have a significant impact on the future of modern Chinese poetry. Since Hu Shih's famous essay of 1917 ushering in the era of the New Literature, no great poetry had emerged to fulfill the tremendous expectations of Chinese readers. The meeting of these Crescent poets was to mainly construct and reintroduce a concept of pure form in poetry. To be free from the classical form in poetry does not mean poetry can be formless. It was Wen I-to who reintroduced the conception of poetry and its relationship with the other arts, and claimed that the beauty of music, painting, and architecture in poetry were in fact implications of rhythm and rhyme, color and rhetoric, form and structure.

Perhaps it is appropriate to recall Acton's anthology and retrace some of his frustrations over the pioneers. Ping Hsin's poems, according to Acton, were only "odds and ends of thought" fitted for pairs of scrolls hanging in breakfast rooms, studies, or bedrooms. As for Kuo Mo-jo, his adaptations to Western influences and imitations of Walt Whitman were quite spontaneous and prolific. Acton observed that Kuo's energy and ardor were impressive, but they impressed the Western reader less than his compatriots, to whom his thought and technique seemed startlingly new.

Payne's anthology, on the other hand, indicated a turning point to the trials and tribulations of the modern poets. Both Pien Chih-lin and Ho Ch'i-fang had been actively advocating experimentation in "modern regulated verse" and stressing the importance of form in poetry. Feng Chih attempted to use the Western sonnet as a new form for his Chinese contents. Wen I-to's "Autumn Beauty" on Jackson Park in Chicago reveals an astounding beauty, a riot of colors. "Dead Water" confirms the stasis of water in the concreteness of form, and "Discovery" highlights the musical and percussive nature of the Chinese language.

Above all, Payne's anthology reveals a diversion of the lyrical stream to the flow of other voices of the time. It is a parting of the way toward continual innovations, yielding particularly the powerful drum-beats of Ai Ch'ing and T'ien Chien. In fact, except for the lingering lyricism of Hsu Chih-mo, Pien Chih-lin, and Feng Chih, Payne's anthology marks a departure from Acton's, taking Wen I-to as the originator of a patriotic soul in constant frustration and sorrow, followed by Ai Ch'ing and T'ien Chien as the protesting voices of the masses. That was the dominant trend of realistic poetry in the 1940s until the Communist liberation of the mainland in 1949; and it even carried over for a period of at least another ten years. These poems, carrying with them messages of the oppressed classes, are usually written in the colloquial language. They are in fact oral poetry which achieves its social function through recitations.

They are not without problems in translation, and it is exactly the oral aspect of the language which causes distress to the translator. T'ien Chien's poems are good examples for illustration. Payne selected "The People's Dance," in which the poet tells the background of the poem as follows:

> On New Year's Day, 1938, when the Japanese were celebrating their "victory," Chinese guerrillas danced this dance outside the West Gate. They were watched by the Japanese guards, who were later killed by the guerrillas, and the guerrillas returned to their hiding-places with their hands wet with Japanese blood. No, I cannot imagine this scene, which seems sacred to me, but I hope that in my lifetime I shall see such a scene.
>
> In April, in Sian, we performed the People's Dance. The dance was of the simplest kind, and chiefly concerned the necessity of co-operation among the Chinese. The characters were workers, farmers, students, merchants, Japanese soldiers and traitors.
>
> I dedicate this poem to the memory of the guerrillas of Peiping.[15]

Thus we know the poem is a narration with sound effects to achieve the description of action on stage. The translator immediately supplies a footnote:

> It is impossible to translate this poem adequately: the phonetic character of Chinese words allows the poet a far greater power of musical suggestion in Chinese than it does in English. The sound of the first six lines in Chinese is roughly: *i go/ i go/ tsa tsa de/ ch'u ch'ang/ tyao yao/ tyao yao*. The poem has been slightly abbreviated in translation.[16]

The first six lines are translated like this:

> | One by one | 一個, |
> |---|---|
> | By one | 一個, |
> | *Tsa, tsa* | 嚓嚓地 |
> | We dance. | 出場。 |
> | | |
> | O we leap, | 跳躍…… |
> | O we jump! | 跳躍…… |

Those who do not know Chinese will find it very difficult to comprehend the sound *tsa, tsa* in the translation. It is the sound from the quick movement of bodies entering the stage, but with *ch'u ch'ang* translated as "We dance," the reader might be misled by wrongly associating *tsa, tsa* with music or with musical instruments.

The handling of another stanza poses a direct challenge to the reader's response to sounds:

> *Ah*
> *Kerch'ang!*
> *Ah*
> *Wuyang!*
> *Ah*
> *Pangtse!*
> *Chutao!*
> *Ah*
> *Chiang!*
> *Ah*
> *Jen-ming!*
> *Ah*
> *Taotse!*

This stanza is repeated twice in the original. When it first appears in the English translation, the translator faithfully renders it as:

Ah	呵,
Singing!	歌唱!
Ah	呵,
Dancing!	舞踊!
Ah	呵,
Sticks!	棒子!
Ah	呵,
Swords!	刀子!
Ah	呵,
Hoes!	鋤頭!
Ah	呵,
Guns!	槍!
Ah	呵,
People!	人民!

Even with the English version in mind, it is still difficult for a Western reader to associate *Bangtse* with "sticks" because it sounds more like gunfire, or *Taotse* with "swords" when the sound *Tao* immediately evokes an association with the passive Taoists.

Because songs of protests are often expressed with heavy exclamations, Chinese mood indicators simply put translators in a quandary. As mentioned, Acton came across the problem with Tai Wang-shu's "Dreams in Autumn," but the situation becomes worse in Payne's case when he has to face an overabundance of repetitive exclamations in these songs. To enhance recitation, exclamations give direct, terse emphasis to dramatic poetry and are just as vital as indirect images and metaphors to lyrics. Due to the limited number of available exclamations in English, the translator sometimes has to neglect the existence of their Chinese counterparts.

In Ai Ch'ing's famous "Snow Falls on China," the beginning couplet goes like this:

Hsueh lo tsai chung-kuo ti t'u-ti shang,
Han leng tsai feng-suo cho chung-kuo ya . . .

雪落在中國的土地上，
寒冷在封鎖着中國呀⋯⋯

Each line has nine syllables, forming a long, stuttering mood of grievance.
In the first line, the emphasis is on the subject *Hsueh* (snow) and its corre-
lating object *t'u-ti* (land, earth). When it comes to the second line, the
variation of snow becomes *Han leng* (chill, cold) and earth becomes China
(*chung-kuo.*) Juxtaposing these two lines, the poet shows the causal effects
of the falling snow on the Chinese land, and the consequence of the chill
"blockading" (*feng-suo cho*) China as a country. The exclamation *ya* indicates the receptive mood of this consequence; it is a key indicator of the
expressive mood of the couplet. However, the translator can only render the
couplet with the omission of the exclamation:

> Snow falls on the Chinese land;
> Cold blockades China . . .[17]

The same treatment applies to another couplet when the original reads:

Chung-kuo ti ku-t'ung yu tsai-nan
Hsiang che hsueh-yeh i yang kuang k'uo erh yu man-ch'ang ya!

中國的苦痛與災難
像這雪夜一樣廣闊而又漫長呀！

The translation goes:

> Pain and suffering of China;
> Wild and long as the snowy night.[18]

Perhaps it is time for us to reconsider the use of transliterated exclamation in translation. If Acton can go for the idea of *feng-shu* instead of maples
or *feng-huang* instead of phoenix, why can't we use the Chinese onomato-
poeic exclamations, such as *ya* and *le*?
In 1963, Kai-yu Hsu published his *Twentieth Century Chinese Poetry* in the
United States.[19] This is quite an accomplishment on Hsu's part as both
editor and translator. Previous anthologies by Acton and Payne were completed through the collaboration of the editors and their Chinese native
speakers. For example, Acton and Ch'en cotranslated the whole volume. In
Payne's case, the poems of each poet were translated either by a native
speaker or by the poet himself. Yuan K'o-chia translated Hsu Chih-mo's
poems; Pien Chih-lin translated his own. Feng Chih and Wen I-to participated, one way or the other, in the translating process. With Hsu, it was

a one-man effort showing his impressive command of both Chinese and English.

Payne reviewed Hsu's anthology in the *Saturday Review* and recommended it as "something of a landmark." It is an ambitious anthology that includes nearly fifty poets who wrote over a span of fifty years. Hsu even grouped the poets, from the pioneers to the independents. Feng Chih and Pien Chih-lin were classified as metaphysical poets, while Li Chin-fa, Tai Wang-shu, and others were considered symbolists. One would doubt very much the authenticity of these categorizations. If there were schools such as the Crescent poets, there should be the Creation school as well, with Kuo Mo-jo and Yu Ta-fu as representatives. Feng Chih and Pien Chih-lin are scholars well read in German and English literature, but to label them metaphysical poets is just as inappropriate as to call Ezra Pound a classicist for his erudition. Ai Ch'ing and T'ien Chien are assigned to the group of independents. However, if there were poets such as the metaphysical or the symbolist, they definitely deserve to be labeled realists or socialists. Hsu's anthology was completed in the 1950s, several years before it was published. During those years, he could have included more "Nine Leaves Poets," such as Hsin Ti, Mu Tan, and Ch'en Ching-yung, or even his friend Yuan K'o-chia in addition to Cheng Min and Tu Yun-hsueh.

On the other hand, with the extensive inclusion of a large variety of poetry and with detailed introductions covering the life and work of individual poets, Hsu's anthology presents a broader historical perspective of a half-century's development of modern Chinese poetry. Not only do we see the efforts of pioneers harvested by latecomers, but these followers also make new turns to improve on the work of their forerunners.

Despite technical problems in translation, the three anthologies discussed here show clearly that it is not only important for an editor-translator to meet the challenge of selecting the best poets and poetry, but it is also crucial to develop a historical criterion by which to determine and describe for the audience the diverse poetic trends in modern Chinese poetry.

NOTES

1. Harold Acton, *Memoirs of An Aesthete* (London: Duckworth, 1936).
2. Ibid., 282
3. Ibid.
4. See Liang Tsung-tai's own endnote to the Chinese translation of Valéry's *Fragments du Narcisse*, in *All the Peaks*, ed. Ch'en Ying (Taipei: Lin-pai Press, 1971), 149. Apparently, the reason for Ms. Ch'en Ying, Liang's ex-wife in Taipei, to edit such a volume was due to Liang's left-wing status as a writer and the consequent censorship of his work in Taiwan in the early 1960s.
5. Harold Acton and Shih-hsiang Ch'en, trans., *Modern Chinese Poetry* (London: Duckworth, 1936).

6. Acton, *Memoirs*, 335.

7. Ibid., 348.

8. Ibid., 349

9. Introduction, *Modern Chinese Poetry*, 26.

10. Ibid.

11. Ibid.

12. Ibid., p. 27.

13. Robert Payne, ed., *Contemporary Chinese Poetry* (London: Routledge, 1947).

14. Ibid., 47.

15. Ibid., 150.

16. Ibid.

17. Ibid., 17.

18. Ibid., 133.

19. Kai-yu Hsu, trans. and ed., *Twentieth Century Chinese Poetry: An Anthology* (Garden City: Doubleday, 1963).

More Than Putting Things Together

The Anthologizing of Chinese Literature in Translation

JOSEPH S. M. LAU

Seldom have I been invited to a conference whose designated area of investigation happens to coincide with my current interest. During the past few years John Minford and I have been putting together an anthology of traditional Chinese literature in English translation that covers material from the ancient myths and legends to late Ch'ing fiction. Circumstances permitting, John and I should have co-authored this essay, for I have benefited a great deal from his experience and expertise as a translator-anthologist. Thus it is inevitable that some of his ideas will be reflected in the following, and the best I can do as acknowledgment is to indicate my indebtedness when I feel certain the points I make originate from him.

We shall begin with hard facts. Call it whatever you will, "Masterpieces of Chinese Literature," "Chinese Literature in Translation," or "The Chinese Experience in Literature," it is generally the case, in American colleges at least, that the courses in which such an anthology would be adopted are considered "service" courses. In plain language, the majority of the students are undergraduates majoring in agriculture, business, chemistry, dermatology, and what not. They need such courses to fulfill the humanities credit requirements as much as to satisfy their intellectual curiosity.

What about the rest of the students? I would say most likely they are students in elementary Chinese language classes still undecided on their future career. Since they are exposed to Chinese literature in English, what they are given to read will affect not only their appreciation of the work at hand but possibly their deliberations about whether they want to enter sinology as a profession.

It thus becomes clear that unlike its counterpart in Chinese, an English anthology of Chinese literature stands or falls on the quality of translation. The usefulness of an anthology is often measured in terms of its effectiveness in acquainting the reader with the representative writers and works of a given literature. But if anthologists have to select materials from translations, all their assumptions about how this literature is to be represented have to be modified. For one thing, they may find the work of a certain writer they consider important either untranslated or available only in dubious translation. If they want to steer a safe course so as not to be accused of oversight, they are left with no choice but to use whatever they have on hand. But while they may perform their task as dutiful anthologists, they may do a disservice to the field in the sense that no sooner have the students finished their humanities credit requirements than they lose interest in this literature.

We need some specific examples. Suppose the student is assigned to read page after page of "literalist" translations such as this one discussed by W. J. F. Jenner:

> One day half a month ago, that young doctor—but he is balding—sought me out for a chat. It's part of a regular hospital procedure. As we spoke, he was dashing everything down in sweeping strokes on a set on note cards.[1]

Translations like that cannot even qualify as mediocre; they are simply unidiomatic. According to Jenner, the idiomatic equivalent for "one day half a month ago" should be either "a fortnight" or "a couple of weeks" (188).

A veteran translator, Jenner is rightfully concerned with the translation of dialogues from Chinese to English. He offers this translation as an example of "how unsayable dialogue kills a translation":

> "I'm not—"
> "Perhaps. Now is not the age of —"
> "Don't get off the subject like this!" He roughly pushes my hands away and grabs the little jumper on the bed.
> "Whom are you knitting this for?" (189)

Jenner comments: "No native speaker would use such a form of words as 'Now is not the age of —' (— refers to a long-dead historical figure). Perhaps 'This isn't —'s time,' or '— has been dead for a long time.' Nor would one say 'Don't get off the subject like this!' Instead we might say, 'Stop trying to change the subject!' And what youngster in a moment of high emotion would use the pedantic form 'whom' instead of the colloquial 'who'?"

It would be hard to imagine a student being carried away by a translation that is so "unsayable." Granted that translation is, alas, always destruction and betrayal and that no reader would be convinced that "Seek. Seek. Search. Search" in the original language is poetry as powerful as *"ming-t'ien, ming-t'ien, yu ming-t'ien"* in Shakespeare's own tongue, enough distinguished exceptions do exist to help restore our confidence in the possibility and feasibility of translation. I cannot agree more with Jenner that translations "need to be polished till we forget that they are translations, like a window so clean that we are not aware that it stands between us and what we are looking at" (193).

Since Jenner has provided no positive example of a good translation, I am compelled to give one myself.

> Mean hovels and abandoned halls
> Where courtiers once paid daily calls:
> Bleak haunts where weeds and willows scarcely thrive
> Were once with mirth and revelry alive.
> Whilst cobwebs shroud the mansion's gilded beams,
> The cottage casement with choice muslin gleams.
> Would you of perfumed elegance recite?
> Even as you speak, the raven locks turn white.[2]

These exquisite lines stand as English poetry—until we are told that they are from the translation of *The Story of the Stone* by David Hawkes.

As regards criteria of selection, English anthologists face another kind of problem alien to their Chinese counterparts. Finding their own favorite writers either untranslated or available only in poor translation is frustrating enough, but the reverse sometimes can be just as baffling. I am referring to those major poets translated by different hands. Now if anthologists take no heed of the truism that all strong poets distinguish themselves by a voice uniquely their own, they should have no difficulty gathering together, in the case of, say, Li Po, some two hundred of his poems translated by various "schools" of translators. But then readers might get the impression that they are being introduced to different Li Pos under one name. Rather than being distinct, the voice of the poet through multifarious ventriloquism would sound cacophonous.

For, just like the poets they impersonate, translators are also entitled to speak in a voice that marks them off from other practitioners. (Here I would like to register my debt to John Minford for alerting me to the problem of "voice" in translation.) A comparison of "Yüeh-hsia tu-cho" (月下 獨酌) as translated by Giles and Waley respectively should bring the question of translated voice into perspective.

Last Words
An arbor of flowers
and a kettle of wine:
Alas! in the bowers
no companion is mine.
Then the moon sheds her rays
on my goblet and me,
And my shadow betrays
we're a party of three!

Drinking Alone by Moonlight
A cup of wine, under the flowering trees
I drink alone, for no friend is near;
Raising my cup I beckon the bright moon
For he, with my shadow, will make three men.[3]

Since our present interest is in the individuality of the translator's voice, we need not comment on the liberties Giles has taken with the original. The voices of Giles and Waley come through clear enough, so much so that we seem to see two personalities of Li Po in separate reincarnations. Nothing is wrong with the "Banished Celestial" having more than one personality. What is at issue is that if the many faces of Li Po are to be represented in translation, the translation should ideally be entrusted to one translator so that his or her flight of imagination, his or her alternate inebriation and sobriety, his or her poetic conceits and stylistic flair, could be captured in a special rhythm and vibration that should be unmistakably as idiosyncratic as the T'ang genius.

In sum, if anthologists feel that a few poems are enough to highlight the unusual accomplishments of Li Po, they should have no problem discharging their duty, for there are a good number of one-person translations for them to pick, so long as no preset guidelines restrict their choice. But if they are keen on showing the poet's multidimensional talents, the selection has perforce to be a chorus of discordant notes.

When it comes to selecting prose work, anthologists might find themselves confronted with yet another kind of "voice" problem. Does the ideal of one translator for one writer apply to fiction translation? If we are talking about such collections are Kan Pao's *Shou-shen chi* (Records of Spirits) or *Shih-shuo hsin yü* (A New Account of Tales of the World), attributed to Liu I-ch'ing, the answer is yes. To enable the reader to sense that the 464 entries in the former are the work of one editor-compiler, the formal features of Kan Pao's style should be systematically recognized. The same can be said of *Shih-shuo hsin-yü*, available in full translation by Richard B. Mather. I will quote from his "Translator's Note":

Nothing in the *Shih-shuo hsin-yü* is so esoteric as to be inaccessible to those who are not native to Chinese culture. The anecdotes, conversations, and characterizations gathered here are mostly of a kind which, given a few substitutions, could occur in any society. For this reason I have tried to retell them as nearly as possible in their original form, even when this results in some "barbarization" of normal English idiom, feeling as I do that preserving the verbal images and conceits of the original text is better than finding the English equivalent which comes nearest to the "intention" of the author but changes his images in the process.[4]

There are 626 characters in this *chih-jen* collection, and by far the strongest one to emerge in the whole work is Hsieh An (320–385), who figures in over a hundred anecdotes. "His prowess in 'pure conversation' (*ch'ing-yen* or *ch'ing-t'an*) was acknowledged even by his enemies . . . " (xvii). Now if Mather occasionally felt compelled to "barbarize" the English usage in order to reconstruct Hsieh An's *ch'ing-t'an* as close to the original as possible, his reader would in due course get used to Hsieh An's peculiar manner of speech so long as he is reading those one hundred episodes in his translation. But the reader's image of the same person will be out of focus once he is given to read another translation that renders the *ch'ing-t'an* in some fashionable lingo, like "Be real, man!"

Having briefly addressed the problem of translation, let's turn to another consideration: principles of selection for an anthology of Chinese literature in English translation. This begs the question: should the principles be any different from the one in Chinese? Theoretically no, especially when it is undertaken by the same anthologist with no supraeditorial or political interference from outside. But in practice, if the work is to be published in a place where freedom of expression is inhibited by concern of propriety or restrained by the necessity that "family disgrace shouldn't be spoken of to outsiders," compiling an English anthology often compromises the integrity of the anthologist.

For this reason it is hard to conceive of an anthology of Chinese literature in Chinese in which chapter 27 of *Chin P'ing Mei* is included unexpurgated. In China, there ought to be "concerned citizens" who are interested in voicing the conscience of China, but such writings can see the light only in places outside the sphere of Communist influence.

The description of violence is also a taboo in the Land of Heavenly Peace, and this would pose serious problems to scholar-critics who have to rely on translations for interpretation. One case in point is the deletion of the passage in the translation of "Wu-shuang the Peerless" (Wu-shuang *chuan*) by Yang Hsien-yi and Gladys Yang (in *The Dragon King's Daughter*, 1954) in which the decapitation of Sai-hung by Officer Ku and Ku's subsequent suicide takes place. Such bowdlerization was not carried out by the translators. As W. J. F. Jenner informed Michael Duke, the editors of Peking's Foreign Languages Press "have absolutely no control over the texts selected for translation or the final form of the published translations. These decisions . . . are made by political authorities and not by the putative editors. . . ."[5]

So the violence that underscores an extreme form of *pao* (reciprocity) in this narrative is blotted out of the picture. What could the rationale be? Simple enough: *The Dragon King's Daughter* is an anthology for foreign readers. It is not the concern for foreigners' fragile nerves but the need to preserve China's "face" that must have dictated the cut by the authorities. But they have missed the point, as I commented elsewhere:

> The question whether Ku is a "good" or "bad" example of Chinese knight-errantry necessitates consideration of his ethical code respectively from a historical and a presentist point of view. . . . It would seem that after succumbing to Wang's [his benefactor's] lavish treatment for over a year, the meaning of Ku's concept of *pao* is simplified to one overriding concern: how to repay his benefactor. So long as this end can be met, a man in his position couldn't care less what means he is forced to take. It is only in this light that the violence he commits on himself and others can be understood: it articulates his sense of moral priority as well as his concept of honor, however narrow it would seem to us today.[6]

I would not have arrived at this conclusion had I relied only on the Yangs' translation.

Let's return to the principles of selection. If English anthologists are free from the "violence" of the supraeditors, what shall they do with their freedom? They can indeed do a lot. This does not mean they should feel duty-bound to include chapter 27 of *Chin P'ing Mei* just for the sake of asserting their prerogatives as free people. But on the other hand, why not? In the words of David Roy, "it is a landmark in the development of narrative art, not only from a specifically Chinese perspective, but in a world-historic context. . . . In roughly chronological order, it has been read as a *roman à clef*, a work of pornography, a Buddhist morality play, an exercise in naturalism, or a novel of manners."[7] So long as *Chin P'ing Mei* is not selected solely for its "pornographic naturalism," anthologists can take comfort in the thought that they are doing justice to the author of the masterpiece as well as to their readers who, as adults, are entitled to view the plain facts of life for themselves.

An anthology is by its very nature a statement of taste and critical judgment on the part of the editor. Though anyone claiming to do an anthology of traditional Chinese literature would need to devote considerable space to, say, T'ang *ch'uan-ch'i* and Sung-Ming *hua-pen*, there are no common standards against which the anthologist can determine the merits of individual narratives. Exactly what should be chosen in order to make the selections "representative"? One expedient way to handle this matter is to "go native," i.e., to pick those staple products of the genres, such as the stories of Ying-ying, Li Wa, Lady White Snake and the Oil Peddler, that have endured in the Chinese popular imagination. What must be noted is that if the selections rely exclusively on borrowed taste and received opinions, then the Minford-Lau anthology, for instance, would differ little from the existing Chinese collections.

Considerations governing making extracts from novels are similar: one can always fall back on those episodes that are supposed to be as familiar to the traditional Chinese readers as bedtime stories. In the case of *Shui-hu chuan*, one such episode has to be the first appearance of Wu Sung when he finds himself hailed as a hero after killing the tiger.

But *Shui-hu chuan* is also known to the discerning reader as a novel of excess, celebrating vengeance, sadism, and misogyny in the name of justice. Within the Liangshan secret society, manhood is defined by personal loyalty, capacity for wine, and indifference to women. Understood in these terms, the anthologist might want to present Wu Sung in a different light. He may want to expose him to the lure and charms of Pan Chin-lien in chapter 24 of the 120-chapter edition. For a *hao-han* like Wu Sung whose ego is nurtured on moral absolutes, his reaction in the confrontation is of course predictable: it is pointless to expect any gesture from him that would externalize the conflicts of the ego and the id that are supposed to be taking place in his psyche. Nor is it realistic to entertain any fond hope that Wu Sung would take pity on the plight of his sister-in-law, a fabulous beauty married against her will to the three-foot midget of a husband.

Chinese culture being what it is, there is no obligation for a Chinese hero to behave differently from what his tradition and society have made him to be. It is of course a valid argument for Wu Sung to reject Pan Chin-lien's advances because she is his sister-in-law. But if the student had been asked earlier to read the *hua-pen* "Chao Tai-tsu ch'ien-li sung Ching-niang" (The Sung Founder Escorts Ching-niang One Thousand *Li*), he might realize that Wu Sung's scruples go deeper than pure ethical considerations. Just like the Sung founder, the tiger-killer is very much obsessed with his self-image as a *hao-han*: a man who is not supposed to succumb to the amorous calls of a woman whatever the circumstances and whoever she is. Friendship has been assigned a value in traditional Chinese literature that at times may even transcend morality, but no similar concession is made for love. Students expecting to see in the brother-in-law versus sister-in-law encounter echoes of the anguish and pain that characterize the *liaison dangereuse* between Tristan and Isolt will be sorely disappointed.

On the other hand, perhaps this cultural difference is what a Western reader would find interesting in Chinese literature. In the essay cited at the beginning of this chapter, Jenner has this to offer regarding the "marketability" of modern Chinese literature in the Anglophone world: "To break into an established market one needs products that are or seem different, better or cheaper" (179–180). If not better in quality or cheaper in price, traditional Chinese literature is at least "different" in that its fictional characters, when confronted with a moral dilemma, may opt to follow a course that runs counter to Western expectations. Had Orphan Chao in the Yuan play *Chao-shih ku-erh ta-pao-ch'ou* (The Revenge of the Orphan of Chao) been raised in Western culture, he would have found himself in an unenviable "To be or not to be" situation. But Orphan Chao is no Hamlet; nor is he meant to be. Thus he wastes no time in taking his revenge as soon as he recovers from the shock of recognition.

Now the *Orphan of Chao* is a violent play for the number of murders and suicides carried out in the name of self-preservation and affirmation of personal loyalty. Should this play be withheld from Western readers just to avoid giving a violent impression of China? Or, in the questionable example of "Wu-shuang the Peerless," presented to the reader in a "disinfected" version? If anthologists are determined to represent traditional Chinese literature as it is and are convinced that a play like the *Orphan of Chao* is useful in demonstrating Chinese moral orthopraxy, they shouldn't flinch from their responsibilities. For, so far as cruelty to others and self is concerned, Western culture can be just as violent as Chinese. In the words of Mark Edward Lewis,

> In what has become the primal mythology of Western civilization, the ancient Greek tales of child sacrifice and cannibalism, of savage amazons and frenzied maenads, of man-eating beasts and bestial heroes, and of murder of parents or spouses all offered a means of depicting the nature and limits of human society. In the systematic play of such oppositions as man and beast, city and wilderness, agriculture and hunting, or woman and man, these stories created an ideal of civilization through mediations on its borderlines and internal divisions.[8]

After giving due attention to sex and violence, let's take up some noncontroversial matters that pertain to the anthologizing of traditional Chinese literature. Since they are noncontroversial, I shall only list them as desiderata.

First, there should be excerpts from the *Analects* and *Mencius*, not only because they represent the central tradition of Chinese thought but also because without their presence as a foil, the sayings of *Lao Tzu* and *Chuang Tzu* would not come off so liberating and refreshing.

China is deservedly well known for its gastronomic culture. If food is allowed by Confucius to be as essential as sex to human existence, it should accordingly be reflected in literature. An anthology is of course different from a cookbook, but it is certainly no sacrilege to cull from literary material to give the reader an idea of how food was prepared and consumed in traditional China. The meals gulped down by the Liangshan *hao-han* do not suffice as an example, as the food they devour is named only in generic terms, such as fruits, vegetables, fowl, fish, and meat.

If not for the full translation of *The Story of the Stone*, the representation of Chinese gastronomic art in literature can only remain as an item of desiderata. I think Wang Hsi-feng's almost lyrical description of how the eggplant is prepared in her kitchen for the enlightenment of Liu Lao-lao is a consummate example. Similarly, simply because preparation of tea involves more than boiling water for the tea bag in Chinese aristocratic society, tea tasting is likewise painstakingly documented by Ts'ao Hsüeh-chin in his magnum opus. The episode that depicts how the fastidious nun Miao-yü goes about making tea ready for Pao-yü should be an eye-opening experience for Western readers.

Fortunately, the ceremonial appreciation of tea also forms one of the "little pleasures of life" for the less affluent. Thanks to Yün-niang of *Fu-sheng liu-chi* (Six Chapters of a Floating Life), we have a commoner's way of preparing tea that Lu Yü (733–804) would have loved to document in his *Ch'a-ching* (Tea Preparation Manual):

> When the lotus flowers bloom in summer, they close at night and open in the morning. Yün used to put some tea leaves in a little silk bag and place it in the center of the flower at night. We would take it out the next morning, and make tea with spring water, which would then have a delicate flavor.[9]

It does not matter how tea prepared in this manner might taste. What matters is Yün-niang's realization that life is worth living only if it is aesthetically conceived and understood. Chinese literary experience of this kind would appear to the Western reader not only different but maybe even refreshing.

Let me conclude this essay by quoting M. H. Abrams's "Preface to the Fourth Edition" of *The Norton Anthology of English Literature:*

> A vital literary culture, however, is always on the move. The interests of readers change; new texts are discovered; old texts are better edited; new scholarly information and critical viewpoints become available; teachers and students want fresh materials that invite experimentation in the way literature is to be presented and studied. The policy, accordingly, has been to issue periodic revisions which, without violating the principle that only major writings be represented, are designed to keep the anthology in the mainstream of contemporary literary, cultural, and intellectual knowledge and concerns.[10]

An anthologist of Chinese literature can only take note of these sensible remarks with envy. The Norton anthology editors can issue revised editions as often as it is profitable, because it will never be their fate to be short of elemental texts. We who put things together in translation would count ourselves fortunate if the major writings that need to be represented are available. Surely, one translator for one writer is an ideal, but as we all are aware, in many cases this ideal will remain as an ideal. The only comfort we may draw in editing a volume like the one Minford and I have been doing is that, in addition to providing "service" to the prospective scientists or engineers, it may, through some extraordinary translations, convince the students in elementary Chinese courses that this is a field worthy of their consideration as a career.

NOTES

1. Quoted in W. J. F. Jenner, "Insuperable Barriers?: Some Thoughts on the Reception of Chinese Writing in English Translation," in *Worlds Apart: Recent Chinese Writing and Its Audiences*, ed. Howard Goldblatt (Armonk: M. E. Sharpe, 1990), 188.

2. David Hawkes, trans., *The Story of the Stone* (Bloomington: Indiana University Press, 1979), vol. 1, 64.

3. The two translations of this poem, by Herbert A. Giles and Arthur Waley, are conveniently collected in *Gems of Classical Chinese Poetry in Various English Translations*, ed. Lü Shu-xiang and Xu Yuan-zhong (Hong Kong: Joint Publishing Co., 1988), 123 and 125.

4. In Liu I-ch'ing, *A New Account of Tales of the World*, trans. Richard B. Mather (Minneapolis: University of Minnesota Press, 1976), xxxi.

5. Michael S. Duke, "The Problematic Nature of Modern and Contemporary Chinese Fiction in English Translation," in *Worlds Apart*, 225, n. 58.

6. Joseph S. M. Lau, "Translation as Interpretation: A Pedagogical View," in *Tamkang Review* 15, nos. 1, 2, 3, 4 (Autumn 1984–Summer 1985): 351.

7. Entry on *Chin P'ing Mei* in *The Indiana Companion to Traditional Chinese Literature*, ed. William H. Nienhauser, Jr., et al. (Bloomington: Indiana University Press, 1986), 287–288.

8. Mark Edward Lewis, *Sanctioned Violence in Early China* (Albany: State University of New York Press, 1990), 4.

9. *The Wisdom of China and India*, ed. Lin Yutang (New York: Modern Library, 1942), 1002.

10. *The Norton Anthology of English Literature*, ed. M. H. Abrams et al., 4th ed. (New York: Norton, 1979), vol. 1, xxix.

Anthologizing and Anthropologizing

The Place of Nonelite and Nonstandard Culture in the Chinese Literary Tradition

VICTOR H. MAIR

Most hard to forget is the speech of your old home.
最難忘是故鄉音
Chao Tzu-yung, *Cantonese Love-Songs* (Eleventh Preface, line 2)

I have become involved recently in editorial work on two major anthologies of Chinese literature. One is a collection of traditional literature for Columbia University Press and the other is a volume of folk and popular literature that is being compiled on behalf of Chinoperl, the Conference on Chinese Oral and Performing Literature.

Assembling a fresh and viable anthology involves hard decisions. One must balance the old standards against previously neglected gems. One must further decide which genres will be represented and whether the focus will be on a limited time period. It is also necessary to determine whether emphasis will be placed on a few authors or whether as many authors as possible should be included.

All of these difficulties are naturally compounded when one is dealing with a translated anthology. In such a case, one must be attentive not only to the quality and representativeness of the literary pieces that will be included but also to the tastes of one's audience as well as their ability to comprehend and appreciate what one is offering up to them. Otherwise there will be a basic incompatibility.

In the course of my editing chores, I have come to feel that by far the hardest task is simply determining what is Chinese literature and what is not. This may seem like a rather inane predicament for a supposed expert on Chinese literature to find himself in, but it is a real dilemma nonetheless, and it exists with regard to both traditional literature and popular literature. This dilemma hinges on complex questions of language, culture, and politics.

Let us address the matter of language first. When we speak of an anthology of Chinese literature, do we mean an anthology of literature written in a Chinese language or do we mean an anthology of the literature of China? The question is not so simple as it may seem. If we are speaking in English, we probably mean by such a designation a collection of literary texts written in a Chinese language (whether it be from Taiwan, Hong Kong, Singapore, the United States, Canada, Europe, or China itself), but even here we cannot be sure. "English literature" is now generally understood to mean the literature of England, "American literature" the literature of America, "Spanish literature" the literature of Spain, "Peruvian literature" the literature of Peru, and so forth. By analogy, "Chinese literature" should mean the literature of China, but such, apparently, is not necessarily always the case. The Mandarin expression *Chung-kuo wen-hsüeh* 中國文學 is superficially less ambiguous, but in actual practice also seems to refer to any literature written in a Chinese language rather than merely literature from China.

Let us assume, for the sake of the argument, that Chinese literature is literature written in the Chinese (linguistically it would be more precise to say "Sinitic") language. This is where the situation becomes still more extraordinarily complicated, because I find it very hard to define precisely what is meant by "*the* Chinese language." Chinese language includes such widely dissimilar entities as Hoklo, Cantonese, Pekingese, Classical Chinese, and Modern Standard Mandarin (hereafter MSM). This is not the place to enter into the thorny matter of whether these are separate languages, but we do need to ask whether literary texts from such diverse origins should be included within the covers of a single anthology.

Our understanding of the issues that are involved may be sharpened by referring to some specific examples. I would like to begin by focusing on *The Lichee and the Mirror* (*Li ching chi* 荔鏡記). This is the earliest and best-known play of the dozens of titles that survive for the genre known as Pear Garden Drama (*Li-yüan hsi* 梨園戲). Pear Garden Drama, now considered to be a type of Ming romance (*ch'uan-ch'i* 傳奇), originated in Chuanchou (Ch'üan-chou 泉州) and spread from there to Chin-chiang 晋江, Lung-hsi 龍溪, Amoy 厦門, and Taiwan. It also became popular among overseas Chinese communities in Southeast Asia. This kind of drama preserves old features of instrumentation and lyric tunes. The movements of the actors are strictly regulated and some are clearly patterned after those of puppets.[1] *The Lichee and the Mirror* (hereafter *LM*) survives in a number of editions, the earliest extant dating to 1566 (Ming Chia-ching 嘉靖 45). Preserved in the Japanese Cabinet Library (Naikaku Bunko 內閣文庫), it was published by the New Peace Bookshop (Hsin-an shu-fang 新安書坊) of Ch'ung-hua village 崇化里 in Ma-sha town 麻沙鎮 (famous for its books printed from softwood plates), Chien-yang district 建陽縣 in Fukien province. A colophon states that *LM* was based on a play entitled *The Lichee Branch* (*Li-chih chi* 荔枝記), but the publisher chose not to reprint that version because it was both full of errors and abbreviated. Ultimately, the play probably has its roots in fifteenth-century folk drama of southern Fukien.

LM relates the story of Ch'en San (Third Ch'en 陳三) and Wu-niang (Fifth Lass 五娘) which had long been popular in southern Fukien and eastern Kwangtung provinces. Indeed, *Ch'en San Wu-niang* is the customary title for this play as it is performed in the Pear Garden Drama repertoire. Many other types of local performing arts in Kwangtung and Fukien provinces have made this story a mainstay of their repertoires as well. Although we do not know the name of the author of the 1566 edition of the *LM*, that is not very important because the story is obviously the collective cultural property of a whole large region of China and has been reworked many times by countless hands.

There is a Chaochou 潮州 ditty which attests to the strong affection that the people of the southeast China coast hold for this story:

> The east produced Meng Chiang-nü of bitter fate,
> The west produced Sixth Sister Su,
> The north produced Chu Ying-t'ai and Liang Shan-po,
> The south produced Ch'en San and Wu-niang.

> 東畔出有苦孟姜
> 西畔出有蘇六娘
> 北畔出有英台共山伯
> 南畔出有陳三共五娘[2]

So attached were the southeastern Chinese to the story of Ch'en San and Wu-niang and so emotional were their responses to its enactment that the Ming and Ch'ing governments repeatedly suppressed performances of it which might enflame their passions.[3] One main reason for official sanctions against the play was undoubtedly Wu-niang's spirited opposition to established customs regarding the way a young lady should behave. Her rebellious attitude toward the whole system of arranged marriages must have left the authorities aghast. The fact that the two lovers remained loyal to each other despite class differences also shows a determined resistance to social convention in general. This, of course, was a kind of behavior that the authorities could not tolerate.

A brief synopsis of *LM* will be helpful in trying to comprehend whether it should be considered as a legitimate specimen of Chinese literary art or whether it should be classified as something else and hence excluded from anthologies of Chinese literature. Ch'en San (full name Ch'en Po-ch'ing 陳伯卿), who hails from Ch'uan-chou, is accompanying his older brother on a long trip to Kuang-nan in Yunnan province, where the latter is going to take up an official position. Their way passes through Ch'ao-chou, and there Ch'en San meets Wu-niang (full name Huang Pi-chü 黃碧琚) at the Lantern Festival (Yüan-hsiao 元宵, the fifteenth day of the first lunar month). They fall in love with each other at first sight. Wu-niang's parents, Huang Chiu-lang 黃九郎 (Huang the Ninth) and his wife, promise their daughter in marriage to the wealthy Big Lin 林大. On the day that the matchmaker comes to present betrothal gifts to the Huang family, Wu-niang smashes the gifts and beats off the matchmaker.

The next year, Ch'en San comes back to Ch'ao-chou. Wu-niang is leaning over a balcony enjoying the warmth of summer and thus the two lovers meet once again. She tosses down a lichee branch and a handkerchief as a pledge of her affection. Thereupon Ch'en San pretends to be a mirror polisher. He intentionally breaks a precious mirror belonging to the Huang family and sells himself into slavery to them to repay the loss. After repeated inquiries, Wu-niang finally learns Ch'en San's real background. Her maid, named I-ch'un 益眷, plays a crucial role in helping the two get together. They elope but are soon caught and Ch'en San is thrown into jail. His brother, Ch'en Po-hsien 陳伯賢, who by now has been elevated to the high rank of executive censor of Kwangtung and Kwangsi provinces, comes to his rescue, and so the two lovers are reunited once again.

A detailed look at a famous scene from the play (allegedly one of the most risqué) should afford further scope for assessing the propriety of considering *LM* as genuine Chinese literature.

Ch'en San: Little sister, what are you going to do with that basin of water?

　　　　‘sio be’ ‘lɯ ˌp’aŋ ‘tsui bə? tsue’ mi̭

　　　　小　妹　你　捧　　水　　卜　做　乜

Maid: I am taking it to the mistress so she can wash her face.

　　　　‘tɕi ‘tsui ˌp’aŋ bə? k’ɪ’ ‘gun ˌa ˌniu ‘se bin’

　　　　只　水　捧　卜　乞　阮　啞娘　洗　面

Ch'en: Let me take it to her for you.

　　　　t’ai’ ‘gun t’e’ ‘sio bue’ ‘lɯ ˌp’aŋ k’ui’

　　　　待　阮　替　小　妹　你　捧　去

Ch'en takes the basin of water and goes offstage.

Maid: How come you're so anxious to be a servant? Aren't you afraid the mistress will scold you if you take the water to her?

　　　　‘lɯ hiŭ’ ai’ hok, sai ˌlaŋ ‘lui bə? ˌp’aŋ k’iu’ m’ ui’ ˌgun ˌa ˌniu ‘a ma’ ‘lɯ

　　　　你　向　愛服　事人　爾　卜　捧　去　不畏阮　啞娘　仔罵　你

The maid goes off and Ch'en reappears.

Ch'en: (Sings to the tune "Golden Filigree")

As I take this basinful of water into her boudoir,

ₜp'aŋ ₜpun ‘tsui tɵiũˊ siuˊ ₜt'iã

捧　盆　水　上　繡　廳

I feel partly happy,

ₜsim laiˊ puãˊ ₜhuã ‘hi

心　內　半　歡　喜

And partly afraid.

tɵit₂ puãˊ tio₂ˀ ₜkɪŋ

一　半　着　驚

My heart is filled with suffering

ₜsin ‘k'ɔ tsaiˊ ₜsim laiˊ

辛　苦　在　心　內

That I dare not reveal;

ₜtɔ m' ‘kã tã'

郡　不　敢　咕

My feelings are tremendously confused,

ₜlaŋ ₜtɵ'iŋ ‘iu ₜtɵ'im ₜpuã

人・情　有　千　般

But she has not the slightest suspicion.

i ₜtɔ m' liam buãˊ ₜsiã

伊都不　念　半　聲

Wu-niang calls the maid and she appears.

Maid: It's Ch'en San.

s'i ₜtan ₜsã

是陳　三

Wu-niang: You wench! I asked you to bring me a basin of water to wash my face. What do you mean by letting Ch'en San bring it?

‘lɯ ‘tɵi ‘kui ‘a ‘gua ka₂ˀ ‘lɯ ₜp'aŋ ₜt'aŋ ₜlai t'ɔˊ ‘gua ‘se bin' ‘lɯ t'ɔˊ

你　只　鬼　仔　我　甲　你　捧　湯　來　度　我　洗面　你　度

ₜtan ₜsã ₜp'aŋ ₜlai mi₂ tai'

陳　三　捧　來　乜　事

Maid: When you asked me to go fetch the water, I happened upon your mother who told me to do some other things.

ₜa ₜniu ‘sai ‘kan k'iu' ₜp'aŋ ₜt'aŋ giu' tiu₂ ₜa ‘ma ‘sai ‘kan ₜtiu

啞娘　使　簡　去　捧　湯　遇着　啞媽　使　簡　除

Wu-niang: What did mother ask you to do?

ₜa ‘ma ‘sai ‘lɯ mi₂ˀ tai₂

啞媽　使　你　乜　事

Maid: She had me go tend to the tea. I was afraid that you needed the water right away, so I had Ch'en San bring it.

‘sai ‘kan k'iu' kuã' ₜte ‘kan ui' ₜa ₜniu bɔˀ ‘tsui ‘kin si' ‘kan ‘sai ₜtan ₜsã

使　簡　去　看　茶　簡　畏　啞娘　卜　水　緊　是　簡　使　陳　三

ₜp'aŋ ₜlai

捧　來

Wu-niang: Despicable wench! Bring me the hot water so I can wash my face!

'lɯ 'tɕi 'kui 'a bə? 'si 'kin ˌtɕiəŋ ˌt'aŋ tɕiap' ke? ˌlai ˌhɪŋ 'gua 'se bin'

你 只 鬼 仔 卜 死 緊 將 湯 接 過 來 那 待 阮 捧

Ch'en: Let me take it over to her.

na' tai' 'gun ˌp'aŋ

還 我 洗 面

Maid: You make me laugh!

'gun ai' tɕ'io' ˌlaŋ

阮 愛 笑 人

Ch'en: Well, go ahead and laugh then.

tio? k'i' 'lɯ tɕio'

着 乞 你 笑

Maid: It's disgraceful!

'ho ˌsue

好 衰

Ch'en: Not to me.

mi,? ˌt'aŋ ˌsue

乜 通 衰

Wu-niang starts to wash herself while Ch'en San looks on.

Wu-niang: I-ch'un, I'd like to wash my face. What's Ch'en San doing standing there?

ia,? ˌtsun 'gua 'tɕi 'tɣ ˌse bin' ˌtan ˌsã 'hiu tɣ' k'ia' mi,? tai'

益 春 我 只 處 洗 面 陳 三 許 處 立 乜 事

Maid: (To Ch'en San) Our mistress wants to wash her face and wishes that you would go away.

'gun ˌa ˌniu bə? 'se bin' ka,? 'lɯ ˌkiŋ ˌk'ui k'iu'

阮 啞 娘 卜 洗 面 甲 你 行 開 去

Ch'en: Your mistress can wash her face by herself. I'm just waiting here to serve her.

'lin ˌa ˌniu bə? ˌse bin' ˌtɔ si' tok, tsu' 'kan ˌdzi 'tɕi 'tɣ t'iŋ' hau'

憑 啞 娘 卜 洗 面 都 是 獨 自 簡 兒 只 處 聽 候

Wu-niang: Scoundrel! I want to wash my face. Who needs you to wait on them? Go away!

ts'at, ˌla ˌlaŋ bə? 'se bin' ˌsui bə? 'lui t'iŋ' hau' 'tsau

賊 奴 人 卜 洗 面 誰 卜 你 聽 候 走

Ch'en San goes off but comes back again to watch her.

Wu-niang: Yi-ch'un, who's over there watching me while I wash myself?

ia,? ˌtsun 'gua 'tɕi 'tɣ 'se bin' ˌsui 'hiu 'tɣ kuã'

益 春 我 只 處 洗 面 誰 許 處 看

Maid: It's Ch'en San.

si' ˌtan ˌsã

是 陳 三

Wu-niang: The scoundrel! How dare he watch me while I'm washing my face? I-ch'un, pretend that you don't know he's there and throw this water in his face. We'll see if he goes away then.

ts'at, ˌlo ‘gua ‘tɕi ‘tɤ ‘se bin’ ˌi ‘kã ‘hiu ‘tɤ kuã’ ia,’ ˌtsun ˌtɕioŋ ‘tɕi
賊　奴 我　只 處 洗 面 伊 敢 許 處·看 啞 春　將　只

‘tsui ‘ke i’ m̩’ ˌtsi tui’ bin’ pua,’ k'i’ ˌi ‘tsau
水　假 意 不 知 對 面 潑　乞 伊 走

Maid: Dear mistress, this basin is so full of water. If I splash it on him, aren't you afraid he'll catch cold?

ˌa ˌniu ‘tsi ˌp'un ‘tsui tsua,’ ‘moa p'ua,’ ˌi ‘laŋ ˌtɔ m̩’ ui’ ‘liau ‘ling ˌi ‘laŋ
啞 娘 只 盆　水 拙　滿　潑　伊 人 都 不 畏 了　冷 伊 人

Wu-niang: It's up to you how you handle it.

ˌsui ‘lɯ k'iu’ ‘le lok,
隨 你 去　禮 約

Maid: I'm afraid he'll scold me if I splash him.

‘kan m̩’ ‘kã pua,’ ˌi ‘liau ma’ ‘kan
簡 不 敢 潑　伊 了 罵 簡

Wu-niang: Vixen! At least dump half of it on him.

ts'ae, pi’ m̩’ ˌhia ‘k'iam tɔ’ naŋ’ e’
賊　婢 不 彼 減　到 二　個

Maid: Dear mistress, since you're so concerned about Ch'en San, you might as well not splash him at all.

ˌa ˌniu tsua,’ t'ia’ ˌi bɔ, tit’ p'ua,’ ˌi
啞 娘　拙　痛 伊 莫 得 潑　伊

Together, Wu-niang and the maid throw the water on him.

Ch'en: Hey! Who made me all soaked like this?

si’ ˌsui si’ ˌsui lia, ‘gua tsit, ˌsin p'ua,’ tit, tɕioŋ’ ˌtam
是 誰　　力 我 一　身 潑　得 障　濕

Maid: We didn't know you were sitting there.

ˌsui ˌlaŋ ˌtsi ‘lɯ to’ ‘hiu tɤ’ tsue’
誰 人 知 你 在 許　處 坐

Ch'en: Little sister, you really can't tell black from white.

‘sio be’ ‘ho ˌbo ˌhun ‘hiau
小 妹 好 無 分　曉

Maid: Who told you to peep at the mistress while she was washing?

ˌsui ˌlaŋ ka,’ ‘lɯ ‘hiu tɤ’ k'uã’ ˌlaŋ
誰 人 甲 你 許　處 看 人

Ch'en: (Sings to the tune of "Red Presentation Jacket")

When I carefully reflect on what happened,

‘tsu sie’ ˌsiu ˌniu ‘tsi tsit,’ tai’
仔 細 思 量 只 一　事

(Ch'en San understands)
I realize this was something you two schemed up.[4]
ˌtɔ si' 'lin naŋ' 'laŋ tsueʔ tsut, 'lai
都 是 憑 二 人 做 出 來

Having read *LM*, I remain puzzled. Surely it is a powerful work of art
that has enthralled millions and an important part of China's literary heritage. Yet does it deserve to be enshrined in an anthology of Chinese literature? If not, on what grounds do we exclude it? It we declare that *LM* is *not*
Chinese literature, what then *is* it, and how should we treat it? Do works
such as *LM* merit preservation at all and, if so, in what form? Should it be
translated into MSM or Classical Chinese (or some combination of the two)
before it is admitted into the national canon of literary masterpieces? If yes,
what then shall we do with the original Minlam text?

If we have difficulty determining the legitimacy of such an elegant and
renowned work as *LM* for inclusion in an anthology of Chinese literature,
other genres I have encountered cause even greater perplexity. Among
them are the Cantonese love songs (*Yud-eo* 粵謳) of Chao Tzu-yung/Chîû
Tsz-yung 招子庸.[5] These are exquisite poems that are almost totally forgotten nowadays in China. I should like to examine them in some detail
in order to gain an appreciation of what Cantonese literature might be
and the degree to which it may be considered an integral part of Chinese
literature.

I would like to begin this section by paying tribute to a remarkable book
in two volumes by Cecil Clementi. Entitled simply *Cantonese Love-Songs*, it is
a model of what a scholarly translation should be. Aside from the fact that
Clementi was once a demy (a type of stipendiary at Magdalen College,
Oxford) and a member of the Land Court for the New Territory in Hong
Kong, I know next to nothing about him. What I do know is that his
renditions of Chao Tzu-yung's poems were done with the utmost love, care,
and thoroughness. Not only does Clementi's book offer splendid translations; it also includes the best edition of the poems available. There are
copious annotations, but they are tucked away in the back of the first volume so as not to interfere with the poetry itself. The annotations provide
full explanations of allusions, historical references, and so on. Clementi also
has a long introduction, which discusses love themes, nature imagery and
symbolism, a comparison of Cantonese with Hebraic and Hellenic love poetry, the social and economic setting of Chao Tzu-yung's poetry, and the
thoroughly Buddhist ethic which informs the poems. It ends with a lucid
exposition of the music to which the poems were sung. There is much more
that I could and would like to say in praise of Clementi's *Cantonese Love-
Songs*, but I will limit myself to the further observation that it is very rare
and richly deserves reprinting and wide dissemination. This is a forgotten
classic of sinology and world literature.

Little is known about the author of the Cantonese love songs, even though he lived less than two centuries ago. Chao Tzu-yung was born in Nan-hai 南海 district near Canton. He was a provincial graduate during the Chia-ch'ing period (1796–1820) and served as magistrate of Wei 濰 district on the coast of Shantung. Clementi tells us that he was also prefect of Ch'ing-chou 青州 and was still active in 1828.

Cantonese Love-Poems contains 97 titles, but some titles include more than one poem, so there are actually a total of 121 poems. Their average length is between ten and fifteen lines, with a few running to twenty lines or more. The collection is preceded by twelve prefaces, most of them by literarily minded friends of the poet. To give an example of the learned, emotion-laden sentiments that the prefaces express, I shall quote the entire Second Preface by Shek the Taoist:

In the autumn of the year 1828, in the eighth month, when the fifteenth day was already passed, when crickets chirped at the door and a cool wind shook the curtains, Meng Shán, a retired scholar, was pleased to visit me. With downcast manner he sorrowfully said: "These autumn sounds increase a man's melancholy! I pray you rid me thereof." I replied: "Aye, aye!" The scholar continued: "My son, do you not observe the Pearl River? Jasmine carpets the fields: sandalwood builds the houses: for ten miles the river smells fragrant: its pearl houses are a thousand: each house, when the white sun sinks westward, displays red lanterns at evening-tide: garments chink and chime bedecked with jewel pendants: the breath of flowers, instinct with primal life, floats around forming a vaporous mist: among diverse fashions of plump and slender, virtue's demeanor takes a myriad phases: pearl maidens and pearl youths in dainty joyance play the Chîû lyre: then, flushed with wine, with tingling ears they change to the melodies of Tshun: have you no pleasure in all this?" —Said I: "Excellent in all excellence! But the sounds are not to my liking." —Quoth the retired scholar: 'When the Lô-lung house-boats descend on the ebbing tide, when the lizard-skin drums strike the midnight hour, as the errant pleasure-boats gradually grow fewer, and the cold moon passes clear of the clouds: at such a time, coifed maidens set the lotus-roots on ice, slim fingers distribute oranges: the heart's oppression is scattered and swept away: pretty roundels are sung and Ng-country ballads form the prelude: then, as the bright lamps change darkness into splendor, suddenly the pipes of Chhoa are blown: instantly the noise of men is silenced: has my son pleasure herein?" —I answered: "Lovely in all loveliness! But not after my heart."

—The scholar replied: "When the three stars of marriage are set in the sky, and a myriad sounds are hushed as the water: when the bright coifed tresses are already unbound at bedtime, and the perfume of ointment may be faintly scented: as comfort in the advance of the lapsing years, and as dirge in the tranquil length of the night: while pursuing the past of bygone events, and while thrilled in the present by passion's advent: even then, as you pour forth those southern songs, as you write of your reliance in a forlorn clue of hope, as your throat swells with singing and you beat the time of the music, as the melody yearns to ebb and yet flows back again, as you choke with suppressed emotion, yet stifle your grief, as the harmony wellnigh broken reunites: at such a time, when the moon at ocean's verge is fain to set, when over the river clouds cease to drift, when suddenly you lament your inexorable fate, who then can banish these sentiments?" —Said I: "The southern songs thrill men through: their sounds are even as you describe. Can you compose such poems?" —Thereupon the retired scholar recited what he had written, in soft tones with long-drawn utterance. The theme was plaintive and gentle: the verses were graceful and passionate, such as Fán Yam has called sad enough to penetrate a man's heart and marrow, piteous enough to melt callous beauty. The reader need not wait for the songs of Hoa Mún, for already his green garment will surely be wet with tears.[6]

These may not be precisely the sentiments of the northern Chinese heartland, but they do represent an authentic aesthetics, one that is fully informed by Chinese tradition and at the same time is securely anchored in local life. This is what makes the whole ethos of the Cantonese love songs more genuine than the countless tomes of stale, repetitive verse that continually tried to imitate the timeless glories of T'ang regulated verse and Sung lyric meters.

The poems themselves actually make fewer concessions to things Cantonese than do the prefaces. Take the first part of the eleventh in the series, for example.

A Lament for Fortune's Frailty

Man is lonely: the moon shines all the brighter.
Those sinful debts of the sea of lust and of the heaven of love are still unpaid.
Since parting and meeting, sorrow and gladness, have their season:
Why is there at all times a blight on famous flowers?
Look you! Yöng Fe's jade bones were buried beside the mountain track.   5
The grass remained green above Chhiu-kwan's tomb.
In fallen fortune Siu Tsheng sadly mourns o'er her likeness.
Shap Nöng drank of misery abundant as water.
In fine, from birth to womanhood more than half among rosy girls are ill-
   fated:
How much the more are we, flowers and paint of love's arbour, injured
   by lustful passions.   10
Since we are willow blossoms, more than the half of us are weak as water:
How can we learn to start stainless from the mire, ever displaying ourselves
   strong and pure?
I fear, I do but fear, that sad autumn will whirl the elm leaves into the
   golden well:
Therefore I must ever be as the winter plum-tree which steadfastly endures
   the spite of snow and frost.
Methinks in all four seasons flowers and trees are as a happy land.
Only sad men, in face of one another, gulp down their grief and stifle their
   words.   15
Ah! needs must I myself be wakeful.
Who can bear witness to fortune's frailty?
I were best recount my way of life o'er the Tomb of a Hundred Flowers.

嗟怨薄命
人寂靜。月更光明。
慾海情天個的孽債未清。
離合悲歡雖則係有定。
做乜名花遭際總是凋零。
你睇楊妃玉骨埋山徑。
昭君留墓草青青。
淪落小青愁弔影。
十娘飲恨一水盈盈。
大抵生長紅顏多半是薄命。
何況我哋青樓花粉。更累在癡情。
旣係做到楊花。多半是水性。
點學得出泥不染。都重表自己堅貞。
怕祇怕悲秋桐葉飄金井。
重要學寒梅偏捱得雪霜凌。
我想花木四時都係樂境。
總係愁人相對就噲飲恨吞聲。
唉。須要自醒。
命薄誰堪證。
不若向百花墳上訴聽生平。

Chao Tzu-yung's Cantonese love songs are largely understandable to someone who knows only Classical Chinese and MSM, hence one wonders how authentic they are in terms of representing pure Cantonese language. There is no doubt that Chao and several of those who wrote prefaces for his collection set great store by their native tongue:

Born and bred in southern villages we ply the country speech:
Yet he who sings, even in the vulgar tongue, must take anxious thought.
生長蠻鄉操土音
俚詞率口幾關心

(Third Preface, ll. 1–2)

Who has composed these lyrics in dialect?
土音曲譜誰修

(Fourth Preface, l. 7)

In skill of plying the country speech, he is become a school of poetry in himself.
土音能操自成家

(Tenth Preface, l. 9)

But what purports to be true vernacular is often highly adulterated with classicisms and Mandarinisms.

One of the best examples of written Cantonese from the nineteenth century is the *Tsuk Wá Khing Thám* 俗話傾談 (Colloquial Chats, or Conversations in Colloquial). In his preface, the author makes a straightforward case for the use of the vernacular:

A good drummer generally strikes the side of the drum: a good story-teller always tells interesting and extraordinary tales. If the language used is too learned and obscure, women and children will find it difficult to understand. If the matters talked about are common speech, then all will easily understand, and furthermore they will feel entertained thereby.[8]

Yet when we analyze the language of the *Tsuk Wá Khing Thám* itself, we find that it is composed of a mixture of Cantonese, simple Classical ("book-language"), and Mandarin. The translator, J. Dyer Ball, writes:

> In "Conversations in Colloquial," the diction employed for several sentences is a simple book language style, when a colloquial phrase will occur, or a conversation or description will ensue in which, if not entirely colloquial, the vernacular nearly entirely predominates. The continual employment of a number of book-language words in the midst of the colloquial also spoils the naturalness. Some, if not all, of the words are occasionally used by educated men in conversation; but the continual use of them and the use of a number of them in juxtaposition with too small a medium of Colloquial to unite them, is what is here complained of—such as, e.g. 不 pat, for *not*, and 是 shí for the verb *to be*. It is not that the native author entirely eschews the use of the colloquial forms, for 唔 m and 係 haí appear in the book as well, though sparingly. The third personal pronoun 其 k'éi and 他 t'á, the demonstrative 此 t'sz, the verb 曰 yüt, *to say*, the verb 來 loi, *to come*, the particle 而 yi—all of these either entirely exclude the use of the equivalent colloquial forms, or minimise their use.
>
> It will thus be seen that the book is not in the book-language, nor is it in the colloquial entirely, though on the whole nearer the latter; it is a mixture of the two. Occasionally a mandarin word or phrase occurs. This may, of course, sometimes be allowable, as a French word may appear in an English book now and then; but when the mandarin form ná appears for the common demonstrative, it is really carrying the matter a little too far, and it sounds unpleasant to the ear accustomed to the pure sounds of Cantonese. If the student of Cantonese colloquial is sufficiently advanced to know what is colloquial and what is not, this book will prove of use to him, as he will find many good idiomatic phrases in it; and it might be useful as a stepping stone from the colloquial to the simple book-language style.[9]

A similar situation obtains for Chao Tzu-yung's Cantonese love songs. We must remember that Chao Tzu-yung was a learned Mandarin who had served as a magistrate in the north. Thus it was inevitable that his poetry would be deeply imbued with the national culture and language. The historical allusions that he employs are usually from mainstream sources. We may characterize his poems as being written in a sort of standard Cantonese book language of about 175 years ago, yet with a sufficiently large admixture of Classical Chinese and Mandarin to accommodate the national culture. Indeed, in spite of Chao's protestations in favor of Cantonese, it is probably more accurate to say that the poems are basically written in Classical Chinese (as would be suitable for someone who had passed the provincial examinations) with occasional touches of Mandarin (as befits a member of the bureaucracy) and a liberal sprinkling of Cantonese (as might be natural for a displaced magistrate who was plagued by nostalgia for his mother tongue). It is doubtful that these poems could have been fully understood when read aloud to someone who had not first been exposed to them in written form or who was not very highly educated. They are certainly a far cry from the spoken Cantonese that we hear on the streets and in the villages of Hong Kong and Kwangtung today.

As a matter of fact, it was Chao Tzu-yung who singlehandedly created the Cantonese love song *as a written genre*. He achieved this by forging a combination of Cantonese folk songs and popular melodies (which could have been understood in the absence of writing) with material drawn from the classical tradition of the literati. These materials were fashioned into beautiful works of art by Chao, who injected them with his own experience and emotion. They became fabulously popular among the educated in Kwangtung province and especially in the city of Canton. But who speaks of them now? I am convinced that Chao's Cantonese love songs ought to be resurrected because they are a precious part of China's literary heritage. In my estimation, we need to contemplate seriously the prospect of including them in anthologies of Chinese verse. At the very least, we must ask why these lovely poems have been so utterly forgotten. This makes us wonder how much else of China's literary past has perished because it did not fit within the narrow confines of what we may call the central culture or prestige culture of the capital.

Now, the prestige culture of the capital is essentially the culture of bureaucrats. Literature belonging to this culture has been homogenized in such a way that it often lacks distinctiveness and persuasiveness.[10] One suspects that much of Chinese culture that was of great worth has been irretrievably destroyed simply because it did not fit the mold of officialdom. To gain some idea of the magnitude of our loss, all we need do is think of the texts that have been recovered from the deserts of Central Asia and the temple libraries of Japan during the past century. I shall not list all of these outstanding recoveries but shall mention only three that have been of paramount value in my own work in particular and in the reconstruction of China's literary past generally: Tun-huang transformation texts (*pien-wen* 變文), *Liu Chih-yüan Medley* (*Liu Chih-yüan chu-kung-tiao* 劉知遠諸宮調), and *Tale Interspersed with Poems of the T'ang Monk Tripiṭaka's Journey to India to Obtain Sutras* (*Ta T'ang San-tsang ch'ü ching shih-hua* 大唐三藏取經詩話). It is painful to imagine how much else of comparable or even greater worth has been lost that the sporadic expeditions of archeologists and the desultory investigations of antiquarians will never be able to resurrect. I believe that we have a very incomplete picture of China's literary past and that even our understanding of the present is terribly skewed by the overwhelming dominance of the central culture.

Clementi refers to the poetry of Chao Tzu-yung as immortal, and rightly so. But how do we explain that this undying verse has virtually vanished in the land of its birth? This is a conundrum of large proportions that cannot be answered without first squarely addressing the question of the relationships among China's national and regional (as well as local) cultures. Provisionally, it seems to me that the central culture of China has always been stiflingly supreme and that it lacks adequate mechanisms for absorbing and assimilating the creative genius of outlying regions. This, of course, is not only a drawback in matters of culture, but is still more serious in the realm of politics. All power and privilege seem to be vested in and flow from the center, leaving the provinces scheming of nothing more than to capture the center. A good dose of federalism would do wonders both for China's ongoing political crises and for combating the monolithic quality of the official culture. To put the matter more bluntly, the riches of China's regionalism and localism should be celebrated, not squashed.[11]

By no means am I the first to raise these admittedly sensitive issues. Many of China's most brilliant and prescient scholars debated them well over half a century ago. It is sad that no progress has been made toward resolving these vital questions since that time. To bring this debate to the fore once again, I can think of no better way than to translate into English substantial portions of three of the prefaces to Ku Chieh-kang's 顧頡剛 landmark publication of Soochow ballads.

Because of its succinctness and exceptional importance, I present the preface of Hu Shih 胡適 almost in toto.

> Seven years ago, I made the following statement:
>
> > ... After literature in the national language arises, as much as possible there should be "topolect literature." The more topolectical literature there is, the more material there will be for the national language literature to select from and the more it will have rich content and lively vitality. Such is the case with the language of England. Although it has gradually extended over the world, on the three home islands there are at least a hundred dialects. Among them are several important dialects, such as Scottish, Irish, and Welsh, all of which possess literature of high quality. After we have created a national language literature and have established a standard, not only will we be unafraid of topolectical literature competing with it, we will actually rely on the various topolects to give it new materials and infuse it with new blood. ('Reply to Huang Chüeh-seng," *Hu Shih wen-ts'un* [Collected Writings of Hu Shih] 胡適文存, first series, I, p. 153.)
>
> At the time, I didn't want to startle those who were promoting literature in the national language, so when I made this statement, I very carefully included some limitations, such as "after literature in the national language arises," "after we have created a national language literature and have established a

standard," and so forth. Viewed from the current vantage point, all of that was unnecessary.

To tell the truth, the national language is but a superior type of topolect; many years ago, today's national language was merely topolectical literature. Precisely because people in those days were willing to use topolects to create literature, dared to use topolects to create literature, during the past thousand and some years there has accumulated a sizable quantity of living literature. Within it, that portion which was most widespread came to be recognized as the foundation for national language literature. Naturally, we should not be satisfied simply to cling to this meager heritage bequeathed to us by history. Inasmuch as national language literature has derived from topolectical literature, we must still seek new materials, new blood, and new life from topolectical literature.

This is to consider the matter from the vantage of "national language literature." If we consider the matter from the vantage of literature in the broad sense, we are all the more obliged to rely on the topolects. Literature should be able to express differences in character. Beggar ladies and prostitutes all say that the classical prose of Ssu-ma Ch'ien and Pan Ku is ridiculous; Joe Blow and John Doe all say that the vernacular of *Dream of the Red Chamber* and *An Unofficial History of the Literati* is ridiculous. The ancients had long ago recognized this, consequently Lu Chih-shen 魯智深 and Li K'uei 李逵[12] used a lot of earthy speech and the main characters in *Gold Vase Plum* are noted for their colloquialisms. "Plain talk" novels (*p'ing-hua hsiao-shuo* 平話小說) such as *Three Knights and Five Gallants* and *Lesser Five Gallants* are intentionally larded with colloquial speech. Since the late Ming, Soochow colloquialisms are often used in southern genres of literature such as K'un-shan Opera and novels. Among these there are some which have exceedingly fine descriptions. Here I shall mention only one passage from *Lives of Shanghai Beauties*:

> Paired Jade approached and sat next to Chastity on the bed. Leaning over slightly, Paired Jade placed her hands on Chastity's shoulders and instructed Chastity to place her right hand on top of Paired Jade's head and her left hand over Paired Jade's heart. Face to face, she asked her. "Do you remember when we were sitting together restfully chatting like this in the Bamboo Hat Garden in the Seventh Month?" 倪七月裡來裏一笠園, 也像故歇實概樣式一淘坐來浪說個間話, 耐阿記得? (chapter 63)

If we were to translate Paired Jade's words into Mandarin (我們七月裡在一笠園, 也像現在這樣子坐在一塊說的話, 你記得嗎?), the thought would admittedly not be at all bad, but the spirit would be drastically diminished.

Consequently, I have often reflected that if Lu Hsün's "True Story of Ah Q" had been written in Shao-hsing colloquial, how much more vivid it would have been! Unfortunately, authors of recent years still do not dare to follow this path. Even writers from Soochow such as Yeh Sheng-t'ao are only willing to learn a Europeanized vernacular but are unwilling to use the topolect of their native place. Recently, in Hsü Chih-mo's collected poems there was one piece that was a ray of golden light in that it was written in the patois of Hsia-shih.[13] In the living literature of today, this must be considered one of the most successful experiments. Its most outstanding lines are the following:

Yesterday morning I went early to her room, *mea culpa*!
Old Atai had already gone, lying frozen amidst the straw,
I know not when the last breath slipped away, nobody knows!
There was nothing else I could do but call some men to come,
Some said that she died of hunger, others that she died of cold;
"More likely her old sickness," I thought, as a light breeze blew
from the northwest.

> 昨日子我一早走至伊屋裡, 眞罪過!
> 老阿太已經去哩, 冷冰冰歐滾在稻草裏,
> 野勿曉得幾時脫氣歐, 野嘸不人曉得!
> 我野嘸不法子, 只好去喊攏幾個人來,
> 有人話是餓煞歐, 有人話是凍煞歐,
> 我看一半是老病, 西北風野作興有點歐。

This is branch of the Wu topolect; whoever understands the Wu topolect can appreciate the spirit of this poem. This is true vernacular and true living language.

Among the various topolects of China, there are three which have already produced a substantial amount of literature. This first is Pekingese, the second is Soochow (Wu/Ngeu), the third is Cantonese (Yüeh/Yud). Pekingese has produced the greatest amount of literature and it has the widest dissemination. Peking has been the capital for five hundred years, the sons and brothers of the eight banners have served in distant positions as officials and in garrison posts, and Peking opera has become very popular in recent years: these are the reasons for the dissemination of Pekingese. The focus of Cantonese literature are the Cantonese love songs which began among the people but, since the time of Chao Tzu-yung/Chiû Tsz-yung, there have been quite a few imitators. So far as verse goes, their achievement is considerable. In spite of the fact that those at home and abroad who can speak Cantonese are quite numerous, however, Cantonese literature lags far behind that of Mandarin and in the final analysis its influence remains minimal. Situated between Pekingese literature and Cantonese literature is Wu literature. In terms of place, Soochow, Sung-chiang, Ch'ang-chou, Tai-hu, Hangchow, Chia-hsing, and Hu-chou may all be considered Wu topolect areas. In terms of its history, it has already been around for 300 years. During the past 300 years, everyone who has studied K'un-shan Opera has received training in Wu phonology. During the last hundred years, Shanghai has become the commercial center of the entire country so that the Wu topolect has also come to occupy a special place of importance on account of this. On top of that, the beauty of girls from south of the Yangtze has long since captured the hearts of the young men of the whole country. The sounds of the "shrike-tongued southern barbarian" of yore have long since become the captivating accents of the girls from Wu. Consequently, apart from Pekingese literature, Wu literature must be considered as the topolectical literature which has the greatest influence and the best prospects.

Wu literature all along has only rarely been completely independent. In K'un-shan Opera, the Wu dialogue is invariably restricted to the jesting portions. Likewise, only rarely is Soochow vernacular inserted in strum lyrics (*t'an-tz'u*). And, in the fiction up till the last few decades which describes the lives of prostitutes, only a portion of the dialogue uses Soochow vernacular whereas the narration uses Mandarin. If we wish to find completely independent Wu literature, we must seek it in the songs and ballads of Soochow.

This volume of *Soochow Songs, I* edited by Ku Chieh-kang is the first book of independent Wu literature. Volume I is divided into two parts. The first consists completely of children's songs which are pure Soochow literature. When we read this part, every utterance seems to bring alive before our very eyes the quick, lively, tender, mischievous spirit of Soochow children. This is authentic[14] topolectical literature. The second part consists of songs sung by adults. Although there are several excellent folk songs[15] in this part, the majority of the longer songs reveal the influence of strum lyric (*t'an-tz'u*) scripts: unrestrained prolixity and overworked clichés have infiltrated the folk songs, diminishing their simplicity.

In his introduction, Ku Chieh-kang divides Soochow songs into five categories: (1) children's songs, (2) songs of village women, (3) boudoir songs, (4) songs of peasants, workers, and drifters, (5) miscellaneous songs. My reading of part two leaves me feeling that he has included too many boudoir songs—long songs of the strum lyric variety—and too few of the second and fourth varieties of genuine folk songs. But this is to be expected, for Ku Chieh-kang was born and grew up in the city of Soochow and the friends who helped him with the collection are all from the city. None of them have very close connections with village women, peasants, workers, and drifters, so it is unavoidable that this collection has the defect of a partiality for boudoir songs. Although the boudoir songs do represent the sentiments and habits of a certain group, because there is too much repetition and too little creativity, insufficient pruning, and stale language, their literary value is not high.

We enthusiastically welcome the appearance of this first volume devoted to Wu literature. We admire Ku Chieh-kang's efforts at collecting and his labors of editing. In his *Miscellaneous Notes on Songwriting*, there are many interesting and valuable discussions (such as "Inspiration" and other chapters) that can increase our knowledge of the *Poetry Classic*. But we hope that when he compiles the second volume, Ku will include many more songs of village women, peasants, workers, and drifters. If the publication of this first volume can stimulate the interest of people throughout Soochow and can induce them to help with the collection of "authentic" folk songs from the various villages, enabling the second and successive volumes to be dedicated to the literature of the common people in pure Wu language, then we may truly say that the appearance of this book will have opened a new era in the history of Chinese literature.

Hu Shih
September 20, 1925
Peking

The following remarks of Yü P'ing-po 俞平伯, dated August 21, 1925, are also of great value.

I believe that any true literature not only must be expressed in living language, it must adopt the language of real living people. Therefore, not only do I advocate national language literature, I also hope for the growth of topolectical literature. I approve of a unified national language, but I do not on that account approve of the unification of literature by the national language. A literary national language and a national language literature ideally go hand in glove. But an ideal, after all, is only an ideal. We cannot make it become an immediate reality simply because it is an ideal. Nor can we close our eyes to the existence of topolectical literature—whether it be in the past, present, or future—even if there are those who truly detest it.

To my mind, not only is there already topolectical literature, there *ought* to be, and we should strive to promote it. Naturally this runs somewhat counter to the wishes of those who fervently espouse the national language. And yet I often·think along these lines. My reasons for advocating the adoption of topolects in writing are two:

1. All characters in literature ought to be presented with lively animation. The language that real living people speak for the most part is an irregular topolect. If one does not care about the verisimilitude of literature, no further questions need be asked. However, if one wishes to achieve verisimilitude, then one is compelled to use the topolects in order to strive for a close resemblance to the way people actually talk. Otherwise, we might well have Soochow farmers addressing their mothers as "Sir" and that would sound very strange indeed. So long as living people do not speak a unified language, there is no possibility of using a single language to create literature. In other words, before the national language has been unified, there can be no pure national language literature. If there is, then it is fraudulent.

2. When an author sets out to create a work of literature, the choice of instrument is at his disposal. He may use elegant, refined Classical Chinese (as, for example, *The Tiger*); he may use the brand new national language; he may use an earthy topolect; he may use English, French, German, Russian, or Japanese; or he may use Pidgin. Forgive my impertinence, however, but I feel that, in the final analysis, the most suitable instrument is his own mother tongue. This is the language that we acquire while we are still teething and playing with dolls or riding on wooden horses. It is only with our mother tongue that we are most familiar; it is only with our mother tongue that there is not the slightest alienation; it is only with our mother tongue that we can pour forth our innermost emotions before others. The spirit of this kind of language is naturally rustic; it is quite far removed from what may be termed "beautiful," "smooth," "succinct," etc. But remember that since you are not (1) being an actor, (2) being an orator, (3) being a diplomat, (4) being a national language specialist, (5) being the lover of wives and young misses, why cast off the companion of your childhood and strive for what is fashionable? If you wish to learn the refined classical language to curry favor with "the tiger," I have no objections. But if that is not your intention and you only want to compose a poem or essay after tea or wine to express your feelings, then I urge you with utmost sincerity not to do so.

We may also consider the typically brash but wise remarks from the preface of Ch'ien Hsüan-t'ung 錢玄同, dated September 2, 1925, and revised on February 8, 1926.

I am an ardent supporter of the national language and I recognize that national language literature is the lifeblood of the national language, so I am also an ardent supporter of national language literature. I believe that national language literature ought to use "the language of real living people." Therefore, I recognize that Pekingese and the topolects of the various localities are the basic materials for national language literature, which is to say that they are also the basic materials of the national language. Because I hold the above beliefs, I affirm that, "to my mind, not only is there already topolectical literature, there *ought* to be, and we should strive to promote it." Not only does topolectical literature *not* run counter to national language literature, it constitutes an important source of material for national language literature. As topolectical literature develops day by day, national language literature grows ever more perfect.

The above is spoken from the point of view of the national language. As for the topolects themselves, they are independent languages and topolectical literatures are independent literatures. Their value is of equal status with the national language and national language literature. They will definitely not perish because we now have a national language literature, nor will they be preserved merely because the national language needs them for its basic material. They have already developed by themselves and they will exist forever.

Therefore, no matter whether I am standing on the side of establishing the national language or on the side of literary appreciation, the long and short of it is that I welcome the various topolectical literatures with the warmest enthusiasm. . . .

I am one who advocates that we should use an alphabetical script to express the vernacular. To construct our formal alphabetical script, I believe that we should adopt roman letters which are current throughout the world and are richly adaptable. But this is a matter for later times, so for the moment I will not elaborate upon it. The writings of the past have already been written down in sinographs, so naturally it will be impossible to get away from them completely in the future. However, they are not symbols for indicating sounds. Even though the "phonetic" part of morphophonetic graphs (*hsing-sheng-tzu* 形聲字) may have had the same function as the national phonetic symbols (*chu-yin tzu-mu* 注音字母) when the graphs were initially created, this function was completely lost later on when the sounds changed. When we read a given sinograph, it is impossible to have everybody pronounce it the same. How much more troublesome it is when we talk of topolectical literature. Each graph should be read according to the pronunciation of the topolect. Thus a single sinograph might have several tens or several hundreds of different ways to be read. If no phonetic annotation is provided, how can it be read? How frustrating it is if we wish to appreciate a work of literature but cannot read it out correctly! That is why I believe that, in the future, books written in sinographs should all have phonetic annotations. Above all, folk literature must have phonetic annotations because it is composed in topolect. The best solution is to write out the entire text alphabetically next to the sinographs as with the "Sino-Western *Four Books*" for ready reference.

Regrettably, the current situation in Chinese literary studies is almost as though Hu Shih, Yü P'ing-po, Ch'ien Hsüan-t'ung, and the other Young Turks of their day had never spoken out. This is lamentable because the level of their discourse was sufficiently high to have brought about a salutary change in the way we view Chinese literature. Instead, when Bertha Hensman and Mack Kwok-Ping were preparing to render the Soochow *t'an-tz'u* 彈詞 (strum lyric) entitled *The Dropped Fan* into English, they followed a most peculiar procedure:

> the Soochow dialect is so different from Mandarin in vocabulary, idiom, and structure that before being able to embark upon translation the authors of this volume had to use an intermediary to help transpose into Mandarin their phonetic transcription of the tale as told in the Soochow dialect.[16]

Their excuse for adopting such a procedure is even more convoluted:

> Two years elapsed between recording this story and completing the translation of it into English via a transcription into phonetic symbols and a further transcription into Chinese ideographs which entailed first, borrowing or inventing (*chieh jung* [sic]: 借用) about 50% of the ideographs because there is no written form for a great deal of spoken Soochow dialect and then "translating" large passages of the story from Soochow dialect into Mandarin.[17]

Perhaps that is why there are so few genuine literary works in the local dialects and regional vernaculars. Judging from the testimony of Hensman and Mack, it is often impossible to write them down in the Chinese script. Be that as it may, I find it highly disappointing that Hensman and Mack did not ask someone fluent in the language of Soochow to help them translate *The Dropped Fan*. Anyway, it is beyond comprehension how they could have accurately rendered the Soochow transcription into Mandarin if they did not understand the original in the first place. If they did understand the original Soochow transcribed text, they should have rendered it directly into English and dispensed with the intermediary Mandarin altogether (what *was* its purpose anyway, to give a false sense of security?). As a result of their untrustworthy (but, unfortunately, all too common among interpreters of Chinese folk and popular literature) procedure, what we have been given is not really a translation of the Soochow story into English at all, but a watered-down, third-hand, incomplete paraphrase. When translating from Chinese into English, whether the original be an obscure Classical Chinese text, an oral performance in a local dialect, or one of the written regional vernaculars, we should go straight to the source instead of first passing it through an MSM filter.[18] By taking the latter course, we are doing justice neither to the literary work which we are rendering nor to the audience for whom we are rendering it.

It may seem to some as though I am beating a dead horse; regional and local literatures are moribund in China, so we should let them lie. I feel that the situation is exactly the opposite. It is precisely in the nonstandard colloquial and vernacular languages that the literary salvation of China lies. I would go still further; we should also pay due attention to the non-Sinitic literatures of China. As far back as the formative period of Chinese civilization, so-called minority peoples played a key role in the development of China's literary traditions. For instance, during the time of the legendary Emperor Yao 堯 (24th century B.C.E. [?]), it is said that ten suns appeared simultaneously. Their fierce heat scorched the earth's surface, parching the crops and bringing hunger in its wake. Emperor Yao called upon the celebrated archer Hou-i 后羿, hero of the Chuang, to save the world. Hou-i drew his bow and shot down the extra suns, thus rescuing the people. This and other notable achievements of Hou-i are recounted in the long epic poem *Moz Yiz Daihvuengz* (The Great King Moz Yiz). Nowadays, Chinese look upon Hou-i as one of their own heroes, but that is only because such tales have been so thoroughly assimilated to Chinese tradition. A tremendous amount of work remains to be done to sort out such ethnic elements that are now part and parcel of Chinese civilization.

A proper assessment of non-Sinitic literatures written within the cultural orbit of China is important not only for an accurate history of Chinese literature; it is also essential simply because some of it is so beautiful. I cite only a brief portion from section 4 ("Ode to Spring and Praise of Ulug Bugra Khan") of the enormously long eleventh-century Uighur poem by Yūsuf Khāṣṣ Ḥājib entitled *Wisdom of Royal Glory (Kutadgu Biliq)*.

> A zephyr came wafting from the east and opened the way of paradise to the world-adorner. The brown earth filled with musk as the camphor melted away. Earth desired to array herself in finery. Bright Spring once again drew Fortune's bow, as balmy breezes banished stodgy Winter. Sol came back to his starting-place, from the tail of the Fish to the nose of the Ram.[19] The withered trees decked themselves in green with ornaments of purple and scarlet, yellow, blue, and red. Brown earth wrapped a veil of green silk over her face; the Cathay caravan spread out its Chinese wares. Hill and dale became overspread, every ridge and hollow bedecked with blue and scarlet. Countless kinds of flowers opened with a smile, and the world filled with the fragrance of musk and camphor. Zephyr sprang up carrying the scent of cloves, and all the world was suffused with musk.[20]

> > *toqardïn əsə kəldi əngdün yili*
> > *aʒun itgükə aqti uxtmak yolï*
> > *yaqïz yir yïpar toldï kapur kitip*
> > *bəzanmək tilər dünya kərkin itip*
> > *irinqig kixïq Sürdi yazkï əsin*
> > *yaruk yaz yana kurdï dəwlət yasïn*
> > *yaxïk yandï bolqay yana ornïnga*

barik kudrukïndïn kozï burnïnga
kuwurmïx yïqaqlar tonandï yaxïl
bəzəndi yipün al sarïq kək kïzïl
yaqïz yir yaxïl torku yüzkə badï
hitay arkïxï yadtï tawqaq ədi
yazï taq kïr oprï təxəndi yadïp
itindi kolï kaxï kək al kedip
tümən tü qəqəklr yazïldï külə
yïpar toldï kafur aʒun yïd bilə
saba yili kopti karanfil yïdïn
aʒun barqa bütrü yïpar burdï kin[21]

I daresay that some such sentiments as these may even have worked their way into Chinese literature in the narrow sense through Uighurs who wrote in a Sinitic language. But even if they did not, the *Wisdom of Royal Glory* is a part of their literary heritage of which all Chinese can be proud. The same is true of the Tibetan epic of Gesar (<Caesar), one of the longest in the world, and the romantic verse of the sixth Dalai Lama, Tshangs-dbyangs-rgya-mtsho (1683–1706). *The Secret History of the Mongols*, which has received a magisterial translation into King James English by Francis Cleaves, is another worthy treasure.

An anomalous case is that of modern emigré authors such as Pai Hsien-yung 白先勇, Yang Mu 楊牧, Chang Hsi-kuo 張系國, Nieh Hua-ling 聶華苓, Yü Li-hua 於利華, Ch'en Jo-hsi 陳若曦, and many others who write in Mandarin about Chinese subjects but live abroad more or less permanently. Should their works be considered Chinese literature? And what shall we do with Chinese authors living abroad who write about their new life and its alien social setting in one of the nonstandard Sinitic vernaculars?

My heart belongs to a handsome young lad.
We exchange messages in English letters.
Sixteen is a peach blossom that's just about to bud;
O, how I long to share his pillow!
Lips meeting,
Like the union of Cowherd and Weaving Maid.
The passion of clouds and rain is thick as glue.
We make another date to meet in the evening after an interlude.

靚仔奴心逐
番信寄通語
二八桃花初開蕊
但得與他同枕睡
咀合咀
儼然牛女會
雲雨情濃如膠水
約定黃昏再復回 [22]

Lines 2 and 4 of this poem are inconceivable in a Chinese setting, but all the others are quintessentially Chinese.

It is even more difficult to decide how to handle ethnic Chinese writing about Chinese subjects in English, whether they dwell in China or abroad, authors such as Lin Yutang, Han Suyin, Maxine Hong Kingston, Bette Bao Lord, Nien Cheng, and Amy Tan.[23] Although this type of author should probably be excluded from anthologies of Chinese literature *stricto sensu*, it must be observed that this is a large and growing category and, furthermore, that several of these individuals have gained international prominence.

Before closing, I would like to mention the bifurcation of our vision concerning even the greatest and most famous of Chinese writers. *Strange Tales from Make-Do Studio* (*Liao-chai chih-i* 聊齋誌異) is the most celebrated collection of classical language Chinese fiction. This is a bit odd, since, I am told, few Chinese can "read it in the original (they appreciate the stories in various retold forms). Its exceedingly difficult classical language (compact, conceptual, and full of historical and contemporary references) makes wide circulation impossible."[24] On the other hand, P'u Sung-ling 蒲松齡 (1640–1715), the author of the *Strange Tales*, also composed at least twenty extremely colloquial texts, including three plays, that have been almost totally and willfully neglected. These are the so-called *Liao-chai li-ch'ü* (Rustic Texts from Make-Do Studio) 聊齋俚曲. Having translated many of the *Strange Tales* and one entire colloquial play by P'u, I find their language equally demanding, the former for the reasons stated above and the latter because late-seventeenth- and early-eighteenth-century Shantung colloquial is poorly represented in conventional dictionaries.[25] Of the two, however, the *Strange Tales* are by far the more challenging for the translator, first, because of the intrinsic difficulty of the language and, second, because converting artificially terse Classical Chinese dialogue and description into smooth and expansive English involves more than mere translation—it requires, as well, a leap of creative imagination to reproduce what was realy going on in the author's mind.[26] There are other ironies surrounding P'u Sung-ling and his work, such as the fact that he was apparently born into an impoverished gentry family of Mongolian or Turkish descent, the fact that he failed the provincial examinations every three years from the age of eighteen until his sixties, and so on, but these dark ironies are usually glossed over in the glare of his brilliant masterpiece. The point to remember is that P'u Sung-ling had an intensely local and perhaps even ethnic aspect to his personality, and that these characteristics may well have contributed to his overall greatness. The revitalization of Chinese literature may consist, in large measure, of energetically seeking out unconventional authors and unusual works by well-known authors.

By way of conclusion, I believe that a strenuous effort should be made to uncover texts comparable to *The Lichee and the Mirror*, Chao Tzu-yung's

Cantonese love songs, and the other works discussed here. Once we have found them, we must ask: do these works of art represent only various regional literatures or are they part of the national heritage? If they are not, how then shall we define the national literature of China? Is it only those works written in Classical Chinese or Mandarin? Having a national literature is all well and good, and arguably necessary or at least desirable for a stable politicocultural entity, but it should not be at the expense of the constituent local, regional, and ethnic literatures which are its very lifeblood. This task of bringing to light vital regional and local literature is of the utmost importance for the architects of China's future literature. It is also something we should take into account in drawing up our anthologies and choosing our translations.

In the end, I would suggest that we all have to become historically minded anthropologists for a while. We need to go into the villages and towns of China to record faithfully what really exists among the vast majority of China's population. And we need to make a completely fresh examination of the entire corpus of Chinese literature, wherever it may be found, with an eye toward its diversity rather than its monolithism. Otherwise, I fear that what is distinctively Chinese will be engulfed by the international culture emanating from the cities, just as the local and regional literatures of an earlier, less global, day were nearly stifled by the bureaucratic, Confucian culture of the center. Like Ku Chieh-kang and his friends, we should be iconoclasts in searching for what is truly vibrant in China's literary heritage. If we proceed in this fashion, I am confident that what we present to our readers in translation will be exciting, attractive, and of enduring human value.

NOTES

1. *Chung-kuo ta pai-k'e ch'üan-shu*, Hsi-ch'ü ch'ü-i, 194ab. For complete publication data on major works mentioned in the notes and text, see the bibliography.

2. Quoted in ibid., 206b.

3. *Chieh-yang hsien-chih* (Gazetteer of Chieh-yang District) 揭陽縣志, chapter on "Customs" (Feng-su p'ien 風俗篇) and *Hsia-men chih* (Gazetteer of Amoy) 廈門志 (1839), 15.13b. The latter text decries *LM* for its "lascivious lyrics and lewd gestures" 淫詞醜態. Women who watched it were said to be in danger of overstepping the boundaries of propriety and eloping with their lovers. The obstacles which the officials put in the way of literary creativity were incredible, as can be seen in this passage from the Amoy Gazetteer which follows its denunciation of *LM*: "Moreover, there are those who tell plain tales (*shuo p'ing-hua che* 說平話者) beneath the shade of a green tree or in front of Buddhist temples, narrating events from the Han, T'ang, and later dynasties. The crowds who surround them gather money for donations. Such storytellers serve to pique the interest of stupid illiterates. Among them those who tell erotic tales and romances based on *Water Margins* 水滸演義 should be

prohibited. Shih Nai-an's *Water Margins* actually teaches outlawry and is especially deserving of prohibition." One can well imagine what insipid vapidities China would have been left with if the Confucian authorities had had their way in every instance.

4. Without the generous assistance of Professor Wu Shou-li, it would have been impossible for me to present this scene from *LM* in the above fashion. Wu is without doubt the world's greatest authority on this significant work. Between 1961 and 1978, he published half a dozen works dealing with this play, including critical editions of the four main texts (1566, 1581, 1651, and 1884) and studies on various aspects of its language (see vol. 2, pp. 1663–1664, of his *Tsung-ho Min-nan T'ai-wan-yü chi-pen tzu-tien* for a list of these works). For facsimile reproductions of the 1566, 1581, and 1651 editions of the play, see *Ming Ch'ing Min-nan hsi-ch'ü ssu chung*, ed. Wu Shou-li and Lin Tsung-i. I have explicitly followed the text as established by Wu and have relied heavily on his glosses to interpret the otherwise impenetrable Minlam (Min-nan) vernacular. Particularly useful in this regard are the explanations of Minlam terms in section 8 (pp. 239–246) of his "Shun-chih pen *Li-chih chi chiao yen*." In section 6B of the same article, there are parallel collated texts of the water-splashing scene as it occurs in the 1566, 1651, and 1884 editions of the play. I have also used the basically Modern Taiwanese Minlam transcription Professor Wu prepared especially for me, together with some additions of my own. Since *LM* was composed in an interesting combination of Ch'ao-chou and Ch'uan-chow speech, it would have been better to use the sixteenth-century pronunciation of these dialects but, inasmuch as that is not known (at least to me), Modern Minlam seems to be a serviceable substitute.

5. For a brief biography of Chao Tzu-yung/Chiû Tsz-yung, extracted from the *Nan-hai hsien-chih* (Gazetteer of Nan-hai District) 南海縣志, see the appendix to the edition of his love songs represented in the Kuo-li Pei-ching ta-hsüeh Chung-kuo min-su hsüeh-hui min-su ts'ung-shu, 56. The biographical sketch is followed by a second appendix consisting of an appreciative essay by Hsü Ti-shan 許地山 entitled "Yüeh-ou tsai wen-hsüeh shang te ti-wei" (The Literary Standing of Cantonese Love Songs) 粵謳在文學上的地位.

6. Cecil Clementi, trans., *Cantonese Love-Songs*, vol. 1, 18–19 (with a few minor stylistic changes). Clementi gives the following notes for the Second Preface (102–103):

望 the fifteenth day of the month; so called because it is the day of full moon, on which, as the Chinese say, the sun and moon are gazing at each other.

明珊 the *nom de plume* 別號 of the author 招子庸.

居士 a retired scholar, i.e. a man who, though qualified to be an official, is not in government employment, either because he has retired from service, or never entered the service. The term would be applicable to Chiû Tsz-yung after his resignation of the office of prefect.

珠江 the Pearl River, on which Canton is situated. The name is only given to that part of the river in the immediate vicinity of Canton, and is derived from a small island, called 海珠 owing to its circular shape, situated in the river just south of the two city-gates known as 油欄門 and 靖海門. The island has been made into a fort. There is a play on the words "pearl houses," "pearl maidens," "pearl youths," which refer to the Cantonese flower-boats, their in-mates and *habitués*.

趙 a part of the State of Tsun 晋, the modern province of Shánsi 山西, which in ancient times was divided between the three families of 趙, 魏 and 韓: the Chiû family holding the north, the Ngai family the south-east, and the Hoan family the south-west of the province.

秦 the state of Tshun, the modern province of Shensi 陝西.

老龍 Lô-lung is a market-town in the north-east of the Wai-chau 惠州 prefecture. The Lô-lung boats are shallow and are built to cross shoals and rapids: their bows are higher out of the water than those of the ordinary Cantonese junks.

吳 Ng is the modern province of Kiangsu 江蘇. "Ng country ballads" are thus described by Tô Yau 杜佑 (Giles, No. 2070) in his treatise called 通典:—吳歌雜曲, 並出江東晉宋以來, 稍有增廣, 梁內人, 黃金珠, 善歌吳聲西曲. "Ng songs are miscellaneous *khuk*, which are also produced in the country east of the Yangtze. From the era of the Tsun (265–419 A.D.) and Sung dynasties (420–477 A.D.) down to the present time, their production has gradually increased. Under the Löng dynasty (502–556 A.D.), Wong Kam chü was a skilled singer of Ng songs and West-country *khuk*." For 曲, see Introduction VI.

楚竹 "the pipes of Chhoa": cf. a poem 楚竹吟 by 孟郊, who writes:—

握中有新聲　楚竹人未聞

"In the fingering (of the stops) are new tones, even tones of the Chhoa pipe such as man has never heard." 楚 corresponds to the modern provinces of Hunan 湖南 and Hupeh 湖北. The best bamboos for pipes are said to grow along the banks of the River Söng 湘江 in Hunan: cf. XVI.1; LVI.3.6; XXXV.4.11: *see* Mayers, Nos. 528, 576.

三星 "the three stars." A quotation from the Shi-king, part i, book x, ode 5 (Legge, vol. iv, part i, p. 179), which describes the delight of a husband and wife at their unexpected union. The reference is probably to the constellation of 參宿 in Orion, visible at dusk in the tenth month, which is regarded by the Chinese as the most auspicious time for contracting a marriage.

繁欽 Fán Yam. The lexicon 典略 says:— 欽, 字休伯, 以文才機辯少得名, 善為詩賦, 率皆巧麗, 為丞相主簿. "Yam: named Yau-pák. By literary talent and disputation he became famous while a youth. He excelled in writing songs and poems, which were always clever and beautiful. He became secretary to the prime minister."

何滿 "the songs of Hoa Mún": cf. a poem 何滿子歌 by 元稹 (Mayers, No. 961; Giles, No. 2543), who says:—

何滿能歌能宛轉　天寶年中也稱罕

"Hoa Mún was able to sing, he was able to round off his songs. Between 742 and 756 A.D., mortals said he was a rarity." 天寶 was the title of the reign of the Emperor 唐玄宗 of the Thong 唐 dynasty, adopted in 742 A.D.

7. Clementi, vol. 1, 34–35. The notes for this poem are found on 120–123:

Line 5. Yöng Kwai-fê 楊貴妃 (Mayers, No. 887; Giles, No. 2394), celebrated as the all-powerful favourite of the Emperor Thong Yün Tsung 唐玄宗 (713–756 A.D.). She was the daughter of Yöng Yün-yím 楊玄琰 a petty functionary of Shuk-chau 蜀州 in Western China, and bore in childhood the name Yuk Wán 玉環, to which no doubt there is an allusion in the 玉骨 "jade bones" of the text. Having attracted notice by her surpassing beauty, she became in A.D. 735 one of the concubines of Prince Shau 壽王, the emperor's eighteenth son. Three years later, on the death of the then imperial favourite, the ministers

of Yün Tsung cast their eyes upon the lovely Princess Yöng. No sooner had
the emperor obtained a sight of his daughter-in-law than he became violently
enamoured of her, and caused her to be enrolled among the ladies of his seraglio, bestowing in exchange another consort on his son. In A.D. 745 she was
raised to the rank of 貴妃, a title second in dignity to that of the empress only,
and year after year the emperor abandoned himself more completely to amorous dalliance with his concubine, ransacking tributary kingdoms for gems to
enhance her beauty and sparing no extravagance to gratify her caprices. These
days of licentious enjoyment terminated in the rebellion of Oan Luk-shán
安祿山 (Mayers, No. 525; Giles, No. 11), the emperor's unworthy minion. During the hurried flight of the court before the advancing insurgents in A.D. 756,
the imperial *cortège* having halted at the entrenched position of Má Ngai 馬嵬,
the beaten and famished soldiery rose in revolt, and satiated their vengeance in
the blood of the imperial consort. With unutterable anguish, the still fondly-
enamoured monarch was constrained to order his faithful attendant, the eu-
nuch Kô Lek-sz 高力士, to strangle Yöng Fê (some say she was hanged on a
pear-tree) and bury her by the road-side.
Ln. 6. Wong Chhiû-kwan 王昭君 (Mayers, No. 45; Giles, No. 2148), a famous
heroine of romance: said to have been taken into the harem of Hoan Yün Tai
漢元帝 in 48 B.C., where, however, she was secluded from the notice of her
imperial lord through the malice of his treacherous minister Mô Yín-shau
毛延壽. The latter had been commissioned to bring her to the palace, on a
report of her beauty reaching the court, and she was found by him to be of
surpassing loveliness, the daughter of poor but worthy parents. Her father refused to pay a sum demanded from him as bribe by Mô Yín-shau, who in
revenge presented to the emperor a portrait so little like the original, that His
Majesty conceived no wish to see the new addition to his seraglio, and she
languished in oblivion for years, until chance threw the emperor across her
path, when he at once became enamoured of her beauty. The faithless minister,
his wiles discovered, fled from the court and took refuge with the Khan of the
Hung Nô 匈奴, to whom he showed the real portrait of Chhiû-kwan. The
Khan, fired by the hope of obtaining possession of so peerless a beauty, invaded
China in irresistible force, and only consented to retire beyond the Great Wall
when the lady was surrendered to him. She accompanied her savage captor,
bathed in tears, until the banks of the Amur 黑龍江 were reached, when, rather
than go beyond the fatal boundary, she plunged into the waters of the stream
and was drowned. Her corpse was interred on the banks of the river, and it is
related that the tumulus raised above her grave remained covered with undying verdure, whence the tomb is called 青冢.
Ln. 7. Siû Tsheng 小青: cf. 情天寶鑑, book xiv, leaf 16:— 小青者虎林某生姬也,
家廣陵, 與生同姓故諱之, 僅以小青, 字雲娘, 夙根穎異, 十歲遇一老尼授心經, 一目
過了, 覆之不失一字, 尼曰是兒早慧福薄. "Siû Tsheng was the concubine of a
certain graduate of Fú-lam: her home was in Kwong-leng. Because her surname was the same as that of her lover it has been suppressed, and the girl is
only known as Siû Tsheng: her second names were Wan Nöng. She was unusually intelligent. When ten years of age she met an old woman who taught
her the Prajñâpâramitâ-hṛdaya-sûtra. After once reading it, she was word-
perfect. The old woman said: 'This girl is precocious in learning, but her fortune will be fragile.'" This prophecy came true, for Siû Tsheng and her lover's
wife became bitter enemies, and one day after a passionate quarrel, in which
the wife carried the day, the story proceeded as follows:— 一日語老嫗曰, 可傳語
宛業, 郎命一戾畫師來, 師至命寫照, 寫畢攬鏡熟視曰, 得吾形似耳, 未盡吾神也, 姑
置之, 又易一圖曰, 神是矣, 而風態未流動也, 若見我面目端莊而太矜持故也, 姑置

之, 命提筆於旁, 而自語嫵指顧語笑, 或扇茶鐺, 或簡書, 或自整衣褶, 或代調丹璧
諸色, 縱其想會, 須臾圖成, 果極纖妖之致, 笑曰, 可矣, 師去, 取圖供榻前, 焚香, 設
梨酒, 奠之曰, 小青小青此中豈有汝緣分乎, 撫几淚潸潸如雨, 一慟而絕.

"Sîù Tsheng said to her maids: 'Bid the artists' studios send me a good
portrait-painter.' The painter came, and she bade him paint her portrait.
When he had finished it, she took a mirror, and, gazing long into it, she said:
'The likeness is there, but not the expression.' So she set it aside; but, when a
second portrait had been painted, she said: 'The expression is there, yet lacks
vivacity. Perhaps it is because the melancholy of my face deceives you.' So she
set it aside, and bade him take his brush and stand beside her, while she spoke
to her maids, looked at them, talked and laughed, or fanned the tea-stove, or
chose a book, or plucked at her clothes, or ground paints for the artist. Soon
the portrait was painted, surpassing in grace and loveliness. She smiled and
said: 'That will do.' When the painter left, she took the picture and made
obeisance to it at her bedside, burning the joss-sticks and pouring a libation of
pear-wine before it. Then with a cry—'Sîù Tsheng! Sîù Tsheng! was this your
fate?'—she fell back upon a chair, weeping like rain, and with the cry she
died."

Ln. 8. Shap Nông 十娘: see 今古奇觀, book v, the section entitled 杜十娘怒沈百
寶箱, where is told the story of Tô Mê 杜媺, who being the tenth among her
brothers and sisters was called 杜十娘. She lived during the reign of 萬歷, an
emperor of the Meng 明 dynasty (1573–1620 A.D.). At the age of thirteen she
became a courtesan and at the age of nineteen, when already rich with her
earnings, she met at Peking a certain Leï Yü-sín 李于先 of the district 紹興府
in the Chekiang 浙江 province, whose father, the lieutenant-governor of
Chekiang, had sent him to Peking to read for his degree as 舉人. Leï and Shap
Nöng fell deeply in love, but after a year in Peking the student had spent all his
money, and his father, hearing of his son's doings, ordered him home. Shap
Nöng went with her lover, and the two were travelling on the river 潞河 and
making their way to 紹興府, when they met a wealthy acquaintance of Leï
Yü-sín, named Sün Fû 孫富, who, availing himself of the poverty of Leï and his
fear of his father's anger, induced them to sell him his mistress for a sum of
$1,000. Shap Nöng, learning of the bargain, when she was handed over next
morning and passed from the ship of her lover to that of Sün Fû, brought out a
casket which she opened under the eyes of both Leï and Sün, showing them its
contents of priceless jewels. Then, reproaching her lover for his cruelty and
avarice, she took the casket in her arms, sprang into the river with it, and was
drowned.

Ln. 13. "The golden well" 金井: cf. the line of 王昌齡 (Giles, No. 2138):—
金井梧桐秋葉黃. "Yellow in autumn are the elm-leaves over the golden well."
The story is told of a certain Portuguese astronomer 欽天監 at the Imperial
Chinese court, who, when asked by a rival astronomer 張天師 when was the
day on which summer changed to autumn, replied: "In Hok-kung 學宮 is a
well: beside this well is an elm 梧桐, which if autumn has not yet come does not
lose its leaves. Take a golden bowl and place it at the edge of the well: then,
when the exact day comes, an elm-leaf will fall into the bowl. That is the day!"

Ln. 19. "The Tomb of a Hundred Flowers" 百花墳: see 廣東新語, book xix, the
section entitled 素馨科:—崇禎間, 有名姬張喬死, 人各種花一本於其冢, 凡得數百
本, 五色爛然, 與花田相望亦曰花冢. "In the time of Shung Cheng (1628 A.D.)
there was a famous courtesan named Chöng Khiû. On her death, each of her
lovers planted a flower on her tomb. In all there were some hundred flowers.
The colour of the flowers was variegated and very beautiful. It was in sight of
the Jasmine Hill, and was called the Tomb of Flowers." Cf. XI.2.14.

8. Translated by J. Dyer Ball in his *Readings in Cantonese Colloquial*, xxi.

9. Ibid., xxii.

10. Cf. the thought-provoking remarks of C. T. Hsia in "Classical Chinese Literature" concerning the value of Chinese literature and its poor reception abroad.

11. I was rather astonished when there was no significant discussion of the role of colloquial and vernacular language during the International Conference on Chinese Folk Literature held at the National Central Library in Taipei, Taiwan, September 4–7, 1989.

12. Characters in *Romance of the Water Margins*.

13. Name of an ancient town near modern Ichang 宜昌 in Hupeh.

14. I have omitted Hu Shih's parenthetical note on the origins of the Mandarin word for "authentic," *tao-ti* 道地, which he claims has something to do with the various administrative circuits of ancient China.

15. I omit the titles of three exemplary pieces.

16. Bertha Hensman and Mack Kwok-Ping, *Hong Kong Tale-Spinners*, iv.

17. Ibid., xiv.

18. We must also scrupulously avoid passing Chinese literary works through Confucian, Communist, or other types of ideological filters. It is most unfortunate that many literary texts were intentionally rewritten (not infrequently authors have been forced to rewrite their own works) for a particular political purpose.

19. The sun is in Pisces from February 19 to March 20, and in Aries from March 21 to April 19 (Robert Dankoff, in Ḥājib, *Wisdom of Royal Glory*, 275, n. 7).

20. Ḥājib, *Wisdom of Royal Glory*, trans., Dankoff, 41.

21. My transcription is based on the complete Peking 1984 edition (p. 52) and the selection given by Keng Shih-min (p. 141) with some substitutions and modifications.

22. Marlon K. Hom, trans., *Songs of Gold Mountain*, 228.

23. It is curious that such a large proportion of these writers are women.

24. Y. W. Ma, private communication, May 30, 1990.

25. When I was working on P'u Sung-ling's colloquial play entitled *The Wall* (*Ch'iang-t'ou chi* 墙頭記), the specialized dictionary of Tung Tsun-chang was not available. Had it been, the translation would have been facilitated, but by no means an easy task.

26. It is even more arduous to render faithfully into English a Chinese text that switches back and forth from Classical to Mandarin (and perhaps even to some other vernacular), whether for stylistic purposes or virtuoso effect.

BIBLIOGRAPHY

Ball, J. Dyer. *Readings in Cantonese Colloquial*. Hong Kong: Kelly and Walsh, 1894.

Chao Tzu-yung/Chiû Tsz-yung 招子庸. *Yüeh-ou/Yud-eo (Early Cantonese Love Songs)* 粵謳. In Kuo-li Pei-ching ta-hsüeh Chung-kuo min-su hsüeh-hui min-su ts'ung-shu (Folklore and Folk Literature Series of National Peking University and Chinese Association for Folklore) 國立北京大學中國民俗學會民俗叢書, 56. Taipei: The Orient Culture Service, 1971 rpt.

Chung-kuo ta pai-k'o ch'üan-shu (Great Chinese Encyclopedia) 中國大百科全書, vol. on

Hsi-ch'ü ch'ü-i (Drama and Performing Arts) 戲曲曲藝. Peking and Shanghai: Chung-kuo ta pai-k'e ch'üan-shu ch'u-pan-she, 1983.

Cinz Yaudingz et al., eds. *Moz Yiz Daihvuengz* (The Great King Moz Yiz). Nanning: Gvangjsih Minzcuz Cuzbajse, 1984.

Cleaves, Francis Woodman, trans. *The Secret History of the Mongols; for the first time done into English out of the original tongue and provided with an exegetical commentary.* Vol. 1. Cambridge, Mass.: Published for the Harvard-Yenching Institute by Harvard University Press, 1982.

Clementi, Cecil, trans., annot., and ed. *Cantonese Love-Songs.* 2 vols. Oxford: Clarendon, 1904.

Giles, Herbert Allen. *Chinese Biographical Dictionary.* London: Quaritch, 1898.

Ḥājib, Yūsuf Khāṣṣ. *Wisdom of Royal Glory (Kutadgu Bilig): A Turko-Islamic Mirror for Princes.* Translated with an introduction and notes by Robert Dankoff. Chicago and London: University of Chicago Press, 1983.

Ḥajib, Yusuf has. *Kutadqu Bilik.* Peking: Millətlər Nəxriyati, 1984.

Hensman, Bertha. *More Hong Kong Tale-Spinners: Twenty-five Traditional Chinese Tales Collected by Tape-Recorder and Translated into English.* Hong Kong: Chinese University of Hong Kong Press, 1971.

Hensman, Bertha, and Mack Kwok-Ping. *Hong Kong Tale-Spinners: A Collection of Tales and Ballads Transcribed and Translated from Story-Tellers in Hong Kong.* Hong Kong: Chinese University of Hong Kong Press, 1968.

Hom, Marlon K., trans *Songs of Gold Mountain: Cantonese Rhymes from San Francisco Chinatown.* Berkeley: University of California Press, 1987.

Hsia, C. T. "Classical Chinese Literature: Its Reception Today As a Product of Traditional Culture." *Chinese Literature: Essays, Articles, Reviews* 10, nos. 1–2 (July 1988): 133–152.

Keng Shih-min 耿世民. *Wei-wu-erh tsu ku-tai wen-hua ho wen-hsien kai-lun* (An Introduction to Ancient Uighur Culture and Literature) 維吾爾族古代文化和文獻概論. Urumchi: Sinkiang People's Publishing House, 1983.

Ku Chieh-kang 顧頡剛, ed. *Wu-ke/Ngeu-keu chia chi* (Soochow Songs, I) 吳歌甲集. In Kuo-li Pei-ching ta-hsüeh Chung-kuo min-su hsüeh-hui min-su ts'ung-shu (Folklore and Folk Literature Series of National Peking University and Chinese Association for Folklore) 國立北京大學中國民俗學會民俗叢書. Vol. 1. Taipei: Orient Culture Service, 1971 rpt.

Kuan Te-tung 關德棟, ed. *Liao-chai li-ch'ü hsüan* (Selected Rustic Texts from Make-Do Studio) 聊齋俚曲選. N.p.: Ch'i-lu shu-she, 1980.

Mair, Denis C., and Victor H. Mair, trans. *Strange Tales from Make-Do Studio*, by Pu Songling. Peking: Foreign Languages Press, 1989.

Mair, Victor H., and Li-ching Chang, trans. "*The Wall*, A Folk Opera, by Pu Songling." *Chinoperl Papers* 14 (1986): 97–152.

Mayers, William Frederick. *Chinese Reader's Manual; an Handbook of Biographical, Historical, Mythological and General Literary Reference.* Shanghai: American Presbyterian Mission Press, 1874.

Tung Tsun-chang 董遵章. *Yüan Ming Ch'ing pai-hua chu-tso chung Shan-tung fang-yen li-shih* (Explanations of Shantung Topolectical Expressions in Vernacular Works of the Yüan, Ming, and Ch'ing Periods) 元明清白話著作中山東方言例釋. Tsinan: Shan-tung chiao-yü ch'u-pan-she, 1985.

Wu Shou-li 吳守禮. Letter of May 25, 1990, with numerous specially prepared enclosures concerning the *Li ching chi* (The Lichee and the Mirror), including a manuscript variorum edition.

————, ed. and annot. *Li ching chi hsi-wen yen-chiu* (Studies on the Texts of the Story of the Lichee and the Mirror) 荔鏡記戲文研究. Ya-chou min-su, she-hui sheng-huo chuan-k'an (Monographs on Asian Folklore and Social Life) 亞洲民俗, 社會生活專刊, no. 7. Taipei: Wen-shih-che, 1987.

————. "Shun-chih pen *Li-chih chi* chiao yen" (Collations of and Studies on the 1651 Edition of *The Lichee Branch*) 順治本荔枝記校研. In the author's *Li ching chi hsi-wen yen-chiu*, pp. 203–248. Originally published in *Taiwan fengwu* (Scenes of Taiwan) 臺灣風物 16, no. 2 (1966): 17–62.

————, comp. *Tsung-ho Min-nan T'ai-wan-yü chi-pen tzu-tien* (The Collective Basic Minnan Taiwanese Dictionary) 綜合閩南臺灣語基本字典初稿. 2 vols. Taipei: Wen-shih-che, 1987.

———— and Lin Tsung-i 林宗毅, eds. *Ming Ch'ing Min-nan hsi-ch'ü ssu chung* (Four Minnan Plays from the Ming and Ch'ing Periods) 明清閩南戲曲四種. Tokyo: Jōjō-dō, 1976.

Translating Taiwan

A Study of Four English Anthologies of Taiwan Fiction

DAVID D. W. WANG

Because of its comprehensive format, the anthology has been considered one of the most efficient ways to promote Taiwan literature overseas. Quite a few English anthologies of Taiwan literature have been published in the past two decades, but rigorous criteria of what an anthology can and should do are yet to be established. This essay discusses four English anthologies of Taiwan fiction: *Chinese Stories from Taiwan: 1960–1970* (edited by Joseph Lau and published in 1972), *An Anthology of Contemporary Chinese Literature: Short Stories* (edited by Ch'i Pang-yüan), *Winter Plum: Contemporary Chinese Fiction* (edited by Nancy Ing, 1982), and *The Unbroken Chain: An Anthology of Taiwan Fiction since 1926* (edited by Joseph Lau, 1983).[1] By recapitulating the editorial assumption of each anthology and examining crucial translations, I will explore two interrelated questions: What is the image of Taiwan each anthology tends to convey and how does it stand with regard to the arguable "original" image of Taiwan? How do the individual translations correspond to this image? Just as intention does not necessarily match textual performance, so the "original" image of Taiwan and its "translation" must elicit dialogue anew.

In terms of both critical insight and editorial expertise, Joseph Lau's *Chinese Stories from Taiwan: 1960–1970* represents a groundbreaking work. The eleven years the anthology covers mark a period in which Taiwan literature took a quantum leap. While mainland writers submitted themselves to rigid formal models and ideological constraints, writers in Taiwan managed to open up new structural and political horizons. They enriched a period in modern Chinese literature which otherwise would have been only a desolate vacuum. By confirming the achievement of the Taiwan writers, Lau's anthology reminds mainland-centered scholars and critics that modern Chinese literature should not be judged only by the standards of geopolitics.

The anthology introduces eleven writers. Most of them became leading figures in the seventies. Both Wang Chen-ho and Huang Ch'un-ming turned out to be forerunners of the Hsiang-t'u (native soil) movement. Pai Hsien-yung won acclaim for chronicling the decaying manners and morals of mainland exiles in Taipei. Wang Wen-hsing aroused controversy with his radical experiment with Chinese linguistic and narrative canons. Both Ch'en Ying-chen and Yang Ch'ing-ch'u propagated a literature about and for politics, finally committing themselves altogether to ideological struggle. As if featuring a preview, the anthology even contains an early work by Ch'en Jo-hsi, before she emerged in the mid-seventies as a celebrity storyteller of what "really" happened in the Cultural Revolution.

The anthology creates a vision of Taiwan at the crossroads between mainland cultural and political hegemony and burgeoning native consciousness, between avant-garde causes and nostalgic sensibilities, and between historical awareness of change and yearning for mythic Time. Rarely has modern Chinese literature witnessed a phenomenon like Taiwan fiction in the sixties, a period that endowed Chinese experiences with thematic tension and formal variety. Thus Ch'en Ying-chen's young police officer is initiated into a world where values such as love, family, marriage, and motherland take on a dubious dimension ("My First Case"), and in the mysterious flood, Ch'i-teng Sheng's existential moralist Li Long-ti faces up to the choice of saving "either" his wife "or" a strange prostitute ("I Love Black Eyes"). Whereas Pai Hsien-yung's "Winter Nights" deplores the passage of Time that has eroded away the romantic dreams of two intellectuals, Wang Chen-ho's "An Oxcart for Dowry" celebrates the perseverance and life force of Taiwanese peasants in withstanding predicaments. The anthology pieces together a picture of Taiwan undergoing drastic change.

Ch'i Pang-yuan's *Anthology of Contemporary Chinese Literature* came out in 1975. It has since become one of the few sources that provide a historical overview of Taiwan literature from 1949 to the early seventies. The anthology features seventeen writers, of whom five (Yu Li-hua, Pai-Hsien-yung, Wang Wen-hsing, Huang Ch'un-ming, Lin Huai-min) also appear in Lau's anthology. Put side by side, the two anthologies show a remarkable difference in projecting a vision of Taiwan. This is not because Ch'i's book covers a longer period than Lau's; they differ in tracing out different lines of historical development for modern Chinese literature. Lau's book sees Taiwan literature in the sixties as a break with the past, while Ch'i's treats it as an integral part of a "great tradition" that is traceable to the fifties and earlier.

Significantly, Ch'i's anthology starts with Lin Hai-yin, a native Taiwanese who grew up in Beijing. With Lin's touching accounts of her childhood, such as "Gold Carp's Pleated Skirt," one comes to appreciate the emotional ties, family relations, and cultural heritages shared by the older and younger generations, both the mainland and the "island" Chinese societies. Also highlighted in the anthology are "soldier writers" such as Ssu-ma Chung-yüan, Chu Hsi-ning, and Tuan Ts'ai-hua, whose stories about their hometowns on the mainland and a legendary Past have fascinated many readers. Though erased at the surface, the image of Taiwan nevertheless looms large in their narratives; it "conditions" their remembrances of things past.

Even writers of the sixties and early seventies appear here in rather different images, despite a large overlap of names with those in Lau's anthology. These writers set out to deal with a wide range of subjects, but their works end up pointing to the same world, one inhabited by people either alienated from their existential circumstances or trapped in social psychological crises. "The Upside-down Ladder to Heaven," the title of a short story by the woman writer Shih Shu-ch'ing, may well summarize the vision shared by these writers. When the "Ladder to Heaven" is hung upside down, the entry to Paradise is lost. Hsi Song's retelling of the mythical Na Cha's fall from Heaven, in this sense, prefigures an allegorical matrix, substantiating Li Yung-p'ing's and Lin Huai-min's stories about the loss of ideal hometown ("A La-tzu Woman" and "Homecoming"). Traditional human relationships are turned upside down, too. Whereas Ou-yang Tzu's "perfect mother" in "Perfect Mother" appears a neurotic distortion of traditional motherhood, Huang Ch'un-ming's father is reduced to a walking machine by the hardships of life ("His Son's Big Doll"). If Lau's anthology envisions a Taiwan on the verge of change, Ch'i's is more pensive, seated in the shadow of History.

Nancy Ing's *Winter Plum* collects twenty-three translations of Taiwan short stories originally published in *The Chinese Pen*. Compared with the two anthologies already mentioned, Ing's is less bothered by thematic formulae and critical criteria; it brings forth a relaxed atmosphere, transcribing Taiwan experiences from the fifties to the early eighties. The anthology carries the stories of such popular writers as Wang Chen-ho and Pai Hsien-yung stories ("Ghost, North Wind, Man" and "Jade Love"), while it also salutes such veteran writers as P'an Lei and Wang Ting-chun. More important, because Ing chooses not to abide by established canons, she succeeds in "loosening up" the tradition a little and calling our attention to voices less well known but just as interesting. She introduces works by Yang Fu, Tzu Yu, Hsieh Shuang-tien, and Chang Jhy-chang, confirming them as integral parts of Taiwan fiction.

Another major difference between Ing's volume and the other two anthologies lies in the way it organizes its translations. Instead of presenting the translations in a chronological sequence, as the other two anthologies do, Ing follows the alphabetical order of their original authors' names. What results is a tentative suspension of temporality, an "escape" from history. Juxtaposing the veteran writers P'an Lei, Meng Yao, and Ssu-ma Chung-yüan with the young rising stars Hsiao Ye and Yüan Ch'iung-ch'iung, the anthology creates a space where "tradition" is manifest only in the simultaneous existence of the past and present, the young and old. Ing's anthology offers an alternative to the diachronic conception of time, thereby inserting a new dimension into the image of Taiwan.

The Taiwan in Ing's anthology is a place crammed with a variety of people and lifestyles. There are aging generals fighting the harshest war in the battlefield of life ("The General," by Chu Hsi-ning), boys falling hopelessly in love with women their mothers' age ("Flaw," by Wang Wen-hsing), refugee Chinese students from Vietnam lost in the brave new world of Taipei ("The Sky's Escape," by Yüan Ch'iung-ch'iung), country kids working hard but in vain to make a living ("Fish," by Huang Ch'un-ming), and overseas prophets loading up with honor in their own country ("Flute," by Chang Hsi-kuo). Whereas Tzu Yu's young men try hard to enter society ("Bewildered"), which is still dominated by self-important "old gingers," as P'an Lei describes them ("Old Gingers"), Fei Hsin-i's and Ssu-ma Chung-yüan's narrators enjoy recollecting adventures and legends that took place long ago. Through Ing's kaleidoscopic lenses, Taiwan appears both lively and inert, both refreshingly young and bewilderingly aged.

Lau's *Unbroken Chain*, is another attempt to anthologize Taiwan fiction in the light of a certain historical plan. Whereas Lau's first anthology of Taiwan fiction paraded a sequence of history from 1960 to 1970, the one published in 1983 does something more ambitious: it presents a complete genealogy of Taiwan fiction. Of the seventeen authors in the anthology, thirteen are native Taiwanese and the other four belong to the generation of mainlanders who were either born or grew up in Taiwan. The year 1949 is no longer used as an arbitrary date for the rise of "Chinese literature in Taiwan"; rather, it is 1945, the year of Taiwan's retrocession from Japan, that marks the turning point of Taiwan literature. More noteworthy is the fact that Lau presents four authors who wrote during the Japanese occupation period: Lai Ho, Wu Cho-liu, Chun Tien-jen, and Yang K'uei. Through their works, one learns how the first generation of modern Taiwan writers endeavored to maintain a native consciousness and how they planted the seeds of the native-soil movements that took place in the seventies.

The textual implication of Lau's second anthology is a polemical one. No longer does he treat Taiwan fiction as a branch of the mainland tradition. If

Taiwan literature is important, that is because it has developed over the past fifty years a unique discourse, one that cannot be homogenized by mixing it in with mainland literature. It carries its own roots and perspective, and it caters to a reading public whose concerns are not identifiable with those on the mainland. Lau, of course, had no intention to propagate political separatism. He simply recognized that the best way to promote Taiwan literature was to foreground its difference from its mainland counterpart, endowing it with a lineage of its own.

The four pioneer writers of the period before 1945 may not handle fictional techniques or even Chinese language well, but their deep concern about Taiwan's fate merits attention. Under their pens, Taiwan is a colonial society suffering from a great identity crisis. Even loyalists to Japan cannot alter the vacuity of their lives ("The Doctor's Mother," by Wu Cho-liu). When the anthology comes to the post-1945 section, it emphasizes the humanist spirit and native-soil consciousness—the thrust of the literary discourse of Taiwan. Besides the familiar names Lin Hai-yin, Ch'en Ying-chen, and Huang Ch'un-ming, Lau features Cheng Ch'ing-wen and Li Ch'iao, two writers overlooked by the previous three anthologies. These two writers may not be as experimental or as radical as their popular peers, but their writings display the tender, straightforward style characteristic of the majority of Taiwan literature. Cheng's "Betel Palm Village" casts a nostalgic look at southern Taiwan as it becomes increasingly industrialized, and Li's "The Spheric Man" provides a bitter caricature of modern Taiwanese trapped in an absurd social and political condition.

The anthology fittingly ends with Chang Ta-ch'un's "Birds of a Feather," a story about a young army reservist's encounter with an old mainland soldier, who indulges his dreams of going home by raising a flock of chickens. Naming the chickens after family members left on the mainland, the old soldier stages a domestic scene which is a degenerate simulacrum of the "real" one. When the troops are ordered to move without carrying extra belongings, he condemns all his "family members" to death, burying them alive in despair. The old soldier personifies the last group of mainland exiles who still hang on to the past, while the young army reservist, presumably a second-generation mainlander born in Taiwan, understands but fails to "feel" the old soldier's pain. Reading Chang's story in the light of the pre-1945 fiction, we see that the theme of identity crisis has run its full circle: people in Taiwan are faced with a new stage of defining who they are. As the story ends, with Taiwan's inevitable "breaking away" from Home, Past, the Mainland, and Origin, it adds an unexpected paradox to the book's title, the "unbroken" chain.

I have described how the image of Taiwan undergoes changes in the four anthologies, each projecting its own implication. But when examined in the light of individual translations, what are the implications? How have the individual translators carried out the editor's overall vision of Taiwan? How obvious are the gaps between the "overall" vision of Taiwan and its various English manifestations in the individual stories?

I will attempt to answer these questions by examining an aspect hitherto neglected by Chinese critics of translation. Conventionally we investigate a translation by gauging to what extent it faithfully renders an original in another language, with the assumption that the original possesses a determinate meaning, luring yet continually eluding a translator's access. But I will address this situation from the point of view of the Derridean problematic: that meaning's "differance" and "dissemination" have always existed in any text and that the concepts of "original/originary" must be put under interrogation.

Insofar as "Taiwan" figures in the discourses formed by the anthologies as mediated productions, the task of "translating" Taiwan does not involve only the stage where a translator is at work. The necessity and the undecidability of translation occurs in all discourse. If "Taiwan" is composed of a complex of voices, calling from the outset for a plural reading, its authenticity can be defined only in terms of approximations. Translation, therefore, does not imply a removal, a distortion, or even a degeneration of some "original" text. Rather the original's meaning surfaces and proliferates "because of" its translation.

Accordingly, the four anthologies in the original and in translation demand equal attention, being different manifestations of the arguable reality of Taiwan. By this argument, I am not denying the semantic and stylistic rigor required of a solid translation; criteria may exist for our judgment of a good or bad translation, insofar as they exist for writings and readings in general. I am suggesting that beyond this first act of linguistic evaluation, one has to enter into the dialogic of interpretation; both acts are openly semiotic and ideological.

Take the two English translations of Pai Hsien-yung's "Winter Nights" (*Tong-ye*), for example. The two versions, one by John Kwan-Terry (and Stephan Lacey) and the other by Li-min Chu, are respectively included in Lau's *Chinese Stories* and Ch'i's *Anthology*. Both are sound renditions of the original, but a comparative reading will show that through linguistic reworkings they project very different visions of Pai Hsien-yung's Taipei and Taipei people. Here are the beginnings of first Chu's and then Kwan-Terry's versions:

> The winter evenings in Taipei are frequently accompanied by cold rains. One day as it darkened and became colder, raindrops started to fall again. And soon, about an inch of water seemed to emerge out of the ground in the lanes of Wenchou street.[2]

> In Taipei, winter nights are usually cold and wet. A chill gust of wind was blowing again this evening and then, without warning, the rain fell, pitter-pattering onto the pavements. The alleys around Wen-chou Street already were under more than an inch of water.[3]

Both versions start with generalizations: Taipei's winter is "frequently" or "usually" cold and wet. But Chu's version immediately jumps into the specific temporal context by starting the second sentence with "one day," while Kwan-Terry's, while giving the reference to a certain day, maintains its generalizing style. Notice how in his version a chill gust of wind was blowing "again" and the alleys around Wen-chou Street "already" were under more than an inch of water. Contrasted with the singular mood suggested by Chu's version, Kwan-Terry's evokes an "iterative" mood, a narrative mode by which, as Gérard Genette puts it, a "single narrative utterance takes upon itself several occurrences together of the same event."[4]

The choice of narrative mode is important, because it sets up the context for the rest of the story. Pai Hsien-yung's story tells of the reunion of two old friends on a rainy winter night, and Chu's version precisely captures the special occasion. Kwan-Terry's version intends to do more. By inserting a singular event, the reunion between two old friends, into an iterative context, he brings into his translation what can be called the "pseudo-iterative" mode, which, as Jonathan Culler notes, enables a story to narrate "as something that happened repeatedly an event whose very particularity makes it seem undeniably singular."[5] The two terms *iterative* and *pseudo-iterative mode* derive from Genette's study of Proust's *A la recherche du temps perdu*. Since Pai Hsien-yung's *People in Taipei* (*Taipei jen*) is a book about people indulging their remembrances of things past, Kwan-Terry's use of iterative and pseudo-iterative modes nicely brings out an effect of life as a nostalgic ritual in the original.

But such a comparison and contrast between Chu's and Kwan-Terry's translation does not have to lead to the conclusion that the former is a less commendable rendition of Pai's story. Putting Chu's version back into the context of Ch'i Pang-yüan's anthology, one finds that it corresponds to the anthology's overall vision of a Taiwan in deep anxiety about what history should be and what history is. By narrating Pai's story in a singular temporal context, Chu may have bypassed the iterative mode, but he conveys a sense of the transitoriness of the narrated event, an awareness that life has not settled into a ritualistic repetition. In contrast to the title of Kwan-Terry's version, "Winter Nights," Chu's is called "One Winter Evening." He calls attention to a Pai Hsien-yung who is not ready yet to compromise with reality, a Pai Hsien-yung who is still willing to singularize, to make sense of a historical moment that is otherwise part of a senseless continuum.

As a second example, take Wang Wen-hsing's "Flaw," an initiation story about a teenager's first love, for a beautiful middle-aged seamstress who turns out to be unworthy. The same translation of the story, done by Ch'en Chu-yun, appears in both Lau's *Chinese Stories* and Ing's *Winter Plum*. Theoretically, the translation should elicit the same response in both anthologies. But when judged in the larger context which is the image of Taiwan the two anthologies convey, the translation elicits different interpretations. This example thus highlights the indeterminacy of meaning in both the translation and the original.

In Lau's anthology, concerned as it is with Taiwan at the crossroads between the past and present, the translation of "Flaw" impresses us with its emphasis on the boy's loss of innocence, through his knowledge of what his beloved really is. It succeeds in transmitting the subdued nostalgia which comes to one's mind only after one has grown up. The same translation, however, invites a different reading in Ing's collection, the one that presents a Taiwan least burdened with a historical concern. "Flaw," read in terms of this vision, suggests to us that the writer's posture of remembering is just as important as the content of his remembrance. The story's sense of nostalgia still hangs around, but interestingly enough, the "pastness" of the past has given way to the "presentness" of the past. Ch'en's use of both past tense ("I was eleven") and past subjunctive mood ("I must have been eleven") foregrounds the ironic interaction between the I as a precocious boy and the I as a wiser but sadder adult-narrator.

Still another example involves the translations of Huang Ch'un-ming's short stories. Acclaimed as one of the most touching tellers of stories about Taiwan in the sixties and seventies, Huang Ch'un-ming is the only writer whose works appear in all four anthologies: "A Flower in the Rainy Night" in Lau's *Chinese Stories*, "His Son's Big Doll" in Ch'i's *Anthology*, "Fish" in Ing's *Winter Plum*, and "I Love Mary" in Lau's *Unbroken Chain*. Needless to say, all the anthologies find in Huang's fiction the specific aspect of Taiwan they want to introduce to English readers. Where does Huang Ch'un-ming's charm lie? Which Huang Ch'un-ming gives a more "authentic" depiction of Taiwan? Can the so-called "quintessential Taiwanness" in his fiction be translated into English?

Earl Wieman is the translator of "A Flower in the Rainy Night." Dealing with a prostitute's wish to have a baby of her own and her efforts to carry out this wish, the story contains a strong romantic potential. The translation manages to transmit the earthy, provincial local color that one might find in the original. But what Wieman does not do is recapitulate the poetic vision that seems to sustain the prostitute Pai Mei's will to carry out her dream. Starting with a naturalistic portrait of Pai Mei's unfortunate youth, the story becomes more and more fantastic. Pai Mei arranges to have a young, robust fisherman become the "surrogate father" of her child. She delivers a baby boy in her hometown, and in the meantime she helps her village folks withstand a typhoon. By the end of the story, after Pai Mei takes her son to "see the sea," Huang's narrative has taken on an "apocalyptic" tone. Given her endurance, forgiveness, and compassion, Pai Mei the prostitute simulates sainthood. With his patently realist style, Wieman smoothly narrates the story in English, but his version retails coolness where it could equally have emphasized imagination or lyricism. His version foregrounds the tentative triumph of an earthy woman's struggle against her heredity and environment by suppressing the narrator's "fantastic" embellishment of that struggle.

Linda Wu's translation of "Fish" shows a similar strategy. The poor kid in "Fish" works hard to buy a fish for his grandpa, but he loses the precious gift on his way home. He fails to convince his grandpa of his misfortune. Taken as a liar, the kid is finally driven to quarrel with the old man. Wu unfailingly reproduces this series of events. But again, the problem lies in how these events blend into a vision of Taiwan, a vision that reads and thereby rewrites Huang's Taiwan. Like Wieman, Wu sees the story in realistic terms, emphasizing local color and the perceivable gestures (linguistic registers, daily behavior, etc.) of Huang's provincial characters. She thus avoids the distractions of psychological intricacy or deep pathos underlying simple surface, which would constitute a contrary kind of reading of Huang. It is unfair to charge either Wieman or Wu with doing less than they might. Their translations demonstrate a "different" reality, one that reengages rather than reduces the story's meaning. More interesting in view of the overall interpretive schemes of Lau's and Ing's anthologies, Wu's and Wieman's translations cohere in style and interpretive tactics with the other translations in their respective anthologies.

Howard Goldblatt translated "I Love Mary," a story about the kind of "imitation foreign devils" who would try anything to please their foreign masters. Amusingly, the story "acts out" the embarrassing situation one would run into in translation. The hero, a social climber in an overseas foreign company, works hard to "translate" himself, linguistically, behaviorally, and conceptually, into an American. He ends up becoming a parody of what he dreams to be, a pathetic impostor. Goldblatt's biggest challenge is just the opposite of the one faced by Wu and Wieman. Goldblatt, an American, has to appreciate the "fakeness" of Huang's characters' American manners, as opposed to the "real" ones Goldblatt is supposedly familiar with, before he can show the hilarious side of Taiwan under Western influence. His translation is sharp and uncompromising; it enacts the original as social critique, lacing it with self-conscious irony.

John Hu's translation of "His Son's Big Doll" poses yet another form for Huang's vision of Taiwan. In contrast to "Flowers in the Rainy Night" and "Fish," which rely on a sympathetic narrator as a modulator of the tone, "His Son's Big Doll" foregrounds the interplay between a much more indifferent third-person narratorial voice and the sandwich man's self-reflexive comments. The sandwich man's voice can be "heard" (read) in parentheses, which graphically suggests its peripheralness. Within the parentheses, one notices the I-narrator's less restrained, changing tonality, a significant reflection of thoughts that are relatively free. Hu's translation wants to "make sense" of the sandwich man's monologue, word for word. In a way it denies the last bit of psychological and linguistic freedom the sandwich man saves for himself.

This is particularly indicated by the climax, in which the hero puts on his clown makeup to pacify his crying baby, a baby who has since birth been used to seeing his father in the clown's costume. Asked by his wife what he is up to, the hero replies, in the original, "*Wo, wo, wo* (I, I, I)," which in Hu's translation becomes "I want Ah-lung [his son] to recognize me." By completing the sentence on the sandwich man's behalf, Hu renders a clear message to his English readers. But in so doing, he forces a predicate on the subject which has not decided what to say or to do. This move to complete the unfinished statement, to cue the reader to what "should" be known, may reflect Hu's uneasiness about the speaker's other potential meanings.

As a decision on the continuum of readerly-writerly interpretations, Hu's way of ending the story serves as a reference back to the ideological framework of the anthology in which it appears. Seeing that Ch'i's anthology is most concerned with the telling of history as a continuous flow from the past to the future, as a coherent "narrative" that manifests China's fate, it is understandable why, in Hu's version, the sandwichman-father is desperate to have his baby son "recognize" him. The "master-plot" of the anthology claims its prerogative: when the clown-father of a future Taiwan generation woefully stammers over the pronoun of personal selfhood, that pronoun can only mean selfhood as recognition, acknowledgment by the social other, and fulfillment in historic time.

I have tried to deal with the problems of stylistics and semantics in translation as they appear in a contemporary perspective. Problems of translation do not lie only at the level of rendition from one language to another. With these anthologies which "translate Taiwan," acknowledged transgressions of meaning occur in translation which are at one with the transgressions that occur in all readings and all critical rewritings of the "text." To look at an "original" is to look for some critical rewriting of the text, some version of it, which the critic can or cannot elicit as a rewriting of the translational text. Insofar as an original's meaning surfaces only in terms of the massive interpretive network it solicits, translation is but one of the many ways to enter into rewriting it. The critic, rewriting this rewriting, is tempted to fault the translation for being at a doubly rewritten distance from some illusory "originary" meaning, when in fact the translation is no more distant than the critic's own initial rewriting of the text.

Maintaining this Derridean posture, I have said that the text itself has been posing as a rewriting—an inscription of some preexistent entity. In this case, the purported entity is Taiwan; and the collected stories are writing of (inscribing) Taiwan. Each anthology inscribes (writes of) a distinct Taiwan, and each Taiwan would have been distinct had the stories all been in Chinese. I have indicated, as critic, my reinscription of the Taiwan in each anthology. But each anthology is an anthology of translations, and therefore of reinscriptions of Taiwan. The fact that translations reinscribe is well known but is felt to be a necessary failure, a postponement of presence.

I have turned this illusion of postponement upon itself, stating the grammatology of translation: that all writing, including all "original" writing, indefinitely postpones the presence of the originary meaning. The translation of Taiwan, therefore, is the reading of all these readings, among which the reading of a translation is only most obviously a reading.

NOTES

1. Joseph Lau with Timothy Ross, eds., *Chinese Stories from Taiwan: 1960–1970* (New York: Columbia University Press, 1972); Ch'i Pang-yuan, ed., *An Anthology of Contemporary Chinese Literature*, vol. 2 (Taipei: National Institute for Compilation and Translation, 1975); Nancy Ing, ed., *Winter Plum: Contemporary Chinese Fiction* (Taipei: Chinese Materials Center, 1982); Joseph Lau, ed., *The Unbroken Chain: An Anthology of Taiwan Fiction since 1926* (Bloomington: Indiana University Press, 1983).

2. Ch'i, *Anthology*, 261.

3. Lau, *Chinese Stories*, 337.

4. Gérard Genette, *Narrative Discourse*, trans. Jane E. Lewin (Ithaca: Cornell University Press, 1980), 116.

5. Jonathan Culler, Preface to Genette, *Narrative Discourse*, 11.

Critical Surveys

On English Translation of Modern Chinese Poetry

A Critical Survey

MICHELLE YEH

This study presents a brief survey of the history of English translation of modern Chinese poetry from 1936 to 1990. It is clear that in the past decade in particular, modern Chinese poetry has received increasing attention and its introduction to the English-speaking world has gained in both breadth and depth.

We need to consider some of the difficulties in translation intrinsic to the unique nature of modern Chinese poetry. For instance, the use of the vernacular as the poetic medium creates a wide discrepancy at the level of literariness; although closer to its Western counterpart, syntax can be ambiguously convoluted; repetition is more common in Chinese than in English poetry; and so forth. These issues are related not only to poetic meaning but also to poetic nuance, and they are the result of linguistic as well as cultural characteristics. For instance, what is poetic in one language may not be so in another, and the associations of imagery are dependent on cultural context.

The introduction of modern Chinese poetry to the English-speaking world is a relatively recent phenomenon. The first attempt to present the new literary form was Harold Acton's and Shih-hsiang Chen's *Modern Chinese Poetry*, published in 1936. A prolific writer and translator (he also translated traditional Chinese plays and tales), Acton was born in Florence and educated at Oxford. He lived in Beijing for the most part of 1932–1939. At the request of Wen Yuanning, chairman of the English Department, he taught English literature at Beijing University until the Sino-Japanese War broke out. One of his students, Chen, introduced Acton to modern Chinese poetry (and to his poet-friends, including Bian Zhilin 卡之琳 [b. 1910] and Li Guangtian 李廣田 [1906–1968]), and they collaborated on the translation. *Modern Chinese Poetry* presents fifteen poets in ninety-six poems, and provides useful historical and biographical information, as well, including the views on poetry of a few poets (e.g., Fei Ming 廢名 [1910–1967] and Lin Geng 林庚 [b. 1910]).

Acton and Chen's pioneering effort had to wait eleven years before a successor came along. In 1947, Robert Payne edited *Contemporary Chinese Poetry*, presenting nine major poets of the 1920s to 1930s. In the fifties no anthology appeared, but the sixties saw the publication of an influential and comprehensive anthology. Kai-yu Hsu singlehandedly edited and translated *Twentieth-Century Chinese Poetry*, which includes more than forty-four poets and 350 poems from the early 1920s through the 1940s. Hsu's introduction gives a succinct historical overview of the development of modern Chinese poetry, dividing it into distinct schools (e.g., the Crescent School, the symbolists, the modernists, the metaphysical poets, etc.). Although the classification of poets and the labels of schools are debatable, the anthology, having gone through two paperback printings since its publication, remains a landmark in English translation of modern Chinese poetry.

As early as 1960, Kwang-chung Yu edited and translated a slim volume of modern poetry in Taiwan, *New Chinese Poetry*. However, due to rather limited distribution outside Taiwan, it did not make a significant impact.

The first anthology devoted to modern poetry of Taiwan published by a major American press appeared in 1970, when Wai-lim Yip edited and translated *Modern Chinese Poetry: Twenty-five Poets from the Republic of China, 1955–1965*. Two years later, another American anthology focused on Taiwan: *Modern Verse from Taiwan*, edited and translated by Angela C. Jung Palandri with Robert J. Bertholf, an English professor and Palandri's former student. The same year saw Cyril Birch's popular *Anthology of Chinese Literature*; its second volume included modern poetry from pre-1949 China as well as postwar Taiwan. In 1975, *An Anthology of Contemporary Chinese Literature*, edited by Chi Pang-yuan et al., was published; it included in its first volume the works of twenty-two poets in Taiwan.

It was also in the seventies that individual poets became the subject of critical study and translation. Tao Tao Sanders published a translation of Wen Yiduo 聞一多 (1899–1946) in 1972; Bonnie S. McDougall's translation of the early work of He Qifang 何其芳 (1912–1977) was published in 1976 under the title *Paths in Dreams*; and Dominic Cheung's critical study of Feng Zhi 馮至 (b. 1905), published in 1979, contained extensive translations.

In the eighties we saw a much broader representation of modern Chinese poetry. With increasing interest in contemporary Chinese literature in general, there was a proliferation of anthologies in translation. Modern poetry is included in such anthologies as Siu and Stern's *Mao's Harvest* (1983), Link's *Stubborn Weeds* (1983), Lee's *New Realism* (1983), Soong's and Minford's *Trees on the Mountains* (1984), Duke's *Contemporary Chinese Literature* (1985), and Barmé and Minford's *Seeds of Fire* (1988). It regularly appears in the translation magazines: *Renditions*, published in Hong Kong; *Chinese Pen*, in Taiwan; and *Chinese Literature*, in mainland China.

More important, several poetry anthologies are now available, including Cheung's *Isle Full of Noises* (1986), Pang Bingjun and John Minford's *100 Modern Chinese Poems* (1987), Nancy Ing's *Summer Glory* (1982), Droogenbroodt et al.'s *China, China* (1986), and Rewi Alley's *Light and Shadow Along a Great Road* (1984). *The Red Azalea: Chinese Poetry since the Cultural Revolution*, edited and translated by Edward Morin et al., appeared in 1990.

Cheung's anthology focuses on poetry written in Taiwan in 1965–1985, with 146 poems by thirty-two poets; Ing's and Droogenbroodt's volumes, much more modest in size, have a similar focus. Morin's concentrates on contemporary poetry in mainland China. In addition, at least two anthologies in preparation will be devoted to avant-garde poetry (much of which remains "unofficial") in China from the early 1970s to the present.[1]

Before the eighties, as mentioned, there were few volumes concentrating on individual poets. Palandri translated the poetry of Luo Men 羅門 (b. 1928) and Rongzi 蓉子 (b. 1928) in *Sun and Moon Collection* (1968), and Kwang-chung Yu translated his own poetry in *Acres of Barbed Wires* (1971), both published in Taiwan. During the eighties, more critical studies appeared: of Wen Yiduo by Kai-yu Hsu (1980), of Bian Zhilin by Lloyd Haft (1983), and more recently of Dai Wangshu 戴望舒 (1905–1950) by Gregory Lee (1989), all containing many poems in translation. Selected works of such poets as Ai Qing 艾青 (b. 1910) (1982), Bei Dao 北島 (b. 1949) (1983, 1988), Duo Duo 多多 (b. 1951) (1989), and Gu Cheng 顧城 (b. 1956) (1990) are also now available.

The translations of modern Chinese poetry indicate that it is attracting more attention in the English-speaking world. The number of both collections and critical studies of individual poets and general anthologies has increased significantly in the 1980s. As more modern Chinese poetry becomes available and accessible to the West, it is possible to have a more specific focus based on period, geographical area, and individual authors. The second direction in the future may be that, as modern Chinese poetry grows, there will also be more attempts to understand the history of its development and the evolution of its style better; and anthologies will be expected to provide more breadth and depth. Both Alley's and Pang and Minford's books cover modern Chinese poetry from its beginning to the eighties, thus having the most comprehensive scope among existing anthologies. Alley's book collects more than four hundred poems. Published in Beijing with a preface written by He Jingzhi 賀敬之 (b. 1924; He's representative works include "Return to Yan'an" and "Song of Lei Feng"), it clearly represents the view of the political-literary establishment, giving priority to thematic correctness ("the thinking and feelings of the Chinese people," p. 35) over artistic excellence. The representation in both works of postwar Taiwan and avant-garde poetry in post-Mao China is minimal. Pang and Minford's book, on the other hand, is not politically oriented. However, considering the large number of excellent pieces written in the past seven decades, the predetermined number of one hundred (of the series of Chinese poetry to which their book belongs) inevitably poses a severe limitation on the selection. The reader might also wish that a more analytical introduction had been given to better situate the poems in a historical and aesthetic framework.

Another point worth mentioning is that for serious students of modern Chinese poetry, it is both convenient and helpful to have bilingual texts. Ing's *Summer Glory* and Pang and Minford's *100 Modern Chinese Poems* provide this double perspective. The Chinese version of Cheung's *Isle Full of Noises* was published separately in Taiwan. It is understandable, however, that for financial and other reasons, bilingual texts are not always possible.

I would like to share a few observations from reading these anthologies and collections and from teaching and writing about modern Chinese poetry over the past few years. It is interesting to observe some of the problems that are unique to the translation of modern Chinese poetry into English, for they illuminate the nature of modern poetry and reveal difficulties inherent in translation in general.

In comparison with classical Chinese poetry, modern Chinese poetry seems to have a higher degree of accessibility for at least three reasons. First, it is written in the vernacular; it uses colloquialisms and is easier to understand. Among the early modern poets, Wen Yiduo stands out for his use of the spoken idiom to convey profound feelings.

> I am sending you these poems.
> Even if you don't understand all,
> It'll be all right;
> You can use your fingers
> To touch them gently,
> Like a doctor taking a patient's pulse.
> Perhaps you can feel
> Their nervous beat,
> Like the beat of your heart.
> ("Red Beans no. 14" *Collected Poems*, 159–160)[2]

> 我把這些詩寄給你了，
> 這些字你若不全認識，

那也不要緊。
你可以用手指
輕輕摩着他們，
像醫生按着病人的脈，
你許可以試出
他們緊張地跳着，
同你心跳底節奏一般。

Second, modern Chinese poetry is easier to translate than classical because, as illustrated in Wen's poem addressed to his wife, the syntax is
looser, more prosaic, and closer to English syntax. Although the ambiguity
created by the omission of the subject of a sentence, common in classical
poetry, still exists, it is not so serious a problem in view of the vernacular
context. In fact, modern Chinese has a significant degree of Westernized
syntax, and it is readily seen in the poetry. The following sentences, for
instance, can almost be translated into English word for word without
changing their order:

Following a dove's whistle, I search for you. (Bei Dao, "The Answer")

沿着鴿子的哨音
我尋找着你

I dared not display love's gifts like this,
Although I dedicated many songs
    To flowers, sea, and dawn. (Shu Ting 舒婷 [b. 1952], "Oh, Mother")

我還不敢這樣陳列愛的禮品，
雖然我曾寫下許多支頌歌
  給花，給海，給黎明。

Let all who thirst for sleep receive a bed and the embrace of a dream;
Let those who march forward, a torch; those who fall, a kiss;
Let those who yearn to fly have wings and distance;
Those who hurt, a reply. (Chen Kehua 陳克華 [b. 1961], "Reply")

讓渴睡的都得到一張眠床和夢的懷抱
讓前行的一隻火把，跌倒的一個吻
讓想飛的擁有翅膀和遠方
讓受着痛的，一個回答。

Third, Western allusions (names, places, events) and symbols (religious,
literary, and others) are sometimes employed in modern Chinese poetry,
and they can be translated rather straightforwardly without losing any of
their meaning.

However, those advantages can turn into disadvantages for the translator. With regard to diction, while modern poetry is written in the vernacular, there is a wide range of literariness which varies greatly from poet to

poet and even from poem to poem. To borrow Charles Altieri's metaphor, modern poetry born in the New Literature movement of 1917 has decidedly enlarged the temple of Chinese poetry; with the expansion of the canon, however, the conventional boundaries for poetic discourse virtually disappear. At the level of diction, there is a wide spectrum between the literary (*wen* 文) at one end and the vernacular (*bai* 白) at the other, and it is not always easy to convey the subtle differences in translation.

To use concrete nouns as an example: Chinese has a large number of synonyms, each implying a different degree of literariness. In some cases, these are not synonyms, different words with the same meaning, but simply alternate versions of the same word. For instance, the early works of Luo Fu 洛夫 (b. 1928), Zheng Chouyu 鄭愁予 (b. 1932), Lin Ling 林泠 (b. 1938), and Yang Mu 楊牧 (b. 1940) use *xingzi* 星子 quite often. Compared with the more common *xingxing* or simply *xing*, *xingzi* is at once more literary, more gentle (with the unaccented second syllable), and more intimate (with the diminutive *zi*). Similarly, to call "eyes" *mouzi* 眸子 instead of *yanjing* 眼睛 makes a subtle difference in diction and style. The effect of Shang Qin's 商禽 (b. 1931) well-known prose poem from the 1960s, "Giraffe" ("Changjinglu" 長頸鹿), depends at least partly on its diction:

> The young prison guard noticed that at every physical exam any increase in the height of the prisoners always took place in the neck. He reported to the warden: "Sir, the windows are too high!" But the answer he received was: "No, they look up to Time."
> The kindhearted young guard did not recognize Time's face, did not know Time's origin or its whereabouts; so night after night he went to the zoo and patrolled and waited outside the giraffe pen. (*Anthology of Modern Chinese Poetry*, vol. 2, 439)

The word "face" in the second stanza is *rongyan* 容顏 in the original, which has a more literary touch than the commonly used *lian* or *liankong* 臉孔. By choosing literary over colloquial terms (also *zhanwang* 瞻望 in the first stanza), the poet creates a disparity in the texture of the poem: between the terse, formal, matter-of-fact, and detached way in which the event is narrated and the event itself, which is incredible in view of the extreme naïveté of the young guard. Such disparity contributes to the absurdist effect intended by the poet.

Different levels of literariness also exist for verbs. In general, disyllabic verbs and (less common) quadrisyllabic expressions tend to be more literary than monosyllabic words. Compare, for instance, *lingting* 聆聽 with *ting* 聽, *siliang* 思量 with *xiang* 想, or *xunmi* 尋覓 with *zhao* 找; the first is definitely more literary than the second. A simple sentence that reads "I will remember" can be as literary as *wo jiang jiqu* 我將記取 or as colloquial as *wo hui jide* 我會記得.

Closely related to the issue of diction in modern Chinese poetry is the idiosyncratic nature of its language in general. Iconoclastic in spirit, modern Chinese poetry places much emphasis on individual expression and artistic experiment. If vernacular Chinese is easier to translate because its syntax is closer to that of English, in the hands of many poets, syntax can be ambiguous and extremely complex. Ya Xian's 瘂弦 (b. 1932) "The Colonel" ("Shang-xiao" 上校, 1960) depicts the petty, impoverished life of a retired colonel, a war hero who lost a leg in the Sino-Japanese War. The first two lines read:

> 那純粹是另一種玫瑰
> 自火焰中誕生 (*Collected Poems*, 145)

Born of the flames of war, the rose is of a different kind from that usually associated with beauty and love. Wai-lim Yip interprets *chuncui* to be a noun and renders the first line this way: "Purity was another kind of rose" (57). On the other hand, it could well be an adverb modifying the copula "is," which would give us a line that reads "That was purely another kind of rose," thus highlighting the contrast between the two kinds of rose—beauty and atrocity, love and cruelty, life and death—mentioned earlier.

In the hands of such poets as Bian Zhilin, ambiguity is derived from convoluted syntax. Take the poem entitled "Autumn Window" ("Qiuchuang" 秋窗, 1933), for instance:

> 像一個中年人
> 回頭看過去的足跡
> 一步一沙漠,
> 從亂夢中醒來,
> 聽半天晚鴉。
>
> 看夕陽在灰牆上,
> 想一個初期肺病者
> 對暮色蒼茫的古鏡
> 夢想少年的紅暈。
> (*A Record of Carving Insects*, 159)

The omission of the subject in the first stanza makes it possible to interpret the poem in different ways. Acton and Chen employ the first person pronoun "I," which is modified by the prepositional phrase ("like a middle-aged man") in line 1:

> Like a man in middle-age
> I look back on the traces of the past ... (126)

However, the second line can just as well be a participial clause modifying the middle-aged man. That is how Kai-yu Hsu, in *Twentieth-Century Chinese*

Poetry, interprets the poem. He also uses the third-person pronoun "he" for the subject of the main clause, which he identifies in line 4:

> Like a middle-aged man
> Looking back at his footprints—
> Every step a desert—
> Awakening from confused dreams
> He listens to the half sky full of evening crows. (167)

When we compare these two translations with the Chinese original, both make sense, and it is hard to choose one as closer to the original. Through syntactic ambiguity, the poem presents a quick succession of images that blur the line between reality and imagination by intermingling what seem to be literal descriptions with metaphors and by intermixing diverse voices and perspectives (the middle-aged man, the unidentified speaker, the tubercular patient, the youth). Is the twilight on the gray wall like a tuberculosis patient or is it other way around? Is the ancient mirror the window, growing misty from the falling dusk, or is it the gray wall with a touch of red from the setting sun? Who dreams of youthful colors, the patient or the speaker, or the middle-aged man in line 1? The ambivalence and confusion, on both syntactic and perceptual levels, intimates the poet's feeling toward life.

The syntax of some of Yang Mu's poems is comparable to Bian's. His "Let the Wind Recite" ("Rang feng langsong" 讓風朗誦, 1973) contains five subjunctive clauses, all beginning with "if," running forty lines long:

> 1. If I could write you
>   A poem of summer, when reeds
>   Spread robustly, when sunshine
>   Bounces around your waist and
>   flows asunder from where the feet part;
>   When a new drum
>   Cracks, if I could
>
>   Write you a poem of autumn
>   Set afloat on a skiff,
>   With water reaching the twelfth notch,
>   When sadness crouches on the riverbed
>   Like a yellow dragon, giving free rein
>   To the torrent down the mountain,
>   Letting it splash from the wounded eyes;
>   If I could write you
>
>   A winter poem,
>   As if at last it could be a witness to the snow,
>   The shrinking lake,
>   And the midnight call

That awakens a hurried dream,
In which you are taken to a distant province,
Given a lantern, and told to sit there quietly,
No tears allowed;

2. If they would not allow you
   To mourn for spring,
   Or allow you to knit;
   If they said:
   Sit down quietly
   And wait—
   A thousand years later
   After spring
   Summer would still
   Be your name;
   They would bring you
   Back, take away
   Your ring
   And your clothes,
   Cut your hair short
   And abandon you
   By the edge of my persevering water
   Then you would belong to me at last.

   You would belong to me at last.
   I would bathe you
   And give you a little wine,
   A few mint candies,
   And some new clothes;
   Your long hair would
   Grow back to what it was before—
   Summer would still be
   Your name.

3. Then I would write you
   A spring poem, when all had
   Begun anew—
   So young, and shy,
   You gaze at a mature self reflected in the water;
   I'd let you shed tears freely,
   Design new clothes, make the candle for the first night.

   Then you would let me write
   A spring poem, on the bosom,
   In the rhythm of heartbeat, the rhyme of blood,
   The image of the breasts, and the metaphor of a mole;
   I'd lay you on the warm surface of the lake
   And let the wind recite. (*Collected Poems*, vol. 1, 490–495)

Each of the "if" clauses introduces more clauses (e.g., "when ...," "where ...") and phrases (e.g., "with ...," "as if ..."). They form a syntactic maze with many twists and turns, suggesting the tortuous path of a romantic relationship—analogous to the progression from summer to autumn and winter—and the persistent rhythm of a faithful heart. The ultimate triumph of love, announced by the coming of spring, is achieved as the prolonged suspension of the subjunctive clauses is finally resolved by the resultative adverb "then," thus completing the sentence in the last twenty-three lines of the poem, mirrored in the coming full circle of the four seasons. In the poem, syntax and imagery, form and content, are inextricable; their organic unity conveys the theme effectively.

A different kind of ambiguity resulting from the highly experimental and idiosyncratic nature of modern Chinese poetry is exemplified in Guan Guan's 管管 (b. 1930) "Lotus" ("He" 荷):

> "There were once lakes of mud here."
> "You mean these lots of lotus flowers?"
> "Now they are stacks of swamps."
> "You mean these ponds of buildings?"
> "Are they ponds of buildings?"
> "*Nope*, they are houses of lotus flowers." (*Selected Poems*, 108)
>
> 「那裏曾經是一湖一湖的泥土」
> 「你是指這一地一地的荷花」
> 「現在又是一間一間沼澤了」
> 「你是指這一池一池的樓房」
> 「是一池一池的樓房嗎」
> 「不,卻是一屋一屋的荷花了」

Written in a colloquial style, the poem does not yield to easy interpretation. The source of difficulty is the incongruity between the measure words (*hu, di, jian, chi, wu*) and the nouns they describe. It can be further analyzed as deriving from a reversal of measure words in every two lines of the poems. Normally, *hu* in line 1 would describe "lotus flowers" in line 2, whereas *di* in line 1 would described "mud" in line 2. By the same token, *jian* in line 3 is usually used to describe "building" in line 4, and *chi* in line 4 to describe "swamp" in line 3; *chi* would also refer to "lotus flowers" in line 6, with *wu* referring to "buildings" in line 5.

In general, it is hard to retain measure words when one translates Chinese into English since they are much more prevalent and important in Chinese than English. Usually, they can simply be omitted. In Guan Guan's poem, however, omission would destroy much, if not all, of the impact of the poem. Through a clever mismatch of the measure words and the objects they refer to, the poem intimates at least two possible meanings. One is the traditional, particularly Daoist, notion of cyclical transformation, the law of constant change in the universe. The contrasts between land and water, human construct and nature, and the presence and absence of beauty suggest the endless cycles of opposite phenomena giving rise to and displacing each other.

The poem can also be read as a lament at the destruction of nature for the advancement of material civilization, the invasion of urban landscape into natural landscape, hinged on the use of measure words. In the first three lines of the poem, the changes from *hu* to *di* and from *di* to *jian* suggest the filling of lakes with dirt and the building of houses. In the last three lines, only buildings exist, yet the speakers insist on seeing them as something else. The last two lines are but alternate readings of the same phenomenon. Refusing to accept the reality, the first speaker (line 5) nostalgically calls the buildings "ponds." Then, upon being questioned by the second speaker, he (or she) revises the mental projection and sees the buildings as lotus flowers. Over and against the urban jungle of buildings, the poem invokes the lost beauty of nature.

No matter how idiosyncratic a poet's style is, it cannot exist beyond the language in which the poet writes. All of the examples we have seen illustrate aspects of the unique character and poetic potential of modern Chinese which are often difficult to render in a language as different as English. While some of those examples relate to how to get at and convey poetic meaning satisfactorily, others pertain more to conveying the optimum poetic effect. If syntax is often responsible for the first problem, the second is derived from more complex sources. For, in the final analysis, poetic effect is determined as much by linguistic as by cultural factors, although the two sets of conditions are related and by no means separate. One cannot determine the level of literariness of diction without extensive experience with the culture, which is in essence the history of language usage. To the same extent, one must also be familiar with the culture to develop a sensitivity to what is poetic and what is not. In translation, what is poetic in one language may not be so in another. Worse still, what is poetic in one language may even be downright banal in another. For instance, Luo Dagang's 羅大岡 (b. 1909) "Short Verse—For S" ("Duanzhang wei S zuo" 短章爲 S 作) affirms love's transcendence over time and distance. It contains this phrase: *zhen jin / ye zhen yuan* 眞近/也眞遠 (lines 18–19, *Anthology of Modern Chinese Poetry*, vol. 1, 146). To translate it as "so near / yet so far" would very likely invite derision from the English-speaking reader because it is a cliché to be avoided. Perhaps "so near / so far" would make it less offensive.

What we are dealing with here, then, is the larger issue of poetic effect based on a solid understanding of both the language and the culture. Repetition, to give another example, is an important device frequently employed in modern Chinese poetry. In English, however, it is not, in general, considered desirable. We have seen that in Chen Kehua's "Reply," of the four "lets" that begin a declarative sentence, one is omitted to avoid too much repetition. Dai Wangshu's "My Memory" ("Wo de jiyi" 我底記憶, ca. 1928) is another case in point, where repetition of key words plays a central role:

> My memory is loyal to me,
> More loyal than my closest friends.
>
> It exists in a smoking cigarette,
> On a penholder painted with lilies,
> In an old powder compact,
> On woodberries by the crumbling wall.
> It exists in a half-empty bottle of wine,
> On a torn manuscript and dried petals,
> On a dim, gloomy lamp, on still water,
> In everything with or without a soul.
> It exists everywhere, the way I do in the world. (Lee, *Dai Wangshu*, 38–39)

> 我底記憶是忠實於我的,
> 忠實甚於我最好的友人。
>
> 它生存在燃着的烟卷上,
> 它生存在繪着百合花的筆桿上,
> 它生存在破舊的粉盒上,
> 它生存在頹垣的木莓上,
> 它生存在喝了一半的酒瓶上,
> 在撕碎的往日的詩稿上, 在壓乾的花片上,
> 在棲暗的燈上, 在平靜的水上,
> 在一切有靈魂沒有靈魂的東西上,
> 它在到處生存着, 像我在這世界一樣。

In the original, the verb "exist" is repeated five times in the first five lines of the second stanza. The translations of Acton and Chen and of Pang and Minford both delete it in lines 2–4, repeating it only once in line 5. The omission seems to be a felicitous choice; to duplicate the original exactly would sound redundant and awkward.

In other cases, repetition is essential and indispensable. Ya Xian's "Songlike Andante" ("Ruge de xingban" 如歌的行板, 1964) uses the word "necessity" (biyao 必要) nineteen times in a poem of twenty-two lines:

The necessity of tenderness
The necessity of certainty
The necessity of a little wine and sweet olive
The necessity of watching a girl walk by seriously
The necessity of the basic realization that you are not Hemingway
The necessity of the European War, rain, cannon, weather, and the Red Cross
The necessity of taking a walk
The necessity of walking your dog
The necessity of mint tea

The necessity of rumors that, like grass drifting, arise from the other end of the
  stock market

At seven o'clock every evening, the necessity of
Revolving doors, the necessity of penicillin
The necessity of assassination, the necessity of
Evening papers, the necessity of wearing velvet
Trousers, the necessity of horse races
The necessity of inheriting your aunt's properties
The necessity of balconies, the sea, smiles
The necessity of laziness—

And, since óne is regarded as a river, one must keep on flowing.
The world is always this way—
The Bodhisattva is on the distant mountain,
Poppies are in the poppy field. (*Collected Poems*, 200–201)

The nineteen phrases, all beginning (in the original, ending) with the
word "necessity" encompass such a wide scope of natures and tones that
they defy any simple generalization. The triviality of such things as "watching a girl walk by seriously" (the adverb reinforcing the irony underlying
the disparity between "watching a girl walk by" and "seriously"), "walking
your dog," and "mint tea" is juxtaposed with the gravity of violence and
death ("European War," "assassination," "the Red Cross"). Tangible images such as rain, sea, and balcony are juxtaposed with intangible ones such
as tenderness, rumors, and laziness. Personal concerns, whether in the form
of self-consciousness ("you are not Hemingway") or vanity ("velvet trousers"), are juxtaposed with impersonal ones ("revolving doors"). Monetary
matters ("stock market," "inheriting your aunt's properties") are juxtaposed with feelings and abstractions ("tenderness," "certainty"). All these
images conjure up a world of confusing complexity and fragmented experiences. They are finally resolved in the concluding stanza. The river seems to
be the only connection running through the long sequence of non sequiturs,
suggesting that the loose ends in life are unresolvable but are all part of life.
The image of the Bodhisattva on the distant mountain may allude to the
mountain in suburban Taipei, along the Danshui River, which receives its
name from the resemblance of the gently rolling hills to a Bodhisattva lying
on her back. The evocation of boundless compassion and transcendental
beauty associated with the Buddhist female deity is juxtaposed with beauty
of the opposite kind—the alluring yet destructive poppies. Like the Bodhisattva, the poppies are always there. Beauty and ugliness, good and evil, life
and death, are always inextricably connected, like all the other juxtaposed
pairs in the poem, with all their repetitions and contradictions, their meanings and their meaninglessness.
  If translators have to decide for themselves whether to omit or preserve
repetitions of phrases and words, they also have to make a choice of what

kind of culturally derived association is appropriate or desirable. The choice of one association over another often makes a significant difference in the meaning or effect of a poem. Mu Dan's 穆旦 (1918–77) "Spring" ("Chun" 春, 1942) depicts the simultaneous attraction and pain of growing up, the experience of both wonder and fear in opening up to the world of the senses and desire. It contains these lines:

> Under the blue sky, forever bewitched by the eternal riddle
> are our tightly closed bodies
> —Like the songs of clay birds.
> You are ignited, curling up, with no home to return to.
> O light, shadow, sound, color—all are stripped naked,
> Painfully awaiting new combinations. (*Selected Poems*, 56)

> 藍天下, 爲永遠的謎蠱惑着的
> 是我們二十歲的緊閉的肉體,
> 一如那泥土做成的鳥的歌,
> 你們被點燃, 捲曲又捲曲, 却無處歸依。
> 呵, 光, 影, 聲, 色, 都已經赤裸,
> 痛苦着, 等待伸入新的組合。

Pang and Minford translate the image in line 3 as "ceramic birds" (139). This translation adds to the poem an intimation of human frailty, physical as well as emotional and psychological. As such, it is in tune with the overall meaning of the poem as a reflection on the vulnerability of youth. On the other hand, the original image is probably closer to "clay" (*nitu*) than to ceramic birds. The analogy evokes Biblical associations that Adam was made of clay and, coming from the earth, humans also return to the earth. The Biblical symbolism not only accords with the idea of the frailty of the flesh which is part of the theme, but perhaps more important, also conveys a profound sense of dichotomy for humans between their infinite desire to learn and experience ("bewitched by eternal mysteries") and their mortality, between their attraction to and at the same time repulsion by the world of the senses, between the trials in life and the reality of death.

Mu Dan majored in English literature at Qinghua and at Southwest United University in 1935–1940. He studied English poetry extensively (for two years under William Empson at Southwest), acknowledged such influences as Auden, Eliot, and Yeats, and was one of those responsible for introducing Anglo-American modernist poetry to China in the late thirties and early forties. After receiving an M.A. in English literature from the University of Chicago in 1951, he returned to China in 1952 and for the rest of his life was a prolific translator of Byron and Pushkin. Given these facts, it would not be far-fetched to assume that he was fairly familiar with Western literature and culture, of which the Bible is a major shaping force. Further, Mu Dan's other poems (e.g., "Eight Poems") contain references to God. All of this information is helpful to the translator in determining the most valid and powerful association of a single image.

In 1948, Acton, recalling the translations of modern Chinese poems that he and Chen had completed in the thirties, remarked: "It was amusing but sometimes discouraging to contrast them with the originals. Poems of extreme simplicity often proved the most difficult ..." (*Memoirs*, 348). Translation is notorious for its inadequacy in preserving the beauty and truth of original poetry. The translation of modern Chinese poetry poses some special challenges at the same time that it shares some of the perennial problems in the translation of poetry. Although by nature it is an art of approximation and partial re-creation, translation has done an invaluable service in introducing modern Chinese poetry to the West in the past five decades, and we can anticipate that efforts will continue to be made.

NOTES

1. The two volumes are edited by Duo Duo and Fei Ye 菲野. The information was obtained from these poets either verbally or in correspondence.

2. Unless otherwise noted in the main text, all translations are mine.

WORKS CITED

Acton, Harold. *Memoirs of an Aesthete*. London: Methuen, 1948.

Acton, Harold, and Shih-hsiang Chen, eds. and trans. *Modern Chinese Poetry*. New York: Gordon Press, 1975.

Ai Qing. *Selected Poems of Ai Qing*. Translated and edited by Eugene Eoyang, Bloomington: Indiana University Press, 1982.

Alley, Rewi, comp. and ed. *Light and Shadow along a Great Road—An Anthology of Modern Chinese Poetry*. Beijing: New World Press, 1984.

Anthology of Modern Chinese Poetry (Xiandai Zhongguoshi xuan). 2 vols. Ed. Yang Mu and Zheng Shusen (William Tay). Taipei: Hongfan, 1989.

Barmé, Geremie, and John Minford, eds. *Seeds of Fire: Chinese Voices of Conscience*. New York: Hill and Wang, 1988.

Bei Dao. *The August Sleepwalker*. Trans. Bonnie S. McDougall. London: Anvil Press, 1988.

Bian Zhilin. *A Record of Carving Insects* (Diaochong jili). Rev. ed. Hong Kong: Joint Publishing Co., 1982.

Birch, Cyril, ed. *Anthology of Chinese Literature*. Vol. 2: *From the Fourteenth Century to Modern Times*. New York: Grove Press, 1972.

Cheung, Dominic. *Feng Chih*. Boston: Twayne, 1979.

———, ed. and trans. *The Isle Full of Noises: Modern Chinese Poetry from Taiwan*. New York: Columbia University Press, 1986.

Chi Pang-yuan et al. *An Anthology of Contemporary Chinese Literature, Taiwan: 1949–1974*. 2 vols. Taipei: National Institute for Compilation and Translation, 1975.

Dai Wangshu. *Selected Work* (Dai Wangshu juan). Ed. Ya Xian. Taipei: Hongfan, 1977.

Droogenbroodt, Germain, and Peter Stinson, eds. *China China: Contemporary Poetry from Taiwan, Republic of China*. Ninove, Belgium: Point Books, 1986.

Duke, Michael S., ed. *Contemporary Chinese Literature: An Anthology of Post-Mao Fiction and Poetry*. Armonk, N. Y.: M. E. Sharpe, 1985.

Duo Duo. *Looking Out from Death: From the Cultural Revolution to Tiananmen Square*. Trans. Gregory Lee and John Cayley. London: Bloomsbury, 1989.

Gu Cheng. *Selected Poems*. Ed. Seán Golden and Chu Chiyu. Hong Kong: Chinese University of Hong Kong Press, 1990.

Guan Guan. *Selected Poems* (Guan Guan shi xuan). Taipei: Hongfan, 1986.

Haft, Lloyd. *Pien Chih-lin: A Study in Modern Chinese Poetry*. Dordrecht, Holland, and Cinnaminson, N. J.: Foris, 1983.

Hsu, Kai-yu, ed. and trans. *Twentieth-Century Chinese Poetry: An Anthology*. Ithaca, N.Y.: Cornell University Press, 1963.

———. *Wen I-to*. Boston: Twayne, 1980.

Ing, Nancy, ed. and tr. *Summer Glory: A Collection of Contemporary Chinese Poetry*. Taipei: Chinese Materials Center, 1982.

Lee, Gregory. *Dai Wangshu: The Poetry and Life of a Chinese Modernist*. Hong Kong: Chinese University of Hong Kong Press, 1989.

Lee, Yee, ed. *The New Realism: Writings from China after the Cultural Revolution*. New York: Hippocrene Books, 1983.

Link, Perry, ed. *Stubborn Weeds: Popular and Controversial Chinese Literature after the Cultural Revolution*. Bloomington: Indiana University Press, 1983.

McDougall, Bonnie S., trans. *Notes from the City of the Sun: Poems by Bei Dao*. Ithaca, N.Y.: Cornell University Press, 1983.

———. *Paths in Dream: Selected Prose and Poetry of Ho Ch'i-fang*. Queensland: Queensland University Press, 1976.

Morin, Edward et al., eds. and trans. *The Red Azalea: Chinese Poetry since the Cultural Revolution*. Honolulu: University of Hawaii Press, 1990.

Mu Dan. *Selected Poems* (Mu Dan shi xuan). Beijing: Renmin, 1986.

Palandri, Angela C. Jung, with Robert J. Bertholf, ed. and trans. *Modern Verse from Taiwan*. Los Angeles: University of California Press, 1972.

———. *Sun and Moon Collection: Selected Poems of Lomen and Yungtze*. Taipei: Mei Ya, 1968.

Pang Bingjun, and John Minford, eds. and trans., with Seán Golden. *100 Modern Chinese Poems*. Hong Kong: Commercial Press, 1987.

Payne, Robert, ed. *Contemporary Chinese Poetry*. London: George Routledge & Son, 1947.

Sanders, Tao Tao. *Wen I-to: Red Candle*. London, 1972.

Siu, Helen F., and Zelda Stern, eds. *Mao's Harvest: Voices from China's New Generation*. New York: Oxford University Press, 1983.

Soong, Stephen, C., and John Minford, eds. *Trees on the Mountain: An Anthology of New Chinese Writing*. Hong Kong: Chinese University of Hong Kong Press, 1984.

Wen Yiduo. *Collected Poems* (Wen Yiduo shi ji). Edited by Zhou Liangpei. Sichuan: Sichuan Renmin, 1984.

Ya Xian. *Collected Poems* (Ya Xian shi ji). Taipei: Hongfan, 1981.

Yang Mu. *Collected Poems* (Yang Mu shi ji). Vol. 1. Taipei: Hongfan, 1978.

Yip, Wai-lim, ed. and trans. *Modern Chinese Poetry: Twenty-five Poets from the Republic of China, 1955–1965.* Iowa City: University of Iowa Press, 1976.

Yu, Kwang-chung, trans. *Acres of Barbed Wire: China in Daydreams and Nightmares* Taipei: Mei Ya, 1971.

———, ed. and trans. *New Chinese Poetry.* Taipei: Heritage, 1960.

Speaking in Tongues

Translating Chinese Literature in a Post-Babelian Age

EUGENE EOYANG

Glossolalia is the technical term designating a phenomenon, usually associated with religious ecstasy, where a communicant, in a state of divine possession, speaks languages with which he or she is not normally familiar. This form of oracular insight is characterized by three factors: (1) its extreme impenetrability for the listener, who is, presumably, not acquainted with the language being spoken; (2) the ignorance, at least on a conscious level, on the part of the speaker of what he or she is saying; and (3) a sense of the miraculous and divine, as if the individual were the mouthpiece for arcane truths which he is merely mouthing, but which are beyond his comprehension. The relevance of this phenomenon to Chinese literature is that some Western studies of Chinese texts strike me as perfect examples of scholarly glossolalia, or an academic "speaking in tongues." It is my purpose in this essay to observe this phenomenon, to examine specific examples, and to consider the reasons for the strange power scholarly glossolalia has over its adherents.

Before we proceed, we might examine what we mean by "Chinese literature." Traditionally, the phrase designates first of all the Four Books—the *Analects*, the *Great Learning*, the *Mencius*, and the *Doctrine of the Mean*. Then there are the so-called Five Classics: the *Book of Poetry*, the *Book of History*, the *Book of Changes*, the *Book of Rites*, and the *Spring and Autumn Annals*. Then there is the entire corpus of writings in the literary language in various genres, the *fu*, the *lü-shih*, the *yüeh-fu*. In modern times, all writings in the

vernacular—from the *zhiguai* tales to the *yen-yi* popularizations of history—
are included. Indeed, the richness in both variety and scope of Chinese
literature is scarcely matched. But despite the variety of levels of readership
—from the semiliterate to the highly literate—there is one claim we can
make about Chinese literature, indeed about any literature, without fear of
contradiction. These works were intended to be understood by the targeted
readership.

It is a basic premise in translation theory that the reader of a work in
translation should have the same access to the meaning in the translated
text as the reader of the original text in the original language. The difficulties in finding exact counterparts from different languages, particularly
languages which are not cognate, languages which represent cultures that
are not historically related, are what make effective translation such a challenge. To test this theory from a commonsensical point of view, let us posit a
nursery rhyme. However arcane that rhyme may be underneath the surface, its surface meaning should be readily understood. A translation of a
nursery rhyme should not sound like a scholarly disquisition, nor should it
appear erudite and forbidding. The difficulty in the process of translation is
not the same difficulty inherent in an original text. Something simple and
inevitable in one language may be difficult to capture in another language
with the same simplicity, yet there is no reason for that difficulty in the
process of translation to be reflected in the *text* of the translation. Art in
translation is that which hides art.

This point, obvious though it is, cannot be passed over, because there are
many who, speaking in tongues, present works of Chinese literature as if
they were elaborate puzzles to confound the ordinary reader, yielding their
secrets only to the scholarly initiates. If readers cannot understand what the
scholarly translator of Chinese literature is trying to convey, it must be
because they, the unintended readers, are dense: they don't, after all, know
Chinese. But what casts strong, dramatic shadows in the glare of only one
light source is far less imposing in the balanced light emanating from different directions: what may be impressive in a monolingual culture is rather
commonplace in a multilingual context. I should like to examine this phenomenon in a multilingual audience and in the light if not of a thousand
suns, then of more than one sun.

In an interesting article titled "Polylingualism as Reality and Translation
as Mimesis," Meir Sternberg posits a term, "translational mimesis," by
which he means the reenactment of the original literary work in another
language. Sternberg is speaking specifically about rendering the occurrence
of a foreign language when translating into another language. But his
discussion raises interesting issues about what is preserved in translation.
Sternberg, in considering the challenge of reproducing in one language the
polylinguality in another, suggests that "the interlingual tension between
language as represented object (within the original or reported speech-

event) and language as representational means (within the reporting speech-event) is primarily mimetic rather than communicative" (222). He posits three categories of "translational mimesis": "referential restriction," in which the objects described are normalized (or, as James J. Y. Liu would say, "naturalized") so that nothing is marked as foreign (Sternberg cites the works of Jane Austen); "vehicular matching," in which the very differences of language have a characterizational force, are, indeed, part of the mythos of the story (Sternberg cites Shaw's *Pygmalion* and Jean Renoir's movie *La Grande Illusion*): these works would be incomprehensible if the polylingual or polydialectical speech were normalized; and finally, "homogenized convention," in which foreign, even fantastic, creatures are assumed to speak the same language (no one finds it implausible, Sternberg points out, to see the White Rabbit speak English in *Alice in Wonderland*). This scheme is very fecund, because it provides a means by which rhetorical strategies can be more clearly examined.

The only—very slight—issue I would take with these categories is with their order. I would reverse "vehicular matching" and "homogenized convention"—arriving at a sequence of increasing factor of sophistication and cosmopolitanism. Referential restriction is provincial in that it limits the object in view to the unilingual; homogenized convention breaks that provinciality by considering so-called foreign objects, but renders those objects comprehensible in the provincial tongue; vehicular matching stretches the unilingual resources to include polylingual phenomena, in their polylingual character.

Let us examine each of these categories for the deconstructed perspective they offer. In the first case, there is an implicit *cultural* coercion. In order to appreciate Jane Austen, one must become, or imagine oneself as, English; to resist that ambivalently self-flatteringly and self-inflating experience would be to resist the charms of Jane Austen's wit and style. There is no reading Jane Austen without becoming English. Her genius was precisely to see the richness and the self-sufficiency of the provincial experience. For her, the life in her precincts was endlessly fascinating, and the earth-shaking events outside those precincts were matters of little or no import. (Which is why critics have remarked, with both admiration and dismay, that no one who reads Jane Austen's novels would have any inkling of the Napoleonic Wars, which were occurring at about the same time as the action in her novels.)

Homogenized convention extends imaginative empathy to include the feelings of other beings, other species. It posits the pathetically fallacious premise that all creation speaks the same language we do. Thus animals speak a language we can understand without effort. On American TV, even Nazis speak English routinely among themselves, and German appears a foreign language even to the Germans: what differentiates foreigner and native is an "accent." With homogenized convention, we encounter what might be called *linguistic* coercion: readers—even if they may be native in the language homogenized and conventionalized—must accept the privileged subjective voice of the prevailing linguistic convention. However, it posits a false universalism and overlooks the "prison-house" that each language represents. This notion homogenizes experience and erases all objective and subjective differences. It allows for no subjective stance from the perspective of the other.

A common symptom of this mind-set is the impatience one feels with someone who doesn't speak one's native language—an attitude more prevalent in dominant world cultures than among the dominated. A recent example of this are the questionnaires circulated in Florida and California about making English the official language: all the applications were in English, and no one thought about the inherent unfairness of such a poll. This conventionalizing of differences erases the multi-ethnic character of a civilization. A German reading an unflattering portrait of Germans in a French novel, or an American reading Akio Morita and Shintaro Ishihara's caustic critique of American society, *The Japan That Can Say No*, which was not intended to appear in English translation, or a Chinese-American being told in English that he doesn't have a Chinaman's chance, know something of the intense feeling of compromise and exclusion homogenized convention represents. Feminists objecting to thoughtless sexist language know something of the pitfalls and provincialities of homogenized convention.

A subtle and historic instance of "marking" in homogenized convention is offered by John F. Kennedy's "Ich bin ein Berliner" speech, universally hailed as a brilliant rhetorical gambit. The metaphor, which suggested that everyone in the world participated in the politically schizophrenic situation of Berliners, was at once ingratiating, tactful, and intensely moving. But Kennedy's locution, whether intentionally or unintentionally, was "self-marked," i.e., it manifested itself clearly as a foreigner speaking German. It wasn't grammar or accent that marked the sentence as being spoken by a foreigner, but usage. What Kennedy said was, literally, "I am a Berliner," but if one asks what Berliners would say to express the same thought, they would say, "Ich bin Berliner" or "Ich bin aus Berlin." For someone who lives in Berlin would be more than passingly familiar with a particular kind of pastry sold in Berlin—a sort of jelly donut—that is called, in the vernacular, "Berliner." A German who says "Ich bin ein Berliner" would be claiming, "I am a jelly donut." In Kennedy's case, no one thought it ridiculous because a foreigner would be assumed to be ignorant of what "ein Berliner" is idiomatically. In other words, one read Kennedy's German as a foreigner's German, or else what he said would have been ludicrous. Conversely, if Kennedy had tried to speak unmarked German, had he said, "Ich bin Berliner" or "Ich bin aus Berlin," his claim would have been manifestly false and presumptuous. "Ich bin ein Berliner" established just the right note of courteous metaphoricalness and avoided at the same time any hint of linguistic presumption.

Vehicular matching appears to be the most satisfactory exercise in translational mimesis: it extends the sensibility of the reader and reflects the true contrasts in the original between what is foreign and what is native in it. Yet, even here, there are pitfalls. Let us consider an instance in which, say, English is used in a Chinese fiction; let us further consider a translation of this fiction into English. The excerpt in English does not need translation, but unless it is editorially marked as foreign in a footnote, the reader will have no idea of the particular "framing" of this context in the original. The modishness of English when it is quoted in a non-English language, for example, the sense of modernity that the use of English evokes—all this is lost if the reader in translation fails to realize that the English in these expressions involves embedded exoticisms, not translated versions of native locutions. Such an instance could be mistaken for "homogenized convention" where everyone—even non-English-speaking characters—speaks English. But this example would actually be the obverse of "homogenized convention," because what is being presented is a "heterogenous unconventionality," someone who, exceptionally, uses a nonnative expression in the original. Lu Hsun's use of the Roman letter "Q" in "The True Story of Ah Q" is a case in point. Originally the phrase was a literary invention intended to pique the reader's curiosity. It is now, of course, so familiar, at least on the mainland, that it is no longer a novelty—either in Chinese or in English. Furthermore, this kind of locution may appear strange to some readers of Chinese unfamiliar with English: indeed, the author may have intended this to alienate the character from the reader. If one leaves the English untranslated, this novelistic effect is lost, even if the exact locution in the original is preserved. And, if one "translates" the already transparent English to another language "foreign" to the Chinese, then the particular characterization of an English-monger is contradicted.

Let us examine this gradient in provinciality: in the first case, there is an implicit assumption that only one language exists and that everyone speaks that language; in the second case, there is a recognition of difference, but that difference is erased by the assumption that despite those differences, everyone understands each other using the same language; in the third case, the differences are recognized for what they are and are preserved as such, either as extensions of the host language or as composites of more than one language. This last point reveals a flaw in Sternberg's categorical division between monolinguality and polylinguality. Individuals may be monolingual and polylingual. When someone says "laissez-faire," is that speaker automatically French? Hardly. American economists routinely say "laissez-faire," and—what is more remarkable—even pronounce the phrase correctly, but the language they speak cannot—on that account alone—be characterized as French. The emergence of Franglais, indeed of Americanisms in all the languages of the world, indicates that there is an incipient, developing polylingualism in every language. Philologists could easily demonstrate the polylingualism of every language, since each language develops out of other languages or blends in admixtures of other languages. English is one of the richest polylingual languages: consisting of Anglo-Saxon (itself a composite), Norman, Celtic, and Romance elements. The Elizabethan was a partially polyglot speaker of Latinisms, Italianisms, Anglo-Saxon, French, and Celt.

It is this polylinguality within monolingualism, as well as the multilinguality and bilinguality of a significant portion of the world's population, that is invoked by the phrase "post-Babelian" in the subtitle of this essay. I define pre-Babelian as a world where everyone speaks one language; a Babelian world is one in which there are different languages mutually incomprehensible; and a post-Babelian world is a world where there are different languages but there are people who speak more than one language. Put simply, the pre-Babelian world is one with a universal language; a Babelian world is a world of many languages, with everyone monolingual; a post-Babelian world consists of many languages, but it also includes polylingual speakers.

There is a hegemonic monolingual myth that has prevailed, which suggests that knowing only one language is the preponderant norm in human civilization and that knowing more than one language is the rare exception. Of course, this monolingual myth has been perpetrated through no arbitrary provinciality but through each language, which naturally tends to restrict or privilege the discourse in its own precincts. Also, it will not be surprising that discourse in a language will reinforce the perception of reality in that language and will downgrade if not neglect altogether the existence of other languages: by considering itself the language of the self and all other languages as "foreign," the language of the other, each language conveys the myth of universal monolingualism. But recent studies have indicated that the monolingual speaker of language may not have dominated human civilization as much as we may have imagined.

Nor has the bilingual and multilingual speaker been quite as exceptional as we might think. In Old Egypt, Milan Dimic reminds us, "the people of that country were divided into seven classes, one of which consisted of interpreters" (15). "The Mesopotamian civilization gave rise," Dimic writes (citing S. Kovganjuk [53f], M. Lambert [17–20], and H. Pohling [126]), "to the Assyrian and Babylonian multinational states. In the third millenium B.C. Sargon of Assyria proclaimed his victories in the many languages of his realm. Ancient Greek evolved from other languages in Asia Minor; even when its culture dominated, it fostered bilingualism.... Wherever they settled, the Greeks and the Romans instituted private elementary schools and educated a bilingual or trilingual elite which held the new commonwealth together. The conqueror and the conquered had to know each other's language" (15). Indeed, all conquest through the ages involved an encounter with bilingualism and multilingualism. All educated Romans

were conversant with Latin and Greek. The spread of Christianity also promoted bilingualism, as did the spread of Islam. Bilingualism may be more
the rule than the exception. "The famous Rosetta-stone from the second
century B.C.," Dimic points out, "is in Greek as well as hieroglyphic and
demotic Egyptian." Chinese, despite its apparent monolithic character in
the West, is a polylingual and multicultural language, involving elements of
Mongol, Turk, Tungus, Thai, and Tibeto-Burman. There are manuscripts
in Tun-huang, dating from the fifth to the eleventh century, with texts that
contain Chinese and Tibetan in interlinear configuration; there are also
texts in Sogdian, Uighur, and other Central Asian languages.

The myth of Babel described an era when all the world's people spoke the
same language, an era which ended when God punished them for over-
reaching and "confounded" their language so that the tongues they spoke
were mutually incomprehensible. The Babelian era is one that divides the
languages of the world into one that is "native" and the rest "foreign." We
have tacitly and implicitly assumed that we live in this Babelian era. But in
fact, the realities are less definitive. Leaving aside the question of relative
degrees of mutual comprehensibilities—surely cognate languages are less
opaque to each other than languages that are not historically related—the
numbers of bilingual and multilingual speakers in history have already
established a "post-Babelian" world.

W. Mackey estimates that 70 percent of the world's population is now
bilingual. In Singapore, many of the inhabitants are descended from the
Chinese and are brought up speaking Chinese, yet the "national" language
is English, the language of instruction in school. For many Singaporeans,
Chinese is "native" but English is their language of public discourse. The
multilingual societies of Switzerland, Yugoslavia, India, Brazil, the Nether-
lands, and the nations of the former Soviet Union are but the most obvious
examples of societies where knowing more than one language is not exceptional. One must add to these instances the worldwide emphasis on instruction in English: I once calculated the number of high school students in the
Far East, where instruction in English is compulsory for all students, and
arrived at a figure in excess of 50 million. The total number of high school
students in the United States does not exceed 25 million. Hence, for every
student in an American high school, there are two East Asians studying
English. The world is not predominantly or uniformly monolingual, yet
most of what is published reinforces a monolingual bias. As a result of the
nationalism of the nineteenth century and the vestigial language chauvinism of the twentieth century (I refer to the attacks against Franglais in
France and those in favor of English only in the United States), patriotism
and monolinguality are viewed as inseparable. In only one language that I
know of is the "foreign" incorporated generically and institutionally in the
"native" language—and that language is Japanese. Can this feature of ac-
commodating the foreign within the native linguistic medium be part of the

reason for Japan's spectacular success in adapting not only to the modern world but also to a multilingual marketplace?

It is in this multilingual and polylingual context, this post-Babelian perspective, in which I would like to consider some pertinent questions of translation.

Sternberg's analysis of the various modes of imitating polylingualism in translation offers a fascinating exercise in perspectivist criticism. By examining the different modes of portraying difference—by erasing it, by marking it, and by enacting it—he focuses our attention on the different strategies available to incorporate the strange into the familiar. His scheme can be seen as a paradigm of the process of understanding: how we progress from learning about the familiar by finding "equivalents" in the familiar; then, realizing that the new object had no real "equivalents" precisely because it is really new "to our ken," we mark its equivalence as "approximate"; until finally, realizing that the similarities between the new object and its approximate familiar equivalents are not as salient as their differences, we incorporate the new object in our native discourse and thereby extend our own language.

These fruitful discriminations are helpful in addressing one of the primary problems of translating from the Chinese. Let us take the word *tao* 道.

Translated variously as "the way," "the Way," and "the Tao," this word can be taken to represent succinctly Sternberg's three approaches to "translational mimesis": to translate 道 as "the way" is an attempt at "referential restriction": the word is treated as if it were exactly equivalent to an ordinary English word—no experience outside the semantic precincts of the host language is admitted; to translate is as "the Way" is an attempt at "homogenized convention": the sense is made accessible, but capitalizing the "w" marks the strangeness of the concept as special; and to translate it as "the Tao" is an attempt at "vehicular matching": the sense is opaque to the uninitiated: the reader is forced to grasp the concept with provisional recognition—true understanding comes only when the reader has encountered the original in its context or, more intuitively, has encountered the same vehicular matching in various contexts of meaning.

But Sternberg's scheme, while useful, fails to explain further anomalies which must be addressed with each of the three categories. In the first case, with the "referential restriction" of "the way" as translational mimesis, one captures the ordinariness of the expression, even if one misses the special philosophical significance of *tao* in Chinese. To the extent that the special meaning of *tao* is missed, referential restriction is clearly inadequate. Yet, in conveying the ordinariness of *tao* in Chinese, referential restriction in this case is *more* adequate than either of the other "more sophisticated" approaches. If anything, translating 道 as "the way" is not ordinary enough: it does not reflect the innumerable semantic and grammatical contexts in which 道 can be used, as in *chih-tao* 知道 "to know"; *tao-ti* 道地 "real,

authentic"; *tao-li* 道理 "reason" or "the right way"; or *shuo-san-tao-ssu* 說三
道四 "to make thoughtless comments."

Philologists, in their categorical way, point out these different uses of *tao*
and imply that they are separate and unrelated senses of the word. Dictionaries have this propensity of offering different meanings, from which the
language user is to select the most appropriate. Yet this digital and analytical approach is precisely what is wrong with dictionary translations: it em-
bodies a fundamental misconception about language. When a word has
many different meanings and different uses, it can often suggest—and not
only in the paranomasic compositions of poets—different meanings *at the
same time*. Indeed, in the case of *tao*, the authority and profundity of the
word inheres precisely in its seeming versatility in different contexts: in that
sense *tao* does not define anything, it does not indicate anything, it is not the
signifier to an elusive signified. It is, in fact, emblematic of what it means:
the word can suggest speech, as in *shuo-san-tao-ssu*; it can suggest a pattern
or principle, as in *tao-li*; it can suggest reality, as in *tao-ti*; or it can suggest
the object of comprehension, as in *chih-tao*. The point is that each meaning is
inherent in *tao*.

The word "way" in English does not occur in compounds involving
speech, nor in phrases that involve principle, nor in construction that suggest reality. It is not a word that resonates with all the other senses, the way
tao does. One doesn't disambiguate the meaning of *tao* when one uses it, in
the way that other words may be disambiguated—either phonetically or
orthographically. For example, we disambiguate graphonyms like "c-o-n-s-
u-m-m-a-t-e" phonetically: an accent on the second syllable denotes the
adjective "consúmmate," whereas an accent on the first syllable denotes the
verb "cónsummate"; we disambiguate homonyms like "stationary," meaning "to be at rest," from "stationery," meaning "writing paper," by writing
one with an "a" and the other with an "e." "Bow," meaning "to bend
forward," is differentiated phonetically from "bow" as in "bow and arrow"
or "violin bow"; whereas "bow," meaning to bend forward, is differentiated
from "bough," meaning "a branch on a tree," by its spelling.

Indo-European languages often enhance the process of semantic dis-
ambiguation—where the context of meaning determines which of two or
more viable alternatives apply—by phonetic or orthographic means. Spoken Chinese, with its wealth of homonyms, relies heavily on context to disambiguate words of similar sounds. Written Chinese has words that require
different phonemes to reflect different semantemes, as in *háo* 好 "good" and
hào 好 "to like" and *chung* 中 "center" and *chùng* 中 "to hit the target."

But the different uses of *tao* are differentiated neither orthographically
nor phonetically. Like the English word "run"—for which I count eighty
entries in the *Oxford Universal Dictionary*—the semantic versatility of *tao* presents an interesting linguistic challenge. If a word has so many meanings,
how can it be accurately or meaningfully used in each? One might also

suggest that such words—which we might dub "maximally meaningful key words"—reflect the cultural emphasis of the language. The root etymon is so rich that the word becomes almost infinitely replicable in different semantic contexts without dysfunctional unclarity. Is there any significance to the fact that in traditional Chinese such a "maximally meaningful key word" is *tao* and that in American English the "maximally meaningful key word" is "run"?

Let us now consider the translation of some key terms in Chinese. One of the most astute philologists, with considerable influence in sinological circles, was Peter Boodberg. His discriminations of meaning, flowing out of a vast erudition that included not only the major East Asian languages but most of the European tongues as well, are lasting contributions to learning. His exegesis of the term *jen*, translated as "benevolence," "human-heartedness," "goodness," etc., is worth close attention. These translations are not the equivalent of *jen* but the fruits of a sense of *jen*. If one has *jen*, one will show benevolence, human-heartedness, goodness, etc. To translate the word in this way is virtually to equate cause with effect. Boodberg writes: "It is my belief that the primary etymology of *jen*, 'humanity,' cannot be successfully conveyed in English, short of creating a neologism, on the prototype of the German Menschlichkeit, such as 'manship,' 'manshipful,' and 'manshipfulness'" (37). He also suggests a "Latin synonym of 'manship'," using a derivative of the plural *homines* rather than the singular *homo*, and comes up with "homininity."

Boodberg has also coined a few neologisms which have proliferated like viruses in certain translations of Chinese literature. Chief among them is the word "Thearch" for Chinese *ti* 帝, usually rendered "emperor." Less well known is his offering of "basilearch" for Chinese *wang*, conventionally rendered as "king." In discussing these terms, Boodberg resorts to his knowledge of ancient languages, as in the following excerpt from his "Cedules from a Berkeley Workshop in Asiatic Philology" (217).

WANG 王 "king," "prince," "emperor" (of the Chou dynasty) may best be metonymized as BASILEARCH. The etymology of WANG, like that of Greek *basileus*, is unknown; it seems, however, to be a Sinitic word, but the native scholiasts can suggest nothing better than association with the homonym WANG, "to go," and the far-fetched school-etymology "king" = "one to whom the people go." Through a curious coincidence, this parallels the attempts of the Greek grammarians to decode *basileus* as some coadunation of *baino*, "to go," and *laos*, "people." HUANG 皇 "emperor," "august," is, on one hand, a cognate of WANG; on the other, an affine of KUANG 光, "bright glow," "glory". The upper part of the graph, now written with the element "white" 白, the *Shuo Wen* interprets as being "original" 自, while the protograph is suggestive of the representation of a corona (of the sun), an aureole, perhaps an anthelion. Since HUANG was traditionally applied to the divine WANG of the highest antiquity, ARCHIBASILEARCH, ARCHIBASILIC (adj.) may prove to be hermeneutically acceptable, with ARGI- (<*argos*, "shining bright") as a paragram for the first element. For TI 帝 "god," "emperor," the logical option is THEARCH or DIARCH (<*dios*, "divine"); for HUANG TI, ARGIBASILIC DIARCH.

I have quoted this dense exegesis at some length, not only because of what it says but also because of how Boodberg says it. It represents a variation of the "vehicular matching" that we encountered in Sternberg's scheme. We may note in passing that aside from the Greek in the exegesis, there are a number of infrequently encountered English words whose meaning can be fairly well adduced from the context but are disconcerting nonetheless: "coadunation," "affines," "protograph," "anthelion," "paragram." "Anthelion" and "affines" are listed in some dictionaries, although in some cases only the adjectival sense of "affines," with reference to finite values in mathematics, is cited. The others are not to be found. One might well ask why an exegesis of words requires its own exegesis.

As for the reliance on Greek, it is true that Boodberg came from a generation in which the educated were more likely to know Greek than not, but even so, why should it be reasonable to require of a reader who doesn't know Chinese that he know another foreign language—especially a language as hoary as ancient Greek—in order to understand the true meaning of Chinese?

There are other epistemological concerns. Given the democratic traditions of ancient Greek culture, is it reasonable to equate the autocrats of the Periclean Age to the specifically Oriental despots of ancient China? To render the *huang-ti* of ancient China as counterparts, if not equivalents, of the monarchs of ancient Greece is to convey certain overtones of reason and of the polis that may have existed in Greece but did not exist in China in the same way. And what about the principle of familiarity: should the reader of a translation not be as familiar with a term in translation as the reader of the original with its counterpart in the original?

Boodberg takes the notion of "vehicular matching" even further than Sternberg develops it. He is addressing an audience at least as polylingual as he is; but he is more polylingual than the normal speaker of the English language, if the locutions which he uses in his own prose are any indication. Indeed, in his era, Boodberg expected his students to be post-Babelian: only the most gifted attempted the study of the difficult non-Western languages —Arabic, Chinese, and Japanese—and only after mastering the most formidable Western languages—Latin and Greek. The study of Chinese was therefore the enterprise of *la crème de la crème*, which by definition would be a very small elite. The consequences of this approach, natural as it was for Boodberg and for sinologists of his generation, makes no sense today, when the study of Chinese is no longer restricted to the classical philologist.

The school of sinology to which I refer has produced considerable contributions to knowledge. I need only cite David Knechtges's work on the *Wen hsüan* and Edward Schafer's many volumes on T'ang poetic imagery. But in its idiosyncrasies and its ideological impatience with translations that depart from their defense of "exact" renderings, there is a specious logic as well as a crucial misunderstanding of language. Philology is not an exact science, but even if it were, even if it were mathematics, the insistence on an absolute accuracy is chimerical. It is not irrational to "approximate" when translating, nor is approximation irrational; indeed, as the English mathematician G. H. Hardy reminds us in his *Mathematician's Apology*, "all approximation is rational" (102). He also provides some uncommonly valuable advice when he tells us that "sometimes one has to say difficult things, but one ought to say them as simply as one knows how" (47). Frankly, some exegeses of difficult points in Chinese literature are simply not said "as simply as one knows how."

Some schools of sinology remind me of the schools of divines which Thomas Hobbes took to task at the end of his *Leviathan*:

> the writings of School divines, are nothing else for the most part, but insignificant trains of strange and barbarous words, or words otherwise used, than in the common use of the Latin tongue, such as would pose Cicero, and Varro, and all the grammarians of ancient Rome. Which if any man would see proved, let him ... see whether he can translate any School divine into any of the modern tongues, as French, English or any other copious language: for that which cannot in most of these be made intelligible, is not intelligible in the Latin. Which insignificancy of language, though I cannot note it for false philosophy; yet it hath a quality, not only to hide the truth, but also to make men think they have it, and desist from further search. (449)

A heuristic principle of epistemology is implicit in this attack. Hobbes is suggesting that one's ability to make clear a difficult or elusive point reflects the degree to which one understands the point. The test of "translatability" into "intelligible Latin"—we have already encountered snippets of unintelligible Greek—is an x-ray that sees through the obfuscations of pseudo understanding. Yet there are those who have insisted that unless one subscribes to a certain school of sinology, one can't understand Chinese—and that includes those who are native Chinese! The perniciousness of this ideological stance is that it exalts academic politics at the expense of free intellectual inquiry. It substitutes method for matter and takes dogma for truth. What is perhaps most mystifying is that it substitutes one unknown for another unknown. Anyone who has experienced the difficulty of comprehending an exegesis intended to elucidate a difficult passage will recognize immediately what I am referring to. The trouble is that, faced with the impenetrability of the original passage, the naïve student takes the impenetrability of factitious scholarship to be the warrant of insight. So, where one began being baffled by one text, now one is baffled by two texts. The problem is that many delude themselves into thinking that they now understand the original just because they have read what purports to be an exegesis. It is time to announce to the world that the emperor has no clothes, that if, on occasion, a reader doesn't understand something, the inadequacy of the exegete rather than the limitations of the reader may be at fault.

How many students of Chinese, encountering "Basilearch" for *wang*, will think that they have the truth and desist from further search? How many Western scholars of Chinese, too often failing to speak in Chinese, speak in tongues?

WORKS CITED

Boodberg, Peter. *Selected Works of Peter Boodberg*, ed. Alvin P. Cohen. Berkeley: University of California Press, 1979.

Dimic, Milan. "Translation and Interpretation in Bicultural and Multicultural Societies." In *Translation and Interpretation: The Multi-Cultural Context*, 13–34. Vancouver: CAUTG, 1975.

Hardy, G. H. *A Mathematician's Apology*. Cambridge: Cambridge University Press, 1967.

Hobbes, Thomas. *Leviathan*, ed. Michael Oakeshott. Oxford: Basil Blackwell, 1960.

Kovganjuk, S. *Praktika perekladu*. Kiev, 1968.

Lambert, M. "La Traduction il y a 4000 ans." *Babel* 10 (1964): 17–20.

Pohling, H. "Zur Geschichte der Übersetzung." *Studien zur Übersetzungswissenschaft*, Beiheft zur Zeitschrift Fremdsprachen 3/4. Leipzig, 1971.

Sternberg, Meir. "Polylingualism and Translation as Mimesis." *Poetics Today* 24 (1981): 221–239.

Translation and Individual Talent

CHING-HSI PENG

I have lamented the misfortune of literary translations—that all of them are fated to be ephemeral; none can lay claim to immortality (see Peng, "Permanency in Change," listed in works cited, at the end of this chapter). With that realization, I turn to a related question: who makes an ideal translator? If translators are unavoidably limited by their own horizons, perhaps an ideal translator is the one least shackled temporally. Paradoxically, as Kenneth Rexroth points out in "The Poet as Translator," "All the great translations survive into our time because they were so completely *of their own time*" (22). I emphasize the last four words because to my mind therein lies the clue. Translators (or poets, for that matter) who belong to their own time can ill afford to overemphasize themselves. In what follows, I will examine two kinds of translators: poets who speak for themselves and scholars who sometimes dig into the original only to find—and eventually go on to represent—themselves. Translation is served by neither kind.[1]

An oft-quoted adage about the translation of poetry is that it lies in the domain of poets. D. S. Carne-Ross, for instance, declares in "Translation and Transposition" that

> only a poet—a poet, possibly, in some way *manqué*, but still a poet—can translate poetry. *The Oxford Book of Greek Verse in Translation* is there as horrid evidence of what happens when people whose only claim is that they can read Greek, try to write English. (15)

Carne-Ross, of course, is not the first advocate for the poet-translator, nor is he likely to be the last; his view is echoed, for instance, by Charles

Tomlinson, editor of *The Oxford Book of Verse in English Translation* and an acclaimed poet himself, who begins his introduction, "The Poet Translator," by claiming: "'With Poesie to open Poesie'—thus George Chapman on his aim as a translator of Homer. All good translators of verse seem to have worked in this spirit" (vii). But in Carne-Ross's argument we detect an amusing qualification—a caveat, almost—that the ideal translator is a "poet *manqué*," though he hastens to insist that the translator must "still [be] a poet." The concession seems to me especially instructive and the idea potentially useful because of its subtle implication for the delicate relationship between the translator and the original poet. It contains a warning that the former must not outshine the latter—not in the act of translating, anyway. Such a self-delimiting awareness, I submit, is necessary in order for the translator to strike a desirable balance between his work and the work of another poet.

After all, the translation of a piece of literature does not require any particularly superior talent. Granted, translators must be equipped with an enlightened mind, without which they cannot appreciate the "content" expressed by the poet. They must also be equipped with a sharp eye, without which they cannot see through the form or construct in which the original is realized. Both the enlightened mind and the sharp eye are products of literary training, things that may be cultivated. With these abilities, translators can then set out to represent an original poem in another language. And in performing this job, their attitude must be one of total submission to the original. They are *manqué* in the sense that, in this case, they find their poem *already written*, by another poet in another place, perhaps also in another time: in a very real sense, they are defeated even before the battle is joined, and I can think of nothing more frustrating for a poet than being thus preempted. Fortunately, all is not lost. Finding one's vision realized, even in someone else's work, must in itself be an exhilarating experience; besides, translators still have their chance—in the act of translating. And in this attempt they remain in essence poets, in the sense that they have the tools, the wherewithal, to turn that poem into their own language and form: "with Poesie to open Poesie."

This, I suppose, comes close to and is reconcilable with what Tomlinson calls "the safest minimum prescription"—"that the translator of poetry must be a poet *so long as he is engaged in that act and art*" (xi; emphasis mine). This is where the risk lies, however: translators who are also poets pose a real threat to the work at hand. If they are possessed of an overabundance of talent, they are likely to compete with the poet being translated; such translators often overshadow the original poet.

The case of Edward FitzGerald (1809–1883) readily comes to mind. This English poet's celebrated rendition of the *Rubaiyat* by the Persian poet Omar Khayyam has been enshrined in English literature. Persian being Greek to me, I am in no position to pass judgment on this much-beloved work as translation. The editors of *The Norton Anthology of English Literature* deftly sidestepped the question by commenting as follows:

> The Italians have a witty saying that translations are like spouses: a beautiful translation is apt to be unfaithful, and a faithful translation is apt to be ugly. Experts have argued at great length whether FitzGerald's adaptation of Omar's poem is a faithful translation, but no one argues its beauty. (Abrams, 1216)

In adapting Omar Khayyam, FitzGerald, as he himself was the first to admit, often "mashed together" the quatrains (see Terhune and Terhune, vol. 2, 318); he also provided the poem with a one-day frame, thus giving it a coherence that is absent in the original.[2] Most specialists have largely exonerated FitzGerald from the charge of willfully interpolating Omar Khayyam's text. As L. P. Elwell-Sutton tells us, "the degree of FitzGerald's faithfulness to his source was finally established" by Edward Heron-Allen in 1899 in his *Edward FitzGerald's Ruba'iyat of Omar Khayyam* (London):

> In a detailed analysis of FitzGerald's poem he [Heron-Allen] listed against each stanza the original Persian quatrains that he thought must have inspired the paraphraser, and came to the conclusion that, while virtually no stanza of FitzGerald's was an exact translation of a Khayyamic quatrain, nevertheless 97 out of the total 101 could be traced back to one, or combinations of more than one, of Khayyam's originals, and that only 4 owed their origins to two other Persian poets, Attar and Hafez. (Elwell-Sutton, 21)[3]

Writing in 1975, the Persian scholar Parichehr Kasra, while taking notice of the stylistic difference between Khayyam and FitzGerald, concedes that "[i]n spite of this, and though his is not a literal translation, FitzGerald's work shows how thoroughly he captured the spirit of Umar Khayyam" (lxxiii). And yet he goes on to present his own prose version of the poem. "Is [FitzGerald] a translation of Omar?" Rexroth once asked, adding: "Here the two cultures are so radically different, all that can be said is that he is probably all of medieval Persia that Victorian England was prepared to assimilate" (22).

One is reminded again of the relationship between translation and its time. In fact, the inclusion of *the Rubaiyat* in most standard anthologies of English literature argues convincingly that FitzGerald Anglicized the Persian masterpiece, so much so that the anthologizers see fit to treat his work not as a piece of translation but as authentic and even indigenous English verse.[4]

What a coincidence, then, that a century later, a Chinese poet should render this "same" Persian masterpiece from FitzGerald's English version into Chinese in much the same manner that the latter treated his original.[5] Huang K'e-sun's 黃克孫 *Lu-pai chi* 魯拜集, which he calls a kind of *yen-yi*

衍譯, or "derivative translation," has captured the fancy of some Chinese literati.

Among the favorably impressed is Fang Yü 方瑜, who observes:

> Poets of great passion and keen sensitivity—how close to each other their minds are! Though separated by light years of time and space, they match to a hair. (110; translation mine)

Sung Mei-hua 宋美璍 also marvels at the high degree of consanguinity between Huang and FitzGerald, noting in particular the facility and grace with which Huang substitutes Chinese classical for English allusions to give his translation a wonderful, unprecedented rapport or kinship with FitzGerald's. She concludes that "from Khayyam through FitzGerald to Huang—here is an example of literary reincarnation; the spirit remains the same, although the body has changed" (244; translation mine).

Both critics have explained, convincingly, the reason why Huang's "derivative translation" should be cherished. For our purposes here, however, *Lu-pai chi* still raises two important issues: first, whether it can be regarded as translation in the ordinary sense of the word; second, whether its choice of the Classical Chinese and a traditional poetic form as its medium is justified.

With respect to the first issue, here is a case, I think, similar to FitzGerald's *Rubaiyat*. *Lu-pai chi* may be better regarded as Chinese literature than as translation, for in it we see conventional sentiment and conventional images of conventional Chinese quatrains. Take, for example, number 70:[6]

> The ball no question makes of Ayes and Noes,
> But Here or There as strikes the Player goes;
> And He that toss'd you down into the Field,
> He knows about it all—He knows—HE KNOWS!

It is translated:

> 眼看乾坤一局棋，
> 滿枰黑白子離離。
> 鏗然一子成何劫，
> 惟有蒼蒼妙手知。

Fang uses this poem to demonstrate Omar Khayyam's "profound understanding of man's insignificance, ignorance, and impotence." "We do not play chess," she says, "but are merely the black and white pawns" (110). The profundity of this verse is then compared to that expressed in two lines by Tu Fu 杜甫 (712–770):

眼枯即見骨
天地終無情

(Your eyes dry up, your bones bare.
Heaven and Earth—what do they care?)

Huang's Chinese quatrain reads extremely well, and his metaphor of a chess game can indeed strike a sympathetic chord in the cultivated Chinese reader. But what about "the Victorian England" that Rexroth mentioned? The ball and the field and the ball player—do they not tell us something about the English and even, indeed, the Persian?[7] Furthermore, one wonders if the metaphor of a chess game is *all* that the Chinese in the late twentieth century can accept.

Similarly, number 96,

> Yet Ah, that Spring should vanish with the Rose!
> That Youth's sweet-scented Manuscript should close!
> That Nightingale that in the Branches sang,
> Ah, whence, and whither flown again, who knows!

is translated as

墓裏古人渾不語，
楊花榭後飄香絮。
子規啼盡一春心，
飛到天涯何處去。

Kasra's literal rendition of this stanza in prose is:

Alas that the letter of youth is folded and that fresh spring of life is turned to winter. That bird of joy whose name was youth—woe, I know not when it came, nor when it went. (63)

In comparison, FitzGerald, apparently attempting to make the stanza more specific, has abused his license as translator by giving a name to that "bird of joy" and identifying "that fresh spring of life" with a particular flower; for "the letter of youth" he has substituted the "sweet-scented Manuscript." The focus of the lament is also shifted from time ("when") to place ("whence" and "whither").

Considered as a translation of FitzGerald, the transformation of rose and nightingale into poplar blossom and cuckoo seems to me unwarranted. The image of the tomb, which occupies the initial position of line one in the Chinese version, is too direct, too blunt. Last but by no means least, while Huang's last line is concerned with "whither" man will go, FitzGerald wonders about the "whence" as well, thus more fully illustrating the bewilderment of the human being unable to resolve that greatest of all riddles—the ultimate meaning of existence.[8]

In short, however elegant and smooth these seven-syllabic quatrains may sound to the trained Chinese ear—and for that reason they may well be thoroughly enjoyable—in them there is little FitzGerald and perforce even less Omar.

While the examples show Huang as an even more liberal translator than FitzGerald, the two differ from each other on yet another significant point: the choice of both form and language. My great admiration for Huang's genius notwithstanding, as a common reader I cannot but feel disappointed that he adopted Classical Chinese, which is no longer current, and couched it in an esoteric, traditional poetic form.

Now it may be argued that if the original poem (in this case, FitzGerald's) is written in a traditional form (in this case, quatrains of iambic pentameter), it is only proper and even desirable for the translator to resort to a similarly traditional poetic form in his translation. To this argument we may counter: what diction and what form should—and would—be used by a modern translator of such Chinese classics as *Shih ching* 詩經 and *Ch'u tz'u* 楚辭? The purpose of the effort being to introduce a foreign work to contemporary readers, the translator, to be successful, must speak "with the veridical force of his own utterance, conscious of communicating directly to his own audience" (Rexroth, 22), as in fact FitzGerald tried to do in his adaptation. Other great translators of this century, such as Ezra Pound, have done the same. Huang's derivative translation may eventually occupy a niche in Chinese literature, as FitzGerald's does in English literature; however, we have no use for something that has to be retranslated—in this regard, FitzGerald acquits himself well. Huang K'e-sun's literary talent as demonstrated in the rendition of *Lu-pai chi* deserves praise, but at a time when many educated Chinese have to resort to translation in modern vernacular to get a taste of their classical poetry, surely the proper medium of "communicating directly to the audience" is the current vernacular.

In contrast to a poet who in his translation obscures or overshadows the original writer with too much of his talent, a scholar steeped in learning may be trapped in a different way, running the risk of marring the translation by displaying too much erudition. Kurt W. Radtke, in *Poetry of the Yuan Dynasty*, is illustrative of the point.[9]

Although Radtke's book is a "study" of the *xiaoling* 小令 poems of the Yuan dynasty, he has along the way translated more than fifty poems, representing, he modestly puts it, "only a little more than one-tenth of the total contained in the *Yangchun baixue*" (7). But this is already a formidable task, and on the whole the translation has been done with care. For instance,

遊魚翻凍影
啼鳥犯春聲

is translated as

> scudding fish *tilt* frozen shadows,
> crying birds *lilt* spring tunes. (167; emphasis mine)

Thus it calls attention to the acoustic similarity between 翻 and 犯 in the original. The commentary accompanying each translation is by and large sound and useful, its strength lying particularly in the detection and elucidation of allusions.

Erudition, however, may mislead, sometimes resulting in quite serious mistakes in translation and interpretation. On page 40, for example, we have a song by Pai Jenfu 白仁甫:

> 1. 參差竹笋抽簪
> 2. 褭垂楊柳攢金
> 3. 旋趁庭槐綠陰
> 4. 南風解慍
> 5. 快哉消我煩襟

It is translated:

> 1. Irregular bamboo shoots: I take off my hairpin.
> 2. Drooping willows: clad in gold.
> 3. I enjoy the *Huai* tree's shade.
> 4. The south wind soothes my wrath.
> 5. How pleasant! It dissipates my grief.

In connection with this short piece, Radtke observes:

> The first line refers to the removal of an [official's] hat that is kept in position by the hairpin. Lines five and six [*sic*] contain allusions that would readily be recognised by an educated scholar as references to the Classic of Poetry, the *Shijing*, and the "Ode on the Wind," the *fengfu* written by Song Yü. One line in particular in the *Shijing* refers to the south wind that "alleviates the depressing situation of the common people," whereas the expression "how pleasant" *kuaizai* is a reference to a line in Song Yü's "Ode on the Wind," which says: "how pleasant, this wind." The allusion in the last line directs the reader's attention again to the importance of the true meaning of the "south wind," which should not be taken merely in the literal sense. One may reasonably expect that "the depressing situation of the common people" refers to the Chinese population, whereas the "pleasant south wind" contrasts by implication with the ruling northern condition—which in this case refers to the Mongol rulers. (40–41)

While the term *chouzan* in line one *may* be taken to mean "taking off the hairpin," and hence "going into retirement," it does not demand such an interpretation. As a matter of fact, this is definitely *not* its meaning here; it is the verb of a sentence whose subject is the 'irregular bamboo shoots": the addition of the personal pronoun "I" in the translation is entirely unwarranted. Lines one and two, in the original, parallel each other strictly, and should perhaps be translated accordingly, into something like this:

> The irregular bamboo shoots are sprouting,
> The drooping willows, clad in gold.

And once the political implication is—as in this case it should be—removed from the translation, the first line becomes lucid, and the winsome piece may be understood and enjoyed for what it is: a simple song in praise of the cooling wind and the sheltering shade. The fantastic theory about the Mongols versus the Chinese stems from the misreading of a single phrase—with plenty of help from erudition. Too much learning, too, can be a dangerous thing.

In 1961, Jean Paris observed in "Translation and Creation" that "until now, translation has fluctuated between two limits, which are also its negation: extreme freedom and extreme slavery" (60). Thirty years later, the question of how much liberty should be allowed in translation still baffles us. In setting up a poet-translator and a scholar-translator as primary examples for discussion, I have no intention to revive the perennial but, unfortunately, often misleading and fruitless debate on the relative "qualifications" of poet versus scholar as translator. Contrary to popular belief, such a distinction may be more apparent than real. The poet and the scholar whom we just scrutinized typify, in different ways, the same extreme: both allow themselves to eclipse the original author, one through excessive poetic energy, the other through excessive learning. Ideal translators are those who know how to curtail their freedom; they use moderation when applying their individual talents.

NOTES

1. A rough draft of this paper, although not meant for publication, appeared, without the consent of this writer, under the title "In Search of an Ideal Translator" in the Autumn 1990 issue of *The Chinese Pen*. It has since gone through substantial revision and augmentation.

2. In a letter dated September 3, 1958, to Edward Byles Cowell, who had taught him Persian and introduced him to Omar Khayyam, FitzGerald had this to say:

> My translation will interest you from its *Form*, and also in many respects in its *Detail*: very unliteral as it is. Many Quatrains are mashed together: and something lost, I doubt, of Omar's Simplicity, which is so much a Virtue in him. But there it is, such as it is.... (Terhune and Terhune, vol. 2, 318)

3. From what little I have read, Elwell-Sutton's view is shared by most experts in the field; see, for instance, Terhune, 221, and Arberry, *Romance*, 7. The only dissension comes from Graves and Ali-Shah, who in the prefatory essays in their translation (1967) have extremely harsh words for FitzGerald, calling his work a "famous mistranslation" (Ali-Shah, 35). But the work of these two severe critics has itself been discredited; see Kasra, lxvii, and Elwell-Sutton, 22.

4. FitzGerald's poem has been represented in apparently mutually exclusive anthologies: Charles Tomlinson's *Oxford Book of Verse in English Translation* (1980) contains sixteen stanzas from it and Helen Gardner's *New Oxford Book of English Verse, 1250–1950* (1972) contains thirteen stanzas.

5. This section on Huang K'e-sun's translation of the *Rubaiyat* contains a number of ideas presented in an earlier and much shorter critique of mine, written in Chinese (see Peng, "Yi-shih sui-hsiang").

6. Huang's translation is based on the fourth edition of FitzGerald's *The Rubáiyát* (1879), which contains 101 stanzas.

7. It appears that FitzGerald's translation of this stanza is rather close to the original. The following is a literal translation according to A. J. Arberry:

Whirling like a ball before the mallet of Fate, go running to right and left, and say nothing; for he that hurled thee into the chase, He knows, and He knows, and He knows! (*Rubā'iyāt*, 22)

8. Indeed, "Where We Have Come, and Whither Do We Go?" is such an important theme in the *Rubaiyat* that Dashti makes it the title of a chapter in his book (209–213).

9. My observations on Radtke's translation are taken largely from my review of his book (see Peng, "Review"). To facilitate the discussion, I follow Radtke in adopting the pinyin system of Romanization.

WORKS CITED

Abrams, M. H., general ed. *The Norton Anthology of English Literature*. 5th ed. Vol. 2. New York: Norton, 1986.

Ali-Shah, Omar. "Historical Preface." In Graves and Ali-Shah, 32–46.

Arberry, A. J. *Rubā'iyāt of Omar Khayyām*. London: Emery Walker, 1949.

———. *The Romance of the Rubáiyát, Edward FitzGerald's First Edition Reprinted with Introduction and Notes*. London: George Allen & Unwin, 1959.

Arrowsmith, William, and Roger Shattuck, eds. *The Craft and Context of Translation*. Austin: University of Texas Press, 1961.

Carne-Ross, D. S. "Translation and Transposition." In Arrowsmith and Shattuck, 3–21.

Dashti, Ali. *In Search of Omar Khayyam*. Trans. L. P. Elwell-Sutton. London: George Allen & Unwin, 1971.

Elwell-Sutton, L. P. Introduction. In Dashti, 11–27.

Fang Yü 方瑜. "Mu-ch'iu ch'ung-tu Lu-pai" 暮秋重讀魯拜 (Re-reading the *Rubaiyat* in late autumn). In Huang, 109–112.

Gardner, Helen, ed. *The New Oxford Book of English Verse, 1250–1950*. Oxford: Oxford University Press, 1972.

Graves, Robert. "The Fitz-Omar Cult." In Graves and Ali-Shah, 1–31.

Graves, Robert, and Omar Ali-Shah, trans. *The Rubaiyyat of Omar Khayaam: A New Translation with Critical Commentaries.* London: Cassell, 1967.

Huang K'e-sun 黃克孫, trans. *Lu-pai chi* 魯拜集 (*The Rubaiyat*). Taipei: Shu-lin, 1987.

Kasra, Parichehr, trans. *The Rubai'yat of 'Umar Khayyam.* Delmar, N.Y.: Scholar's Facsimiles and Reprints, 1975.

Paris, Jean. "Translation and Creation." In Arrowsmith and Shattuck, 57–67.

Peng, Ching-hsi. "Permanency in Change: Reflections on the Original and Its Translation(s)." *The Chinese Pen* (Spring 1989): 30–40.

———. "Yi-shih sui-hsiang" 譯詩隨想 (Two notes on poetry translation). *Wen-hsing tsa-chih* 文星雜誌 (December 1987): 150.

———. Review of Kurt W. Radtke, *Poetry of the Yuan Dynasty. Journal of the American Oriental Society* 109, no. 3 (1989): 484–487.

Radtke, Kurt W. *Poetry of the Yuan Dynasty.* Canberra: Faculty of Asian Studies, Australian National University, 1987.

Rexroth, Kenneth. "The Poet as Translator." In Arrowsmith and Shattuck, 22–37..

Sung Mei-hua 宋美嬅. "Yi-mao ch'ü-shen: p'ing *Lu-pai chi*" 遺貌取神：評「魯拜集」 (Dropping the appearance, grasping the spirit: A review of *Lu-pai chi*). *Lien-ho wen-hsueh* 聯合文學 (*Unitas*) 29 (March 1987): 243–244.

Terhune, Alfred McKinley. *The Life of Edward FitzGerald, Translator of The Rubáiyát of Omar Khayyám.* New Haven: Yale University Press, 1947.

Terhune, Alfred McKinley, and Annabelle Burdick Terhune, eds. *The Letters of Edward FitzGerald.* 4 vols. Vol. 2, 1851–1866. Princeton: Princeton University Press, 1980.

Tomlinson, Charles, ed. *The Oxford Book of Verse in English Translation.* Oxford: Oxford University Press, 1980.

Foundations for Critical Understanding

The Compilation and Translation of Encyclopedic Dictionaries of Chinese Literary Terminology

JOHN J. DEENEY

The linguist Geoffrey Sampson observed in *Writing Systems* that "it has been estimated ... that up to about the end of the 18th century more than half of all the books ever published in the world were written in Chinese. Even today, ... Chinese and Chinese-derived writing occupies a very respectable second place in terms of numbers of users" (145). Russian- and English-language publications are close rivals to Chinese in this century and will probably continue to be so for the foreseeable future. The corpora of these three important languages deserve a great deal of attention from a terminological point of view. And considering China's extraordinarily long tradition of excellence in *belles lettres*, the compilation and translation of Chinese literary terminology is of major importance.

We might recall with amusement the way the horse was defined by an eager-to-please student in Dickens's *Hard Times*:

> "Bitzer," said Thomas Gradgrind. "Your definition of a horse."
>
> "Quadruped. Graminivorous. Forty teeth, namely twenty-four grinders, four eye-teeth, and twelve incisive. Sheds coat in the spring; in marshy countries, sheds hoofs, too. Hoofs hard, but requiring to be shod with iron. Age known by marks in mouth." Thus (and much more) Bitzer.
>
> "Now girl number twenty," said Mr. Gradgrind. "You know what a horse is." (3)

The ludicrous inadequacy of this "definition" in describing the many Pegasuses of literature points up the basic difference between scientific and literary definition. Although the natural and social sciences have their own peculiar problems in compiling terminology dictionaries, they do not face the kind of difficulty encountered by the humanities, which are so much more culture-specific. Humanists must often be satisfied with a "descriptive" definition and, consequently, leave themselves open to accusations of inexactness and imprecision from more formula-minded scientists. But as C. E. Whitmore says in "The Validity of Literary Definitions," "The formulas of science serve for prediction and for production.... The most that a literary formula can do is to bring together a large group of facts under the manageable form of a statement which conveniently summarizes some phase of their behavior" (129).

The difficulties are compounded immeasurably when attempts are made to cross cultural barriers through translation, particularly when there has been so little literary exchange between China's millennia-long tradition and the Western world. What exchange has taken place has been largely unilateral—far more attention being given to the translation of Western literary terminology into Chinese than vice versa. And from the mid–twentieth century on, this problem of literary vocabulary has been considerably exacerbated by the incredible proliferation of new literary theories spawning never-ending clusters of new terms.

Moving from the level of literary theory to that of practical criticism, we may well ask: how can Westerners talk about Chinese literature sensibly unless they have mastered the basic critical vocabulary of that long and rich literary heritage? And how can Chinese explain their literary heritage to Westerners unless they too have a commonly agreed-upon set of terms in order to engage in fruitful dialogue? K. W. Radtke, in "Concepts in Literary Criticism," suggests that a comparative approach is, perhaps, the most challenging and fruitful.[1]

> Despite the difficulties of a comparative approach it seems highly interesting and promising to test to the limit the usefulness of Western literary concepts in other literary traditions and *vice versa*; such an approach will—hopefully—lead to a better understanding of the process of literary criticism itself. (120)

In comparative literature studies, one of the most vexing and fundamental problems is the need for a clearer and more discriminating use of critical concepts, since a complete standardization of terminology is well-nigh impossible.

It is obvious that we must come to terms with basic critical concepts used by different cultures if there is to be any significant understanding, and this is most obvious and pressing in the field of comparative literature. Presumably, all scholars would agree that any intelligent (and intelligible) discourse must begin with a mutual understanding of the basic literary terms. But even among professional comparative literature scholars, the problem of understanding—or, at least, clarifying terminology across cultures— remains elusive. The very term *comparative literature,* as well as attempts to distinguish it from general literature, world literature, and so forth, prompted Janos Hankiss to tell his colleagues at the Second International Congress of Comparative Literature (1959): "L'érudit qui, vers la fin de ce siècle, s'avisera d'écrire l'histoire de notre discipline entre 1920 et 1950, se trouvera embarrassé par la terminologie extrêmement flottante que nous appliquons à l'ensemble ou à certaines branches de cette discipline" (98). The same collective concern over the definition and illustration of literary terms has been aired in subsequent congresses, and the International Comparative Literature Association finally made it one of its long-term projects. I deal with this at some length in the section "Historical Background," where I bring together representative projects and publications by describing their various methodologies and illustrating them with extensive quotations.

A number of scholars have pointed up the special terminological difficulties associated with China's literary criticism. As C. H. Wang has noted in "Naming the Reality of Chinese Criticism,"

> The most serious problem in wrestling with traditional Chinese criticism and theory is the translation of terminology.... Since all scholars realize that one of the characteristics of Chinese criticism is the ambiguity of vaguely defined concepts scattered in generally disorganized treatises—including lengthy monographs, prefaces, and postscripts, *shih-hua* [詩話], letters to literary friends and colleagues, and notes and commentaries written on the classics or other favorite masterpieces—they set out to name and classify concepts. It is undoubtedly a proper approach to a systematic understanding of a difficult subject. (534 and 532)

Furthermore, Ngan Yuen-wan complains about the imprecision of Chinese terminology in her essay "Some Characteristics of Chinese Literary Criticism":

> Looseness of language must be faced as a problem of Chinese literary criticism.... Chinese critical language is often unsatisfactory because of the lack of useful definitions even for the key terms. Traditional critics never took the trouble of defining a word or term before they employed it, paying no attention to the fact that the word or term might have been so much bandied about that it had ceased to have any solid and accurate meaning. Even critics trained in modern scholarship commit the same error.... The imprecision of language caused by the absence of accurate definitions makes Chinese critical writings elusive. Chinese literary criticism is far too often presented in an undesirably ornate style. (195–196)

Adele Austin Rickett discovered in the process of writing her doctoral dissertation on Wang Kuo-wei's [王國維] *Jen-chien Tz'u-hua* [人間詞話] that Western scholars have an extremely difficult task in attempting translations of Chinese literary terminology. She writes:

> Some terms are common to literary critics from early times on, while others have assumed special meanings in the hands of certain critics. Sometimes the whole essence of a critic's theory of poetry is stated in a single pair of words.... Some of these terms find their origin in philosophy. This is true of words such as *ch'i* [氣] (vital force or breath) and *shen* [神] (spirit).... Other descriptive terms seem to have come out of poetry itself, such as *ch'i-wan* [淒婉] (extremely tender) or *kao ku* [高古] (lofty and timeless).... One of the most unique characteristics of Chinese criticism is the wide use of metaphors and similes to describe poets and poetry.... The imagery is extremely vivid and unusual, so unusual indeed that sometimes explanation proves difficult and meaningful translation almost impossible. [And Rickett adds a note:] Here again we find a technique prevalent in other forms of Chinese scholarship, e.g., philosophy: picturesque analogy and metaphor becomes a substitute for analysis and definition. (72–74)

Rickett takes up this point again in her introduction to *Chinese Approaches to Literature from Confucius to Liang Ch'i Ch'ao*:

> It was not common practice in the past for a scholar to make any attempt at systematic exposition of them [terms]. Through examples taken from well-known poems he would illustrate his concept of literature as enshrined in the term. Or he would, in casual style, write a paragraph or less on what he meant by it. Sometimes a disciple or commentator would try to give an explanation, but usually such explanations were couched in metaphorical language not designed to clarify the picture at all. (5)

Rickett goes on to say that it is only in the twentieth century that the frame of reference has changed: "With that change has come a keen awareness of the complexities of Chinese literary criticism, of the wealth of insight to be gained from an understanding of it, and a determination to bring Western techniques of criticism and analysis to bear upon specific subjects" (6).

My remarks so far serve as something of a prolegomenon of problems in tracing some of the issues involved in the compilation and translation of literary terminology. The next section points out representative examples of publications which have been completed or are in preparation. The remaining two sections lay out ideas and methods that may serve as a blueprint on how to proceed in the work of compilation and translation in an orderly, systematic, and comprehensive fashion. In this way literary scholars may come closer to achieving the goal of mastering the terminological tools of their trade.

Historical Background

As a Westerner interested for many years in promoting Chinese-Western comparative literature studies, I certainly would not have the temerity to comment on the making of dictionaries in China, a country long familiar with dictionaries. On the other hand, there are international organizations concerned with terminological problems worth consulting.[2] Furthermore, there is nothing in Chinese, to my knowledge, that matches some of the more advanced literary dictionaries published in the West and, particularly, the kind of encyclopedic dictionary I describe below (based on English and French sources). I trust that at least some of the methods and principles used in Western scholarship which I consider worth extrapolating will become a useful reference source of information in the compilation and translation of literary terminology from Chinese into English and other languages.[3]

Many scholars of Chinese, over the years, have lamented the lack of good terminological dictionaries and have done their best to remedy the need by writing specialized articles or monographs on certain literary terms.[4] But the task of compiling a dictionary covering the entire tradition of Chinese literary terminology has proved too difficult a task. On the other hand, there are many brief essays relating to literary terminology (often found in prefaces or introductions to dictionaries of literary terms), but in my brief treatment here, I can only mention a few representative examples of both the essays and model dictionaries to illustrate certain points I wish to make.

As for Western dictionaries of literary terminology, there are many kinds compiled for different levels of readership. In the past decade, there have been a number of solid but fairly basic texts, such as those by Abrams, Beckson and Ganz, Fowler, Lentricchia and McLaughlin, Scott, and Shipley. One of the more common college texts used in the United States is Holman's *Handbook to Literature*. It contains descriptive definitions of Western terms (for the most part), extending from one or two sentences to several paragraphs. Far more sophisticated, though limited in coverage, is Preminger's *Princeton Encyclopedia of Poetry and Poetics*, which contains detailed descriptions of terms, including their historical origins and development, written by specialists for scholars. Explanations often extend to two or three pages and conclude with a short but useful bibliography. There is also *The Critical Idiom* series, under the editorship of John D. Jump, which has been translated, in part, into Chinese. These booklets (averaging 100 or more pages each) are written by specialists to provide "reasonably full discussions," including illustrative quotations, references to more than one literature when possible, and a brief bibliography of several pages. All of the above-mentioned dictionaries are useful in their own way, depending on whether we are dealing with beginners, intermediate learners, or advanced scholars.

One might also wish to examine certain Japanese works, in English, as points of reference for the proposed Chinese encyclopedic dictionary of literary terminology. One such book is by Hisamatsu Sen'ichi, *The Vocabulary of Japanese Literary Aesthetics*. This is actually a brief history of Japanese literature with a focus on aesthetic terms. These terms are described in the context of chapters entitled "Basic Problems," "Aesthetic Stereotypes" (in traditional literature), and "Aesthetic Concepts" (in modern literature); the book concludes with a ten-page "Glossary of Literary Terms." The other Japanese reference source is Earl Miner's *Princeton Companion to Classical Japanese Literature* which provides much useful information and discusses literary terms throughout.

The work which comes closest, however, to the ideal of an encyclopedic dictionary of literary terminology is the ambitious *International Dictionary of Literary Terms (Dictionnaire international des termes littéraires)*. This enterprise has had a long and bumpy history and it would be instructive for any would-be compiler to review that history. The idea was first brought up in 1951, by Robert Escarpit, a professor at the University of Bordeaux, and was more formally proposed by Escarpit in 1958, on the occasion of the second International Comparative Literature Congress. It was finally accepted as a project of the ICLA in the sixties, and work began under the editorship of Escarpit.

Under Escarpit, five fascicles have been published to date, extending from letters A to D. In addition, there was the first eighty-five-page experimental volume, published under the letter L (*Lai—Lyrique*). For each of the nineteen terms included (for example, *littérarité, littérature, littérature comparée, littérature générale, littérature mondiale*, and even the Chinese poetic form, *lu shi[h]* (律詩), it usually gives etymologies, brief semantic studies, linguistic equivalents (from other languages), lengthy historical commentary, and bibliography. The entries are in French or English.

A detailed description of the long-range project is contained in a special *rapport* by Escarpit. His original statement of purpose, made to the ICLA in 1964, is still worth contemplating:

> The report I am about to present to you is the result of twelve years of consideration, seven years of various investigations, and four years of methodological work.... The need was felt ... for an inventory and a stricter definition of the terms which we have in everyday use in academic criticism.... Such an undertaking could reach a successful conclusion only by means of collective work, on an international level.

A more recent (October 1987) flyer description, "Vocation du Dictionnaire," states:

> Répondant à un souhait fréquemment exprimé par la critique universitaire, le Dictionnaire a pour objet de recenser, de définir et de clarifier certains termes

de critique littéraire, d'un usage universel mais susceptible de recouvrir des acceptions parfois nuancées d'un pays à un autre, d'une littérature à une autre.... Il ne s'agit donc pas d'une entreprise encyclopédique: le Dictionnaire doit se présenter comme un instrument de travail et de référence conçu à l'usage d'un public international d'enseignants, spécialistes et étudiants.

Despite the negative connotation attached to the term *encyclopedic*, including much information not exactly pertinent to terminological considerations (e.g., literary authors, general historical background, etc.), I understand the term in a positive sense. While I too would restrict coverage to literary terminology only, the encyclopedic dictionary I propose would go beyond the brief treatment of ordinary literary term dictionaries.

Unfortunately, judging from the entries which have appeared in the *IDLT* so far, the work is rather uneven in quality. It would seem that far stricter editorial control must be exacted if the work is to be successful as a whole. Escarpit retired from the task in 1987, and it has been taken over by Jean-Marie Grassin of the General and Comparative Literature Department at the University of Limoges. Among his editing principles, expressed in a recent report on the subject, are his concern about "problems of literary theory related to the IDLT"; "new guidelines ... in order to harmonize the format of the articles"; "national committees entrusted with specific tasks"; "improvements and new features ... being introduced progressively." Grassin estimates that as many as twenty specialists may be called upon to complete certain terms. The majority of these specialists would be involved in finding equivalents in the ten languages covered by the *IDLT*.

In a 1990 form letter of instructions to scholars who have agreed to prepare terms for the *IDLT*, Grassin gives "un aperçu de l'esprit" of the *IDLT*, modifying and elaborating upon some earlier statements.

> *Il s'agit surtout de clarifier et de définir l'usage effectif du mot comme terme dans la critique littéraire internationale* ("Qu'entend(ai)ent les littéraires quand ils parl(ai)ent de ...?"). Le projet est donc plus lexicographique qu'encyclopédique.
>
> Doivent rester secondaires par rapport à l'aspect descriptif (mais ne sont nullement interdits): les développements d'ordre documentaire ou thématique autour de la notion, l'exposé de votre position théorique ou méthodologique personnelle à mettre en regard des autres courants, les propositions normatives, l'usage du terme dans des sciences connexes (philosophie, sémiologie, histoire de l'art, etc).
>
> Dans un ouvrage de référence comparatiste, il convient d'examiner l'usage du terme dans différents pays, même si, pour une raison historique ou par compétence personnelle, vous vous attachez plus particulièrement à une aire linguistique ou nationale.

In a review of the *IDLT* which appeared at the same time as Grassin's report, Bernhard F. Scholz raises an important point in reference to definitions of non-Western terms published so far: "Are we dealing with items that are expected to come within the purview of the Western reader or with items that stand out in their original context?" (153). Ulrich Weisstein, on the other hand, takes a more international view:

> As soon as we leave the boundaries of Western literature to look for terminological equivalents in Arabic, Chinese, Japanese and Sanskrit, we enter a totally unfamiliar realm of linguistic usage. Here lies the best food for thought and a source of creative frustration for the comparatist of the future. (471)

Both of these comments point up the difficult problem of selecting the proper number and proportion of non-Western literary terms that should be included in a truly international dictionary.

> In a recent letter, Grassin stresses two points about the *IDLT*: It is based on an objective inventory of the actual vocabulary of literary criticism in an international context.... The matter of the international dictionary of terms versus the dictionary of international terms, of the coherence between Western and Eastern nations is no longer relevant. A term is in the dictionary because it (a) *is* a term and (b) is *actually* used by scholars in *international* contexts, whether it refers to a theoretical notion, a genre of a particular culture, an international current, a local school, a problem raised initially in China or Brazil.... [Secondly,] it is a worldwide cooperative project. If Western tradition and terms are a huge majority, it is not because French and North American contributions make a majority, but because terms in actual international use are a majority.... What I would like to obtain, above all, is Asiatic scholars writing articles not only on Chinese, Japanese or Korean literature but on Western terms in an international perspective.

It would appear that the laudable efforts of the editors of the *IDLT* to include terms beyond the Western hemisphere might be best served by inviting experts from various national literatures to participate in contributing to the *IDLT*, even though this will often entail the difficult task of translation. In fact, the editors have been trying to do this from early on, but it requires both competent scholars to volunteer for the task and the active cooperation of national associations to assist in selecting the best specialists for the job. To this purpose, the *IDLT* has been sponsoring annual meetings on literary terminology since 1987, and Grassin himself created what he calls the Observatory of Literary Terminology, which meets in workshop formats annually. These workshops, along with the reactivation of national literary committees, are intended to monitor terminological and national changes in literary criticism as well as to update and complete the *IDLT*. The fourth observatory convention was held in October 1990.

Grassin has also organized small one-day seminars, involving particular *IDLT* problems. A seminar relating to Chinese literature was held on January 19, 1990, in Limoges, with both French and Chinese scholars participating. On this occasion, some of the questions discussed by the group were: should other "national" terms be added, or should any be deleted, or should any terms be grouped under the one lemma? What standard keywords (e.g., narrat(ology)(ive), love and eroticism, movement, rhetoric, etc.) could be introduced into the field "area"? What correlations can be established between these terms, and between these terms and other terms in the international inventory? Which "international" terms in the general inventory would necessitate a special treatment in connection with the literatures covered by the committee (e.g., "epic" in African oral literatures)? Can a specialist be recommended for vacant terms?

The work accomplished by *IDLT* and the various meetings described above might also serve as a stimulus to urge countries which do not yet have comparable dictionaries of literary terminology, even in their native languages, to produce them. National pride is at stake here. One's literary heritage should not be ignored or neglected when such opportunities are available to represent them to the international scholarly community.

Participation in these meetings, especially by non-Western cultures, would also help to point up some of the distinct differences between Eastern and Western literary concepts, as well as the utter otherness of many non-Western terms and the virtual impossibility of ever creating a single, acceptable metalanguage for literary criticism, let alone a universalist common poetics. The best we can hope for is a composite poetics—and what better place to begin than the juxtaposition of literary terms in an international dictionary, which will at least make each culture better informed about its distant neighbors' literary uniquenesses?[5]

Before turning to Chinese examples of literary terminology, it is worth reminding ourselves that this problem of defining our terms goes back to Confucius. Although Confucius connected *cheng ming* [正名], "rectification of names," with proper governance and ethical significance, the phrase does not lose its fundamental meaning that there should be a careful choice of words and expressions which are actually related to reality.[6]

The coverage of literary terms published in the great *T'zu Hai* [辭海] dictionary and published in a separate volume is probably the closest thing to a monolingual dictionary of literature vocabulary we find on a sustained, general level. On the other hand, in 1985 the Taiwan-based journal *Wen Hsun* [文訊] began publishing a series of short essays on both Western (February, no. 16) and Chinese (June, no. 18) terms. Unfortunately, this feature was discontinued and nothing of this nature has appeared since the December 1986 issue (no. 27). Nevertheless, a list of its twenty-four published essays on Chinese terms (in Chinese) is worth perusing.

Recent developments in China show promise of a revival of interest in producing a representative selection of literary terms from China's classical tradition as well as from modern times. In his excellent survey "Some

Recent Research Aids to Traditional Chinese Literature," William Nien-hauser, Jr., mentions a few works which discuss literary terminology but do so in a rather cursory fashion. On the other hand, in addition to several dictionaries already published on aesthetics, there are at least two large-scale literary terms projects in progress. The first is under the general editorship of Yue Daiyun, head of China's Comparative Literature Association and long-time teacher at Peking University's Chinese Department; the second is under the direction of Sun Jingyao, who is an executive member of the Chinese Comparative Literature Association teaching at the Chinese Department of Suzhou University. Both have traveled extensively abroad and enlisted the aid of many scholars.

Yue, in her guidelines for the compilation *A Dictionary of World Poetics* [世界詩學大辭典], states:

> In accord with the current trend of globalism and cultural pluralism in literary theoretical research, we plan to compile *A Dictionary of World Poetics* with the aim of providing essential information about the theories and concepts of literature in the cultures of China, Japan, the Arabic countries, Europe including Russia, and America. We hope by this enterprise to help Chinese students of literature to have some grasp of poetics and its evolution in the different cultures. We hope that the dictionary will also provide a basis for the comparative study of poetics.

Yue goes on to describe, in considerable detail, the nature of the entries, the requirements for each, the procedures for writing, and so forth. There will be over 3,000 entries, broken down roughly as follows: China, 700; India, 500; Japan, 300; Europe and America, 900; Russia, 400; and the Arabic-speaking countries, 300. From my point of view, the 700 entries from China are the most interesting. Yue and her team want to join with other scholars throughout the world to have at least a portion of these Chinese terms translated into English and other languages.

Sun Jingyao has a similar plan. I will paraphrase the description he has given in a number of Chinese documents: We plan to compile *A Dictionary of Chinese and Western Literary Terms* 中外文學術語辭典 which will include at least 1,420 entries. Terms from both Chinese and Western literature will be included, ancient as well as modern. In this way we hope to make a helpful contribution to the bridging of Chinese and Western literary concepts and promote the further development of comparative literature studies, East and West. Experts will be invited to participate in the work of translating Chinese terms into Western languages, beginning with English. The first phase of this project has already begun with the selection of terms from Classical Chinese literature.

It is interesting to compare Yue's and Sun's extensive lists of terms with other lists. When deciding upon which terms should be selected and translated for an international community of literary scholars, it would also be instructive to examine the fifty-five terms found in the body of Nienhauser's *Indiana Companion to Traditional Chinese Literature*, as well as those contained in the introductory essay on rhetoric.

Compilation Principles

Before compiling a dictionary of Chinese literary terminology, one must decide upon suitable space and time frames. The former determines whether one wants to produce a monolingual dictionary for one's native culture or to take a bilingual approach in order to achieve a cross-cultural international effort. The latter course requires considerable translation skills and is examined in the next section.

As for the time frame, because Classical Chinese literature is so much more difficult to describe, the emphasis here (as well as the examples) will be on the pre–twentieth century tradition. On the other hand, I believe the principles of compiling and translating both traditional and modern critical terminology is basically the same, except that the latter is much easier to deal with, since it does not have to trace the evolution of a term over a long time span. Even though the Yue and Sun projects have much in common, so much has to be done in this area of critical terminology that there is little likelihood of too much overlapping. Scholars using either traditional or modern approaches (preferably both) will learn much from each other's experience.

In both cases, one of the basic principles of compilation is that the definitions or descriptions be made to fit the literary works and not vice versa. In the words of Robert Alter in *Fielding and the Nature of the Novel*,

> What happens too often, however, is that critical intelligence is seduced by the shapeliness of the definitions it has inherited or conceived, and as a result it fails to respond adequately to works that cannot be accommodated to the definitions, those very exceptions which, in the proper sense, prove the rule—put it to the test. (vii)

Therefore the best we can do, in R. P. Blackmur's words, is to "use definition in the end in order to surround the indefinable. If you 'define' the novel or the sonnet you will not be able to read the next one that alters the limits" (in Alter, 178).

Another basic principle about defining the indefinable is that all terms are conditioned by the historical period out of which they evolved, along with the subsequent historical periods which enlarged upon or radically modified them. As Scholz points out in his critical review of the *IDLT*,

As heirs to the invaluable distinction between meta-language and object-language we would wish now for a clearer distinction between the history of the use of a term or *Begriffsgeschichte* and the history of the literary phenomena subsumed under that term, that is to say literary history proper. (155)

On a more pragmatic level, the scope of the dictionary as well as the type of audience for whom it is being prepared must be clearly determined. One should first consider the various ways of dividing the work into several phases, accörding to principles of breadth and depth of coverage. These in turn are determined to a large extent by one's potential readership. Hence, depending on one's audience, one could list the following examples (by no means exhaustive) to illustrate some of the differences:

1. Elementary glossary type for quick reference purposes (Abrams)
2. Intermediate handbook type for pedagogical purposes (Holman)
3. Advanced encyclopedic dictionary type for (a) general scholarly purposes (Preminger), or (b) specialist scholarly purposes (Escarpit/Grassin)
4. Monograph-size individual treatment of specific terms (Jump)
5. Cultural emphasis broadly conceived but including literature (Bullock)

I suggest steering a middle path and concentrating on number three (ideally, something between 3a and 3b) as the type of work which would be most useful for serious scholars of literature, especially comparatists.

Other broad principles of action would refer to the need for a strong and clear-minded editorial committee which would determine high standards, a solid grounding in research methodologies and, finally, a specific enumeration of the organizational and classification principles that would go into the actual compilation of each entry.

Many of these principles and their related corollaries are summed up in the following checklists concerning the formation of a dictionary project. Any individual point on these checklists may not appear significant in itself, but the cumulative effect can make the difference between a successful and unsuccessful publication.

Checklist A

Establishment of an editorial committee to determine standards
The task of compiling and translating an encyclopedic dictionary of literary terms would be too daunting for most individuals even if they had the time and talent to carry it through. Hence the obvious need for collaboration among a team of experts and collaborators to bring such an immense project to a successful conclusion. This necessitates the need for a committtee

which would coordinate and supervise the project. The purpose of such a committee would be to ensure continuity and uniformity as well as to exert editorial control over the entries submitted in order to ensure a high level of performance. A suitable structure of communication would have to be set up (employing electronic mail, faxes, etc.) to make sure duties would be performed with dispatch and deadlines observed by the many collaborators involved. The editorial committee would have the final word on the acceptability of submissions and the right to revise or reject. Among many other things, this committee would also have to decide:

1. Total number of terms to be included, that is, identification and a judicious selection, including both the usual literary terms (e.g., *lu-shih* 律詩) as well as critical items (e.g., *hsing* 興).
2. Types of classification:
   a) problem words (e.g., realism, formalism).
   b) essay words (e.g., book, edition).
   c) account words (e.g., prosody, rhetoric, parallelism, etc.).[7]
3. Length of treatment should be concise but adequate, maintaining a sense of proportion among the entries:
   a) long or major entry (over 1,500 words).
   b) medium-sized entry (500–1,500 words).
   c) shorter minor entry (under 500 words).
4. Professional copy editing according to a standard format.
5. Consistency.
6. Uniformity.
7. Pronunciation, accent, syllabification (IPA).
8. Meticulous proofreading.
9. Later revisions.
10. Role of the computer, devising program, etc.; especially important if there are to be translations into several languages.[8]
11. Selection of cooperative contributors.
12. Sample of model entries and written guidelines.
13. Style of explanations should be readable and not overly technical; on the other hand, meaning must not be distorted by over-simplification.

CHECKLIST B

Application of basic principles of research methodology
The underlying principle behind bibliography and research methodology is to find out what has been already done, not to repeat it, as well as to try and improve upon it. This would seem to be self-evident, but it is surprising to discover how often it is neglected. In the case of the compilation and translation of literary terminology, this will entail a survey of the editorial introductory material of dictionaries or encylopedias of literary terms as

well as an evaluation of critical treatises and translations of particular terms, often scattered or buried in out-of-the-way and unexpected sources.

1. Searching for and evaluating what has already been done.
2. Visiting (at least electronically) other local, regional, and international organizations for accessing materials.
3. Combing through bibliographies, indexes, encyclopedias, dictionaries, etc., for books, monographs, journals, theses, essays, etc., as well as tapping into general and terminological databases (online as well as CD-ROM) for relevant materials.
4. Checking book reviews for critiques from specialists in the field.
5. Acquiring expertise in computer applications: compiling, revising, editing, retrieving, sorting, comparing, etc.
6. Entering into correspondence with scholars whose names are discovered in the research process.

Checklist C

Specification of principles of organization and analysis
A good way of organizing oneself in preparing a literary definition is, in C. E. Whitmore's words, to ascertain its properties, constituents, and antecedents.

> We have to deal, then, with properties ascertained by direct experience, with constituents revealed by analysis, and with antecedents reached by historical study.... The framing of a literary definition which shall be viable in the domain of theory is a task which depends on a number of factors—on a thorough knowledge of the literary field with its antecedents and issues, on a due sense of our aim in any particular case, on a careful emphasizing of the aspect which we may have especially in view. (136–138)

In the following list, sentences in French are taken from one of Grassin's recent "models" which are sent to those preparing a terminological essay for the *IDLT*. They serve as something of an update on the *IDLT* current recommendations. In fact, Grassin sums up much of his ideal essay when he describes the nature of the *"Commentaire"*:

> Chercher à clarifier l'emploi du mot comme *terme* de critique littéraire, l'évolution historique des notions qu'il recouvre et les différentes directions de recherche qui peuvent être pratiquées aujourd'hui à son sujet.
>
> Le commentaire est plus descriptif que normatif. Il doit être suffisamment technique pour que le spécialiste y trouve une synthèse utile sur la question, suffisamment clair pour que le profane puisse s'informer sur le fond. Définir, ne serait-ce que par une apposition, les termes employés qui ne relèvent pas du langage quotidien.

Le DITL *[IDLT]* est international. Veiller à représenter l'usage du terme par la communauté universitaire dans son ensemble et non seulement dans un pays ou une école.

L'opinion du rédacteur, sa culture, sa position philosophique, etc.... peuvent transparaître à condition que les autres positions soient loyalement évoquées.

C'est l'usage littéraire comme terme qui doit inspirer le commentaire. Dans le cas d'un terme issu des sciences humaines, (psychanalyse, sémiologie, linguistique), c'est son usage effectif dans le théâtre, la critique ou l'histoire littéraire qui intéresse le dictionnaire.

But now for the checklist proper:

1. Alphabetical arrangement (most convenient) vs. the more logical but cumbersome topical arrangement (e.g., fiction, including novel, short story, etc.) which treats related terms in one general context.[9]
2. Philological and etymological study when useful. Notice orientée sur le "comportement" littéraire du terme. Ne remonter au sanscrit par ex. que pour faire sentir le fondement sémantique du mot. Consulter des philologues ou leur confier la notice au besoin.
3. Semantic analysis indicating various uses of terms and extensions or derivatives (e.g., symbol, symbolism). Définition du mot dans ses principales acceptions courantes en mettant l'accent sur les emplois comme terme littéraire.
4. Linguistic equivalent terms in other languages. Equivalents linguistiques obtenus par le rédacteur s'il les connaît. Consulter les spécialistes des différentes langues dans l'Université ou à l'occasion de congrès. Les équivalents renvoient aux différents sens numérotés ci-dessus. Pour l'arabe, le chinois, le japonais et le russe, donner la transcription la plus courante en caractères latins après le mot, et fournir une graphie originale du mot sur une feuille à part avec un numéro de renvoi. Allemand, anglais, arabe, chinois, espagnol, français, italien, japonais, portugais, russe, autre langues (équivalents dans des langues pertinentes pour le terme en cas d'utilité seulement).
5. Origins of the term, its development, and historical shifts in meaning (including dates), and reconciliations if they occur.
6. Cultural and intellectual milieu of individual using term vs. the critical evolutions within and without the given era vs. the preferred use based on common consensus.
7. Period terms, as Wellek reminds us, are to be conceived "not as arbitrary linguistic labels nor as metaphysical entities, but as names for systems of norms which dominate literature at a specific time of the historical process" (129).[10]
8. Genre terms should be dealt with in a similar way.
9. Divisions and distinctions to delimit categories.

10. Functions of literary devices (e.g., parallelism can function in terms of simple emphasis, balance and antithesis, and/or rhythm and euphony).[11]
11. Illustrative examples, apt quotations, and distinguished practitioners.
12. Overlapping and cross-references. Correlats propositions de renvoi à d'autres termes traités par le dictionnaire ou à introduire.
13. Select bibliographical references. Une bibliographie peut suivre le commentaire. Elle doit être limitée, en principe, aux références actuelles les plus utiles (10 maximum).
14. Number and types of indexes.
15. Possible need for introductory essays treating broad topics such as the Classics and Literature, Buddhism and Literature, etc. (See Checklist F, no. 6, as well as the introductory essays in Nienhauser).[12]

CHECKLIST D

Determination of principles of classification
In "On Defining Terms," Edward E. Seeber reminds us of some basic distinctions (the square bracketed portions are my paraphrase of Seeber's examples):

> In specific contexts, terms may demand close study for different reasons: indeed, they sometimes must be considered simultaneously in more than one of the following categories: (1) Terms that may undergo a change of meaning in different eras ["Gothic" through the 17th and 19th centuries; "nature" for Rabelais, Pascal, Rousseau, and Balzac].... (2) Terms that may mean different things within the same era ["reason" and "imitation" as interpreted by Neoclassicists and Romantics].... (3) Terms that may have different meanings in different countries [French *ballade* and the English ballad; French *drame* and English drama].... (4) Terms that may mean different things to the same writer using them ["virtue" and "natural goodness" for Rousseau]. (58–60)[13]

The list contained in J. A. Cuddon's Preface to *A Dictionary of Literary Terms* may serve as our checklist here inasmuch as it is a convenient and comprehensive summary of the problems of adequate classification. Cuddon begins by stating that there are ten main categories and then cautions about their inadequacy:

1. Technical terms (e.g. iamb, pentameter, metonymy, *ottava rima*).
2. Forms (e.g. sonnet, *villanelle*, limerick, *tanka*, *clerihew*).
3. Genres or kinds (e.g. pastoral, elegy, *fabliau*, *Marchen*, *conte*).
4. Technicalities (e.g. pivot word, tenor and vehicle, communication heresy, aesthetic distance).
5. Groups, schools and movements (e.g. Pleiade, School of Night, Parnassians, Pre-Raphaelites, School of Spenser).

6. Well-known phrases (e.g. pathetic fallacy, willing suspension of disbelief, negative capability, *quod semper quod ubique*).
7. -isms (e.g. realism, naturalism, primitivism, Platonism, plagiarism).
8. Motifs or themes (e.g. *ubi sunt*, *carpe diem*, Faust-theme, *leitmotif*).
9. Personalities (e.g. *scop*, *jongleur*, villain, *guslar*).
10. Modes, attitudes and styles (e.g. *dolce stil nuovo*, irony, Marinism, grotesque, sentimental comedy).

These ten categories account for a fair proportion of literary terms but there are hundreds which do not belong to any easily recognizable family or phylum, and any kind of taxonomical approach almost at once breaks down as soon as one begins to classify. (3)

Translation Principles

Presuming that we had a Chinese encyclopedic dictionary compiled according to the above checklists, certain fundamental problems come up that have to be dealt with in the translation process. For Chinese readers, the use of transcription systems is not particularly helpful; a Chinese character index arranged according to stroke order would also be necessary. This brings us to some of the special problems associated with Chinese, particularly with the problems of translating from Chinese into English (the principles are also applicable, more or less, to other languages). A variety of checklists of problems and possible solutions could be prepared for the task of translation.

CHECKLIST E

Problems peculiar to Chinese
The words of Benjamin Schwartz serve as a useful warning:

> When we unreflectively apply our modern Western categories to ancient Chinese texts, we certainly cannot assume the existence of word-for-word lexical equivalents. The notion that such words can simply be used unreflectively without a concern for the complexity of their long and turbulent history in the West or in China can only be an impediment to the enterprise of comparative thought. Yet the opposite notion that they cannot be used at all may be equally "culture-bound." The semantic range of a Chinese term may in fact overlap with the semantic range of a Western term. Instead of arguing whether a term like "religion" applies to China or whether a word like *tao* may apply to the West, one must be as conscious as possible of one's particular use of such words within particular contexts. (12)

1. Nature of the written character; problem of using modern simplified or standard traditional characters (the latter is preferred for Classical Chinese).

2. Types and uses of transcription systems when literal translation is impossible.[14]
3. Cultural phenomena requiring explanation.
4. Length of the tradition and its evolution.
5. Lack of emphasis on abstract literary theories.
6. Use of highly figurative language to express critical concepts (e.g., *fenggu* 風骨).

CHECKLIST F

Some possible solutions
1. Cooperation between philologists, literary historians, and theorists.
2. Team translation by Chinese and foreign scholars.
3. Approximations vs. equivalents or near-equivalents.
4. Give the literal word-for-word meaning of a term and then its common dictionary definition where that helps; finally, an elaboration on the import of the word would be in order which goes beyond any pat definition.
5. Annotation or explanatory notes when elaboration is necessary.
6. Explanation of complex literary and cultural phenomena in separate essays as part of publication (see Checklist C, no. 15).
7. Use of an acceptable transcription system as well as inclusion of the original Chinese characters (see Checklist C, no. 4).
8. Use of quotation marks to alert readers about unusual meaning(s); for example, "parallelism."
9. Accompany the transcribed form with the word "Chinese," creating a kind of composite form; e.g., the "Chinese novel" or, better, the "Chinese *hsiao-shuo* 小說 novel."

A valuable distinction, made by James J. Y. Liu, between "barbarizers" and "naturalizers" regarding Chinese poetry translation can be applied to translating literary terminology.[15] From the English reader's point of view, a "barbaric" translation would be one that was overly literal in its insistence on sticking as close to the original as possible; a "naturalizer" would prefer to find equivalents or near-equivalents in English. Incompetent proponents of the latter approach are often accused of the opposite extreme of under-literalness because, as Derk Bodde—himself an expert "naturalizer" —rather severely points out in his essay "On Translating Chinese Philosophic Terms," they are lazy or ignorant or too easily content with loose paraphrase and fall into the temptation to gain fame or money by glamorizing or jazzing up the text with inappropriate modern idioms or ideas alien to the original (244, n. 43). An interesting debate occurred between Bodde (the "naturalizer") and Peter A. Boodberg (the "barbarian"), which was conveniently summarized in Bodde's essay.[16]

Whatever one's policies may be regarding the translation of critical terms, the advice given by Liu to himself (and others) is appropriate here. The quotation is taken from a section entitled "The Translation of Critical Terms" in the introduction to his *Chinese Theories of Literature* and is worth quoting at length.

> Turning to the problem of translation, once we realize that a Chinese critical term cannot be expected to yield a single, clearly defined concept but several interrelated and overlapping ones, we shall naturally no longer aim at a consistent translation of the same term in all contexts. Instead, we shall translate a term according to what predominant concept it appears to denote in a given context and what subsidiary concepts it may also connote, using different English words each time if necessary, and offering alternative versions, while indicating what the original term is. Conversely, when we find essentially the same concept denoted by different Chinese terms, we shall not hesitate to translate them by the same English word, again taking care to point out the original term. In attempting to discern the concept or concepts underlying each term, not only do we have to ask about the immediate context, some or all of the questions raised above, but we also have to take into consideration the critic's general intellectual orientation, the examples he gives (if any), and earlier and contemporary usages of the same term, in literary criticism as well as in other kinds of writings. In this connection, etymology may be helpful, but cannot be relied on as an infallible guide, for obviously what a word originally meant need not throw any light on its subsequent meanings. (13–14) [17]

Conclusion

Scholars acknowledge the importance and usefulness of this terminological enterprise, but some are intimidated by the sheer massiveness of the project. In fact, many have been collecting and refining definitions within their areas of specialization. The task is formidable, however, and it would be a rare individual indeed who would have the time and talent to cover the entire field of Chinese literary terminology. But how can we bring all these individual efforts together into one large collaborative project?

Obviously, there is a need for a team of specialists to collaborate according to a well-thought-out, systematic, and comprehensive plan of sharing the task under a competent and dynamic editorial committee which would also seek financial support for a long-term project. Until adequate financing is forthcoming, a practical and feasible way of implementing this plan is to start publishing a few model terms in both Chinese- and English-language journals in order to attract constructive comment and possibly to entice potential contributors to come forward. Such brief entries could become regular features of these journals and eventually be revised and incorporated into reference book form.

I conclude with some of my favorite words from the great Samuel Johnson. After describing "the fate of those who toil at the lower employments of life ... where success would have been without applause, and diligence without reward," Johnson sadly reflects:

> Among these unhappy mortals is the writer of dictionaries, whom mankind have considered not as the pupil, but the slave, of science, the pioneer of literature, doomed only to remove rubbish and clear obstructions from the paths through which learning and genius press forward to conquest and glory, without bestowing a smile on the humble drudge that facilitates their progress. Every other author may aspire to praise: the lexicographer can only hope to escape reproach—and even this negative recompense has been yet granted to very few. (3)

If such a genius as Samuel Johnson was willing to devote so many precious years of his creative life to the making of a dictionary, contemporary laborers in the field surely are in good company and will not be forgotten by posterity.

NOTES

1. While Radtke talks about the usefulness of comparing concepts and terms for a better understanding of different literatures, André Lefevere has promoted the idea of serious study of translation as another useful way of doing criticism, especially in a comparative way.

2. Although the emphasis of most international organizations concerned with terminology has been placed on pragmatic areas such as science and technology, business and industry, they are also keenly interested in the humanities, since this is crucial if effective international communication is to take place. UNESCO, for instance, has long recognized the importance of standarizing the terminology among the world's nations. As part of UNESCO's General Information Program, there is also the International Information Centre for Terminology (INFOTERM). This group was founded in Vienna in 1971 by contract between UNESCO and the Austrian Standards Institute with the function of coordinating worldwide terminological activities. As one of its major projects, INFOTERM began to implement the International Network for Terminology (TERMNET) in 1979 and tries to coordinate various activities throughout the world. INFOTERM and TERMNET make it their business to probe into all the theoretical and methodological problems involved in producing terminological works. For information regarding INFOTERM, write to INFOTERM, Österreichisches Normungsinstitut (ON), Postfach 130, A-1021 Wien, Austria.

3. My primary focus in this essay is on the compilation and translation of Chinese literary terminology into English. The reverse process has been fairly well covered (especially regarding contemporary literary teminology, aesthetics, etc.) by scholars in China as well as in Taiwan.

4. There seem to be relatively few publications dealing at length with the special problems of Chinese literary terminology as a whole. For a sampling of how some

scholars try to interpret certain complex Chinese literary terms for the Western reader, one may consult the following authors in my list of works cited and consulted: Chang Ching-erh; Chang Hui-chuan; Chen Yu-shih; Chi Ch'iu-lang; Chiang T'ai-fen; Ching, Eugene; Chou, Balance Tin-ping; Chou Ying-hsiung; Chow Tse-tsung; Fu, James S.; Gibbs, Donald A.; Heine, Elizabeth; Huang Pi-wan; Ku Tim-hung; Plaks, Andrew; Pollard, David; Rickett, Adele Austin ("Technical Terms" and "Method"); Wang, John C. Y.; Wong, Simon H. H.; Wong Siu-kit; Wong Wai-leung; Yeh Ching-ping; Yeh, Michelle Hsi; Yu, Pauline Ruth; Yuan Heh-hsiang.

5. See my ideas on "composite poetics" in the conclusion to the "Ideology" chapter in *Comparative Literature from Chinese Perspectives*.

6. For a brief explanation of *jeng (cheng)* 正, see D. C. Lau's translation and comment, 121 and 115.

7. Some dictionaries of literary terms give a separate treatment to the more formal features of terminology, that is, those associated with genre, versification, rhetoric, etc. Many of these have been treated in reference works by Hightower, Frankel, Kao, etc.

8. For an interesting article on working from other languages into Chinese, see Yu Yongyuan. There are many articles written on all aspects of Chinese and computerization, some of which are concerned with terminology, but not literary terminology.

9. It is instructive to see how Miner treats this problem by combining the alphabetical with the topical arrangement in his *Companion to Classical Japanese Literature*: "The terms are entered under their Japanese names, because it is not feasible to give translations that are at once brief and adequate. For readers with little or no Japanese, and as a quick guide to others, a brief preliminary Glossary by category is given" (267). Some of the general categories which list clusters of related terms are: Poetry, Topics and Categories, *Kabuki*, Technical and Critical Concepts, etc. Individual terms are arranged alphabetically (in transcribed forms) with brief paragraph explanations. Another compromise frequently resorted to is to list the terms alphabetically and then to add a list of entries arranged by subject. See, for instance, Beckson, 304–308. In Nienhauser's *Indiana Companion to Traditional Chinese Literature*, the editor works out a compromise: most terms are put in alphabetical order, along with much other information, but certain terms are treated in special introductory essays (e.g., rhetorical terms; see Kao).

10. Wellek is famous for his thorough, historically based analyses of important literary terms. His *Concepts of Criticism*, for instance, discusses many terminological problems related to Literary Criticism, Evolution, Form and Structure, Baroque, Romanticism, Realism, etc. See also Auerbach's *Mimesis* and Levin's treatment of terms (e.g., Convention and Realism).

11. The *function* of literary terms is often neglected in dictionaries and deserves far more attention than it has received. See Plaks's article on parallelism as an excellent example of what can be said in this regard.

12. Whitmore takes an example from Aristotle's *Poetics*:

Aristotle's definition of tragedy ... takes into account practically all the specifications I have suggested. Before coming to the definition itself, Aristotle briefly sketches the antecedents of tragedy; then enumerates its constituents (an action serious and complete, in embellished language, enacted not narrated") and its properties ("through pity and terror effecting the proper purgation of these emotions"); and is throughout concerned with placing tragedy in the general literary field. Some details of his view may rouse our dissent; but the soundness of his general method is undeniable.... The upshot of our discussion is thus the conception of literary definitions as providing us with clues, with kinships, with orders, and with types. The basis of the division is functional, and the validity of the resulting forms is likewise functional—derived, that is, from the fulfil-ment by each of its due office, within its attendant limits. (138)

13. The essay collection with Seeber's essay also contains a useful essay by Remak, "West European Romanticism." See also the article by C. E. Nelson, which takes up problems associated with distinguishing "literature" and "*littérature*" as well as "reason" and "*raison*."

14. The problem of using transcription is not ideal and does place a burden on the reader who knows no Chinese, especially if there are few if any dictionaries available which adequately explain the term. On the other hand, there are many terms, transcribed from different languages, which have gradually been incorpo-rated into an educated literary person's vocabulary. For instance, because of the many shifts in meaning and interpretation over the centuries for Aristotle's *catharsis*, few would object to keeping the transcribed form. But there is an unfortunate ten-dency—I would go so far as to say, concession—to rather facilely translate Chinese critical vocabulary by pseudo-Western equivalents and this is very misleading. While Easterners long ago accepted Western terms like *Bildungsroman* into their ac-tive vocabulary, the reverse is not true, with rare exceptions such as *haiku*, *Zen*. This unfortunate unilateralism should be gradually corrected by introducing a suitable number of transcribed terms into the vocabulary of the international community of scholars and enriching our literary vocabulary. A number of scholars have taken up this issue of transcription; see, for instance, Ching and Wright. See also n. 9.

15. The essay is entitled "Polarity of Aims and Methods: Naturalization or Barbarization?"

16. The conclusion of Bodde's essay is particularly instructive because it sums up many problems regarding theories of translation useful to both literary scholars and philosophers translating from Chinese into English. Bodde suggests three criteria for good translations of Classical Chinese:

(1) *Stylistic intelligibility, simplicity and naturalness*. This means avoidance of clumsy locutions, awkward or hard-to-understand neologisms, exoticisms, and the other faults that often arise from over-labored and over-literal adherence to the original text....
(2) *Consistency*. This means that a technical vocabulary consistently used in the original should as much as possible be reproduced by a similarly consistent vocabulary in the translation.
(3) *Accuracy*. By this I do not merely mean accuracy of meaning—vital though such accuracy of course is—but also fidelity to the spirit and form in which the original is written. (242–243)

17. Liu's point about the same critical word having different meanings is easy enough to distinguish by listing the various meanings one by one. When the word (e.g., *xing* 興) and its many meanings occurs in the body of one's text, a useful expedient would simply be to add a numbered subscript distinguishing the word and its meanings.

WORKS CITED AND CONSULTED

Abrams, M. H. *A Glossary of Literary Terms*. 5th ed. New York: Holt, Rinehart and Winston, 1981.

Alter, Robert. *Fielding and the Nature of the Novel*. Cambridge, Mass.: Harvard University Press, 1968.

Auerbach, Erich. *Mimesis: The Representation of Reality in Western Literature*. Trans. Willard R. Trask. Princeton, N.J.: Princeton University Press, 1953.

Beckson, Karl, and Arthur Ganz. *Literary Terms: A Dictionary*. 3d rev. ed. New York: Noonday Press, 1989.

Blackmur, R. P. *A Primer of Ignorance*. Quoted from Alter (q.v.).

Bodde, Derk. "On Translating Chinese Philosophic Terms." *Far Eastern Quarterly* 14, no. 2 (1955): 231–244.

Bullock, Alan, and Oliver Stallybrass, eds. *The Fontana Dictionary of Modern Thought*. London: Fontana Books, 1977.

Chang Ching-erh. "The Concept of *Ch'i* in Chinese Literary Criticism." Dissertation, National Taiwan University, 1976.

Chang Hui-chuan. "Chinese Fiction: A Tentative Generic Appraisal." *Tamkang Review* 13, no. 4 (Summer 1983): 339–350.

———. "Literary Utopia and Chinese Utopian Literature: A Generic Appraisal." Ph.D. dissertation, University of Massachusetts, 1986.

Chen Yu-shih. "The Literary Theory and Practice of Ou-yang Hsiu." In *Chinese Approaches to Literature from Confucius to Liang Ch'i-ch'ao*. ed. Rickett (q.v.), 67–96.

Chi Ch'iu-lang. "The Concept of '*Feng-ku*': A Bridge across History and the Reader." *Tamkang Review* 14, nos. 1–4 (Autumn 1983–Summer 1984): 249–260.

———. "Liu Hsieh's *Shen-ssu*: Its Positive and Negative Capability." *Tamkang Review* 16, no. 2 (Winter 1985): 23–37.

Chiang T'ai-fen and Ch'iu Chin-jung. "Vincent Y. C. Shih's Translation of the *Wen-hsin tiao-lung*: A Note on Literary Translation." *Tamkang Review* 15, nos. 1–4 (Autumn 1984–Summer 1985): 233–253.

Ching, Eugene. "Translation or Transliteration: A Case in Cultural Borrowing." *Chinese Culture* (June 1966): 107–116.

Chou, Balance Tin-ping. "Heterocosm and *Ching-chieh*: Towards a Concept of Interiority for the Literary Work of Art. M.Phil. thesis, Chinese University of Hong Kong, 1983.

Chou Ying-hsiung. "The Linguistic and Mythical Structure of *Hsing* as a Combinational Model." *Chinese-Western Comparative Literature: Theory and Strategy*. Hong Kong: Chinese University Press, 1980, 51–78.

Chow Tse-tsung. "The Early History of the Chinese Word *Shih* (Poetry)." In Wen-lin, *Studies in the Chinese Humanities*, ed. Chow Tse-tsung. Madison: Department of East Asian Languages and Literature, University of Wisconsin, 1968, 151–209.

Ci Hai 辭海. See *Tz'u Hai*.

Confucius. *Confucius: The Analects* (*Lun yü* 論語). Trans. D. C. Lau 劉殿爵. Hong Kong: Chinese University Press, 1983.

Cuddon, J. A., ed. *A Dictionary of Literary Terms*. London: Andre Deutsch, 1977.

Deeney, John J. *Comparative Literature from Chinese Perspectives*. Shenyang (China): Liaoning University Press, 1989.

Dickens, Charles. *Hard Times*. Ed. George H. Ford and Sylvère Monod. New York: Norton, 1990.

Escarpit, Robert. Rapport sur le *Dictionnaire international des termes littéraires*. Faculté des lettres et sciences humaines, Université de Bordeaux, 1964. An updated report was presented to the ICLA Belgrade congress by Alain Boisson in 1967. The *Dictionnaire* is published under both its French and English titles.

————, ed. *Dictionnaire international des termes littéraires—L.* The Hague, Paris: Mouton, 1973.

————, ed. *Dictionnaire international des termes littéraires—Fascicule 1: Académie—Autobiographie*. Bern: Editions Francke, 1979.

————, ed. *Dictionnaire international des termes littéraires—Fascicule 2: Autobiographie—Bourgeois*. Bern: Editions Francke, 1980.

————, ed. *Dictionnaire international des termes littéraires—Fascicules 3 & 4: Bourgeois—Corrido*. Bern: Editions Francke, 1984.

————, ed. *Dictionnaire international des termes littéraires—Fascicule 5: Cosmopolitisme—Dialectique*. Bern: Editions Francke, 1986.

Fowler, Roger, ed. *A Dictionary of Modern Critical Terms*. Rev. ed. London: Routledge & Kegan Paul, 1987.

Frankel, Hans H. "Classical Chinese [Versification]." In W. K. Wimsatt, Jr., ed. *Versification: Major Language Types: Sixteen Essays*. New York: New York University Press, 1972, 22–37.

Fu, James S. "The Device of *Hsing* in Classical Chinese Poetry." *Asian and Pacific Quarterly* 10, no. 1 (Summer 1978): 14–19.

Gibbs, Donald A. "Notes on the Wind: The Term '*Feng*' in Chinese Literary Criticism" (285–293) and "The Term *Hua-pen*'" (295–306). In *Transition and Permanence: Chinese History and Culture (A Festschrift in Honor of Dr. Hsiao Kung-ch'uan)*, ed. David C. Buxbaum and Frederick W. Mote. Hong Kong: Cathay Press, 1972.

Grassin, Jean-Marie. [A series of typescript materials containing valuable information on the progress of the *IDLT* has been sent to me by Grassin: they are clearly identified in the body of my text.]

————. Letter to the author. 17 September 1990.

————, ed. *Dictionnaire international des terms littéraires—Fascicule 6: Dialectique—Emploi*. Bern: Editions Francke.

————, ed. *Dictionnaire international des terms littéraire—Fascicule 7*. Bern: Editions Francke.

Hankiss, Janos. "Théorie de la littérature et littérature comparée." In *Comparative Literature: Proceedings of the Second Congress of the International Comparative Literature Association*. Ed. Werner P. Friederich. Chapel Hill: University of North Carolina Press, 1959, 98–112.

Heine, Elizabeth. "The English Meaning of *Hsing* in Liu Hsieh's *Wen-hsin Tiao-lung*." In *China ancienne*. Section organisée par Michel Soymié. Paris: L'Asiatheque, 1977, 155–161.

Hightower, James R. *Topics in Chinese Literature*. Rev. ed. Cambridge, Mass.: Harvard University Press, 1962.

Hisamatsu, Sen'ichi. *The Vocabulary of Japanese Literary Aesthetics*. Tokyo: Centre for East Asian Cultural Studies, 1963.

Holman, C. Hugh, and William Harmon, eds. *A Handbook to Literature*. 5th ed. New

York: Macmillan, 1986.

Huang Pi-twan. "The Use of Simile in T'ang Literary Criticism." *Journal of National Sun Yat-sen University* 1 (1984): 1–25.

Johnson, Samuel. *Johnson's Dictionary: A Modern Selection.* Ed. E. L. McAdam, Jr., and George Milne. London: Victor Gollancz, 1963.

Jump, John D., founder ed. *The Critical Idiom.* London: Methuen, 1969–. The two-volume Chinese translation is entitled *Hsi-yang wen-hsueh shu-yu ts'ung-k'an* 西洋文學術語叢刊. 2d ed. Ed. Yen Yuan-shu 顏元叔. Taipei: Li-ming Wen-hua 黎明文化, 1978. 2 vols. Twenty of the original booklets are included in this translation series.

Kao, Karl S. Y. "Rhetoric." In Nienhauser, 121–137. Also see Kao's "Rhetorical Devices in the Chinese Literary Tradition." *Tamkang Review* 14, nos. 1–4 (Autumn 1983–Summer 1984): 325–327.

Ku Tim-hung. "Toward a Semiotic Poetics: A Chinese Model in Comparative Perspective." Ph.D. dissertation, University of California at San Diego, 1981.

Lau, D. C. See Confucius.

Lefevere, André. "The Study of Literary Translation and the Study of Comparative Literature." *Babel* 17, no. 4 (1971): 13–15.

———. "Translation and/in Comparative Literature." *Yearbook of Comparative and General Literature* 35 (1986): 40–50.

Lentricchia, Frank, and Thomas McLaughlin, eds. *Critical Terms for Literary Study.* Chicago: University of Chicago Press, 1990.

Levin, Harry. "Notes on Convention." *Perspectives of Criticism.* New York: Russell & Russell, 1950, 55–83.

———. "What is Realism?" *Contexts of Criticism.* Cambridge, Mass.: Harvard University Press, 1957, 67–75.

Liu, James J. Y. "Polarity of Aims and Methods: Naturalization or Barbarization?" *Yearbook of Comparative and General Literature* 24 (1975): 60–68.

———. *Chinese Theories of Literature.* Chicago: University of Chicago Press, 1975.

Miner, Earl, et al. *The Princeton Companion to Classical Japanese Literature.* Princeton, N.J.: Princeton University Press, 1985.

Nelson, C. E. "Literature and 'Littérature': The Comparative Critic's Problem of Definition." *Books Abroad* (Winter 1966): 34–36.

Ngan Yuen-wan. "Some Characteristics of Chinese Literary Criticism." *Tung-ya wen-hua* (East Asian Culture) 18 (August 1981): 185–197.

Nienhauser, William H., Jr., ed. and comp., et al. *The Indiana Companion to Traditional Chinese Literature.* Bloomington: Indiana University Press, 1986.

———. "Note on Some Recent Lexica and Indexes to Traditional Chinese Literature. Part I: Lexica." *Chinese Literature: Essays, Articles, Reviews* 9, nos. 1–2 (July 1987): 93–114. The author surveys 61 publications and provides evaluative annotations. Items numbers 15 and 50 could serve as representative samples of some of the better work being done.

Plaks, Andrew. "Towards a Critical Theory of Chinese Narrative." In *Chinese Narrative: Critical and Theoretical Essays.* Princeton, N.J.: Princeton University Press, 1977, 309–52.

———. "Full-length *Hsiao-shuo* and the Western Novel: A Generic Reappraisal." In *China and the West: Comparative Literature Studies*, ed. William Tay et al. Hong Kong: Chinese University Press, 1980, 163–176.

———. "Where the Lines Meet: Parallelism in Chinese and Western Literatures." *Chinese Literature: Essays, Articles, Reviews* 10, nos. 1–2 (July 1988): 43–60.

Pollard, David, *A Chinese Look at Literature: The Literary Values of Chou Tso-jen in Relation to the Tradition.* London: C. Hurst, 1973. Pollard defines a number of key terms throughout this book.

———. "*Ch'i* in Chinese Literary Theory." In *Chinese Approaches to Literature from Confucius to Liang Ch'i-ch'ao,* ed. Rickett (q.v.), 43–66.

Preminger, Alex, ed. *Princeton Encyclopedia of Poetry and Poetics.* Enlarged ed. Princeton, N.J.: Princeton University Press, 1974.

Radtke, K. W. "Concepts in Literary Criticism: Problems in the Comparative Study of Japanese, Chinese and Western Literature." *Oriens Extremus* 28, no. 1 (1981): 107–123.

Remak, Henry H. H. "West European Romanticism." In *Comparative Literature: Method and Perspective.* Rev. ed. Ed. Newton P. Stallknecht and Horst Frenz. Carbondale: Southern Illinois University Press, 1971, 275–311.

Rickett, Adele Austin. "*Wang Kuo-wei's* 王國維 *Jen-chien Tz'u-hua* 人間詞話: A Study in Chinese Literary Criticism." Ph.D. dissertation, University of Pennsylvania, 1967. This dissertation was later published in book form with the same title by the Hong Kong University Press (1977). The book is largely based on her dissertation, but the latter has the advantage of including Wang's original Chinese text, more on critical terms, and a number of other features (e.g., Chinese characters) left out of the book version.

———. "Technical Terms in Chinese Literary Criticism." *Literature East and West* 12 (1968): 141–147.

———. "Method and Intuition: The Poetic Theories of Huang T'ing-chien." In *Chinese Approaches to Literature from Confucius to Liang Ch'i-ch'ao,* ed. Rickett (q.v.), 97–119.

———. *Chinese Approaches to Literature from Confucius to Liang Ch'i-ch'ao.* Ed. Adele Austin Rickett. Princeton, N.J.: Princeton University Press, 1978.

Sampson, Geoffrey. *Writing Systems: A Linguistic Introduction.* Stanford: Stanford University Press, 1985.

Scholz, Bernhard F. Review of *IDLT,* fascicles 1–5. *Yearbook of Comparative and General Literature* 36 (1987): 152–155.

Schwartz, Benjamin. *The World of Thought in Ancient China.* Cambridge, Mass.: Harvard University Press, 1985.

Scott, A. F., ed. *Current Literary Terms: A Concise Dictionary of Their Origin and Use.* London: Macmillan, 1981.

Seeber, Edward E. "On Defining Terms." In *Comparative Literature: Method and Perspective.* Rev. ed. Ed. Newton P. Stallknecht and Horst Frenz. Carbondale: Southern Illinois University Press, 1971, 58–83.

Shipley, Joseph T. *Dictionary of World Literary Terms.* 3d ed. Boston: The Writer, 1970.

Sun, Jingyao. Description of literary terms project. Ts. N.d. 6 pp.

Tz'u Hai: Wen-hsueh fen-ts'e 辭海:文學分冊. Shanghai: Shanghai Tz'u-shu Publishing House 上海：上海辭書出版社, 1981.

Wang, C. H. "Naming the Reality of Chinese Criticism." *Journal of Asian Studies* 38, no. 3 (May 1979): 529–534. This is a review article of Liu's *Chinese Theories of Literature.*

Wang, John C. Y. "The *Chih-yen-chai* Commentary and the Dream of the Red Chamber: A Literary Study." In *Chinese Approaches to Literature from Confucius to Liang Ch'i-ch'ao*, ed. Rickett (q.v.), 189–220.

Weisstein, Ulrich. Review of *IDLT*, fascicles 1 and 2. *Canadian Review of Comparative Literature* 12, no. 3 (September 1985): 469–471.

Wellek, René. *Concepts of Criticism*. New Haven: Yale University Press, 1963.

Wen Hsun 文訊. Journal published in Taiwan which featured articles on Chinese and Western terminology: nos. 16–27 (February 1985 to December 1986).

Whitmore, C. E. "The Validity of Literary Definitions." In M. M. Liberman and Edward E. Foster, *A Modern Lexicon of Literary Terms*. Glenville, Ill: Scott, Foresman, 1968, 127–138. The original essay is found in *PMLA* 39 (1924): 722–736.

Wong, Simon H. H. "*Wan-ko*: A Study on a Chinese Genre in the Perspective of Western Genre Theory." M.Phil. thesis, Chinese University of Hong Kong, 1983.

Wong Siu-kit. "*Ch'ing* in Chinese Literary Criticism." Dissertation, Oxford University, 1969.

———. "*Ch'ing* and *Ching* in the Critical Writings of Wang Fu-chih." In *Chinese Approaches to Literature from Confucius to Liang Ch'i-ch'ao*, ed. Rickett (q.v.), 121–150.

Wong Wai-leung. "Chinese Impressionistic Criticism: A Study of the Poetry-Talk ('*Shih-hua Tz'u-hua*') Tradition." Ph.D. dissertation, Ohio State University, 1967.

———. "The Carved Dragon and the Well-Wrought Urn—Notes on the Concepts of Structure in Liu Hsieh and the New Critics." *Tamkang Review* 14, nos. 1–4 (Autumn 1983–Summer 1984): 555–568.

Wright, Arthur F. "The Chinese Language and Foreign Ideas." In *Studies in Chinese Thought*, ed. Arthur F. Wright. Chicago: University of Chicago Press, 1953, 286–303.

Yeh Ching-ping. "Informal Essay and Contemporary Society." *Asia Culture Quarterly* 6, no. 2 (Summer 1987): 71–75.

Yeh, Michelle Hsi, "Metaphor and Metonymy: A Comparative Study of Chinese and Western Poetics." Ph.D. dissertation, University of Southern California, 1983.

———. "Metaphor and '*Bi*'": Western and Chinese Poetics." *Comparative Literature* 39. no. 3 (1987): 237–254.

Yu, Pauline Ruth. "Metaphor and Chinese Poetry." *Chinese Literature: Essays, Articles, Reviews* 3, no. 2 (1981): 205–224.

———. *The Reading of Imagery in the Chinese Poetic Tradition*. Princeton: Princeton University Press, 1987.

Yu Yongyuan. "An On-line Multilingual Terminology Data Bank Including Chinese Data." Ts. Infoterm Papers, n.d. 11 pp.

Yuan Heh-hsiang. "A Study of Some Literary Expressions in the Wei Tsin Period." *Tamkang Review* 4, no. 2 (October 1973): 11–36.

Yue Daiyun. "Guide-lines for the Compilation of *A Dictionary of World Poetics*." Ts. N.d. 5 pp.

CONTRIBUTORS

Cyril Birch is Professor Emeritus of Chinese and of English Literature at the University of California at Berkeley. He is well known for his two-volume *Anthology of Chinese Literature*, which has been a staple in introductory courses since its publication by Grove Press in 1965.

Dominic Cheung teaches at the University of Southern California. He published a monograph on *Feng Chih* in Twayne's World Authors Series in 1979, as well as a collection of translations, *The Isle Full of Noises: Modern Chinese Poetry from Taiwan*, which Columbia University Press published in 1987.

William G. Crowell is a foreign service officer for the United States Information Agency assigned as deputy chief of the Division of Academic Exchange Programs. He holds a Ph.D. in Chinese history from the University of Washington and has published articles and reviews on Han and the Nan-Bei Chao period.

James I. Crump, Jr., Professor Emeritus of Chinese at the University of Michigan, published his version of the *Chan-kuo Ts'e* with Oxford University Press in 1970; his most recent publication is *Song-Poems from Xanadu* (Ann Arbor: Center for Chinese Studies, 1993).

Robert Joe Cutter teaches at the University of Wisconsin in Madison. He is the author of *The Brush and the Spur: Chinese Culture and the Cockfight*, published by the Chinese University Press in 1989.

John J. Deeney is on the faculty of the Chinese Department of the Chinese University of Hong Kong and a member of its Centre for Translation. He has edited *A Golden Treasury of Chinese Poetry: 121 Classical Poems*, published by the Chinese University of Hong Kong Press in 1976, and a collection of essays, *Chinese-Western Comparative Literature: Theory and Strategy*, also published by the Chinese University of Hong Kong Press, in 1980.

Glen Dudbridge is Lecturer in Chinese at Oxford University. Among his publications are *The Legend of Miao-shan* (London: Ithaca Press, 1978), *The Hsi-yu chi: A Study of Antecedents to the Sixteenth-century Chinese Novel* (Cambridge University Press, 1970), and *The Tale of Li Wa: Study and Critical Edition of a Chinese Story from the Ninth Century* (London: Ithaca Press, 1983).

Eugene Eoyang is a founding editor of *Chinese Literature: Essays, Articles, Reviews* (CLEAR). He has published *Selected Poems of Ai Qing* (Foreign Languages Press and Indiana University Press, 1983) and *The Transparent Eye: Reflections on Translation, Chinese Literature, and Comparative Poetics* (University of Hawaii Press, 1993). He teaches at Indiana University.

David R. Knechtges teaches at the University of Washington in Seattle. He has published *The Han Rhapsody: A Study of the Fu of Yang Hsiung, 53 B.C.–A.D. 18* (Cambridge University Press, 1972) and *Wen Xuan, or, Selections of Refined Literature* (Princeton University Press, 1982–), of which two volumes have appeared.

Joseph S. M. Lau has published anthologies with Columbia University Press: *Chinese Stories from Taiwan, 1960–1970* (1976), *Traditional Chinese Stories: Themes and Variations* (1978), and *Modern Chinese Stories and Novellas, 1919–1949* (1981). He was also a co-translator of Ts'ao Yü's *Yüan-yeh: The Wilderness*, which appeared in 1980 (Indiana University Press).

Lin Yao-fu is Dean of the College of Arts and Sciences at National Taiwan University. Formerly Chair of the Department of English, he was the conference organizer for the first International Conference on the Translation of Chinese Literature, held in Taipei in December 1990.

Victor H. Mair teaches at the University of Pennsylvania. His publications include *T'ang Transformation Texts: A Study of the Buddhist Contribution to the Rise of Vernacular Fiction and Drama in China*, published by the Council on East Asian Studies, Harvard University, 1989, and *Tun-huang Popular Narratives*, published by Cambridge University Press, 1983. He has also translated the *Tao te ching: The Classic Book of Integrity and the Way* (Bantam Books, 1990).

Richard B. Mather is Professor Emeritus of Chinese at the University of Minnesota. He published his translation of the *Shih-shuo hsin-yü: New Account of the Tales of the World* with the University of Minnesota Press in 1976. He is also the author of *The Poet Shen Yüeh (441–513): The Reticent Marquis* (Princeton University Press, 1988).

John Minford published the fourth and fifth volumes of *The Story of the Stone*, a translation of the *Shih-t'ou chi* (Hung-lou meng, The Dream of the Red Chamber) with Indiana University Press in 1982 and 1987. (David Hawkes had completed the first three volumes.) With Geremie Barmé, he published *Seeds of Fire: Chinese Voices of Conscience* (Hill and Wang, 1988); and with Stephen C. Soong, he collected *Trees on the Mountain: An Anthology of New Chinese Writing* (Chinese University of Hong Kong Press, 1984). He teaches at the Australian National University.

William H. Nienhauser, Jr., is a founding editor of *Chinese Literature: Essays, Articles, Reviews* (CLEAR), and he is editor of the *Indiana Companion to Chinese Literature* (Indiana University Press, 1986) as well as *Critical Essays on Chinese Literature* (Chinese University of Hong Kong Press, 1976). He is also author of *Liu Tsung-yuan* (1973) and *P'i Jih-hsiu* (1979) in the Twayne's World Author Series.

Ching-hsi Peng has published *Double Jeopardy: A Critique of Seven Yuan Courtroom Dramas* (Center for Chinese Studies, University of Michigan, 1978). He teaches at National Taiwan University in Taipei, and is currently Chair of the Department of Foreign Language and Literature.

David D. W. Wang has published *Fictional Realism in Twentieth-century China: Mao Dun, Lao She, Shen Conwen* (1992) and *From May Fourth to June Fourth: Fiction and*

Film in Twentieth-century China (1993), which he edited with Ellen Widmer. He teaches at Columbia University.

Stephen H. West teaches at the University of California at Berkeley. He has published *Vaudeville and Narrative: Aspects of Chin Theater* (Wiesbaden: Steiner, 1977) and *The Moon and the Zither: The Story of the Western Wing* (University of California Press, 1991).

Michelle Yeh is the author of *Modern Chinese Poetry: Theory and Practice since 1917* (Yale University Press, 1991), and she has edited *Anthology of Modern Chinese Poetry* (Yale University Press, 1992). She teaches at the University of California at Davis.

INDEX